REINVENTING
DETROIT

Comparative Urban and Community Research Series

Michael Peter Smith, editor

The Comparative Urban and Community Research Series is devoted to cutting-edge theoretical and empirical research in the social sciences on processes of urbanization and community change throughout the world. The series focuses on the key driving forces of urban change, including economic and cultural globalization, transnationalism in all of its forms, and the grassroots politics of place-making. Each volume in the series is focused on distinct themes such as the regional development of cities along the Pacific Rim, the politics of urban social movements, the global restructuring of city life, and the agency possible in marginalized urban spaces.

REINVENTING DETROIT

THE POLITICS OF POSSIBILITY

Michael Peter Smith
and
L. Owen Kirkpatrick,
editors

Comparative Urban and Community Research, Volume 11

Transaction Publishers

New Brunswick (U.S.A.) and London (U.K.)

Library of Congress Catalog Number: 2015006289
ISBN: 978-1-4128-5693-5
eBook: 978-1-4128-5660-7
Printed in the United States of America

Library of Congress Cataloging-in-Publication Data

Reinventing Detroit : the politics of possibility / Michael Peter Smith, L. Owen Kirkpatrick, editors.
    pages cm. -- (Comparative urban and community research ; volume 11)
    Includes bibliographical references and index.
    ISBN 978-1-4128-5693-5 -- ISBN 978-1-4128-5660-7 1. Urban policy--Michigan--Detroit. 2. Urban renewal--Michigan--Detroit. 3. Shrinking cities--Michigan--Detroit. 4. Municipal government--Michigan--Detroit. 5. Municipal finance--Michigan--Detroit. 6. Detroit (Mich.)--Economic conditions--21st century. I. Smith, Michael P., editor. II. Kirkpatrick, L. Owen, editor.
    HT168.D45R45 2015
    307.3'4160977434--dc23
                                                                    2015006289

Contents

Introduction

Reinventing Detroit: Urban Decline and the Politics of Possibility

Michael Peter Smith and L. Owen Kirkpatrick

Detroit, Michigan, has followed an arcing historical path that is as dramatic as it is iconic. The "Motor City," once an industrial powerhouse, has been unsparingly beset by demographic shrinkage, economic contraction, and socio-spatial abandonment and deterioration since its peak in the mid-twentieth century. This slow, chronic pattern of urban decline culminated in an acute "hyper-crisis" in the wake of the Great Recession, triggering concerted efforts to restructure the forms and functions of municipal governance. Urban restructuring in Detroit has largely been implemented via institutional and political channels, such as the formal process of municipal bankruptcy, the State of Michigan's emergency management of the city's affairs, and the increasing role of public-private partnerships in providing social services and shaping urban space. The rapid and far-reaching structural changes arising from Detroit's hyper-crisis provide an apt occasion to fundamentally rethink the dilemmas facing the city and the range of political possibilities available to those collectively trying to address them.

Detroit is also ripe for reinterpretation and collective reinvention in ways relating to the lived spaces of the city. Detroit is now experienced—by both residents and visitors alike—via the targeted retrenchment of public infrastructures and services, the skeletal erasure of the built environment, and the percolating pressure of natural reclamation. And yet Detroit cannot be fully understood only in terms of loss, decay, and dereliction. Rather, urban decline and abandonment is uneven and intermittent, containing the embryonic possibilities of new and/or renewed forms of social integration and economic development. Some scholars insist, for instance, that abandoned industrial spaces be seen as both desolate and empty, and fecund and expectant. From this perspective, Detroit should be simultaneously understood as "[v]oid, absence, yet also promise, the space of the possible, of expectation." Abandoned spaces exist "outside the city's effective circuits and productive structures"—a condition that presents residents with new modes of perceiving, and acting on, the city (de Solà-Morales, 1995, 120).

To "reinvent," of course, is to create anew or remake something in a form different than its original. In the case of cities, reinvention often refers to the ways in which urban places, particularly those in decline, are remade—their communities and built environments reordered and their histories and cultures re-branded—so as to be better positioned in the global economy. In the context of austerity and public retrenchment, as we will see, fiscal crisis can narrow the debate among policymakers by effectively funneling limited public resources into the city's commercial core in an effort to create spaces of mass entertainment, high-end residential enclaves, and entrepreneurial, high-tech "innovation zones," while most of the city's residential neighborhoods are left to decay. But despite these trends, urban reinvention remains a contested and contingent process, and as such is a moment pregnant with emergent political possibilities. In order to best assess the political potentiality of the current historical moment in Detroit—a difficult objective given the indeterminate and multiform nature of the task—two analytic procedures are necessary.

First, alternative theoretical models and new epistemological insights are necessary in order to enhance our ability to account for cases of extreme urban decline and abandonment. Hence, Part I spells out three novel approaches for conceptually framing and conducting research on shrinking cities. These include: a comparative model of social change in the context of extreme inter- and intra-urban inequality; a powerful call for a definitive epistemological break from conventional explanations of Detroit's hyper-crisis; and a compelling statement outlining some of the ways the empirical insights gleaned in Detroit are of special relevance to urban planning theory and practice. Each of these pieces diverge in important ways from generally accepted ways of investigating and understanding the city, and in so doing, they provide a useful foundation for the critical reconsideration of the Detroit case.

Second, reimagining the future of the city requires rereading its past and reinterpreting its present. Our substantive analysis begins, therefore, by explicitly making the *past* present as a part of the analysis. The two chapters comprising Part II begin with the same basic historical inquiry: "What went wrong in Detroit and other industrial urban centers of the twentieth century?" Popular (and certain political and scholarly) discourse would largely have us believe that the answer lies in the pathological behaviors of inner-city residents nurtured by a "culture of poverty" and the undisciplined and/ or corrupt machinations of urban officials and public sector unions. The contributions comprising Part II of *Reinventing Detroit* focus, instead, on the retrenchment of national urban policy and the spreading ideology of market fundamentalism, respectively. By analytically "presencing" the city's past, these authors help us better understand the structural origins of current conditions.

Part III more fully fleshes out the present condition of Detroit as a baseline for thinking about the city's future trajectory. The four chapters in this section analyze: the politics of Detroit in bankruptcy; the tradeoffs between democracy and efficiency involved in the emergency management of the city; the ritual politics entailed in Detroit's de-democratization; and the distortions and misrepresentations involved in common discursive framings of Detroit's bankruptcy, which ostensibly justify the shift of costs and risks onto the city and its most socioeconomically marginalized citizens.

Part IV culminates in the question of reinventing the city's future in the context of systemic industrial decline. The four chapters comprising this section begin with a pessimistic reading of the prospects for a full Detroit recovery, wherein "recovery" is defined in fairly conventional terms. This general stance is shared by even the most optimistic contributions to this section, which show that conventional urban politics and policies oriented toward socioeconomic expansion and economic intensification have failed to reverse Detroit's downward decline, and there is scant evidence that pro-growth, supply-side tactics would suddenly begin functioning as intended in the post-crisis period. Hence, the final three chapters of the book address unconventional forms of economic recovery and redevelopment. The first of these is a critical rethinking of the city's economic base, which argues for abandoning "smokestack chasing" economic development strategies and replacing such strategies with a "community wealth building" vision of Detroit's future. This alternative vision is based on small-scale enterprises, anchored by local institutions such as hospital complexes, universities, and government institutions, which build complex economic interdependences that promote regional socioeconomic stability. The penultimate chapter carries this approach further, sketching a comprehensive framework for urban revitalization in which Detroit becomes a cooperative commonwealth of worker- and community-owned business enterprises and social service organizations. And lastly, the final chapter rejects conventional models of urban revitalization. Instead, the author engages in a utopian thought experiment concerning a "New Social City" based on social justice, social abundance, and democratic decision-making.

Reinventing Detroit: The Politics of Possibility seeks to contribute to the current moment of restructuring and reinvention by bringing together a distinguished group of urban social scientists, planners, and public intellectuals who have thought deeply about the decline of Detroit, together with preeminent urban scholars who have written about alternative future pathways to urban social justice. In so doing, Volume 11 in the Comparative Urban and Community Research book series offers a wide range of theoretical perspectives, insightful diagnoses, and practical proposals for the city's revitalization and stabilization under conditions of extreme urban decline. At times, the essays comprising this volume offer competing (re)interpretations of Detroit's current predicament and adopt different stances with respect to the relative feasibility of particular strategies or desirability of particular visions. Yet, taken together, they allow us to more accurately map the sociopolitical geography of opportunities and constraints facing cities in extreme decline, and hence, enable us to better navigate Detroit's many possible futures.

Reenvisioning a Theoretical and Epistemological Framework

We begin by noting that many disciplines have been slow to designate urban decline and abandonment as a proper and worthwhile object of analysis. Thus, shrinking cities and abandoned spaces tend to exist, analytically, in the interstitial gaps between disciplines and models. This can be traced, in part, to the fact that most conventional urban models and imaginaries cannot easily or effectively capture extreme or persistent patterns of urban decline and decay. Urban sociologists interested in norms and social order find, instead, a space in which the strictures of normativity have been partially and unevenly suspended. Similarly, urban political economists discover that traditional explanations of urban politics are not as helpful in the context of abandoned cities. Models based on the premise that dominant urban coalitions have the power and capacity to get things accomplished (urban regime theory), or that land-based elites and politicians possess a high degree of collective efficacy with respect to socio-spatial and economic development (the urban growth machine hypothesis), lend only limited insights into land-use patterns in the context of systemic abandonment. This tendency appears to stretch across all relevant disciplines. As one scholar notes, "Dealing with voids within a city lies outside the experience and even the language of most urban planners, architects, and social scientists. Planners and architects build and manage growth, while social scientists—economists, sociologists, epidemiologists—learn to use data. . . . Nobody trains to deal with emptiness" (Robin Boyle, paraphrased in Gallagher, 2010, 23).

One possible reason for this scholarly oversight derives from the epistemological characteristics of urban decline, and the fundamental difficulty many disciplines have when they encounter the emptiness and "in-betweenness" of abandoned urban space. According to Waldheim and Santos-Munné (2001), for instance, architects and planners have de-emphasized abandoned space because they "no longer required the techniques of growth and development that had become the modus operandi of the[ir] discipline[s]." Building on Michel de Certeau's observation that the scope of a doctor's attention ends at the site of the dying patient, the authors argue that municipal retrenchment combined with other forces of destruction and decay create "a region of meaninglessness"—a collection of "non-sites," that "could not be *thought* by the architectural and planning disciplines" (Ibid, 107; emphasis in the original). Part I of *Reinventing Detroit* offers several important correctives to this tendency.

In chapter 1, Lucas Owen Kirkpatrick and Michael Peter Smith develop a theoretical framework for understanding the political economy of extreme urban decline. Inspired by the sociological writings of Karl Polanyi, this framework can also be used for comparative urban analysis in the context of extreme inter- and intra-urban inequality. In the case of Detroit, we see Polanyi's "double-movement" playing out throughout the twentieth century. First, GM, Ford, and the big automakers had the advantage, and the political pendulum swung toward free markets and deregulated labor practices. By mid-century, organized labor had won significant gains, but in the latter half of the century, union power gradually declined, thus completing one pendulous cycle of the double movement. Today, however, the pendulum appears broken—or at least stalled. There are many reasons for this, but we emphasize those involving de-democratization. The gains made at mid-century were at the ballot box and the negotiating table via collective bargaining. But both types of political power have since been eviscerated in the city. Hence, there are very few, if any, traditional, grassroots democratic mechanisms that Detroit residents can use to protect themselves from market forces or the lack thereof.

While a Polanyian-inspired framework is well suited to analyze national movements seeking to regulate functioning markets in liberal democracies, it can also be extended to incorporate more localized and radical political possibilities. As Nancy Fraser has recently argued, a Polanyian lens need not dwell solely on the efforts and impacts of large, formal social movement organizations, because in doing so we would miss "that which is present" on the urban political scene, namely the spread of emancipatory movements that are antiracist, multiculturalist, participatory democratic, antiimperalist, and so on (Fraser, 2013, 127–128). She asks us to rethink the impacts and locations of a variety of diverse movements struggling for sociopolitical recognition and inclusion, rather than focusing solely or disproportionately on formal interest group politics negotiating for increased social protections and resource redistribution.

Mathieu Desan and George Steinmetz provide us with additional theoretical tools that can be used to "see what is present" in Detroit. In chapter 2, the authors develop a theoretically sophisticated analysis that demonstrates the importance of locating the multiple dimensions of Detroit's hyper-crisis and situating it in multiple regions and scales of social space—from the global to the local. Desan and Steinmetz demonstrate, for example, how narrowing one's focus hyper-locally to central city blight (e.g., the "ruin porn" of Detroit's train station and abandoned factories) elides structural factors such as the city's location in a metropolitan system, the structurally entrenched dynamics of economic disinvestment, extreme racial segregation, and administrative fragmentation. These factors both produce race and class inequalities and preclude regional approaches to addressing the crisis, such as revenue sharing or joint service ventures. Tendencies to localize the crisis—to stress Detroit's uniqueness—essentially blames the victim while ignoring underlying structural causes including: (a) racialized disinvestment, (b) the splintered political geography of suburban exclusion and regional inequality, (c) sharp state cuts in revenue sharing, (d) the disappearance of federal urban policy initiatives, and, more generally, (e) the rollback and collapse of the Fordist welfare state. In large measure, these structural changes were ushered in by industrial capital's disinvestment in a city that was historically a crucial site of working-class power.

The authors of chapter 3 challenge the disciplinary inattention to shrinking cities by investigating the many ways Detroit can inform traditional lines of urban inquiry. Put differently, they explore the extent to which the lessons gleaned from the Motor City can be applied to other cities and regions. In their careful explication of planning theory and practice in the context of shrinkage and contraction, urban planning scholar Margaret Dewar and her colleagues Matthew Weber, Eric Seymour, Meagan Elliott, and Patrick Cooper-McCann ask, in practical pedagogical terms: What can urban studies learn from Detroit? Their core argument is that Detroit's severe decline presents urban researchers with unique opportunities to observe phenomena, such as gentrification, that are usually studied only under conditions of urban expansion. In Detroit, researchers can address a series of novel and important research questions, including: (a) How do cities facing steep decline function socially, economically, politically, and administratively? (b) What happens to the social relations of urban property under conditions of low demand, and what can be done to revitalize urban neighborhoods when little or no demand exists? (c) How do the remaining residents of these neighborhoods deal with ongoing physical decay? (d) What types of "self-provisioning" strategies and "alternative urbanisms" have sprung up in the face of decline? (e) And what roles have federal and state policies and institutions (e.g., mortgage lending organizations and property foreclosure policies) played in accelerating or mitigating the urban disinvestment process? Time and again, Dewar and her colleagues demonstrate the concrete benefits that can accrue when urban decline and abandonment are clearly "seen" and "thought" by urban scholars.

Rereading Detroit: Past, Present, and Future

A central premise of this book is that the case of Detroit—its past, present, and future—deserves a thorough rereading. According to J. K. Gibson-Graham, rereading is a technique of "uncovering what is possible but obscured from view" (2006, xxxi). This is an especially useful tactic in the case of Detroit, where the city's dramatic decline is often dismissed as either the natural result of a pathological subculture or as an inevitable outcome of deindustrialization. Both assumptions, of course, sharply delimit the universe of viable political responses. "Rereading offers us something new to work with," note Gibson-Graham. "Possibilities multiply along with uncertainties, and future possibilities become more viable by virtue of already being seen to exist, albeit only in the light of a differentiating imagination" (Ibid). Taken together, the essays that comprise the remainder of the volume provide the basis for a thorough rereading of Detroit's troubled past (Part II), its contested present (Part III), and its uncertain future (Part IV).

Rereading the Past

William Tabb initiates the task of "rereading" Detroit's storied history by focusing on the national urban policy context. In chapter 4, Tabb offers a compelling historical narrative of how the New Deal and the postwar liberal urban policy consensus, entailing both expanded social policies and a growing redistributive role for federal revenue sharing, was dismantled in the 1970s and 1980s. This Keynesian-inspired system was replaced by a market-oriented urban policy regime characterized by a very high degree of inter-local competition for shrinking governmental resources nationally and uncertain private investment in the global marketplace. Viewed in this wider context, Tabb argues that Detroit's current plight, while severe, is hardly unique. Rather it is a microcosm of a general US urban condition—including (inter alia) global capital flight from the cities, forced urban fiscal austerity, growing racial and income inequality, and a narrow "go-it alone" set of neoliberal policy options for economic recovery and social well-being. But despite the many structural challenges he identifies, Tabb is not entirely pessimistic about the current state of affairs. Rather, he locates the seeds of progressive urban change in already emergent blue state (and blue city) initiatives prompted by a renewed concern about growing income inequality following the Great Recession, the subsequent suburban housing bubble, and the spread of urban-style social problems to older suburbs and even rural areas.

In chapter 5 Jason Hackworth advances a theoretically sophisticated account of the recent history of market fundamentalism in Detroit, concluding that optimistic expectations for Detroit's future (such as the Polanyian model we sketch in chapter 1) are misplaced. In the Motor City, neoliberal ways of framing reality have become so pervasive that the city's prevailing policy options, particularly with respect to land management, have been restricted to "market-first" and "market only" policy regimes. Effectively excluded from the policy conversation is the possibility of meaningful regulation of real estate markets and land use, such as rent controls, social housing, or increased public spending. Hackworth largely traces the rise of market fundamentalism to extra-local, and often extra-democratic, forces. For example, a 2003 Michigan law that limited nonmarket "land-banking" practices in favor of market-based mechanisms for the adjudication of abandoned land was written by a conservative think tank funded by ALEC (American Legislative Exchange Council). Hackworth's account of the recent historical ascendance of market fundamentalism in Detroit complements Tabb's analysis of the retrenchment of federal urban policy in the last decades of the twentieth century. In both cases, the authors help us better understand the structural constraints that need to be shaken for alternative policies and strategies to take hold.

Reinterpreting the Present

Part III of *Reinventing Detroit* turns the analysis to current crisis conditions in the city. In chapter 6, Reynolds Farley analyzes Detroit in bankruptcy, with an emphasis on the structural roots of the problem. In his empirically precise case study, Farley examines the bankruptcy process itself, its origins, its implementation, and its immediate and possible long-term effects. He posits four key reasons why the city went bankrupt: the collapse of its tax base; the limitations of the state of Michigan's support for local government, which served as a disincentive for inter-local cooperation; the region's long historical legacy of racial inequality and conflict; and the financial mismanagement of its public officials. The chapter also details the State of Michigan's response to urban fiscal crisis, with particular attention paid to emergency management legislation of the past fifteen years, its contested reception by voters, and ultimately, its implementation in Detroit. Assessing the current winners and losers in Detroit's bankruptcy process, Farley provides a balanced overview of the current crisis and the efforts of the state to contain it. Compared to other chapters in this book, Farley's assessment is relatively optimistic (vis-à-vis jobs and capital investment, population trends and neighborhood development, and urban governance), though he leaves open the question of whether the signs of reform and progress that he identifies will work in the long run to revitalize Detroit and overcome its long history of black poverty and racial inequality.

Picking up on the themes of municipal crisis and the emergency management of the city in chapter 7, John Gallagher—a highly esteemed Detroit-area journalist—examines the tradeoffs between democracy and efficiency in times of urban crisis: efforts by outside forces to resolve the city's fiscal and public service woes entail de-democratizing Detroit's political system. Gallagher traces the process of de-democratization to the turn of the last century (1990s–2000s), when various city-owned and -operated entities and functions were spun off and privatized to realize financial savings. Efforts to financialize and de-democratize municipal functions and public assets have accelerated in the postcrisis period, with some systems such as street lighting being privatized, while others, like the municipal water system, are placed under regional control. The coup de grace was the appointment of a powerful emergency manager to the city in March of 2013. As would be expected, this did not go over well with local communities and officials, and Gallagher carefully documents the extensive local protests against the usurpation of public authority by Detroit's emergency manager. He describes these protests as "long, loud, and unrelenting," if not powerful enough to win the day.

Ultimately, Gallagher argues that strictly in terms of cost savings ("economy and efficiency"), measures to manage Detroit through extra-democratic channels have actually worked. He contends that local democracy in Detroit has not entirely disappeared, because local elected officials still retain some appointment, zoning, and approval functions over policies pursued by spun-off special purpose entities like museums, parks, and exhibition centers. Rather than disappearing altogether, local democracy has merely shrunk and receded into the background. Nevertheless, he cautions that placing various democratic controls "on hold" during an emergency period can cascade down a slippery slope if Michigan officials do not ensure that emergency measures are temporary.

The erosion of urban democracy is also the core theme of Lucas Owen Kirkpatrick's chapter on the "ritualization" of the local electoral process. In Kirkpatrick's view (chapter 8), the appointment of Detroit's emergency manager (EM) rendered the subsequent local election (for mayor and city council) little more than a ritual political act—an instrumentally empty symbol of legitimacy. Kirkpatrick demonstrates, first, how popular expectations that the EM's control will be short and followed by the full and unambiguous restoration of local popular sovereignty are belied by evidence from other cases of emergency management across Michigan, where EMs exercise a form of "pseudo-dictatorial" power that has long and lingering structural effects in cities like Pontiac, Flint, and Benton Harbor. Importantly, in dispensing the city's financial obligations, EMs will, on balance, favor the interests of municipal bondholders and Wall Street firms over those of local municipal employees and pension holders. This tendency does not derive from the personal convictions of individual EMs, but rather is a structural feature of the position itself, as cities are dependent on access to capital markets to pay for needed infrastructures and services. The financial imperative of emergency management cannot be challenged or mitigated while a city is under EM control. In point of fact, officials elected under such conditions are effectively powerless and categorically prevented from performing their duties (unless or until these powers and duties are specially restored by the EM). And yet, local elections continue to be held at great time and expense. Under such conditions, the local electoral process is no longer functionally instrumental, becoming instead a highly ritualized symbol serving primarily to legitimatize accelerated patterns of financial value extraction.

Finally, in chapter 9, Jamie Peck examines Detroit's crisis from the analytic intersection of the political, the financial, and the social. In a devastating deconstruction of neoliberal readings of Detroit's financial crisis, Peck demonstrates that the causes of the city's financial woes have been erroneously localized and endogenized. According to the dominant narrative, local residents, particularly low-income blacks (and their enabling local politicians, city workers, and labor unions), are to blame for the city's plight, a position that justifies shifting the costs of Detroit's potential recovery and redevelopment downward, and onto the backs of those least equipped to shoulder it. This approach to framing Detroit denies the reality that the urban crisis is multi-scalar and, accordingly, that any effective solution to the crisis must also be understood in structural, multi-scalar terms.

Reimagining the Future

When we analytically pivot from the present (Part III) to the future (Part IV), the contributions necessarily become more speculative and prescriptive, and the range of assessments of Detroit's prospects becomes wider and more dramatic—from abject pessimism to minimally bridled optimism. The section begins with Peter Eisinger's broad assessment of the challenges facing Detroit and the obstacles in the way of a robust and equitable recovery (chapter 10). Like other authors, Eisinger traces the roots of Detroit's current condition to structural factors such as industrial disinvestment, metropolitan hyper-segregation enabled by decades of federal housing policies, and massive housing foreclosures in the wake of the recent housing bubble. Looking forward, he further identifies five fundamental obstacles to the city's socioeconomic recovery. Three of the five factors he analyzes are largely "inside" factors: a local institutional and human capacity deficit, weak or dismantled local government institutions, and a long-term internal mismatch between local resources and problems (e.g., limited local sources of taxation, outmoded technological management systems, low educational attainment of the city's population, limited local business entrepreneurship, and the absence of large-scale immigration). The fourth and fifth factors discussed by Eisinger are "outside" developments—market marginalization produced by global capital flight and the privatization of previously public functions.

Each of the obstacles identified by Eisinger are complex phenomena that pose daunting, multiform challenges for the social, political, and economic revitalization of Detroit. Take, for instance, the issue of privatization. Eisinger's comprehensive analysis of privatization in the Detroit case includes different modes of private involvement in public decision making: (a) the contracting out of services such as trash collection; (b) an increasing reliance on foundation and corporate funding for service provision, service planning, and economic development efforts; (c) the private provision of funds for Detroit's "grand bargain"; (d) the growing reliance on citizen-initiated projects, such as "mower gangs" and citizen safety patrols; (e) and the oligarchic domination of the urban redevelopment scene by a handful of billionaire investors and developers. Ultimately, Eisinger comes to the sobering conclusion that a true recovery for Detroit is an elusive and unlikely objective.

A more hopeful vision is laid out in chapter 11, wherein Gar Alperowitz and Steve Dubb propose a model of revitalization based on an environmentally and socioeconomically sustainable "community wealth building" strategy. As an iconic example of America's "throwaway" culture, Detroit has been subjected to the usual array of one-dimensional pro-growth tactics. But Alperowitz and Dubb argue for a more fundamental restructuring of the city's economy involving the expansion of its employee- and community-owned enterprise sector. They also encourage collaboration between community-owned businesses and local "anchor" institutions. These partnerships generate investments clearly tied to place, in contrast to the hyper-mobile capital that dominates the global economy. The authors offer concrete examples of this strategy, with a particular emphasis on Cleveland. In the "Cleveland Model"—partly developed by Dubb and Alperowitz in their capacity as board members of an NGO known as the Democracy Collaborative—the city's hospitals and universities have developed a long-term working relationship with a variety of worker-owned cooperatives. The authors argue that community wealth building can work in Detroit because a significant number of relevant grassroots projects and community-based businesses already exist there, including an effort to develop a "Mandragón in Detroit," patterned after Spain's world-famous worker-cooperative network. Shifting to wider policy scales,

Alperowitz and Dubb call for new forms of regional and national planning devoted to environmentally sustainable public infrastructure investments, well-planned rail networks and urban public transit, and the redistribution of public economic development resources to depressed cities and regions.

Building on several of the same key themes and ideas, David Fasenfest considers how a city organized around democratic forms of socioeconomic organization and cooperative enterprise might blunt, if not reverse, Detroit's decline (chapter 12). In a provocative thought experiment, Fasenfest imagines an alternative timeline for Detroit, in which at a critical historical juncture public funds were used to finance a worker-owned and -controlled automobile factory. (In reality, the city provided massive subsidies to General Motors to build a traditionally owned factory in the city's Poletown area. It has long since closed.) He argues that such a move would have generated more stable living-wage jobs and would have reduced the future vulnerability of the community to market forces. Rehearsing the successes experienced by a variety of cooperative movements in a number of countries, Fasenfest notes that small steps in this direction have been taken in Detroit, which could serve as the seeds of a thriving cooperative sector. The thought experiment is filled out by considering the institutional landscape (the enabling legislation, avenues for accessing credit, financial support, and public sector involvement) that would be needed to develop a robust cooperative self-management sector in the city.

Peter Marcuse's reflective theoretical essay "Which Way, 'Detroit'?" (chapter 13), which closes the book, broadens our political imagination with another hopeful and thought-provoking look forward. Marcuse begins by arguing that it is best to view Detroit not as a singular entity, but rather as "multiple Detroits": Corporate Detroit, Working Detroit, and Excluded Detroit. These groups struggle to define the city and chart a path forward. As conventionally understood, the options available to cities are quite limited, especially under conditions of neoliberal austerity. Today, cities must generally pursue development via the "growth game," the "global city game," or the "identity game." Marcuse rejects these familiar strategies due to their respective weaknesses. In their stead, he engages in a utopian thought experiment on the creation of a "New Social City" based on three central normative goals—social justice, social abundance, and democratic decision making. Marcuse recognizes that social divisions, conflicting class interests, and the unequal power relations currently stand in the way of his normative vision. Yet he develops a multi-scalar policy agenda designed to support the goals of social justice, abundance, and democracy. As a crucial first step in making the city a model of progressive socioeconomic and political change, Marcuse stresses the role of democratic political engagement.

Urban reinvention represents a moment of political possibility. But when the process of reinvention and restructuring is dictated primarily by the strict demands of the global economy, the core strategic vision is everywhere the same: the publicly subsidized construction of sports and entertainment megaprojects, high-rise office complexes, high-end residential developments, and high-tech information hubs. Importantly, assessing the prospects for Detroit's recovery purely in terms of market-based reinvestment solutions (and/or other market-based metrics) could reasonably lead to the conclusion that the prospects for recovery are slim indeed. By contrast, when we expand our political imagination to include alternative forms of socioeconomic development and political integration that move beyond market-based logics, the door remains open for more optimistic readings. Several of the contributors to this volume demonstrate the need to consider the significance and impact of social practices that move beyond market exchange—from the reciprocity of Detroit's mower gangs, to various modes of self-provisioning, to the redistributive remnants of the Keynesian welfare state, to the production of autonomous zones of counter-power found sprinkled across the city.

Detroit stands at a crossroads. Decisions made now will have profound and long-lasting political, economic, and infrastructural impacts on the form and functions of the city. The Detroit of the future will be much different than the Detroit of today or the Detroit of yesterday. But will it be a city of inclusion and equitable development, or will it remain stagnant and splintered, reflecting the socio-spatial re-inscription of traditional inequalities? It is our hope that the path it takes will be determined by way of public deliberation and honest democratic engagement. And it would be to our great benefit if competing blueprints for Detroit's future (such as the several proposed in this book) were to be historically and structurally contextualized and critically reappraised. In this way, the arc of Detroit's history may indeed begin bending toward a robust and socially just future.

References

de Solà-Morales Rubio, Ignasi (1995). "Terrain Vague," in C. Davidson (ed.), *Anyplace*. Cambridge: MIT Press.

Fraser, N. (2013). "A Triple Movement," *New Left Review,* 81 (May–June): 119–132.

Gallagher, J. (2010). *Reimagining Detroit: Opportunities for Redefining an American City*. Detroit: Wayne State University Press.

Gibson-Graham, J.K. (2006). *A Postcapitalist Politics*. Minneapolis and London: University of Minnesota Press.

Waldheim, C. and M. Santos-Munné (2001). "Decamping Detroit," in G. Daskalakis, C. Waldheim, and J. Young (eds.), *Stalking Detroit*. Barcelona: Actar Publishers.

Editors' Note:
In some of the chapters in this book, references to Polanyi in the editors' Introduction actually refer to our use of Polanyi in chapter 1.

Part I

Theoretical and Epistemological Frameworks

1

Rereading Detroit: Toward a Polanyian Methodology

L. Owen Kirkpatrick and Michael Peter Smith

The case of Detroit sits uneasily within the analytic confines of existing models of urban change. Such models tend to epistemologically prioritize urban growth, irrespective of whether the analyst's attention lingers on its potential pitfalls or payoffs. The paradigmatic statements that constitute the canon of urban studies thus invariably emerge from the crucible of social expansion and economic intensification. But the story of Detroit—its chronic population decline, long-term economic contraction, and acute social and fiscal distress—challenges the explanatory boundaries of the dominant schools of thought. Hence, it is not uncommon, in both popular and academic discourse, for Detroit to be implicitly or explicitly dismissed as anomalous.

While Detroit is certainly an extreme case of urban decline and abandonment, we do ourselves a disservice by categorizing it as anomalous, and thus outside the purview of our theoretical models. First, avoiding an analytic reconciliation between general processes and a particular outcome, no matter how extreme, is not a compelling strategy. The key, notes Peck, is to engage with, rather than avoid, "the tensions between holistic, integral modes of analysis and the difference-finding methodologies that yield exceptional or disruptive cases" (2013b: 1546). Second, there is an empirical imperative to account for shrinking and distressed cities, the ranks of which are large and growing in the global North (Oswalt 2006). Third, dismissing Detroit as a social or fiscal anomaly serves to camouflage the fact that the city may well represent the leading political edge and/or logical endpoint of advanced (postcrisis) neoliberal austerity. In sum, an approach is needed that can theoretically integrate a wide range of empirical cases (including Detroit) into a framework of urban change under conditions of advanced neoliberalism. We propose that the work of Karl Polanyi can be used as an effective foundation for such an approach.

While Polanyi's core ideas—such as embeddedness and the double movement—have long been staple concepts in the fields of economic anthropology and economic sociology, they have frequently appeared in the study of cities and regions, as well. But despite the broad appeal of Polanyi's thought across a variety of city-related disciplines (urban studies, geography, urban and regional planning, urban sociology), his theory and methods are rarely developed in a sustained or systematic manner with respect to the urban condition (Peck 2013a: 1537). One recent exception can be found in the field of economic geography, where Polanyian approaches are being (re)cast and (re)considered. This exception yields several useful guidelines for developing a Polanyi-inspired analysis of the Detroit case.

We begin by noting that developing such an approach will involve more than the mechanistic transposition of Polanyi's original concepts onto the domain of the modern metropolis. Our task is neither so simple nor so straightforward. If we were to fashion an overly rigid Polanyian model for the purpose of analyzing cities—in all of their undulating, polymorphic, interconnected, and multi-scalar complexity—the framework would surely crack from the pressure. Rather, a more fluid approach is required "that is forgiving, flexible, and responsive both to normatively informed exploration and to empirically conditioned elaboration" (Peck 2013a: 1540). When deployed in this manner, a Polanyian perspective takes the form of a "reflexive methodology, rather than a fixed framework or template" (Peck 2013b: 1547). With this reflexivity in mind, we begin with a brief inventory of the theoretical, conceptual, and methodological insights that a Polanyian orientation affords us in the Detroit case. We continue with an overview of the ways in which the Detroit case, in turn, helps us identify possible lacunae in the Polanyian perspective vis-à-vis urban and regional analysis.

Rereading Detroit through the Lens of Polanyi

A Polanyian orientation theoretically illuminates several pivotal aspects of the Detroit case—including the city's historical trajectory, contemporary political and economic dynamics, and possible futures. But this is not purely a deductive process, as even the strongest and most complementary linkages between the theory and the city demand flexibility in applying one to the other.

The Double Movement, Embeddedness, and the City

We begin with the notion of the *double movement*. According to Polanyi, the contours of modern history resemble a pendulum, which swings between two opposed socio-political forces (Polanyi 2001: 138-40). On one hand are those who seek to expand the reach of markets by limiting social and political intrusions (the laissez-faire movement). On the other are those who seek to mitigate the disruptive impact of markets on social life (the protective countermovement). Ultimately, struggles over the double movement hinge on the proper relationship between markets, communities, and the state—a relationship Polanyi conceptualized in terms of *embeddedness*. According to this formulation, economic activity is naturally embedded within a dense thicket of social, moral, and regulatory expectations and restrictions (Ibid.: 60). "Market society" (which first arose in the early nineteenth century) is characterized by the efforts of powerful entities to invert this traditional relationship by "liberating", or disembedding, markets from a range of constraints imposed via community engagement, cultural tradition, and state intervention.

Polanyi primarily deployed these concepts on the scale of the nation state; a country's level of embeddedness is largely determined by national variables, such as its position within the global economy, the nature of its political system, and the sub-stance of its national policies. Embeddedness at this scale is also understood in terms of social structure; for Polanyi, a country is a "social unit" that, "in the long run, [is] even more cohesive than the economic unit of class" (2001: 255). All of this is not to say that Polanyi turned a blind eye to sub-national scales. For instance, *The Great Transformation* (1944/2001) includes detailed empirical discussions of local struggles over (dis)embeddedness.[1] "Trade unions, Chartism, the cooperative movement, [and] Owenism are [identified by Polanyi as] local reactions to the devastation wrought by the market" (Burawoy 2003: 237).

A certain image of urban political economy emerges from Polanyi's corpus. Market forces are unleashed on the scales of the national (via laissez-faire policies) and inter-national (via global economic and geopolitical pressures). Simultaneously, however, "we also see counter movements that have sought to check, control, or modify the impact of market forces" (Block 2008: 2), many of which unfold on subnational levels (i.e., neighborhood, city, region, state/province). In this view, urban struggles influence national levels of embeddedness, but only in the aggregate. Local protective efforts can take myriad forms, notes Burawoy, "[b]ut *setting out along local tributaries, they eventually flow into national movements*" (2003: 237; emphasis added). This is a telling analogy; just as water "seeks its own level," embeddedness is assumed to flow from struggles at various scales into the vessel of the state, where it settles at a uniform level—a single, undifferentiated surface stretching smoothly across the entirety of a territorially bounded society. For a time, this image roughly aligned with urban real-ity in the United States. This is merely to say that for a good portion of the twentieth century, intergovernmental transfers provided a socioeconomic and socio-spatial floor under which cities were not generally allowed to fall; the well-being of urban communities was pegged to the nation state (via the War on Poverty, infrastructural interventions, etc.).

Today, the image of embeddedness "seeking its own level" across a national territory is no longer accurate. Under conditions of neoliberalism, cities are cut loose from the protectionary embrace of the nation state. For better or worse, cities are set adrift and left to sink or swim by their own devices. Those that succeed—such as growing cities and those otherwise looked upon favorably by financial markets—are in a good position to provide their citizens with basic public services and infrastructure systems. Cities that cannot tread water, on the other hand, are locked out of capital markets and left without assistance from higher scales of governance, as authorities are no longer compelled by the norms of embeddedness to blunt the sharpest edges of uneven development. So a rather new image emerges; instead of embeddedness being evenly distributed across a national territory, we find a highly variegated inter-urban geography characterized by sharp peaks and deep valleys.

Despite the fact that the geography of embeddedness has changed since Polanyi's first implicit mappings, his core concepts can still play an invaluable role in its navigation. Take, again, the double movement. Polanyi's ambitious intellectual agenda drew his focus to macro political economies. But when we emphasize sub-national scales of governance, we are presented with new ways of thinking about the double movement. For instance, the jagged and irregular geography of urban embeddedness can be interpreted as the socio-spatial fragmentation of the double movement. And once we allow for the geographical splintering of the double movement, we must also grant the possibility of its segmental breakdown (an issue to which we'll return below). The concept of embeddedness can be similarly modified. Gemici proposes a useful interpretive inflection in the concept of "gradational embeddedness"—according to which the "degree of embeddedness changes from one type of [social unit] to another" (2008, 9). In sum, Polanyi's core concepts can be utilized to explore new, radically uneven geographies of urban and regional (dis)emeddedness. From this perspective, there are no anomalous cases; all cities can be explained in terms of their imbricate position within sociopolitically fragmented, gradationally embedded spaces.

Modes of Socioeconomic Integration in Detroit

We make a significant analytic advance when our models explicitly attend to extreme inter-urban variation. This is certainly true with respect to the double movement, as some cities have managed to maintain rather high levels of embeddedness (despite countervailing national trends), while others have been unable to protect their most vulnerable communities from the vicissitudes of the market. But while concepts such as gradational embeddedness help us assess inter-urban (between cities) variation, we need to introduce additional analytic tools in order to gain purchase on patterns of intra-urban (within cities) variation. For this more granular task, we turn to the four principle types of economic behavior: exchange, redistribution, reciprocity, and householding (Polanyi 2001: 45–58). These foundational activities represent "modes of socioeconomic integration" that form the basic building blocks of societies. As a rule, according to Polanyi, the economic sphere of a given society is comprised of a hybrid mix of these four types of socioeconomic behavior. For our purposes, the concept allows us to systematically explore the "various social and institutional ways in which provisioning for material wants have been (and can be) organized" in Detroit (Peck 2013b: 1555).

Of the four principle forms of socioeconomic activity, market *exchange* is both the newest and most cocksure. Only bursting onto the scene in the early nineteenth century, exchange is a form of economic behavior based on individual self-interest. Famously identified as the essential, eternal core of human nature by Adam Smith, our "propensity to truck, barter, and exchange" is believed to provide the social-psychological groundwork for a completely disembedded market society. But Polanyi insists that economic reality is much different than the idealized image projected by economic orthodoxy. Actually existing economies are never unadulterated constructs (of one type or another), but rather are partial and hybrid. Purity of the sort peddled by mainstream economics, argues Polanyi, is a dangerous illusion, as it "means no less than the running of society as an adjunct to the market" (Polanyi 2001: 60). In a typical capitalist city, market exchange is the dominant form of economic activity. Other forms of socioeconomic integration do not disappear (as many economists would predict), but they must live in the long shadow of the market, and the illusion remains intact. But in shrinking cities such as Detroit, where markets are contracting and capital is in full retreat, the illusion can be shattered quite dramatically. The retreat of capital and markets opens up a space that is filled not only with other forms of socioeconomic activity (e.g., reciprocity, householding), but also with various forms of hybridized exchange, such as diverse cooperative ventures (worker and consumer), local trading systems, alternative (local) currencies, underground exchanges, and informal markets (Gibson-Graham 2006a: xiii).

Second, systems of *redistribution* are "typically marked by appropriational movements to and from a recognized central authority, tribal or governmental" (Peck 2013b: 1556). Under Keynesianism, when cities suffered economic dislocation, the most adversely affected communities could expect to be the beneficiaries of a (relatively) progressive system of taxation and redistribution. The socioeconomic and institutional space being opened up in Detroit by retreating markets, however, is not being filled by the public safety net. Redistribution still occurs, but not in the progressive, Keynesian sense. In Detroit, the key central authority is no longer the federal government, but rather an EM who enjoys vast, near dictatorial control over municipal resources. Furthermore, the direction of redistribution has, in effect, been reversed. The welfare state sought to establish a system of cross subsidies benefitting poor and marginalized urban communities. Appropriation and redistribution under conditions of neoliberal austerity, by contrast, seek to transfer resources from poor and working class urban communities to extra-local financial entities. In Detroit, all collectively held and bargained assets are in danger of being privatized so as to better meet the city's financial obligations—including, but not limited to, public infrastructure networks and service system assets, natural resources and amenities, cultural artifacts, and public pensions and health benefits.

With markets in retreat and progressive patterns of redistribution a thing of the past, there is a critical void with respect to the "provisioning of material wants" in Detroit. It appears that this void is being filled, in significant measure, by burgeoning systems of *reciprocity*. "Reciprocal modes of integration", reports Peck, "are embedded in recurring, social logics of give-and-take [and are] predicated on broadly symmetrical social relations" (2013b: 1556). Prototypically embodied in the "gift relationship," norms of reciprocity can take either "thin" or "thick" forms. In its thin manifestation, reciprocity is consistent with the logic of the market, "since the parties are able to do a relatively precise cost-benefit analysis to make sure that they will gain materially from the exchange" (Block 2008: 8). Market complementarity is possible because thin reciprocity meets the tripartite criteria of dyadic symmetry, value equivalence, and temporal limits (Ibid.). Reciprocated behavior of the thick variety, by contrast, breaks these rules. Gifts still need to be reciprocated, "though not necessarily by the same individuals" (Polanyi, 2001, 55), the gifts need not be of the same (exchange) value, and "the timing of the obligation is open-ended" (Block 2008: 8).

Researchers have only scratched the surface with respect to the systems of thick reciprocity that seem to flourish in contemporary shrinking cities. But initial reports out of Detroit indicate that reciprocity is emerging as a crucial mode of economic provisioning and social integration. Take, for example, local reactions to the decay of the urban built environment. Detroit's real estate market has been crippled by more than a half-century of white flight, a grinding deterioration punctuated by the subprime mortgage crisis. At the same time, government (at all scales) has proven unwilling or unable to intercede in a manner that mitigates market decline. This is true on the most basic of levels, such as the failure of the city to provide reliable fire and police services in damaged neighborhoods (further eroding property values). Into this void has arisen all manner of social initiatives that appear principally motivated by the norms of reciprocity. These reciprocal enterprises tend to occupy and reshape "the spatial residue of capital's withdrawal—valueless property, abandoned buildings, vacant lots, unserviced neighborhoods" (Herscher 2012: 9). For instance, a variety of efforts have been launched focused on vacant and abandoned lots—including an array of community agriculture projects guided by the principles of food security and social justice (Ibid.: 38–63). These efforts can bleed into broader neighborhood maintenance initiatives, such as block clubs, park crews (e.g., the "Detroit Mower Gang"; Ibid.), and various other "guerilla-style spatial interventions" (Kinder 2014). Thus, we begin to get a glimpse of "how a decline in the exchange value of property" has created the conditions "for new sorts of commons" based on reciprocal forms of integration (Herscher 2012: 10).

The final mode of socioeconomic integration is *householding*: any self-sufficient system of provisioning in an autarkic ("closed") social formation. It is a principle of economic activity that amounts to "producing and storing for the satisfaction of the wants of the members of the group." While such systems exist outside of the market proper, self-provisioning activities involving "accessory production for [profit] . . . need not destroy the basis of householding" (Polanyi 2001: 55–56). As a principle of economic behavior, householding may thus "straddle both the market and nonmarket domains" (Gregory 2009: 143). While redistribution and reciprocity are often used as general historical categories, householding is understood as a "historically specific concept"—applicable to specific social spaces at specific historical moments—the "patriarchal family, village settlement, seigniorial manor" (Ibid.: 135). Polanyi does not mention householding in the context of cities, as they appear to have been virtually eliminated from urban centers in the industrial era. Today, however, householding is making definitive inroads into the socioeconomic fabric of shrinking cities. In Detroit, for example, "urban homesteading" is blossoming. This practice is encouraged by "blotting," whereby homeowners acquire empty and abandoned lots that are property adjacent (often for the purpose of food production). Consider also "micropolitanism": small, relatively self-contained social systems tucked away in spatial crevices around the city—places that "comprise a world . . . at a downsized scale."

> [Detroit is] punctuated by havens, pockets, isolated islands, narrow interstices . . . urban farmers clustered on a city block, a subculture thriving at the tail of a dead-ended street, a complex of houses sheltering immigrants . . . place[s] . . . to refuse, to differ, to disappear, to live otherwise (Herscher 2012: 192).

The popularity of householding and micropolitanism in Detroit suggests an insurgent, subaltern set of sociopolitical practices, in which the "goal is not to wrest control, but to create autonomous zones of counterpower" (Gibson-Graham 2006b: xx).

Polanyian Methodologies

According to neoclassical economics, market exchange is based on formal cost-benefit analyses, a calculus that must be free of social and political interference. Polanyi stakes out an opposing perspective that begins with the notion of the substantive economy. "The fount of the substantive concept", observes, Polanyi, "is the empirical economy. It can be briefly (if not engagingly) defined as an instituted process of interaction between man and his environments, which results in a continuous supply of want satisfying material means" (1957: 248). A great methodological schism opens up from these competing (formal vs. substantive) definitions of the economy. In contrast to the formal, abstract modeling of "pure" market behavior favored by mainstream economists (based on methodological individualism), Polanyi insists on the social and institutional "rootedness" of economic activity (Halperin 1994: 209). This leads to three methodological principles that can be usefully applied to studies of urban change.

The first insight can be found in Polanyi's dictum that the economy is an "instituted process." The principles of economic behavior (exchange, redistribution, reciprocity, and householding) "cannot become effective unless existing institutional patterns lend themselves to their application" (2001: 51). Peck elaborates, "Institutionalist analyses must duly attend to those organized (or 'instituted') patterns of valuation, understanding, and behavior that are culturally stabilized and contested within different socio-economies" (2013b: 1553).[2] A second methodological precept involves historicizing and spatializing our analysis. "The substantive economy is situated in both time and place", observes Halperin, "[while] the formal economy . . . operates in a time and space vacuum" (1994: 209). When we explicitly attend to the empirical (historical, spatial, and institutional) particularities of a given case, it becomes clear that "actually existing" cities are complex, hybrid entities—"combinatory sites of multiple rationalities, interests, and values, rather than . . . singular and invariant economic laws" (Peck 2013b: 1555).[3] Third, the substantive model of the economy lends itself to the logic of comparative analysis. Variegated socioeconomic formations of (and in) cities can only be fully appreciated in relation to one another and in relation to the larger societal units in which they are nested. Ultimately, a proper model of urban change "must provide for more than the 'internal' deconstruction of heterogeneous economies; it must also attend to questions of uneven spatial development across those economies" (Peck 2013b: 1563).

These broad methodological tenets draw our attention to a common fallacy with respect to Detroit. Many observers (especially on the political Left) are sympathetic to the notion that the city's decline was inevitable—the unfortunate but ineluctable result of economic globalization and deindustrialization. In one variant of this thinking, Detroit's decline is chalked up to a rare confluence of factors that rendered the city structurally reliant on a single industry, which ultimately sealed its unenviable fate. A Polanyian orientation would view such assumptions skeptically. Methodology is important here because historical and comparative analyses (of labor and management regulations and related urban and public policy contexts) produce substantial evidence challenging the fallacy of inevitability. When we break out of the local spatio-temporal orbit, we are able to compare actually existing responses to neoliberalism. What we find is a diverse array of innovative social, economic, and political initiatives in other shrinking cities and regions across the globe, including postcapitalist socioeconomic possibilities in Greece, "social economy" initiatives in Quebec, and state-managed labor and management regulations in Germany (the latter case demonstrating that deindustrialization doesn't necessarily lead to deskilling and massive employment decline).

A Polanyian methodology thus suggests that urban shrinkage is not the inevitable result of inexorable economic forces, but rather is the outcome of sociopolitical choices, struggles and negotiations at various scales.

Rereading Polanyi through the Lens of Detroit

Following Peck (2013a; 2013b), we have argued that applying a Polanyian perspective to the urban condition demands a certain analytic reflexivity. We have outlined some of the ways Polanyi's thought can be used to better understand the decline of Detroit (and other shrinking cities). But it is also important to engage in the inverse exercise; namely to interrogate how Detroit informs Polanyian theory. Here we argue that the Detroit case inductively highlights and empirically illuminates several aspects of Polanyi's thought that require critical rereading. This is a flexible and generative undertaking that pushes the Polanyian approach forward so as to expand its analytic breadth and depth.

(Firmly) Inserting Race

The story of Detroit cannot be deeply understood unless the issue of race is foregrounded (Sugrue 1996; Thomas 1997; Farley, Danziger, and Holzer 2000). Race permeates the politics and economics of the region, a fact that is reinforced demographically. As the population of Detroit shrank, the proportion of African American residents soared: from 16 percent in 1950 (pop. 1.8 million), to 83 percent in 2010 (pop. 713,000). Today, urban-suburban tensions in the area track the color line; a recent study ranked Detroit as the most segregated metropolitan region in the United States (Logan and Stults 2011). Clearly, race has had a profound influence on Detroit's trajectory; it would be folly to suggest otherwise. This observation has important theoretical implications, at least insofar as our model must be able to explicitly account for race. On this point we observe that while the traditional Polanyian model does not assign race an explicit role in the double movement, the framework does allow for its consideration (along with other axes of social exclusion). We believe, moreover, that the framework is robust enough that race can be placed closer to, or further from, the core of the analysis, as the empirical circumstances dictate.

Polanyi believed that the battle over the double movement would primarily be waged by shifting, cross-class coalitions. This opens up the possibility of political groupings being formed along extra-economic axes, such as race. As Fred Block notes, "Polanyi followed Weber in recognizing that in actual politics, classes often divide along multiple lines"; class antagonisms are crosscut by and against other axes of social difference (2008: 5). While this dynamic may open up possibilities for marginalized populations to engage in innovative alliance building, it also presents distinct challenges, because "[t]hose who most need protection from the market are often separated from each other by religious, ethnic, racial, gender, age or other divisions" (Ibid.: 7).

In the case of race, social divisions are also reflected spatially. Hence, questions concerning social separation must also be framed in terms of the creation and enforcement of socio-spatial boundaries. From a Polanyian perspective, this dynamic is best understood in terms of gradational embeddedness—the geographical unevenness of the contemporary double movement. Rendering the racial geography of the double movement for closer analysis involves a more granular mapping of how "the embedding and disembedding of economy and society are formed out of the struggles over geographically constituted social relations" (Smith 2013: 1657). These struggles can be infused with racial tension and conflict. When minorities are concentrated in particular spaces, and these spaces are stigmatized and subjected to alternate techniques of governance (i.e., emergency management), than the table is set for the *racial segmentation of the double movement*.

There is also room in a Polanyian account for race to play a formative role in ideological struggles over embeddedness. For Polanyi, the double movement is an "open" political affair in which peoples' perceptions and beliefs matter. In each instance, the confrontation between the forces seeking to disembed markets and those seeking to (re)embed them are dependent not only on the resources and skills of the primary combatants, but also the perceptions, beliefs, and worldviews of secondary social actors. "[T]he two competing movements struggle to influence the state in their own preferred direction, but their relative power will be heavily dependent on the political and economic conditions and how those specific conditions have been perceived by social actors. . . . In these battles, ideology is an essential resource" (Block 2008: 4). Race fulfills a discursive function in this respect whereby poor, majority-black cities are blamed for their own decline. This can be communicated stealthily, via a discourse of municipal ineptitude, corruption, and greed—a "culture of poverty" perspective that tends to emphasize black "pathologies."

The Retreat of Markets

If we are to appropriate Polanyi's thought for the purposes of analyzing Detroit, we must confirm that it is able to explain cases of chronic and acute market contraction. This is no small matter, as Polanyi's scholarly raison d'être was the critical examination of market expansion (and political struggles over said expansion). But can a theory designed to interrogate the unrelenting advancement of markets and the stubborn expansion of commodification be used to study the obverse? The short answer, we believe, is yes. While long-term contractionary conditions were not Polanyi's focus, his conceptual tools can be used to gain analytic leverage in such cases. Consider the case of fictitious commodities.

Polanyi attached special importance to the relative embeddedness of land, labor, and money. He referred to these items as *fictitious commodities* (the "factors of production" in the parlance of mainstream economics) because—as they are not created for sale on the market—they do not respond faithfully (or in equilibrious fashion) to market forces such as supply and demand. While market exchange may be well suited for "real" commodities, it is unable to govern the production and distribution of their fictitious counterparts (Polanyi 2001: 71–80). Efforts to disembed land, labor, and money will invariably lead to socioeconomic dislocation, which in turn triggers the protective countermovement. Thus, in "normal" times of capitalist growth and expansion, we would expect to find battles over the double movement to be particularly pitched around the factors of production. In times of declination, land, labor, and money continue to be vital pressure points in the double movement. For instance, in a recent review of community development practices in the contractionary, postcrisis period, Kirkpatrick (2012) traces community-based efforts to (re)embed land (community land trusts), labor (worker co-ops), and money (community development finance institutions) back into the norms, networks, and institutions of local communities. We can also profitably explore the ways burgeoning systems of reciprocity and householding intersect with the fictitious commodities; here we would be less concerned with efforts to (re) embed market relations (with respect to land, labor, and money), and more concerned with their role in entirely distinct, alternative systems of socioeconomic integration. As noted, when formal markets retreat, a space opens in which alternative systems can take root.

According to Polanyi, there is nothing in the laws of history or society that would prevent the type of socioeconomic breakdown we're witnessing in Detroit. From this perspective, societal struggles related to the double movement are not historically predetermined. Breaking from the enlightenment orthodoxy of the day (which saw society as progressing on a linear path to some predestined endpoint), Polanyi viewed history as non-teleological and "open" to socioeconomic contingencies and the vagaries of sociopolitical contestation. This preference for the cyclical over the linear is particularly useful in the context of Detroit (and other shrinking cities) whose violent trajectory belies simple teleological assumptions.

The Crisis of (Urban) Democracy

Perhaps the biggest hurdle in applying a Polanyian frame to the Detroit case lies in the question of urban democracy. Scholars note the multiform ways that democracy has come under assault in recent decades, leading some to decry the emergence of the "post-political" (Swyngedouw 2007) or "post-democratic" city (MacLeod 2011). As Block observes, the process of depoliticization profoundly threatens the functioning of the double movement.

> In its specifics, the double movement is a theory of politics in societies that are at least nominally democratic and where citizens have a set of basic political rights. . . . The double movement is about the normal politics of market societies with democratic governance, where adherents of both *laissez faire* and the protective counter movement are able to press their case in the political arena (2008: 5).

In Detroit, the gains made at mid-century were at the ballot box and the negotiating table via collective bargaining. But both types of local political power have since been categorically decimated. We can broadly identify two categories of factors contributing to the de-democratization of urban and regional governance. The first are the usual suspects—general political and economic trends that blunt democratic processes. The second is a set of techniques that have emerged more recently, under conditions of advanced neoliberal austerity. Taken together, they raise the prospect that the double movement is irreparably broken.

First, we must acknowledge the effects of socioeconomic changes associated with globalization and deindustrialization, which not only caused large-scale economic dislocation, but also devastated the power of private sector unions in the city. This fits a general pattern of institutional abandonment, class and race-based patterns of depopulation, and the systemic flight of industry/jobs from the confines of the city. Also well documented is the retrenchment and redirection of federal urban policy since the latter decades of the twentieth century. The shift away from the Keynesian welfare state and toward the neoliberal austerity state has had unfavorable impacts on local democracy, while signaling a general retreat from the ideal of direct democratic participation. This effort has more recently been reinforced by new techniques and modes of de-democratization. On the national and state level, for instance, we see the growing political importance of corporate capital, elite-funded PACs, and aggressive lobbying and legislation-writing operations in US cities. On the local level, meanwhile, the alarming suspension of local democratic self-rule via "emergency management" measures is an assault on citizenship rights and legal-juridical status of Detroit residents and opens the door for the systematic assault on public labor unions and pension protections. Under these conditions it may seem hard if not impossible to imagine local communities launching a broadly successful "counter-movement." There are very few, if any, traditional political mechanisms that Detroit residents can use to protect themselves from market forces (or the lack thereof).

Despite these alarming trends, we believe that there are two reasons why a Polanyian orientation remains applicable to the case of Detroit. First, emergency management laws (and related measures) are a socio-spatially targeted technique of governance. As such, they must still be legitimated in the wider political arena; consent must still be sought, on some level, for targeted de-democratization. This being the case, the political future of Detroit is still in play vis-à-vis the checks and balances of the democratic system. Secondly, on a temporal level we can also observe that many of the more aggressive anti-democratic tendencies observed in Detroit are as of yet still quite recent phenomena; they may yet amount to mere historical footnotes in the continuing tome of democracy.

In the final analysis, we recall Polanyi's theoretical injunction that history is not written in advance. Struggles over embeddedness at various scales are indeterminate, agency oriented, and open to social, economic, and political contingency. Thus, only time will tell whether the double movement survives the current crisis of urban democracy. With all that being said, there are several reasons for optimism. First, perhaps the double movement can be jump-started. If the neoliberal advances we have identified can be beaten back by a protective countermovement, then we could imagine a re-invigorated federal urban policy platform, a revitalized labor movement, and a re-energized and re-democratized local political arena. But a Polanyian perspective also raises another, more radical possibility, namely, the segmental transformation away from market society entirely, in which economically and institutionally abandoned cities develop new systems of socioeconomic integration and new ways of defining, valuing, and interacting with space, place, and markets.

Notes

1. This includes an analysis of both the Speenhamland system and the enclosure movement (Polanyi 2001).
2. "Conceptually and methodologically," Peck continues, "the foundational sociological principle here is that institutional formations preexist the patterning of individual behavior" (2013b: 1553).
3. Polanyian categories are thus utilized best as Weberian "ideal types"—abstract tools of categorization that never perfectly match-up with empirical reality.

References

Block, F. (2008). "Polanyi's Double Movement and the Reconstruction of Critical Theory." *Revue Interventions économiques*, 38: consulté le 04 février 2014. URL: http://interventionseconomiques. revues.org/274.

Burawoy, M. (2003). "For a Sociological Marxism: The Complementary Convergence of Antonio Gramsci and Karl Polanyi." *Politics & Society*, 31 (2): 193–261.

Farley, R., S. Danziger, and H. J. Holzer (2000). *Detroit Divided*. New York: Russell Sage Foundation.

Gemici, K. (2008). "Karl Polanyi and the Antinomies of Embeddedness." *SocioEconomic Review* 6 (1): 5–33.

Gibson-Graham, J. K. (2006a). *The End of Capitalism (as we knew it): a feminist critique of political economy* (with a new introduction). Minneapolis; London: University of Minnesota Press (1st University of Minnesota Press ed.).

————. (2006b). *A Postcapitalist Politics*. Minneapolis; London: University of Minnesota Press.

Gregory, C. (2009). "Whatever Happened to Householding?" in C. Hann K. and Hart (eds.), *Market and Society: The Great transformation Today*. Cambridge; New York: Cambridge University Press.

Halperin, R. H. (1994). *Cultural Economies Past and Present*. Austin: University of Texas Press.

Herschner, A. (2012). *The Unreal Estate Guide to Detroit*. Ann Arbor: University of Michigan Press.

Kinder, K. (2014). "Guerrilla-Style Defensive Architecture in Detroit: A Self-provisioned Security Strategy in a Neoliberal Space of Disinvestment." *International Journal of Urban & Regional Research*, 38 (5): 1767–1784.

Kirkpatrick, L. O. (2012). "The Local Politics of Embeddedness: Karl Polanyi and the Community Development Movement." In J. Peter Rothe, L. Carroll, and D. Ozegovic (eds.), *Deliberations on Community Development*. NY: Nova Science Publishers.

Logan, J. R. and B. Stults (2011). "The Persistence of Segregation in the Metropolis: New Findings from the 2010 Census." Census Brief prepared for Project US2010. At: http://www.s4.brown.edu/us2010.

MacLeod, G. (2011). "Urban Politics Reconsidered: Growth Machine to Post-democratic City?" *Urban Studies*, 48 (12): 2629–2660.

Oswalt, P. (ed.), (2006). *Atlas of Shrinking Cities*. Ostfildern: Hatje Cantz.

Peck, J. (2013a). "Disembedding Polanyi: Exploring Polanyian Economic Geographies." *Environment and Planning A* 45 (7): 1536–1544.

————. (2013b). "For Polanyian Economic Geographies." *Environment and Planning A* 45 (7): 1545–1568.

Polanyi, K. (2001). *The Great Transformation: the Political And Economic Origins of Our Time*. 2nd Beacon Paperback ed. Boston, MA: Beacon Press.

————. (1957). "The Economy as Instituted Process," in K. Polanyi, C. M. Arensberg, and H. W. Pearson (eds.), *Trade and Market in the Early Empires; Economies in History and Theory*. Chicago: Henry Regnery Company.

Smith, A. (2013). "Polanyi, Double Movements, and Political Economic Transformations." *Environment and Planning A* 45 (7): 1656–1661.

Sugrue, T. J. (1996). *The Origins of the Urban Crisis: Race and Inequality in Postwar Detroit*. Princeton, NJ: Princeton University Press.

Swyngedouw, E. (2007). "The Post-Political City." *Urban Politics Now*, BAVO Reflect Series, Netherland Architecture Institute (NAI)-Publishers, Rotterdam.

Thomas, J. M. (1997). *Redevelopment and Race: Planning a Finer City in Postwar Detroit*. Baltimore: Johns Hopkins University Press.

2

The Spontaneous Sociology of Detroit's Hyper-Crisis

Mathieu Hikaru Desan and George Steinmetz

The crisis of Detroit is not just a dual crisis of the city and the US automobile industry, or of bankruptcy and abandonment. It is a social hyper-crisis. By that we mean something very specific. A social hyper-crisis is one in which the determinants of crisis are a complex conjuncture of causes, and the crisis itself is irreducible to a single region of social space. A social hyper-crisis is not the same thing as a really big crisis, such as an economic depression, as opposed to a recession. Nor is it the same thing as a meta-crisis, in which some essential economic, political, or cultural force can be identified as the true principle of which all levels of the social structure are but an expression. Nor is a hyper-crisis the same thing as Gramsci's "organic crisis" (Gramsci 1971), which denotes a crisis of hegemony leading to "the collapse of the representative function and leaving the field open for providential or charismatic men." In the case of Detroit we cannot foresee the crisis being resolved by charismatic leadership.[1]

Detroit's social hyper-crisis is a massively overdetermined social crisis: not just a crisis of the city, not just an economic and fiscal crisis, but a political and cultural crisis as well. It is also a specifically epistemological crisis. The object "Detroit" was contested by a series of politically very distinct voices between the 1920 and 1970s, ranging from the labor unions and management to social scientists and the mass media.[2] In contrast to this rather sharply defined contest of images, recent decades have seen a simplification of discourse and the reproduction of "common-sense" clichés.

One peculiarity of Detroit's hyper-crisis is that it is unfolding in a global context in which the entire world seems to have fixed on the city as a symbol of crisis. The existing tropes of ruin and decline are now melded with the tropes of fiscal irresponsibility, urban pathology, and political dysfunction. Many professional academics and policy-makers deplore the proliferation of these images, but the key point is their global spread. Photographers and filmmakers from around the world come to Detroit hoping or fearing to glimpse their own future or to revel in the decline of a former superpower. People everywhere refer to depressed or indebted cities in their own countries as "Detroit." In the past two years the German media have referred to cities from Bochum to Stuttgart as "the German Detroit." The Spanish media call cities from Arnedo to Valencia "*el Detroit*

15

Españo." In the French media, cities from Clermont to Roubaix have been labeled "*le Détroit français.*" The French Communist Party recently included a photo by Yves Marchand and Romain Meffre (2010) of the abandoned William Livingstone House in Detroit in an article on French pension reform, as if the dilapidated house were a generic symbol for capitalist crisis.[3]

The dramatic impression left by Detroit's current plight has encouraged the sense that the meaning of Detroit's crisis is taken to be legible on its surface. To the economic, political, and cultural crises, then, must be added a crisis of interpretation. Popular accounts of Detroit's decline have too often tended either to reduce blame to a single factor or, in what amounts to the same thing, to inflate its crisis into an essentialist meta-crisis. Readings of Detroit by political actors, journalists, and social scientists have likewise remained mired in surface appearances. They often end up reproducing or merely inverting the immediate phenomenological appearances of the object. Grasping Detroit's social hyper-crisis in its overdetermined complexity first requires critically deconstructing the pre-constructed fallacies of a spontaneous analysis that the spectacular quality of Detroit's crisis so temptingly invites.

Epistemological Obstacles: The Spontaneous Sociology of Detroit's Decline

Drawing on philosopher Gaston Bachelard's (2002) notion of the necessary "epistemological break" that must precede all social research, Pierre Bourdieu, Jean-Claude Chamboredon, and Jean-Claude Passeron argue in *The Craft of Sociology* (Bourdieu et al. 1991: 14) that "epistemological vigilance is particularly necessary in the social sciences, where the separation between everyday opinion and scientific discourse is more blurred than elsewhere." The social scientist's "struggle with spontaneous sociology" is complicated by his own embeddedness in the social universe he is studying. Where the object of study systematically produces misleading knowledge about itself (as in Marx's famous analysis of commodity fetishism), the epistemological break will be especially difficult. But as we will see, this break is especially necessary in the case of Detroit, many of whose surface characteristics systematically generate misleading ideologies.

Elsewhere Bourdieu turns his attention to the "site effects" that mark the study of urban marginality. He remarks that "referring to a 'problem suburb' or 'ghetto' almost automatically brings to mind, not 'realities' . . . but phantasms, which feed on the emotional experiences stimulated by more or less uncontrolled words and images" (Bourdieu et al. 1999: 123). Bourdieu also warns against the "empiricist illusion" according to which it is enough to "go see" a place in order to "break with accepted ideas and ordinary discourse" and thus know "what it's all about" (Bourdieu et al. 1999: 123). In fact, the "essential principle of what is lived and seen *on the ground . . .* is elsewhere" (Bourdieu et al. 1999: 123). Bourdieu could have written these words about Detroit, which too has come to take on a phantasmagorical appearance in the popular imagination. But as Bourdieu also recognized, the issue goes beyond the circulation of sensationalized media images. It is the very lived relation to the city, i.e., the categories and forms of common-sense perception and experience, that is often at the source of the most entrenched "epistemological obstacles" (Bachelard 2002) to an adequate account of Detroit's urban crisis.

In what follows we identify several of these "epistemological obstacles": the empiricist treatment of Detroit's ruinscape; the recent spotlight on the 2013 municipal bankruptcy as the apotheosis of the city's long decline; a narrow focus on the central city that glosses over Detroit's location in a metropolitan system of inequality; and the pervasive cultural branding of Detroit that has become the common idiom of corporate boosters and civic do-gooders alike. Each of these spontaneous sociological "pre-notions" is rooted in certain empirical realities even as they produce scientific fictions, and each one systematically distorts our vision of Detroit's urban crisis. Structuring the mental categories with which the city and its crisis are apprehended, they have shaped the ordinary discourse about Detroit and infiltrated the discourse of academic specialists. Yet it is precisely the task of the social scientist to break with the spontaneous and seemingly self-evident categories of perception that are generated by the social order but that nonetheless systematically misrecognize the real processes determining that order.[4] It is thus necessary to distinguish between a problematic dedicated to solving "social problems" and one oriented towards "sociological problems" (Bourdieu et al. 1991: 247–259). Whereas the latter follows the exigencies of scientific inquiry and emerges from a careful theoretical construction of one's object, the former takes for granted the pre-constructed objects imposed by the social order, and as such ends up smuggling in the ideological distortions inherent to it.

Few cities in the world seem more desperate than Detroit for solutions to its "social problems." It is our contention, however, that it is first necessary to ask what is implied and what is obscured in how these problems are defined. Only then can we fully appreciate the overdetermined nature of Detroit's urban crisis.

The Ruin Effect

It is impossible not to be struck by the archipelago of blight that stretches across Detroit. Indeed, the numerous vacant lots and abandoned structures have become some of the city's most distinguishing features, amply documented by a cottage industry of professional and amateur photographers (Marchand and Meffre 2010, Moore and Levine 2010, Vergara 1999) in a genre that has been ideologically dubbed "ruin porn" (Binelli 2012).[5] The city's most iconic structure is arguably not the fortress-like Renaissance Center dominating the downtown skyline, but rather the skeletal eighteen-story façade of the vacant Beaux-Arts Michigan Central Station. The station and the abandoned 325,000-square-meter Packard Automotive Plant have become tourist destinations of sorts, attracting throngs of gawkers and "urban explorers." They are obligatory waypoints on the many driving tours of the city.[6] But the grandeur of Detroit's ruins is more than matched by the sheer ubiquity of blight. The recently convened Detroit Blight Removal Task Force, for example, counted 114,000 vacant lots (i.e., 30 percent of city parcels) and 78,506 blighted structures (i.e., 30 percent of total structures) in the city. The vast majority (92 percent) of these blighted structures are single-family houses spread out over Detroit's residential neighborhoods (Detroit Blight Removal Task Force 2014).

Detroit's many overgrown lots, torched homes, hollowed out high-rises, and collapsing factories are not just inescapable features of the urban landscape, they have become powerful tropes orienting interpretations of the city and its fate. Whether nourishing white suburbanites' nostalgic longing for a bygone era of prosperity (Steinmetz 2008) or material condensations of the contradictions of capitalism, Detroit's ruins are readily available for signification.[7] Indeed, images of the ruins accompany almost every story about the city, often without commentary, as if their meaning were obvious.

But if Detroit's blight problem is undeniable, the prevailing fixation on it can be deeply deceptive. John Patrick Leary notes that in viewing Detroit ruin photography,

> one is conscious of nothing so much as failure—of the city itself, of course, but also of the photographs to communicate anything more than that self-evident fact. This is the meta-irony of these often ironic pictures: Though they trade on the peculiarity of Detroit as living ruin, these are pictures of histori-cal oblivion. The decontextualized aesthetics of ruin make them pictures of nothing and no place in particular. (Leary 2011)

In the tradition of "ruingazing," the fascination with Detroit's ruins often says more about the projected fantasies of observers than about any inherent meaning disclosed by the ruins (Hell 2010, Steinmetz 2008). Deeply evocative and aesthetically effec-tive, the ruins nonetheless remain silent about the particular sociohistorical forces that have ravaged Detroit. The ruins, together with the perennial stories about the city's reclamation by the "urban prairie," the hordes of feral dogs, and the return of pheas-ants, encourage an aestheticized contemplation of the city as a depopulated wasteland settled into an equipoise with nature (Simmel 1965). And yet as haunting as they can be, the city's blighted structures are not akin to ancient ruins, and Detroit is not a fallen civilization that has vanished into history. Indeed, despite losing more than half its population in the past sixty years, Detroit remains a large city. Who would know from the phenomenological impression left by the ruinscape that 700,000 people still live in the city, or that at 5,142 people per square mile Detroit remains more densely populated than Portland, Atlanta, and Indianapolis? Obscured by Detroit's ruins is the very simple fact that a great many people still live there and struggle with problems a good deal more prosaic than those evoked by the poetic wreckage of the city's past.

None of this is to deny that the omnipresent blight has real negative effects. If, as Bourdieu argues, social structures are inscribed in spatial structures and these are in turn inscribed in mental structures, then it follows that the daily exposure to abandon-ment is a demoralizing form of symbolic violence perpetually reminding Detroiters of their disposability. But the point is precisely that although blight is a problem *for* Detroiters, it does not in itself divulge the truth *of* Detroit's crisis. Nor can it disclose its own source in unchecked suburban development that, in a process George Galster calls "the housing disassembly line," has rendered the urban housing market largely redundant (Galster 2012). In Bourdieu's terms, then, the "essential principle" not only of Detroit's malaise, but also of the blight itself, is not contained within the ruined landscape. It is, indeed, "elsewhere" (Bourdieu et al 1999: 123).

The Bankruptcy Effect

The recent interest in Detroit has doubtless been due to the spectacle of the July 2013 bankruptcy filing. The largest municipal bankruptcy in US history, Detroit's total long-term debt burden is said to stand at $18–20 billion, with roughly $8 billion owed to creditors and $12 billion in unfunded pension and health care obligations. Given the city's long-term economic decline, it is unsurprising that it should be fiscally challenged. A recent report by the *Detroit Free Press* showed that between 1958 and 2012 assessed property values fell from $45.2 billion (adjusted for inflation) to $9.6 billion (Bomey and Gallagher 2013). To make things worse, only half of Detroit property owners actually pay their property taxes (Detroit Blight Task Force 2014). Consequently, property taxes today constitute a diminished share of a much-reduced total revenue stream. Whereas in 1960 property taxes accounted for 49 percent of the $2 billion (in 2013 dollars) collected by the city, today they make up only 13 percent of $1.1 billion. While Detroit has tapped other sources of cash, it has not been able to collect enough to meet more than basic obligations. In 2012, 83 percent of city spending, compared to only 38 percent in 1960, was dedicated to emergency services, pension and health care contributions, and debt servicing. In the same period, the city has more than halved its payroll (Bomey and Gallagher 2013). Even so, at the time of the bankruptcy declaration many needs notoriously still went unmet (City of Detroit Bankruptcy Filing 2013).

But if the bankruptcy has sparked global interest in Detroit's fate, it has also had distortionary effects. For example, a report by liberal think tank Demos argues that the headline long-term debt figure of $18–20 billion is deeply misleading, as it is irrelevant to what remains essentially a municipal cash flow crisis. Without denying Detroit's structural issues, the report warns against conflating a $198 million annual cash shortfall largely caused by the Great Recession, cuts to state revenue sharing, and unscrupulous financial arrangements pushed by Wall Street, with an exaggerated and politically-motivated long-term debt crisis blamed on the city's pension and health care obligations (Turbeville 2013). More generally, the bankruptcy has narrowed the discourse on Detroit's crisis and risks recasting the city's troubles as a consequence of fiscal profligacy and political irresponsibility. Thus the *Detroit Free Press* report on Detroit's bankruptcy ends up blaming high taxes, financial mismanagement, corruption, overcompensated municipal employees, and the failure to "make the tough economic and political decisions" necessary to "rightsize" city government (Bomey and Gallagher 2013). Detroit's bankruptcy, in other words, is less a product of its persistent social and economic crisis than of the city's inability to accommodate itself to it.

The bankruptcy is thus a chapter in the politics of "austerity urbanism" that have intensified the neoliberal push for structural adjustment as a result of the relentless downward shifting of costs and risk following the Great Recession (Peck 2012). In fact, the bankruptcy was literally imposed on the city by a state-appointed emergency manager vested with quasi-dictatorial fiscal powers. As of this writing, the outcome of the bankruptcy process remains uncertain. What seems likely, however, are further budget cuts and reductions in retiree pensions and benefits. City trash collection has already been privatized, and the emergency manager has threatened to privatize the Water and Sewerage Department too. The bankruptcy, then, has furnished the usual prescriptions of fiscal retrenchment, government downsizing, deregulation, and privatization, with an aura of necessity and, crucially, the political authority for their realization.

In a sense there is not much else that the city by itself can do to solve the fiscal crisis. But that is precisely the point. The discursive framing of the bankruptcy is inherently predisposed to "endogenize and localize" the causes of the crisis, thereby devolving political responsibility for its resolution onto the city's shoulders (Peck 2014). Moreover, seeing the city's troubles primarily through the prism of bankruptcy risks substituting Detroit's fiscal crisis for the overdetermined hyper-crisis afflicting Detroiters. Though obviously related, the two are not the same, and resolving the fiscal crisis does not necessarily entail addressing the structures of spatial inequality and racialized disinvestment that subtend the latter. The American state's fiscal and administrative decentralization means that cities faced with chronic shortfalls are left with little choice but to find solutions on their own and practice fiscal restraint (Steinmetz 2009). By narrowing the issue to one of fiscal solvency, the discursive effect of the bankruptcy has been to effectively naturalize the underlying structural causes of the urban crisis by relegating them to background conditions, and to call on the city and its residents to resign themselves to their austere fate.

The Bureaucratic Effect

The depths of Detroit's social crisis are by now familiar. From a population of 1.85 million in 1950, the city's population today is about 715,000 (US Census Bureau). As of this writing the unemployment rate stands at roughly 18 percent, after reaching close to 30 percent at the height of the Great Recession (US Bureau of Labor Statistics). Whereas national median household income was $51,371 in 2012, the same figure for Detroit was only $23,600. Furthermore, 42.3 percent of Detroiters live below the poverty line (US Census Bureau). Detroit has clearly suffered from an economic catastrophe, made only more acute by the recession. The economic deprivation has in turn been accompanied by a plethora of well-documented social problems—crime, disease, infant mortality, etc. (Deprez and Christoff 2014, Jahnke 2009).

Detroit's social and fiscal crises might thus appear to be primarily determined by the broad economic transformations inaugurated by the post-Fordist era (see below). This is, however, only partially correct. Again following Bourdieu, one must be careful not to adopt willy-nilly the preconstructed bureaucratic categories of the state (Bourdieu 2012). More generally, social scientific research (like natural scientific research) is organized around deliberately constructed objects, not around empirical objects that are "preconstructed by perception" (Bourdieu et al. 1991: 34). Detroit, after all, is only an arbitrary political artifact—surrounded by other no less arbitrary political artifacts—not a theoretically rigorous "system of expressly constructed relations" (Ibid.). What looks one way within the city limits looks very different when the entire metropolitan region is taken into account. Whereas Detroit has steadily hemorrhaged people, the metro area's population has remained relatively stable over the past forty years. Metro Detroit's 2012 median household income stood at $50,310, barely lower than the national level and comparable to those of Phoenix, Nashville, and Indianapolis. At 17 percent, the metro area's poverty rate is also not much different than the nation's, though less than half of Detroit's (US Census Bureau).

The region's wealth is for the most part concentrated in the suburbs. Suburban Oakland County is among the wealthiest counties in the country, with a population over a million, and even Macomb County, home of the working-class "Reagan Democrats," has a median household income slightly higher than the nation as a whole (SEMCOG). The job outlook in suburban communities remains substantially stronger than in the city, as seen by unemployment rates in Macomb and Oakland counties that are about half that of Detroit's (US Bureau of Labor Statistics). Job opportunities thus haven't simply disappeared; they've moved to the suburbs. For several decades now there has been a "spatial mismatch" in Metro Detroit's jobs landscape, with even low-skill manufacturing jobs more often located in the suburbs than in the central city (Farley, Danziger, and Holzer 2002). A 2009 Brookings Institution study, for example, found that metro Detroit had by far the most decentralized employment distribution in the country with over 77 percent of jobs at least ten miles from downtown (Kneebone 2009). What is true for jobs is also true of economic activity in general; the vast majority of the area's commercial retail and entertainment establishments are located outside the city limits (Galster 2012).

Grasping Detroit relationally in its metropolitan context reveals that the city's problem relative to other cities is in large part one of political geography and inequality (Reich 2013, Schifferes 2013, Stiglitz 2013). Detroit's tax base has been decimated despite the region's wealth because of a politico-administrative arrangement that has unevenly distributed the pain of economic dislocation across a fiscally balkanized metropolitan region. The city has historically been blocked from recapturing some of its escaped tax base by state-level home rule laws that favor incorporation over annexation and that have fixed Detroit's boundaries since 1926 (Thomas 1997: 28–33). As Galster argues, "most of what we see in the city is a result of what transpires in the suburbs and is beyond the power of the city to control." It is thus "impossible to understand what drives the City of Detroit by looking only within its jurisdictional boundaries; a metropolitan perspective is required" (Galster 2012: x).

Of course, metro Detroit's structure of spatial inequality is also deeply racialized. The racial turnover in the city has been stunning. Between 1950 and 2010, the white population fell from 1.5 million to 75,000 as whites left in droves for the suburbs, and the share of the city's black population has skyrocketed from 16 percent to 83 percent. Furthermore, the metro area remains one of the most segregated in the country. While only 16 percent of the total metropolitan population lives in Detroit, almost 60 percent of the metro area's black population is in the central city. The same figure for whites is 3 percent (US Census Bureau). With some exceptions, blacks are severely underrepresented in Detroit's suburbs, many of which are still overwhelmingly white.

Looking only at Detroit and losing sight of the metropolitan context of racialized inequality can severely distort analysis. Naturally, commentators on the right have tended to blame Detroit for its own decline, and to the extent that they acknowledge the relational connection between urban poverty and suburban growth, they have seen racialized disinvestment as a reasonable response to urban pathologies (e.g., Malanga 2013). In these self-serving narratives, in which the culpability of the 1967 riots and Coleman Young, a dynamic former labor activist elected in 1973 as the city's first black mayor, have become touchstones of suburban common sense, the prosperity of the suburbs and the wretchedness of the city serve only to confirm an underlying racist worldview according to which Detroit is but the victim of its own moral failures.

More surprisingly, this kind of blinkered vision can be found even among the more progressive minded. Detroit's much-ballyhooed urban agriculture boom is exemplary in this regard. Urban farming has come to take on an almost eschatological significance, as if what had befallen Detroit were a kind of biblical cataclysm. Indeed, one gets the sense that the apocalyptic clichés have been taken too seriously. Take, for example, architects Kyong Park and Steve Vogel's fanciful vision for "Adamah," a three-thousand-acre agricultural community carved out of Detroit's east side. In line with what Park calls an "Architecture of Resurrection," the proposal calls for a Brigadoon-like village emerging from the scarred landscape, built around community gardens, greenhouses, grazing land, a tree farm, a shrimp farm, artisanal workshops, lumber and wind mills, and parallel political and educational institutions, the idea being that the village would be almost entirely self-sufficient (Boggs and Kurashige 2011, Gallagher 2010, Gallagher 2013, Guyette 2001).[8] One of the project's most enthusiastic supporters has been Grace Lee Boggs, the doyenne of Detroit radicals and the leading interpreter of the city's urban farming movement. More than just a source of food, urban gardens represent for Boggs a redemptive project making up for the spiritual deformations of industrial capitalism's materialistic culture (Boggs and Kurashige 2011). This has been a long-running theme for Boggs, who was in the 1970s already arguing that an American revolution would "require the masses to make material sacrifices rather than to acquire more material things" (Boggs and Boggs 1974: 16). Detroit, in this worldview, as the site of what is conceived as nothing less than a civilizational collapse, is an especially propitious terrain to "begin anew," "grow our souls," and accelerate our "evolution to a higher plateau of Humanity" (Boggs and Kurashige 2011: 105, 28, 70).

The quasi-religious significance attached to urban farming in Detroit is symptomatic of a failure to grasp the city relationally. Divorced from its metropolitan context, the city's troubles could indeed appear to be an act of God. The distortionary effect produced by limiting the scope of analysis to the arbitrary bureaucratic entity "Detroit" underlies the many approaches to Detroit that, defining the city primarily by absence, see it as a blank slate on which to project various visions of postindustrial urbanism. Of course, this is a "well-founded illusion" (Bourdieu 1996), rendered plausible by the actual structure of spatial inequality that has made of Detroit a zone of concentrated deprivation and, furthermore, a zone in which rural phenomena like pheasants have appeared "spontaneously."[9] One might say, then, that discourses such as that of urban farming, in a kind of *amor fati*, exhibit a "taste for necessity" (Bourdieu 1984). In doing so, however, they are but flip sides of the austerity coin. Predicated on a fatalistic acceptance of austerity, they merely transvalue what is in the last instance an injunction for Detroiters to accept their fate and to live within their means. The mistake is to transmute what is a localized experience of deprivation into a general societal condition, thereby obscuring the racialized dynamics of spatial inequality that are at the root of Detroit's crisis.

Also typical in this regard is the current vogue in Detroit for what Leary (2013) calls, using a term coined by Evgeny Morozov (2013), "technocratic solutionism." Manifested in a variety of local startups, consulting companies, and tech incubators, this ideology combines "utopian idealism with the technocratic fantasy that systemic problems can be managed away with the right experts and right digital tools," and as such resonates with austerity-minded policymakers in the context of state retrenchment (Leary 2013). Nothing epitomizes the neo-liberal vision of the world of which this phenomenon is the expression better than Jason Lorimer and his consulting company, Dandelion.[10] According to Lorimer, "providing solutions to [Detroit's] problems is a market, like any other, where productive disruption—new and improved processes, programs, and platforms to solve problems—can be socially beneficial and financially fruitful" (Lorimer 2012). Or as Josh McManus, "chief inventor" of Little Things Labs, another "solutionist" outfit, puts it: "Detroit is the wild west of social entrepreneurship . . . you can try anything here" (quoted in Mercer 2010).

Characterized by an abiding faith in localized entrepreneurial solutions and a disdain for established public institutions, what this small-bore solutionism has in common with Adamah-style blank-slate urbanism is a complicity with the neo-liberal doxa according to which austerity is not only the ineluctable condition of modern life but is in itself a sign of virtue. This embrace of austerity also suggests a perfect inversion of the fantasy of endlessly expanding consumerism that was the core message to the working masses during the Fordist era (see below), and as such is doubly embedded within the spontaneous sociologies swirling around this topic. "Detroit," though, is neither a problem to be cleverly hacked nor a fallen city to be spiritually redeemed. In reality, it is simultaneously more and less than that. Its "problems" are neither reducible to technical glitches nor are they grandiose allegories for civilizational decline; rather, "Detroit" is an object of political contestation whose overdetermined history cannot be understood without reference to the metropolitan system of racialized inequality of which it is a part.

The Brand Effect

Detroit, as a symbolic condensation of Fordist ideology, has long been a brand. Aesthetic modernism returned repeatedly to Detroit between 1910 and the 1930s (Smith 1993). But although its prominence in the cultural imaginary has accounted for the popular fascination with the city's fate, the cultural meanings evoked by "Detroit" can do just as much to obscure the nature of its crisis. This "brand effect" can redouble the epistemological obstacles discussed above. Thus the dramatic effects of the ruins and the bankruptcy have their source in the dissonance between the imagined grandeur of the city's golden age and its present wretchedness. Likewise, it is the city's density of historical signification that has encouraged an excessively allegorical reading of its decline.

As Fordism has given way to post-Fordism (and beyond), the city has become an object of nostalgia (Steinmetz 2008). In an ironic twist, however, it is Detroit's present hardships that have become integrated into the city's brand and given it new life. Expressed by the city's unofficial motto—"Detroit hustles harder"—emblazoned on countless shirts and caps, the city has become synonymous with American grit and resilience in the face of adversity.

Chrysler's 2012 Super Bowl ad, part of its celebrated "Imported from Detroit" campaign, exemplifies this new turn in Detroit's brand. Featuring an exaggeratedly gruff Clint Eastwood, the ad uses the Super Bowl's "half-time" as a metaphor for America's economic malaise. Against an extended montage of American recessionary life, including shots of Detroit and auto plants, we hear Eastwood growl that though "the people of Detroit know a little something" about America's struggles, "now Motor City is fighting again." Not just the symbol of American decline, Detroit is also its salvation, proving through its moxie that "this country can't be knocked out in one punch," and that when "we get back up again . . . the world is gonna hear the roar of our engines." The ad thus depends for its effectiveness on the mobilization of every conceivable cliché about American exceptionalism—"Detroit" foremost among them—whose resonance only seems to get stronger the less they correspond to reality.

This hard-edged nostalgia for Fordist Americana has made the Detroit brand newly fashionable, with companies like the Austrian Redbull and the French Pernod Ricard also launching products spinning Detroit's economic deprivation and urban decay as toughness and authenticity. Few of these companies have gotten as much press as Shinola, an old shoe polish brand recently reborn as a luxury watch, bicycle, and leather goods company that markets its products as being assembled in Detroit. Trading on the city's reputation for skilled, unionized labor, Shinola, with nonunion starting wages at around $12–13, is in fact only a simulacrum of what it evokes (Hackman 2014).

Through a series of metonymic fallacies, the brand "Detroit" risks displacing the real place. The expansive cultural footprint of "Detroit" as a source of symbolic identification overflows its politico-administrative boundaries, such that suburbanites can cheer for the Detroit Tigers while simultaneously wanting nothing to do with the actual city. The fact that "Detroit" often refers not just to the city but to the wider metropolitan area can serve to elide the stark inequalities that crosscut the region.[11]

The branding of Detroit has also been an integral part of a booterish discourse that, channeling Richard Florida, systematically conflates the city's increasing trendiness with its revitalization. There is no doubt that parts of the city are becoming trendier, attracting young educated people back into the city with hip new restaurants, bars, and coffee shops. What is unique to Detroit is the quasi-evangelical fervor that has accompanied this process. Building a business in the urban frontier of Detroit is no longer just an investment; it is the ultimate act of civic mindedness. Where else but in Detroit could a barbecue restaurant be repeatedly portrayed by the *New York Times* as the harbinger of a city's renewal (Alvin 2014, Ryzik 2010)? But the revitalized Detroit of the boosters' imagination is not one that addresses the systemic causes of the city's crisis. Rather, it is simply a place that has more things that people with economic and cultural capital like. In a sleight of hand, then, the discourse of boosterism replaces the concrete Detroit of seven hundred thousand Detroiters with the hip "Detroit" brand, and makes the latter the measure of Detroit's renewal.

For many, "Detroit" remains first of all a metonym for the auto industry. The mural that greets international arrivals at Detroit Metropolitan Airport shows the great men of Detroit industry.[12] Yet Detroit has not really been the Motor City for many decades. Despite record profits since the 2008–2009 auto bailouts, employment at the "Big Three" is down to 190,000, compared to 410,000 in 2001, and only 10,000 of those jobs are in Detroit proper. In fact, only 4 percent of Detroit jobs are in the auto industry, compared to 11 percent for the suburbs (Walsh 2013). Detroit has thus become a charity case for the auto industry, more important for its brand identity than for any actual operations (Vlasic 2013). It has become a common metonymic fallacy to conflate the automotive crisis with Detroit's urban crisis (Steinmetz 2009), and conversely since the auto bailouts to take the industry's restored profits for "Detroit's" recovery (Aschoff 2013). Herein, then, lies the problem with all manners of Detroit boosterism: the language of "renewal" or "renaissance" that defines ordinary discourse about the city is pitched not at the welfare of flesh-and-blood Detroiters, but at the promotion of a certain cultural ideal of the city that reflects the interests and biases of the privileged.

An Overdetermined Crisis

Each of the interpretive tendencies discussed above sustain systematic distortions that make it more difficult to understand Detroit's crisis. Against a spontaneous analysis that relies on preconstructed categories, we argue that Detroit's crisis must be understood as a complex, overdetermined hyper-crisis, a crisis that entails a confluence of causes and that is irreducible to any one cause taken alone.

The hyper-crisis also exists at different temporalities. An adequate analysis of the crisis should include: the *longue durée* of urbanization and the city's built environment; the medium duration of capitalist modes of regulation and the formation of individual habitus and wealth; and the "eventful history" of events like the 1943 and 1967 riots, the 2008 recession, and the 2013 bankruptcy.[13]

At the most immediate level is the city's fiscal crisis. Though blame for this crisis has been ideologically directed at the city and its workers, it is, as suggested earlier, a politically manufactured crisis. This is not to deny the reality of the crisis. The point, rather, is that the fiscal crisis is not a morality play in which irresponsibility and profligacy finds its just desserts, but a concatenation of political mechanisms that have unevenly distributed exposure to economic risk. Thus the crisis has its source outside the city itself, in factors such as the State of Michigan's attempt to balance its budget on the back of Detroit's by slashing state revenue sharing, the risky financial products pushed by Wall Street in 2005 that have blown up in the city's face, the absence of a real urban and industrial policy at the national level, and the politico-administrative fragmentation of Southeast Michigan that has precluded effective regional government and led to the fiscal balkanization of the metropolitan area. It was the overdetermined combination of these factors with the Great Recession that pushed Detroit into insolvency.

Yet the fiscal crisis is embedded in a broader urban crisis. Operating at a longer temporality, the urban crisis itself overdetermines the causes of the fiscal crisis. Indeed, the above-mentioned factors are continually refracted through the historical forces of unfettered capitalism, the disintegration of Fordism, and racial oppression that have defined Detroit's urban crisis. Any serious effort to make sense of Detroit's current predicament must thus break with the presentist and pragmatic biases of ordinary popular discourse and instead grasp those historical forces whose combined effect accounts for the stubborn persistence of the city's decline. In what follows we sketch these forces that constitute the historical matrix through which Detroit's recent past has unfolded. We suggest that these forces are eminently political in that they are the enduring consequences of the class and racial conflict that have marked the city's history and that of capitalism in the past century.

Capitalism and the End of Fordist Regulation

At the core of capitalism is a spatially uneven set of processes in which waves and thrusts of commodifying "primitive accumulation" and unfettered growth in certain times and places are combined with bouts of disinvestment, decentralization, and decommodification in others. Viewed strictly through the lens of capitalism, Detroit benefitted from the growth of manufacturing in the region after the late nineteenth century—a process that was repeatedly interrupted, of course, by cyclical crises of accumulation. Conversely, the city suffered gravely from the tendency of capitalists to move jobs to sites of less organized labor and lower wages. This basic process was already underway during the years the French call *les trentes glorieuses* and the Germans call the *Wunderjahre*, and that Regulation Theorists call Fordism (Steinmetz 2006)— roughly 1945 to 1973. Economic abandonment of the entire manufacturing region then accelerated (Bluestone and Harrison 1982; Cowie and Heathcott 2003), followed by a restructuring of US labor markets away from manufacturing and toward services, finance, and information technology (Krippner 2011). Financialization contributes to Detroit's crisis negatively, given the city's meager involvement in the rising sectors (with exceptions like Quicken Loans) and positively via the waves of foreclosures and the ongoing bankruptcy discussed above.

The crisis of the end of the Fordist mode of societal regulation is related but not reducible to these generic dynamics of disinvestment and restructuring of capital. The term *Fordism* emerged between the two world wars and referred specifically at that time to the economic and social system pioneered by Henry Ford, which extended Frederick Taylor's methods from the individual laborer to the "collective worker" on the moving assembly line. In January 1914, Henry Ford famously introduced the unprecedented wage of five dollars for eight hours of work, which was more than double the going wage in the automobile industry at the time. Admirers used the term *Fordism* to refer to a system that they found baffling due to its combination of a "constant reduction of prices" with "powerfully superelevated wages" (von Gottl-Ottlilienfeld 1924: 3). The tradeoff for these high wages was a relentless increase in the pace of production. Even if wages were slashed at Ford during the Great Depression, the ideal of the diligent worker-consumer became a standard component of the postwar model of Fordism in Western Europe and the US. Ford's social interventions in the lives of his workers and their communities during the Great Depression were a private alternative to the New Deal. This points toward the centrality of the welfare state in postwar Fordism. Ford's involvement in improving his employees' homes points to another dimension of Fordism: its sweeping effects on patterns of urbanization. Like many other industrial metropolitan areas that emerged in the twentieth century, Detroit was not so much a city as a series of mainly low-rise buildings "held together by transportation and communications" (Bucci 1993: 11). During the interwar period the term *Fordism* therefore usually referred to the combination of mass production on the assembly line, rationalization of the labor process, comparatively high wages, and efforts to shape working-class culture to fit the requirements of industry (for an example of an idealized image of Fordist prosperity, see Figure 1.1). Since Ford resisted labor unions, and was the last Detroit automaker to recognize the United Auto Workers after a 1941 sit-down strike, unionists and socialists used the term *Fordism* as an epithet designating the company's fierce repression of unions and relentless speedup of the pace of work.

In the 1930s Antonio Gramsci suggested that developments like this in the United States constituted a novel form of "hegemony"—a word Gramsci used to refer to the exercise of political power not simply by the use of force but through a dense

Figure 1.1. Fordist industrial prosperity (*Ford News* vol. 9 no. 8, April 15, 1929).

web of informal and formal persuasive devices located not just in the state but also in the interstices of civil society and within families, bodies, and psyches. These loosely coordinated devices, Gramsci argued, help stabilize and reproduce capitalism (Gramsci 1971).

The version of Fordism that developed in the postwar United States and in Europe differed in certain respects from the version pioneered by Ford during the first half of the century.[14] The virtuous cycle between standardized mass production and mass consumption, grounded in a disciplined working class, remained the essential principle. But the postwar model encompassed a more elaborate system for stabilizing labor relations through greater recognition and integration of labor unions. Crucial developments included New Deal labor legislation, industrial agreements like the "Treaty of Detroit" in the American auto industry, and the "neocorporatist" practices of policymaking by representatives of labor and management together with government officials and political parties. Labor unions now promised to control their members' militancy in exchange for increased benefits, some participation in managerial decision-making, and wages that were pegged to profits. This social contract was buttressed by the welfare state and fiscal policies that buffered workers' incomes during cyclical downturns, unemployment, illness, disability, and retirement. In geographical terms, Fordism meant the political evening out of regional inequalities within a given country (Brenner 1998).

The late 1970s and early 1980s marked the beginning of a rollback of this entire Fordist paradigm. Unionization levels began a steady decline; individual and regional economic inequalities began their steady increase (Brenner 1998; Piketty 2014). Industry moved toward just-in-time production, flexible specialization, and niche market manufacturing; neo-liberalism became the dominant economic ideology. Centers of Fordist-style manufacturing like Detroit, the German Ruhr Valley, and the English Midlands suffered massive disinvestment, leaving behind vast factory ruins. In Europe and the US right-wing and anti-immigrant extremists rooted in the disenfranchised working class began to look back nostalgically at an idealized Fordist era of prosperity, equality, and national homogeneity (Steinmetz 1997).

This nostalgia for Fordist prosperity glosses over the fact that Fordist regulation was itself a compromise formation responding to acute class struggle. The deskilling effects of the mass assembly line were designed to break the power of craft unions. But in decomposing its class antagonist Fordism only created another in the "mass worker," thus inaugurating a new era of class struggle (Negri 1968). Detroit, of course, has a central place in this history. As the birthplace of the United Auto Workers and the heart of industrial unionism, Detroit is home to some of the most momentous struggles in American labor history and was synonymous with union power. Looking back from the political turmoil of 1960s Italy to the massive cycle of working class militancy that emerged in 1930s America, famed Italian Marxist Mario Tronti spoke of "Marx in Detroit" and argued that in the practice, if not theory, of those American struggles could be found "the most exact interpretation of the most advanced of Marxian texts" (Tronti 2006: 304).

The elaboration of the Fordist regulatory compact was aimed at neutralizing this working-class challenge. The 1950 "Treaty of Detroit" was both the apotheosis of working class power and the beginning of its decline. Fully incorporated into the regulatory regime, the UAW became more bureaucratic and less militant. Moreover, the postwar boom and resulting proletarian prosperity were short-lived, as Detroit's manufacturers as early as the 1950s sought to undermine the power of the "mass worker," which lay in its spatial concentration and ability to disrupt the production chain, by automating production and decentralizing facilities to the suburbs and beyond—a dynamic recognized and analyzed by James Boggs in 1963 (Boggs 1963, Sugrue 1996). The relentlessness of this process, which only intensified in the 1970s with the advent of robotics and the further relocation of plants to union-hostile locales outside the region and country, also cowed Detroit's workers, despite periodic spikes in militancy such as the series of wildcat strikes initiated by the Dodge Revolutionary Union Movement and the League of Revolutionary Black Workers in the early 1970s (Georgakas and Surkin 1975, Geschwender 1977). Metro Detroit's workers have since been backed into making concession after concession, culminating in the steep givebacks imposed as part of the recent auto bailouts.

Fordism represented a fleeting equilibrium in the balance of class forces. Detroit's deindustrialization is the byproduct of a half-century class struggle during which capital, through decentralization and automation, successfully decomposed the sources of working-class power. The transition from Fordism to post-Fordism and the resulting disinvestment from cities like Detroit must be understood in this class context. Although the entire metro region has suffered from the decline of American manufacturing, the long legacy of decentralization has meant that its effects are especially felt in the central city. So, while after World War II Detroit employed 338,400 people in manufacturing (Sugrue 1996: 144), only 27,000 manufacturing jobs remain in the city today, compared to 180,000 in the suburbs (SEMCOG). Detroit's dramatic deindustrialization is not simply the manifestation of global economic trends, but also, in a sense, a punishment for the audacity of its workers in challenging capital's dominance. Detroit was abandoned by capital—first for the suburbs and then beyond—just as workers took a giant step in the fight for industrial democracy, and for precisely for that reason. Detroit's economic crisis is thus both a sign and effect of the defeat of working class power in America.

Racism and Segregation

Detroit's crisis is not reducible to broad economic transformations. The pattern of racialized spatial inequality that defines the metropolitan region cannot be understood without accounting for the sordid history of racism that continues to make Detroit one of the most segregated metropolitan areas in the country. Like the process of contemporary hyper-ghettoization analyzed by Loïc Wacquant, Detroit's marginality is thus "economically underdetermined and politically overdetermined" (Wacquant 2008: 4). It is the interaction of the economic dislocations discussed above with the dynamics of racialized disinvestment and segregation that begins to specify Detroit's urban crisis.

As Detroit's population boomed mid-century, chronic housing shortages led to tensions in the urban geography of race. Historically, black Detroiters were largely confined by systematic segregation to the overcrowded and decaying neighborhoods of the city's near-east side. Urban renewal, though clearing these slums, only intensified the pattern of segregation as local authorities concentrated what little public housing was built in black neighborhoods (Sugrue 1996, Thomas 1992). Moreover, as black Detroiters with the means to do so began moving into white neighborhoods in the 1950s once outright housing discrimination became legally untenable, many were greeted with violent harassment by white homeowners banding together into neighborhood associations. As Sugrue argues, this was in part the consequence of a New Deal ideology that privileged homeownership over public housing as a solution to the working-class housing shortage. As workers' modest wealth became tied up in their homes, class anxiety and racial resentment mutually overdetermined each other such that white homeowners, fearful of declining property values and an increasingly tenuous hold on the middle class in the context of a deindustrializing economy, desperately enforced Detroit's unofficial racial boundaries. Nonetheless, the white racial order could not hold, and whites abandoned the city en masse for the suburbs, pulled by newly constructed freeways and federally backed mortgages, and pushed by unscrupulous real estate agents profiting from Detroit's rapid racial turnover (Sugrue 1996).

As whites disinvested from the city, black Detroiters largely remained confined to the city through discriminatory lending practices and suburban hostility. For example, long-time Dearborn mayor Orville Hubbard, of whom a statue still stands outside City Hall, was famous for his outspoken advocacy of segregation and campaigned on his successful policing of Dearborn's racial borders. More recently, controversial Oakland County Executive L. Brooks Patterson, repeating remarks he's made in the past, was quoted as saying, "What we're gonna do is turn Detroit into an Indian reservation, where we herd all the Indians into the city, build a fence around it, and then throw in the blankets and corn" (Williams 2014). Evidence suggests that housing discrimination remains widespread and that whites in the Detroit area are still much less willing to live in integrated neighborhoods than blacks (Farley, Danziger, Holzer 2002). Indeed, the pattern of racial turnover has even extended out to suburbs such as Southfield, where the white population declined as the city went from 29 percent black in 1990 to 70 percent in 2010 (US Census Bureau). Hubbard and Patterson also stand as reminders that racial politics have historically overdetermined urban-suburban relations in metro Detroit, scuttling regional planning efforts and perpetuating administrative and fiscal fragmentation to the detriment of the urban core (Thomas 1992).

Black Detroiters have always been more exposed to the predations of American capitalism. Even in the heyday of Fordism, blacks suffered rampant job discrimination. Relegated to the lowest-skilled and most dangerous manufacturing jobs, they were then disproportionately affected by automation. Moreover, persistent segregation meant that blacks were especially hit by the flow of jobs out to the suburbs and beyond (Sugrue 1996). Those managing to keep jobs in the auto plants were forced to work longer and harder in what black autoworkers colloquially called "niggermation" (Georgakas and Surkin 1975).

The long history of segregation and racialized disinvestment has concentrated risk and disadvantage in the central city. A poor, black city surrounded by wealthier white suburbs anxious to maintain their racial borders, Detroit in a way resembles what Wacquant calls the "hyper-ghetto" (2008), not just in the sense of a zone of concentrated economic deprivation, but in the more robust sense of a "historically determinate, spatially-based concatenation of mechanisms of *ethnoracial closure and control*" (Wacquant 1997: 343). Indeed, the irony is that now the entire city has been turned into a ghetto of sorts. Metro Detroit's racial and class borders have become congruous with its political, administrative, and fiscal boundaries, making it that much easier for the rich and white to divest themselves of any solidarity with a city and a population that they have long since abandoned (Desan 2014). At the heart of Detroit's urban crisis, in other words, are the racialized dynamics of spatial inequality by which white suburban prosperity has come at the expense of the black urban core.

Conclusion

Taken together, these processes yield a seemingly unassailable, quasi-structural barrier to any but the most cosmetic improvements to the city's problems. Of course momentous social events are almost entirely unpredictable, even if they are explicable post hoc. It is thinkable, if highly unlikely, that a conjuncture of overlapping developments could dislodge this massive impediment. It is crucial, however, that analysts retain a pessimism of the intellect rather than indulging in expressions of naive goodwill.

We can nevertheless make a distinction between neo-liberal policy recommendations and progressive political interventions. Policy science often displays a behaviorialist bias, wherein prescribed solutions to narrowly defined social problems are designed primarily to nudge behavior in certain directions and are thus only indirectly related to the ultimately desired outcome. Planners who promote the idea of "smart decline," for example, suggest concentrating population and turning empty spaces into greenways. Uprooting and resettling people is presumably not the policy's goal in and of itself, but that is the only actual result that can be predicted. Likewise with tax incentives, whose desired outcome is to stimulate investment but the direct result of which is corporate welfare. A similar logic underlies "technocratic solutionism," which treats the city as if it were simply a puzzle to be solved. Sensible planning, smart design, and "disruptive" innovation are imagined to have downstream benefits contributing to the city's revival. Though individual measures may be unobjectionable and even welcome, the general effect of these kinds of approaches has been to depoliticize Detroit's crisis by suggesting that it can be effectively addressed by the city itself through clever interventions in a few strategic areas.[15]

We argue that Detroit's hyper-crisis is a politically overdetermined crisis of racialized and spatialized inequality. Quick fixes that do not address the entrenched dynamics of economic disinvestment, racial segregation, and administrative fragmentation are therefore unlikely to provide lasting benefits to Detroiters. By contrast with neo-liberal policies, in progressive interventions there is no hiatus between cause and effect, explanans and explanandum, policy and outcome. The intervention itself *is* the desideratum. For Detroit, this would mean exploring policies that—instead of relying only on internal remedies that make the city more attractive—directly redistribute wealth, revenue, and jobs more equitably across the metro region and redress the historical wrongs that have consistently pushed risk and disadvantage onto the backs of black Detroiters. In other words, policies must be pitched not only at reviving the city's image, but also at concretely making whole those Detroiters who, though not having made the crisis, have been made to pay for it. Any strategy that seeks to "reinvent" or "reimagine" Detroit without combatting the systemic inequality and racism that are at the source of the city's crisis might find success of some kind, but it would be a hollow and fleeting one for many Detroiters.

The processes of disinvestment, segregation, and fragmentation were not simply accidents of history. Rather, they were outcomes of past political struggles over class, race, and space. As such, any effective intervention at those levels would entail tilting the political balance of forces in favor of the marginalized. The federal government's refusal to bail out Detroit as it did Wall Street and the auto companies, however, suggests that the political conjuncture is not especially propitious at the moment. Being the product of an overdetermined concatenation of forces operating at multiple temporalities, Detroit's hyper-crisis is immune to isolated remedies. As with any overdetermined structure, substantial change is contingent on the condensation of multiple struggles at multiple levels into a "ruptural unity" (Althusser 1969). This would need to be the work of an articulatory practice than can unite those struggles around an alternative hegemonic vision of greater Detroit (Laclau and Mouffe 1985). This vision, however, cannot be limited to the inward-looking illusions promoted by boosters and urbanists alike; it must be thoroughly *political* in the sense that it presents itself as a pole of antagonism against the scandalous mechanisms of racialized inequality. Only in such a political conjuncture can the dominant order be enduringly challenged.

Notes

1. Of course, any crisis and indeed any social process, practice, or event has to be analyzed as being overdetermined, insofar as is it the product of a conjuncture of determining processes. This is a basic premise not just of Althusserian and post-Althusserian theory (Althusser 1969, Laclau and Mouffe 1985), but of the critical realist philosophy of science (Bhaskar 1978, 1979).
2. See Steinmetz and Chanan (2005), which reconstructs the history of these twentieth-century battles over the image of Detroit.
3. Article retrieved: http://www.pcf.fr/44090.
4. The key problem is empiricism. While social science positivism may have become part of the American epistemological unconscious without daring to say its name (Steinmetz 2005), social science empiricism is still widely endorsed and even fashionable.
5. The polemical slogan ruin porn, with its Puritanical overtones, is itself one of the ideologies generated by the constellation of blighted city versus wealthy suburbs discussed below. The slogan fails to capture the specificities of these images and the differences among them. There is no space here to delve into the theoretical discussions of ruins, but see especially Edensor (2005), Hell and Schoenle (2010), Macauley (1953), Simmel (1965), and Smithson (1979).
6. One of the more bizarre episodes of Detroit's bankruptcy proceedings has been the argument in court over whether the judge overseeing Detroit's bankruptcy should take a bus tour of the city to survey the blight. Creditors opposed the idea, presumably because it would predispose the judge to sympathize with the city (Bomey 2014).
7. Ruins may contain certain inherent and even universal meanings, as Simmel (1965) suggested, which is why ruins rather than ice cream cones are regularly connected to ideas about mortality, decline,

and apocalypse. That said, the historical determinants and interpretations of a specific ruin are never inherent in the object. One of the critiques of the treatment of urban ruins in still photographs as opposed to documentary films or historical-sociological analysis is that still images remain open to a very wide an array of possible significations (Steinmetz 2008).

8.   One can watch the informational video for the project here: http://vimeo.com/9609433.

9.   That Detroit's rural appearance is far from "natural" is emphasized, for example, by the fact that the tens of thousands of empty lots produce above-average levels of ragweed pollen when mowed, exacerbating the above-average levels of asthma among city residents (Erikson 2014).

10. Lorimer became the subject of a viral meme, known as "White Entrepreneurial Detroit Guy" (http://whitedetroitguy.tumblr.com/), making fun of, among other things, his and Dandelion's copious use of opaque techno-jargon.

11. An example of the kind of confusion created by using the same term to designate both the central city and the metropolitan area is Farley, Danziger, and Holzer's (2002) criticism of Sugrue (1996) for being overly pessimistic in characterizing Detroit as a kind of reservation for the poor (see also Farley 2009). In fact, the former cite metropolitan region level economic data to make their case, whereas Sugrue's historical analysis is predicated precisely on the racialized dynamics of urban-suburban inequality.

12. Of course, the airport is located in the suburbs, and Ford Motor Company has not been located in Detroit for a century, but the airport's symbolism refers repeatedly to the city proper.

13. On the layering of differential historical temporalities, see Braudel (1972); on differential temporalities congealing in an overdetermined empirical event, see Althusser (1969), Althusser and Balibar (1970); Bourdieu (1988: 159–193); on "eventful history" see Sewell (2005).

14. The rethinking of the concept of Fordism since the 1970s is associated with "regulation theory," a social-theoretical approach that presents Fordism as a "mode of regulation," a cluster of economic, political, social, and cultural institutions that organize society in ways that allow business to continue making profits despite the intrinsically contradictory dynamics of capitalism.

15. Our rejection of behavioralist approaches to social science and policy science is rooted in a fundamentally non-positivist social epistemology. If the social world does not generally correspond to the positivist image of "constant conjunctions of events," and if causes and events are both overdetermined conjunctures, it is difficult, if not impossible, to predict the eventual indirect effects of "incentives" and the like. This is especially true in contexts where even the normal *demi-regularities* (Lawson 1998: 149) of everyday life are being relentlessly destroyed.

References

Althusser, L. (1969). *For Marx*. London: Allen Lane.

———— and E. Balibar. (1970). *Reading Capital*. London: New Left Books.

Alvin, J. (2014). "A Gleam of Renewal in Struggling Detroit." *New York Times*, 17 June. Retrieved Jun 28, 2014, from http://mobile.nytimes.com/2014/06/22/travel/a-gleam-of-renewal-in-struggling-detroit.html.

Aschoff, N. (2013). "Imported from Detroit." *Jacobin* 10: 4–11.

Bachelard, G. (2002). *The Formation of the Scientific Mind*. Manchester: Clinamen.

Binelli, M. (2012). *Detroit City is the Place to Be: The Afterlife of an American Metropolis*. New York: Metropolitan Books.

Bluestone, B. and B. Harrison. (1982). *The Deindustrialization of America: Plant Closings, Community Abandonment, and the Dismantling of Basic Industry*. New York: Basic Books.

Boggs, G. L. and S. Kurashige. (2011). *The Next American Revolution: Sustainable Activism for the Twenty-First Century*. Berkeley: University of California Press.

Boggs, J. (1963). *The American Revolution. Pages from a Negro Worker's Notebook*. New York: Modern Reader Paperbacks.

———— and G. L. Boggs. (1974). *Revolution and Evolution in the Twentieth Century*. New York: Monthly Review Press.

Bomey, N. (2014). "Creditors protest proposed Detroit bus tour for bankruptcy judge." *Detroit Free Press*, 17 June. Retrieved Jun 27, 2014, from http://www.freep.com/article/20140617/NEWS05/306170142/Detroit-bankruptcy-bus-tour-Judge-Steven-Rhodes.

———— and J. Gallagher. (2013). "How Detroit Went Broke: The answers may surprise you – and don't blame Coleman Young. *Detroit Free Press*, 15 September. Retrieved Jun 27, 2014, from http://www.freep. com/interactive/article/20130915/NEWS01/130801004/Detroit-Bankruptcy-history-1950-debt-pension-revenue.

Bourdieu, P. (1977). *Outline of a Theory of Practice*. Cambridge: Cambridge University Press.

————. (1984). *Distinction. A Social Critique of the Judgment of Taste*. Cambridge: Harvard University Press.

————. (1988). *Homo Academicus*. Stanford: Stanford University Press.

————. (1996). "On the Family as a Realized Category." *Theory, Culture & Society* 13 (3): 19–26.

————, et al. (1991). *The Craft of Sociology. Epistemological Preliminaries*. Berlin: de Gruyter.

————, et al. (1999). *The Weight of the World. Social Suffering in Contemporary Society*. Stanford: Stanford University Press.

Braudel, F. (1972). *The Mediterranean and the Mediterranean World in the Age of Philip II*. New York: Harper & Row.

Brenner, N. (1998). "Between Fixity and Motion: Accumulation, Territorial Organization and the Historical Geography of Spatial Scales." *Environment and Planning D: Society and Space* 16 (4): 459–81.

Chanan, M. (2005). *"Detroit: Ruin of a City* - A Reception Diary." *Journal of Media Practice* 6 (3): 135–144.

City of Detroit Bankruptcy Filing, Eastern District of Michigan US Bankruptcy Court. (2013). Retrieved Jun 27, 2014, from http://www.scribd.com/doc/154574836/Detroit-Chapter-9-Bankruptcy- Filing-WXYZ.

Cowie, J. and J. Heathcottand, eds. (2003). *Beyond the Ruins: The Meanings of Deindustrialization*. Ithaca: ILR Press.

de Nardis, F. and L. Caruso (2011). "Political Crisis and Social Transformation in Antonio Gramsci. Elements for a Sociology of Political Praxis." *International Journal of Humanities and Social Science* 13–23.

Deprez, E. E. and C. Christoff. (2014). "Babies Pay for Detroit's 60-Year Slide With Mortality Above Mexico's." *Bloomberg*, 11 June. Retrieved Jun 27, 2014, from http://www.bloomberg.com/news/2014–06-11/babies-pay-for-detroit-s-fall-with-mortality-above-mexico.html.

Desan, M. H. (2014). "Bankrupted Detroit." *Thesis Eleven* 121 (1): 122–130.

Detroit Blight Removal Task Force. (2014). *Every Neighborhood Has a Future . . . And It Doesn't Include Blight*. Retrieved Jun 27, 2014, from www.timetoendblight.com.

Edensor, T. (2005). *Industrial Ruins: Space, Aesthetics and Materiality*. Oxford: Berg.

Erikson, J. (2014). "Controlling Ragweed Pollen in Detroit: A No-Mow Solution for Motown?" *The University of Michigan Record* June 23: 13.

Farley, R. (2009). "G.M., Detroit and the Fall of the Black Middle Class." *New York Times Magazine*, Letters section, July 12.

————, S. Danziger, and H. J. Holzer (2002). *Detroit Divided*. New York: Russel Sage Foundation.

Gallagher, J. (2010). *Reimagining Detroit: Opportunities for Redefining an American City*. Detroit: Wayne State University Press.

————. (2013). *Revolution Detroit: Strategies for Urban Reinvention*. Detroit: Wayne State University of Press.

Geschwender, J. A. (1977). *Class, Race, and Worker Insurgency: The League of Revolutionary Black Workers*. Cambridge: Cambridge University Press.

Gramsci, A. (1971). "State and Civil Society: Observations on Certain Aspects of the Structure of Political Parties in Periods of Organic Crisis." Pp. 210–218 in Q. Hoare and G. Nowell Smith (eds.), *Selections from the Prison Notebooks*. New York: International Publishers.

Guyette, C. (2001). "Down a green path. An alternative vision for a section of east Detroit take shape." *Metro Times*, 31 October. Retrieved Jun 27, 2014, from http://www2.metrotimes.com/news/story. asp?id=2625.

Hackman, R. (2014). "Detroit: the bankrupt city turned corporate luxury brand." *The Guardian*, 14 May. Retrieved Jun 27, 2014, from http://www.theguardian.com/money/2014/may/14/detroit-bankrupt-brand-ad-chrysler-nostalgia.

Hell, J. (2008). "Ruins Travel: Orphic Journeys through 1940s Germany." In *Writing Travel*, edited by J. Zilcosky (Toronto: University of Toronto Press): 123–160.

————. (2010). "Imperial ruin gazers, or why did Scipio weep?" In J. Hell and A. Schoenle (eds.), *Ruins of Modernity*. Durham, NC: Duke University Press.

———— and A. Schoenle eds. (2010). *Ruins of Modernity*. Durham, NC: Duke University Press.

Jahnke, K. (2009). "Metro Detroit can be hard on your health." *Detroit Free Press*, 7 June: D4.

Kneebone, E. (2009). "Job Sprawl Revisited: The Changing Geography of Metropolitcal Employment." *Metropolitcan Policy Program at Brookings*. Retrieved Jun 27, 2014, from http://www.brookings.edu/*/media/research/files/reports/2009/4/06%20job%20sprawl%20kneebone/20090406_jobsprawl_kneebone.pdf.

Krippner, G. R. (2011). *Capitalizing on crisis: the political origins of the rise of finance.* Cambridge, Mass.: Harvard University Press.

Laclau, E. and C. Mouffe (1985). *Hegemony and Socialist Strategy: Towards a Radical Democratic Politics.* London: Verso.

Lawson, T. (1998). "Economic Science without Experimentation/Abstraction." Pp. 144–185 in *Critical Realism, Essential Readings*, eds. R. Bhaskar, A. Collier, T. Lawson, M. Archer, and A. Norrie. London: Routledge.

Leary, J. P. (2011). "Detroitism." *Guernica*, 15 January. Retrieved Jun 27, 2014, from http://www.guernicamag.com/features/leary_1_15_11/.

———. (2013). "All the Young Technocrats." *Huffington Post*, 15 April. Retrieved Jun 27, 2014, from http://www.huffingtonpost.com/john-patrick-leary/all-the-young-technocrats_b_3082414.html.

Lorimer, J. (2012). "Expect More Detroit." *Huffington Post,* 11 October. Retrieved Jun 27, 2014, from http://www.huffingtonpost.com/jason-lorimer/detroit-innovation_b_1951220.html.

Macauley, R. (1953). *Pleasure of Ruins.* London: Weidenfeld and Nicolson.

Malanga, S. (2013). "The Real Reason the Once Great City of Detroit Came to Ruin." *Wall Street Journal*, 26 July. Retrieved Jun 27, 2014, from http://online.wsj.com/article/SB10001424127887324110404578625581152645480.html.

Marchand, Y. and R. Meffre (2010). *The Ruins of Detroit.* Göttingen: Steidl.

Mercer, M. (2010). "Chattanoogans help pull off 'intervention' in Detroit." *Times Free* Press, 8 November. Retrieved Jun 27, 2014, from http://www.timesfreepress.com/news/2010/nov/08/chattanoogans-help-pull-off-intervention-in/.

Moore, A. and P. Levine (2010). *Detroit Disassembled.* Bologna: Damiani Editore.

Morozov, E. (2013). *To Save Everything, Click Here: The Folly of Technological Solutionism.* New York: PublicAffairs.

Mouffe, C. (2013). *Agonistics: thinking the world politically.* London: Verso.

Peck, J. (2012). "Austerity Urbanism." *City: analysis or urban trends, culture, theory, policy, action*, Vol. 16, No. 6: 626–655.

———. (2014). "Bailing on Detroit." *cities@manchester blog*, 26 January. Retrieved Jun 27, 2014, from http://citiesmcr.wordpress.com/2014/01/26/bailing-on-detroit/.

Piketty, T. (2014). *Capital in the Twenty-First Century.* Cambridge, MA: Belknap Press.

Reich, R. (2013). "Income Gap is What's Tearing Cities Like Detroit Apart." *Detroit Free Press*, 3 August. Retrieved Jun 27, 2014, from http://www.freep.com/article/20130803/OPINION05/308030014/robert-reich-detroit-bankruptcy-middle-class-income-gap.

Ryzik, M. (2010). "Detroit's Renewal, Slow-Cooked." *New York Times*, 19 October. Retrieved Jun 27, 2014, from http://www.nytimes.com/2010/10/20/dining/20Detroit.html.

Schifferes, J. (2013). "Political Geography Bankrupted Detroit." *Royal Society of Arts Blogs*, 19 July. Retrieved Jun 27, 2014, from http://www.rsablogs.org.uk/2013/social-economy/political-geo-graphy-bankrupted-detroit/.

Sewell, W. H. (2005). *Logics of History: Social Theory and Social Transformation.* Chicago: University of Chicago Press.

Simmel, G. (1965). "The Ruin." Pp. 259–266 in *Essays on Sociology, Philosophy and Aesthetics*, ed., Kurt H, Wolff. New York: Harper and Row.

Smith, T. (1993). *Making the Modern: Industry, Art, and Design in America.* Chicago: University of Chicago Press.

Smithson, R. (1979). "A Tour of the Monuments of Passaic, New Jersey." Pp. 52–57 in *The Writings of Robert Smithson*, ed. N. Holt. New York: New York University Press.

Southeast Michigan Council of Governments [SEMCOG]. Retrieved Jun 27, 2014, from http://www.semcog. org/Data/bycommunity.cfm.

Steinmetz, G. (1997). "Social Class and the Reemergence of the Radical Right in Contemporary Germany." In *Reworking Class: Cultures and Institutions of Economic Stratification and Agency*, edited by John R. Hall. Ithaca, NY: Cornell University Press, pp. 335–368.

———. (2005). "Scientific Authority and the Transition to Post-Fordism: The Plausibility of Positivism in American Sociology since 1945." Pp. 275–323 in *The Politics of Method in the Human Sciences: Positivism and its Epistemological Others*. edited by G. Steinmetz. Durham, NC: Duke University Press.

———. (2006). "Fordism." *Europe since 1914: Encyclopedia of the Age of War and Reconstruction*, edited by J. M. Merriman and J. M. Winter (Detroit: Charles Scribner's Sons), pp. 1111–1114.

———. (2008). "Harrowed Landscapes: White Ruingazers in Namibia and Detroit and the Cultivation of Memory." *Visual Studies*, vol. 23, no. 3, pp. 211–237.

———. (2009). "Detroit: A Tale of Two Crises." *Environment and Planning D: Society and Space*, 27 (5): 761–770.

———. and M. Chanan. (2005). "Detroit; Ruin of a City. A Documentary Road Movie about Detroit and the Automobile Industry." Distributed by Art Films.

Stiglitz, J. (2013). "The Wrong Lesson From Detroit's Bankruptcy." *New York Times*, 11 August. Retrieved at: http://opinionator.blogs.nytimes.com/2013/08/11/the-wrong-lesson-from-detr oits-bankruptcy/.

Sugrue, T. (1996). *The Origins of the Urban Crisis: Race and Inequality in Postwar Detroit.* Princeton: Princeton University Press.

Tronti, M. (2006). *Operai e capitale*. Derive Approdi: Roma.

Turbeville, W.C. (2013). "The Detroit Bankruptcy." *Demos*. Retrieved Jun 27, 2014 from http://www.demos.org/sites/ default/files/publications/Detroit_Bankruptcy-Demos.pdf.

US Bureau of Labor Statistics. Retrieved Jun 27, 2014, from www.bls.gov

US Census Bureau. Retrieved Jun 27, 2014 from www.census.gov

VanArragon, E.J. (2006). "The Photo League: Views of urban experience in the 1930s and 1940s." Thesis (Ph.D.)--The University of Iowa.

Vergara, C. J. (1999). *American Ruins*. New York: Monacelli Press.

Vlasic, B. (2013). "Detroit is Now a Charity Case for Carmakers." *New York Times*, 22 September. Retrieved Jun 27, 2014, from http://www.nytimes.com/2013/09/23/business/detroit-is-now-a-charity-case-for-carmakers.html.

Wacquant, L. (1997). "Three Pernicious Premises in the Study of the American Ghetto." *International Journal of Urban and Regional Research*, 21 (2): 341–353.

———. (2008). *Urban Outcasts: A Comparative Sociology of Advanced Marginality*. Cambridge, UK: Polity.

Walsh, T. (2013). "Detroit Goes Bust as Auto Industry Booms, and Here's Why." *Detroit Free Press*, 28 July. Retrieved Jun 27, 2014, from http://www.freep.com/article/20130728/COL06/307280070/.

Williams, P. (2014). "Drop Dead, Detroit!" *The New Yorker*, 27 January: 32–39.

3

Learning from Detroit: How Research on a Declining City Enriches Urban Studies

Margaret Dewar, Matthew Weber, Eric Seymour,
Meagan Elliott, and Patrick Cooper-McCann

Detroit's experiences have long mirrored those of many cities: rising industrialization and population growth in the early twentieth century, suburbanization of industry and of white population following World War II, industrial restructuring that dismantled the region's economic base from the 1970s on, and racial tensions throughout that hindered regional progress. This shared experience made research on Detroit relevant to a broad audience of urban scholars. Texts such as *The Origins of the Urban Crisis* (Sugrue 1996) or *Detroit: Race and Uneven Development* (Darden, Hill, Thomas, and Thomas 1987) not only told Detroit's story; they also offered insights into what happened in cities elsewhere.

Today, however, Detroit stands alone among large American cities in both the depth and breadth of its distress. Thousands of homes and many acres of land are vacant and abandoned. Residents are disproportionately poor and racially segregated. The tax base is decimated. The government is bankrupt. These extreme conditions place at issue Detroit's continued relevance to urban studies. What can scholars and practitioners learn about urban processes and phenomena from research on such an outlier city? Is that research relevant only to distressed cities such as Cleveland, St. Louis, and Newark, or can it aid in understanding places like New York, Los Angeles, Sao Paulo, or Beijing?

This chapter argues that research on Detroit continues to advance urban studies in significant ways. Moreover, the city's importance comes not *in spite of* Detroit's decline but rather *because of* its decline. That decline offers research opportunities that are hard to find elsewhere. Researchers, for example, are able to observe phenomena in Detroit that likely exist elsewhere but go unnoticed. The magnifying effects of the city's decline make the invisible visible. Detroit also allows researchers to untangle certain phenomena, such as gentrification, from the context of growth where they are usually observed, casting those phenomena in a new light. The large swaths of vacant urban land in Detroit are also an asset to researchers. They allow researchers to test hypotheses that would be difficult to assess in more intact, densely populated areas. Such research can have broad application to heavily developed urban areas elsewhere. Furthermore, Detroit research can expose the shortcomings of policies that presume strong real estate markets but do not work as expected in disinvested neighborhoods where property demand is very weak. In all these ways, Detroit's extreme conditions present ready opportunities for researchers to advance urban studies.

Detroit's extreme conditions also pose a challenge for some of the disciplines that contribute to urban studies. These disciplines have tended to focus on conditions of growth—seeking to understand how and why cities and regions grow, who benefits when they do, and how to renew growth when it ebbs. Not enough attention has been paid to understanding decline. Scholars have figuratively modeled urban phenomena only across the range that variables exhibit during growth, leaving out the range during decline. The challenge that Detroit poses for urban studies is to flesh out that model—to understand the spatial, social, political and economic dynamics of change and how decline may differ from growth (Galster 2012).[1]

The balance of this chapter develops these themes more fully. It proceeds in three parts. Part 1 summarizes the extreme conditions that prevail in Detroit. Part 2 provides examples of the ways that these conditions open up research opportunities. Part 3 takes up the challenge that Detroit poses to urban studies to deepen the understanding of processes of decline. It does this by offering an example of a possible direction for theorizing and empirical investigation: a "sociology of urban property relations" (Logan and Molotch 1987: 13) or a sociopolitical economy of real property under conditions of decline.

Most of the examples of research in this chapter are completed or ongoing case studies of Detroit. Although the studies focus on Detroit, they contribute ideas and challenges to urban studies more generally by positioning the research in relation to bodies of knowledge. As Robert Yin has stated more generally, case studies of phenomena in Detroit "generalize to theoretical propositions" (Yin 2009: 15), giving them broader relevance.

The majority of these examples come from urban planning, reflecting the disciplinary bias of the authors. Urban planning is an excellent example of how a discipline can learn from Detroit. It is a field where most scholarly attention has focused on growth and on property development despite persistent decline in many cities (Dewar and Weber 2012). Even in places characterized by decline, scholarship has tended to investigate how redevelopment and rebuilding happen or can happen (Bright 2003, Gittell 1992, Keating and Krumholz 1996). Detroit offers a case of decline so extreme that it can jerk urban-planning scholars out of their habitual focus on growth and redevelopment, prompting them to address how cities function politically, economically, socially, and administratively over a broader spectrum of conditions that includes decline as well as growth.

Detroit's Conditions

Detroit has changed greatly since World War II. In 1950 the Census registered the city's largest population, 1.85 million. Since then the population has declined by over 60 percent, to 714,000 in 2010. Among American big cities, only St. Louis has lost a larger share of its peak population. Detroit's population loss contrasts starkly with the population change that occurred in the same period in the three-county metropolitan area that includes Detroit. The region's population *grew* during this period to 2.7 times its 1950 level. As population decline began within the city, the number of households in Detroit continued to increase slightly as households became smaller, so the loss of population did not initially decrease demand for housing. By 2010, however, the city had lost 48 percent of households since 1960, more than the loss in any other large city (US Bureau of the Census 1952, 1962, 1963, US Census Bureau 2010).

The loss of employment has been even more marked than population loss, although changes in the way the federal government defines industries make these comparisons imprecise. Between the immediate post World War II years and 2007, the city lost nearly 95 percent of its manufacturing jobs and nearly 90 percent of its retail jobs (US Bureau of the Census 1949, 1951; US Census Bureau 2007a, b). The city's share of metro area manufacturing jobs fell from three-fifths to one-tenth, and its share of metro retail employment fell from 70 percent to 7 percent. The city's share of these jobs is now well below its share of the region's population.

Detroit is an extraordinarily poor city. The poverty rate rose from slightly less than 15 percent in 1969 to about 42 percent in 2012. In 1969, median household income in Detroit stood at $7,944; by 2012, this had grown to about $23,600 (US Bureau of the Census 1973, US Census Bureau 2012). If income had kept up with inflation, median household income in 2012 would have reached $50,000 (US Bureau of Labor Statistics 2014). In numerous years, Detroit has ranked as the poorest big city in the country, vying for this position with Cleveland (for example, Smith and Starzyk 2010, Smith 2009, Smith and Perkins 2008, Galbincea and Smith 2007).

The changes in population, employment, and income caused a major drop in demand for housing and for commercial and industrial property. Disinvestment led to a 37 percent drop in the number of housing units from 1960 through 2010. This decline lagged the loss of households, however, so the housing vacancy rate stood at 23 percent, signaling that huge numbers of additional units would need demolition (US Bureau of the Census 1962, US Census Bureau 2010). In 2009 about 12,000 of the city's housing structures with one to four units were in poor condition or immediate need of demolition (Data Driven Detroit 2010). About 20 square miles of the city's 139 square miles were already vacant land (not counting parks and highway buffers) as of 2012 (Detroit Works Project 2012, 98). By 2014, public entities owned about 84,000 properties in the city (Detroit Blight Removal Task Force 2014: 195); the average sales price of residential properties sold through realtors in Detroit was just $24,843 in March 2014 (Michigan Realtors 2014).

These changes led to city government fiscal problems. The loss of demand for property led to a huge loss in property values from the 1960s through the 1980s and eroded property tax revenues. The city adopted an income tax in 1962, a utility tax in 1971, and a casino revenues tax in 1999. The income tax became the largest source of tax revenue in the mid-1970s, but these revenues fell by more than half from 2000 through 2010. Property values fell precipitously as a result of huge numbers of mortgage foreclosures and the recession that began in 2008. Federal and state intergovernmental transfers fell considerably as well; state leaders, for instance, cut shared revenue by 48 percent from 1998 to 2012. The city faced chronic deficits after the mid-1980s, ongoing cuts in spending, and ultimately the state's imposition of an emergency financial manager. Detroit became the largest city to declare bankruptcy in US history in 2013 (Bomey and Gallagher 2013).

The city's transformation includes dramatic racial shifts. In 1950, African Americans made up 16 percent of Detroit's population but only 5 percent of the three-county metro area's population outside Detroit (US Bureau of the Census 1952, 1966). By 2010 African Americans constituted 83 percent of the city's population, compared to 12 percent of the three-county area outside the city (US Census Bureau 2010). The metropolitan region has a legacy of intense racial animosity and distrust (Thomas 1997; Farley, Danziger, and Holzer 2000). Among the fifty metropolitan areas with the largest black populations in 2010, blacks and whites were most segregated in the Detroit region in every census year from 1990 through 2010, although the intensity of segregation decreased slightly between 2000 and 2010 (Logan and Stults 2011: 6).

Detroit's conditions are extreme even among other distressed cities such as Cleveland, St. Louis, and Buffalo. The city's current conditions are far removed from those of places like Los Angeles or Houston. This is precisely what makes it a valuable place to conduct urban research.

Ways of Learning from Detroit

In this section, we review four ways researchers learn from Detroit. They observe the phenomena that the magnifying effects of the city's decline make visible. They use the city's extreme conditions to isolate phenomena from the context of growth where they are usually observed. They take advantage of the spatial dimensions of decline to test hypotheses that would be difficult to test elsewhere. And they document the mismatch between policies that presume a demand for real estate and the issues the policies aim to address in neighborhoods where little demand for property exists. This research contributes significantly to the literature on urban studies in ways that might not be possible in other cities with less extreme conditions.

Magnifying Effects in the Context of Decline

Research on Detroit can advance urban studies by observing and explaining the phenomena that Detroit's decline reveals. Many cities have distressed neighborhoods and small areas of widespread abandonment. However, the small scale of these areas and their context amid otherwise growing areas can make discerning some aspects of their social, spatial, political, and economic dynamics difficult. Equally challenging is figuring out whether observed phenomena are part of a larger pattern or are quirks of the particular areas studied. In Detroit, the processes of decline are writ large. Phenomena that researchers might overlook elsewhere are pushed to the surface, making them and their significance more evident. In this regard, Detroit serves as an "extreme" case—an unusual circumstance whose study allows researchers to develop a richer, deeper understanding of hard-to-observe phenomena (Yin 2009). What researchers learn in Detroit they can then test in other places.

Several recent or ongoing studies of property-related issues in Detroit gain insights from the magnifying effects of Detroit's decline. Kimberley Kinder (2014) documents the ways that people secure, care for and sometimes dismantle vacant or abandoned houses in Detroit neighborhoods. The residents' aim is often to make the houses appear occupied. To that end, they may mow the lawn, plant flowers, and place furniture and children's toys in conspicuous locations. In other cases, residents board up vacant houses to secure them against vandals, squatters, and "scrappers"—individuals who remove wiring, plumbing, and other valuable materials from houses to sell to scrap yards. Still others dismantle houses, so that they cannot be used for drug or other illicit activity and will not be targeted by arsonists. Kinder identifies all of these tactics as self-provisioning strategies that residents employ to compensate for the retrenchment of governmental and social control brought on by Detroit's decline.

Andrew Herscher (2012) documents the ways that the devaluing of real estate in Detroit allows residents to repurpose it, creating "alternative urbanisms" (p. 9)—transitory artistic and public spaces, community and guerilla gardens, intentional communities, and more. Herscher wandered the city to find sites where people had reused property that had little value and sought out places others told him about. Because these uses often occupied property that some other private or public entities owned and would not meet city code or use restrictions, he does not reveal where the sites are or who is responsible for the reuse. His assemblage of photographs and brief descriptions show how much activity and creativity exist where outsiders see only vacancy, ruins, and abandonment. These new uses, Herscher argues, offer lessons for what cities and urban spaces can and should become.

Matthew Weber (2014) analyzes the incidence of informal property ownership in Detroit. "Informal property ownership" refers to ways of holding property in which residents have possession of property but their legal claim to ownership is in doubt. Informal owners include squatters who take over vacant houses, residents who hold over in their homes following tax or mortgage foreclosure, people who fence, build on, or otherwise lay claim to vacant lots without purchasing them or securing the owners' permission, and property purchasers who fail to get clear title to property because the recorded interests of prior owners or lien holders have not been released. Researchers have long dismissed efforts to study informal property ownership in the United States. They reason that it occurs too infrequently here and that sites elsewhere better teach what we need to know about informal property ownership (Abrams 1964, Jindrich 2010, Manaster 1968, Peterson 1991). However, Weber finds that informal property ownership is widespread in parts of Detroit that have seen significant depopulation and disinvestment. Some of the emptiest census tracts in the city—those that retain 30 percent or less of their peak number of households since 1970—show some of the highest rates of informal ownership. More than 9 percent of properties in those tracts are either vacant lots that an adjacent property owner has taken over or are homes whose residents have taken over an adjacent vacant lot. More than 11 percent of residential properties in those same tracts were purchased with clouds on the title. These spatial patterns suggest that the flow of people, wealth, and value out of an area erodes the mechanisms that ordinarily reinforce formal property ownership, a possibility that has not been part of theorizing about property.

Eric Seymour (2014) assesses the ways that the property management and disposition practices of banks and government-sponsored enterprises (such as Fannie Mae) may have undermined the stability of Detroit's remaining intact middle-class and working-class neighborhoods, especially those that experienced high rates of mortgage foreclosures in the 2000s. The volume of these properties makes possible the study of varied practices of institutions while holding neighborhood conditions constant. Many of these entities sold numerous properties at very low prices, often to out-of-state investors. These sales relieve these entities of carrying costs that outweigh the properties' value. Nonetheless, such sales have the potential to inflict serious harm on neighborhoods by pushing down property values, extending vacancy periods, and transferring ownership to those who have little interest in reinvesting in the properties. These conditions undermine the confidence of homeowners in the future of their neighborhoods and encourage them to defer maintenance or move away (Galster 1987, 2001). Seymour's research may challenge lenders and government entities to devise property disposition practices that do less unnecessary damage to neighborhoods in cities where demand is weak.

In each of these examples, Detroit's decline makes the phenomena of interest more apparent and accessible than they would be elsewhere. This is a matter of scale. Vacancy and abandonment are widespread in Detroit. Squatting and title issues have long plagued the city. Mortgage foreclosures hit the city hard. Due to these conditions, it becomes possible to find many people engaged in self-provisioning tactics to defend their neighborhoods against decline, or repurposing space to create alternative urbanisms, or holding property without maintaining good title to it. The consequences of banks' property management and disposition practices become more apparent when the foreclosed properties are geographically concentrated.

This research advances urban studies in at least two significant ways. First, it frames inquiries for future investigation. The researchers cited above have identified phenomena observed in Detroit. These phenomena appear to be rooted in circumstances that commonly occur elsewhere, albeit with less intensity and in smaller geographical areas. These circumstances include poverty concentration, population loss, vacancy and abandonment, and weak real estate markets. The Detroit research raises the question of whether similar phenomena occur in other cities under similar circumstances. Notably, but for the magnifying effects of Detroit's decline, researchers might not think to look for these phenomena elsewhere.

Second, this research helps to round out theory on processes of urban change. To date, that theory has focused heavily on the context of growth, leaving understanding of processes of decline underdeveloped. For example, Harold Demsetz (1967) long ago theorized that private property rights develop as the social value of establishing such rights outweighs their social costs. Much of the unraveling of formal ownership that Weber documents in Detroit results from the inversion of this principle: as the cost of maintaining property rights outweighs the gains, property rights diminish. Nonetheless, the possibility that decline might unravel property rights arrangements has not been part of the scholarship on property. Indeed, the evolutionary theory of property rights contemplates change flowing only toward stronger and more refined property rights (Merrill 2002, Platteau 1996). Evidence from Detroit forces theorists to consider how property rights may evolve differently in the context of decline.

Untangling Phenomena that Occur Together Elsewhere

Detroit's conditions can allow researchers to distinguish among phenomena that seem inseparable in settings of growth. Gentrification provides a ready example. Gentrification is the process whereby incoming middle-class residents create demand for redeveloped housing and commercial property in the urban core, with the ultimate effect of displacing working-class residents. It is now a central feature of public discussion and media attention surrounding redevelopment across the United States and Europe (Brown-Saracino and Rumpf 2011). Gentrification often occurs in cities and regions experiencing strong growth in population and economic prosperity in some areas. The co-occurrence of these phenomena interferes with discerning gentrification's essential features. In Detroit, focused nodes of growth occur in the context of widespread, profound disinvestment. This allows a fresh assessment of what gentrification is and how it operates.

A neighborhood where numerous residents and others believe gentrification is occurring in Detroit is the North End. However, rents and housing values have remained so low that as of 2014 no one would be displaced because of rising costs. The area had lost 89 percent of its 1950 population by 2010, a loss much higher than the city's. Only 5,585 people lived there in 2010. Of those, 94 percent were African American and 2.4 percent were white. The North End's vacancy rate was 37 percent of the housing units as of 2010. The North End also had extensive amounts of vacant land; as of early 2014, 38 percent of residential properties were vacant lots. Housing disinvestment continued in 2014 as 9 percent of residential properties faced auction for owners' failure to pay property taxes (US Census Bureau 1952, 2010; Data Driven Detroit 2009; Motor City Mapping 2014; Loveland Technologies 2014).

The North End helps researchers better understand gentrification in a context where residents perceive gentrification to be occurring but where, as of 2014, no physical displacement has occurred that can be attributed to rising rents. As disinvested as the North End is, residents are concerned about gentrification. Long-term residents discuss the ways that changes in their neighborhood have threatened their sense of place, connection with other residents, and use of public space. As one example, numerous North End residents suggested to one of the authors in 2012 that, in a process they termed gentrification, young whites had taken over a large vacant lot for a garden with no consultation with anyone in the North End, although residents had envisioned other uses of the space. Over time, some nearby residents started accepting food from the garden and volunteering there while others remained skeptical that any good would come to the North End from such activities (Eligon 2014). Although no data existed to document the phenomenon, the authors observed numerous professionals in their twenties and thirties purchasing houses in the North End, and several former industrial structures were rehabilitated into lofts. In this way, while no physical displacement has occurred, some long-term residents suffer from "cultural displacement," in which they remain physically in place but culturally isolated from other residents of the neighborhoods where they have long resided (Elliott 2012).

The North End is a neighborhood without a "rent gap," referring to the difference between the value of property as currently used and the value it would have if put to its highest and best use (Smith 1979). When a rent gap becomes large enough, it serves as a significant driver of redevelopment in low-income and working-class neighborhoods. Poor maintenance and outdated housing stock in these neighborhoods can push down current rents and property values, while their proximity to downtown, other major employment centers, or higher value neighborhoods promises high returns from rehabilitation or redevelopment. Large rent gaps can lead to rapid neighborhood transformation, as real estate developers and landlords leverage the opportunities to profit and middle-class households move in. Amid these changes, the neighborhood's long-time, lower-income residents may be unable to pay the much higher rents or may need to sell their homes to draw on the equity that rising values create.

Whatever rent gap exists in Detroit, however, is not enough to drive this kind of transformation. As of 2014, no significant development occurred in any neighborhood in Detroit without subsidy (staff of Midtown, Inc., and the City of Detroit Planning and Development Department, personal communication with M. Elliott). The low value of property in a higher and better use has the effect of keeping the pace of redevelopment slow, due to developers' dependency on transfers of very low priced city-owned property and on subsidies from foundations and the federal government. This can be an opportunity for researchers, allowing for a rich qualitative assessment of the processes and dimensions of change.

That gentrification may be occurring in the North End without physical displacement speaks directly to academic debates regarding gentrification. Kathe Newman and Elvin Wyly (2005: 25) state that displacement was at one point a litmus test for what distinguished redevelopment from gentrification. This measure was then dismissed for several years, until discussions returned to the issue in research in the past decade. Much of present research contests the mechanisms for measuring displacement, rather than seeking a more robust understanding of gentrification's other contours as a social process. Displacement is not the only aspect of concern in gentrification. Indeed, definitions of gentrification need not include the process of displacement as part of what constitutes the phenomenon. For example, Willem Van Vliet (1998: 198) calls gentrification "the process by which central urban neighborhoods that have undergone disinvestments and economic decline experience a reversal, reinvestment, and the in-migration of a relatively well-off middle- and upper middle-class population." Van Vliet therefore emphasizes conditions prior to the in-moving population rather than what happens after. These types of definitions are more useful for a context like Detroit's, where displacement exists as a widely held fear (Elliott 2012) but is not a physical reality for more than a very small number of residents.

Detroit offers an opportunity for more fine-grained research into the social and cultural dynamics of gentrification. As Jackelyn Hwang and Robert Sampson (2014: 1) argue, the coexistence of neighborhood upgrading with the persistence of neighborhood inequality by race and class is not well understood. Nonetheless, it is a condition that Detroit's widespread vacancy all but guarantees will prevail as neighborhoods in some parts of Detroit gain population.

Detroit's extreme conditions of decline and loss of government capacity enable the sorting out of other relationships as well. For instance, Cleveland has a much stronger community development industry than Detroit, as evidenced by much greater success in reusing vacant and abandoned land. Research that compared Detroit and Cleveland to explain this difference in the context of similar, weak demand for property showed that collaboration between city officials and nonprofit developers and among city and county officials was key to enabling nonprofit developers to carry out projects (Dewar 2006, 2013). In another example, Detroit served as a case for Janice Bockmeyer's (2000) examination of hypotheses about a "culture of distrust" that grew out of Mayor "Young's failed pursuit of long-term business investment and coalition formation in the face of neglected neighbourhood development" (p. 2424). The protracted lack of trust between city hall and neighborhood leaders helped reveal defensive group formation through development of norms and networking among community development leaders. This civic culture and a history of racial division determined interactions in planning for the Empowerment Zone. In both of these examples, Detroit's experience enabled scholars to understand better the key dimensions of phenomena.

Learning from Experiments in the Context of Weak Demand for Property

Detroit's extensive vacant land makes policy experiments or quasi-experiments possible. Researchers can take advantage of Detroit's conditions to test environmental interventions and their effects on health, neighborhood stability, and environmental quality. Community-based participatory research projects in fields such as public health, environmental design, and ecology are demonstrating this potential.

For example, public health advocates argue that establishing buffer zones that limit residential development around major roadways would limit the incidence and severity of pollution-related ailments such as asthma, impaired lung function and development, and cardiovascular disease (Los Angeles County Department of Public Health 2013). Testing the effectiveness of such a practice in real-world conditions, however, would be socially destructive, politically infeasible, and financially costly in nearly all other cities, where areas around major roadways are developed and heavily populated. Detroit, by contrast, offers many sites where depopulation has established de facto buffer zones—places where few, if any, residents remain within several hundred feet of major roadways. Over the next few years a community-based participatory research project in Detroit will measure the effects on air quality of planting various types of trees and plants in such areas (Bowyer 2014). Although Detroit offers the site for such a project, the findings will be applicable to other cities with similar environmental and ecological conditions.

Likewise, researchers are testing the social, economic, health, and ecological impacts of green infrastructure in Detroit. "Green infrastructure" refers to the vegetation, soils, and natural processes used to manage storm water and create healthier urban environments (US Environmental Protection Agency 2014). It might be a cost-effective way to limit combined sewer overflows that pollute waterways, while enhancing neighborhood attractiveness, increasing property values, and adapting to climate change. Widespread public land ownership and many new demolitions in Detroit enable researchers to select sites strategically to test the impacts of varied green infrastructure designs. Moreover, the low cost of privately held land means that strategic sites that are not publicly owned can often be acquired within the constraint of a research budget. An ongoing research project at the University of Michigan, in partnership with Detroit city departments and in consultation with neighbors, is measuring the volume and quality of water that flows through vacant lots with conventional post-demolition fill and with two types of ecological designs that aim to retain water. The research will solicit nearby residents' reactions to the different treatments. Because so many demolitions are occurring in the city, the researchers have a range of choices of properties as treatment and control sites (Nassauer 2014). The results of this research can apply in other cities where vacancy is less abundant and such tests would therefore face more research challenges but where green infrastructure could absorb storm water and improve neighborhoods.

A third example of this type of research looked at how different ways of maintaining vacant land might affect health (Katz, Barrie, and Carey 2014). Detroit's many vacant lots receive varied levels of maintenance. Mowing of publicly owned lots occurred once a year or every two years in the period of the study; these account for 51 percent of all vacant lots. Some lots experience no mowing and are becoming reforested. Some owners or neighbors mow frequently. As the authors stated, "The large number of vacant lots and the wide array of mowing regimes make Detroit an ideal place to answer our study questions" (p. 6). In vacant lots that were mowed annually or biennially, ragweed, a prolific producer of allergenic pollen, appeared more frequently than in the other mowing regimes, suggesting that this treatment of vacant lots could cause significant health problems, a finding with implications for the maintenance of vacant lots in many cities.

The availability and use of extensive vacant land could offer many more opportunities for experiments. The growth of urban agriculture in the city offers one example. Researchers have investigated residents' views about urban agriculture (Colasanti, Hamm, and Litjens 2012; Draus, Roddy, and McDuffie 2014). As urban gardening and agriculture become widespread in the city, researchers may be able to investigate ecological conditions, air and water quality, and health effects in quasi-experimental settings. In all these studies, Detroit offers a context, but the city is not necessarily the subject of study or the unit of analysis. The tests of hypotheses could not take place without Detroit's substantial vacancy, but the findings are often generalizable to situations in growing and dense residential settings as well because of the phenomena the research investigates. Researchers can learn from the Detroit context about effects of land uses that exist only at a small scale in other cities.

Demonstrating the Limits of Policy in the Context of Disinvestment

Studying Detroit can expose the shortcomings of policies not evident in growing places and reveal gaps in ways of thinking about decline. Policy research can also use Detroit as a setting to test policies that are least likely to succeed there; if they succeed in Detroit, they may have even greater potential elsewhere.

Michigan's reform of the state's property tax foreclosure process provides one example where the Detroit case exposes incorrect assumptions about demand for property. Michigan's 1999 law aimed to "strengthen and revitalize the economy of this state and its municipalities by encouraging the efficient and expeditious return to productive use of property returned for delinquent taxes" (Michigan Public Act 123

1999). The legislation reduced the period of tax foreclosure from at least six years to two or three years. It also ended sale of tax liens and implemented a two-tier auction system. The primary auction each year offers tax-foreclosed properties for bids of no less than the amount of delinquent taxes, interest and fees owed on the properties. A second auction offers properties that do not sell in the first auction for opening bids of $500, regardless of the amount of taxes, interest, and fees owed. Michigan's law has served as a "best practice" for other state governments to consider adopting because it shortens the period of property abandonment and can provide clear title, thus reducing the time for damage to structures and potentially bolstering property tax returns (Brophy and Vey 2002: 11; Mallach 2006: 79; National Vacant Properties Campaign 2005: 8).

Wayne County's experience in implementing the legislation was positive in the first year after the law took effect. It sold most of the foreclosed Detroit properties offered at auction. However, as the economy weakened through the first decade of the 2000s, the demand-based assumptions underlying the legislation became apparent. As of 2012 the number of properties foreclosed (slightly over 20,000) had increased to more than 70 times the number offered at auction in 2002 (282). By 2007, the number of properties sold at the second auction each year dwarfed the number sold at the first auction. Most of the properties did not sell at all. For the first time, in 2009, the proceeds from the auction did not cover the unpaid taxes for which the properties had been foreclosed. By 2013, the county was not foreclosing on all properties with taxes unpaid for two years because the foreclosure and auction processes could not handle so many properties (Dewar, Seymour, and Druță forthcoming).

Even for properties sold when the economy was stronger, in 2002 and 2003, productive reuse did not necessarily result. New owners most likely to use property in ways that would add to future tax base—owner occupants, side lot purchasers, and those undertaking new development—purchased only 11 percent of a random sample of properties sold at the auctions. Nearly 50 percent of sampled sold properties were not redeveloped and not acquired by an adjacent owner. Of these properties, 80 percent were vacant lots with no sign of use following sale. Twenty percent of properties sold at auction in 2002 and 2003 were foreclosed again by 2007 (Dewar forthcoming).

These failures reveal that the widely praised Michigan legislation was based on incorrect assumptions about the demand for property. Legislators and proponents of the change in the law assumed that foreclosed properties would sell at auction. They assumed that auction revenues would cover the unpaid taxes and costs of foreclosure. They assumed property sold at auction would "return to productive use." None of these assumptions proved true in Detroit. The Detroit case suggests that such provisions would work to encourage reuse only in places with stronger demand. Even in jurisdictions with strong economies, the case suggests, the neighborhoods where tax foreclosures occur most often could also have quite weak demand for property, and therefore, the outcomes could resemble those in Detroit.

Detroit-based research on federal policies and practices for handling mortgage foreclosures also reveals flawed assumptions about how policies work in the context of decline. As noted above, Detroit had one of the highest mortgage foreclosure rates in the nation preceding and during the recent recession. Many of these properties reverted to the ownership of federal entities that handle individual properties in their large national inventories of foreclosures in an identical manner, regardless of local housing market context. Using a national network of third-party contractors, federal entities have their foreclosed properties appraised and placed on the market, with price reductions occurring at set intervals. These practices assume demand for mortgage-foreclosed properties regardless of value, condition, or location. In the context of weak demand for housing, properties languish on the market and therefore experience extensive deterioration. Investors often purchase properties with low sales prices and in poor condition and then attempt to flip their acquisitions (Dixon 2011, Evans 2013). Such investors mislead buyers about needed improvements and unpaid taxes, leading to financial difficulties and possible foreclosure for new owner occupants. Investors allow properties they cannot flip to go into tax foreclosure, shifting responsibility for the properties to local governments. In these situations, federally owned and sold foreclosures impose negative externalities through their degraded conditions and unstable occupancy. In neighborhoods where demand for housing had remained strong prior to the recession, these policies and practices undermine the confidence of nearby owner occupants in the future of their neighborhood and encourage them to disinvest. Although neighborhood stabilization is an explicit objective of federal disposition of mortgage-foreclosed properties, the implicit assumption of adequate demand for the large number of foreclosures in Detroit frustrates the realization of this goal. Research on federal entities' handling of mortgage-foreclosed properties in Detroit reveals the particular, place-based consequences of federal policies that assume that demand for property exists and points to the need for nuanced understanding of local conditions and flexible approaches to sale of housing (Seymour 2014).

Other research offers examples of investigation of policies that work differently than expected in a context of decline. Lan Deng has looked at how the Low Income Housing Tax Credit (LIHTC) has been implemented in Detroit. Unlike growing cities, Detroit has a substantial supply of low-cost housing. In Detroit neighborhoods, the justification for the use of LIHTC to subsidize housing is to redevelop neighborhoods. Deng's analysis has shown, however, that LIHTC is only associated with the strengthening of neighborhoods when a large number of subsidized units are concentrated in an area and when other redevelopment programs also focus there (Deng 2013). In another example of such research, Gary Sands and Mark Skidmore have explained how the property tax system, similar to that usually functioning adequately in most of the country, has contributed to Detroit's financial crisis and limits the possibility of financial recovery (Sands and Skidmore 2013). Part of the explanation for the problems lies in state law that imposes a tax value cap, but most of the difficulties are due to Detroit-specific conditions such as very low property values, a range of tax abatements, and public ownership of tens of thousands of properties.

Stronger analysis of how urban policies may work needs to depend on theories that encompass situations with both strong and weak demand for property. The policy problems discussed above can be thought of as resulting from misspecified relationships with incorrect parameters because the analysis on which the policies depended did not consider the full range of conditions where the policy would be implemented.

Advancing Synthesis of Varied Research on Detroit

The previous sections have shown several ways that studying Detroit can enrich and expand urban studies. Much of the cited work relates to property dynamics in the context of decline. This is an area in need of further theorizing and empirical research, in order to account for the range of political, social, and economic conditions that both affect and are affected by property relations. To date, theory has focused more heavily on property relations in the context of growth than decline (see, for example, Logan and Molotch 1987). Decline is not merely the reverse of growth. Because buildings are durable, disinvestment takes place over a long period after demand for housing and industrial and commercial property declines, in contrast to the speed with which real estate development can respond to an increase in demand. The time between loss of demand and demolition allows many actors to extract remaining value. It also leaves a physical legacy with significant social, economic, environmental, and political implications. In this section, we call for new theorizing to develop a sociopolitical economy of real property that encompasses both growth and decline, in order to give a more complete and robust account of property dynamics across a range of contexts.

Numerous studies that might contribute to such a project exist, but how these pieces fit together as a whole is not yet clear. The literature is perhaps most developed with regard to the economic and financial systems that operate as property becomes degraded and eventually abandoned. Some work has also considered the intersection of social relations and property dynamics in the context of decline. The beginnings of a literature on the interplay of property with political and governance issues in the context of decline also exist. Nonetheless, significant work remains both to fill holes not yet addressed by scholars and to develop the theoretical moorings that link these bodies of research with each other and with the larger literature on the political economy of property relations.

The literature on the economic and financial systems that operate as property becomes degraded encompasses topics such as landlord behavior in the context of decline, private lending and mortgage foreclosure practices and their consequences, and municipal property tax foreclosure practices. Much of this research comes from other cities experiencing decline and from earlier eras of property disinvestment. George Sternlieb and his coauthors (Sternlieb, Burchell, Hughes and James 1974; Sternlieb and Burchell 1973) and Michael Stegman (1972), for example, analyzed the situation of landlords in Baltimore and Newark as demand for housing fell with a decrease in immigration and with suburbanization. They found that neighborhood conditions (including vacancy rates and maintenance levels) and landlord-tenant relations have a bigger influence on the decision to abandon property than does the condition of the property that landlords abandon.

More recent research on the effects of huge numbers of mortgage foreclosures has helped reveal the behaviors of numerous actors and governmental entities in extracting housing equity from declining cities' strongest neighborhoods. In the 1990s and first half of the 2000s, mortgage companies and brokers pushed predatory mortgages in middle- and working-class neighborhoods, often with a majority of minority-race homeowners. In a first boom of high-risk lending from 1992 through 1999, such loans were concentrated among minority borrowers and in minority neighborhoods in cities

(Immergluck 2009, ch. 3; Whitehouse 2007). Therefore, mortgage foreclosures hit these neighborhoods and this type of borrower hardest. As Dan Immergluck (2011: 143) wrote, "Federal policymakers chose to permit the flourishing of subprime and high-risk mortgage markets and to actively preempt state governments' efforts to protect their consumers in the absence of meaningful regulation." In metropolitan areas with weak housing markets such as Detroit's, foreclosures concentrated in central cities (Bratt 2012, Immergluck 2009). The influence on decline continues to become evident. In Cleveland, a large percent of real-estate owned (REO) houses—those that banks owned following mortgage foreclosure—sold at extremely low prices, under $10,000. Such low prices contribute to blight by eroding property values and the confidence of investors and homeowners in the future of their neighborhoods. Many of the buyers were not from the Cleveland region and had not seen the properties. By early 2010, 9 percent of REO houses that had sold at very low prices between 2004 and 2009 had been demolished; nearly half of such homes in the Cleveland area were vacant, and 56 percent were tax delinquent—indicating they could be on their way to abandonment and demolition (Coulton, Schramm, and Hirsh 2010).

Building on research in the 1970s (Sternlieb and Lake 1976, Olson and Lachman 1976), a growing literature on tax foreclosures also contributes to understanding the roles of government entities, investors, and speculators in the disinvestment process. The handling of tax foreclosures in Detroit seeded more blight by reducing owner occupancy and introducing irresponsible property owners into strong neighborhoods (Dewar, Seymour, and Druță forthcoming). Joshua Akers (2013) argued that tax foreclosure practices in Detroit and Michigan were part of a system of "production of decline" (p. 1073). Jason Hackworth and Kelsey Nowakowski (2014) investigated what types of purchasers were "investing in disinvestment" through purchases at tax auctions in Toledo and found they very rarely had interest in redevelopment. Collectively, this research helps advance understanding of the interplay between decline, tax foreclosure, and individuals' efforts to extract value as property becomes degraded.

This body of work leaves many holes to fill. Many real estate practices that characterize decline are not well understood. Corruption appears to be widespread. Most noteworthy in the last fifteen years is the now well-known marketing of high-cost, high-risk mortgages, the mischaracterization of the risk in mortgage tranches, and the foreclosures on households that could have made the monthly payments on restructured loans. Newspapers' investigative reports and discussions in neighborhood organizations' meetings provide evidence of many other types of crimes as well. As one example, in the late 1990s, the largest securities fraud case in Michigan's history involved the bankruptcy of RIMCO, a company that owned thousands of homes in Detroit. Most of these homes became blighted (King 2001). For another example, with the rise of mortgage foreclosures and the increase in housing vacancies in strong neighborhoods after 2007, the state chair of the Michigan Welfare Rights Organization promoted squatting in houses. She told a reporter that she said to people unable to pay their rent, "Here's a list of houses that we have intercepted that have been repossessed by banks; pick one and move in" (Thomas 2012).

Research at the intersection of social relations and property dynamics in the context of decline also helps to round out a sociopolitical economy of real property. Studies, cited above, by Kinder (2014), Herscher (2012) and Weber (2014) contribute to this literature. Each documents changes in property and social relations in places where decline has emptied neighborhoods, pushed down property values, and diminished governmental capacity, or where it threatens to do so. Kinder links these conditions to self-provisioning tactics residents employ to defend property values and neighborhood stability. Weber connects them to an unraveling of formal property relations. Herscher shows their relationship to property repurposing activities that create alternative urbanisms. Another piece of the same puzzle comes from research into the relationship between neighborhood disinvestment, abandonment, and crime. Erica Raleigh and George Galster (2014) find that a block in Detroit with many vacant homes has a higher crime rate than an otherwise identical block with few vacant homes. Whether those homes are abandoned—rather than merely vacant—appears to make little difference in the crime rate. However, if a block has vacant lots instead of vacant homes, the crime rate is lower. All of this research—by Kinder, Weber, Herscher, and Raleigh and Galster—helps point the way for future work that links changes in property conditions to changes in social relations, and vice versa, in the context of decline.

Kinder's and Herscher's research also contributes to thinking about the relationship between property and political/governance issues in the context of decline. It provides examples of adaptations and consequences when the public sector's capacity to govern severely diminishes, whether in providing city services or in enforcing city statutes and regulations. Literature on "urban austerity" policies (Peck 2012, 2014) provides a grounding for understanding how such government incapacity is produced. Such incapacity grows out of neoliberal ideology and the fiscal federalism policies that neoliberalism promotes.

Scholars could do more to articulate other forces largely outside the city's control—for instance, the ways that the Detroit region's changing role in the global economic system has implicated governance and property relations. Industrial decline was a major force in the city's transformation (Farley, Danziger and Holzer 2000; Darden, Hill, Thomas, and Thomas 1987; Thomas 1990). The decline, restructuring, and relocation of auto manufacturing has reshaped relationships between elected officials and industrial leaders and changed the character of growth coalitions in ways not fully explicated.

Further work remains as well to link state and federal government actions to the social, economic, and political dimensions of real property in the context of decline. Although Detroit's decline stems from structural forces beyond its control, the State of Michigan nonetheless requires the Detroit city government to balance its books on the basis of an eviscerated tax base, in accordance with fiscal federalism's demand that each level of government be self-financing (Frug 1999). Only market-oriented interventions like outsourcing and public-private partnerships can achieve this in an environment that restricts intergovernmental transfers and tax increases.

Another useful line of research is suggested in Douglas Rae's *City* (2003). Rae demonstrates that the challenge of governing changes as cities decline. In cities where decline has not undermined social capital, informal networks of households, churches, small businesses, voluntary associations, and the like supplement the work of government, as neighbors watch out for one another and care for their properties (a point also famously made by Jane Jacobs [1961]). Those networks and the capacity to govern change considerably in cities like Detroit as a consequence of capital and job flight and the departure of residents. Block clubs and neighborhood organizations that remain in neglected areas no longer supplement government services; instead, they often provide the services themselves. They do so even as loss of population undermines capacity to meet private needs informally. Residents in some neighborhoods adopt parks, organize security patrols, pick up trash, board up vacant homes, and take other defensive measures in place of the public authorities that are ostensibly responsible for these tasks (Kinder 2014). Other neighborhoods lack similar coordination and receive only the minimal services the fiscally strained government provides. The level of neighbors' interventions shapes the quality of neighborhood life unevenly across Detroit. Thus in many areas neighbors seek to socialize tenants to local norms when they move into housing that was owner occupied before the owners lost their home to mortgage foreclosure. Neighbors become code enforcers as they pester demolition contractors to do their work with the proper health and safety precautions and press city inspectors to assure contractors comply. Residents develop and share tactics for getting squatters out of houses that can be preserved and sold, ignoring official statements about their own illegal trespassing.

This evidence suggests that decline prompts substantial shifts in both social relations and the allocations of power and responsibility in urban settings. Further documenting and understanding these dynamics is a promising line of inquiry for proposed broader understanding of the political economy of real property.

Learning from Detroit

These suggestions of ways to learn from Detroit and the implications for urban studies address a small number of the topics, research designs, and styles of research on Detroit. Learning from a specific city has a contentious history with reference to city-based schools of urban studies. However, we do not suggest that Detroit is representative of urban processes generally or that it is "radically unique" (Beauregard 2011). We do not mean to say that Detroit is what Neil Brenner calls "prototypical" (a case with characteristics soon to become more generalized) or "stereotypical" (typical of more general development) (2003). Rather, the examples demonstrate ways that Detroit's extreme decline helps to expose phenomena not noticed elsewhere, parse phenomena that occur together elsewhere, undertake experiments that depend on the existence of much vacant land, and evaluate contrary policy results under very weak market conditions. In these examples Detroit sometimes serves as Brenner's "archetypical" city, "an extreme case of a more general development" (p. 209). The extreme conditions in Detroit also serve as an invitation to comparison, not as a privileging of Detroit-based research. Research conducted on any site makes implicit reference to other sites of research by addressing theory derived from investigation of those places. Following Colin McFarlane (2013), we propose the comparative aspect of research on Detroit as explicit and strategic, that is, "as a critique . . . that seeks to unsettle and destabilize knowledge and theory as it is produced, and that seeks to reconstruct and develop new lines of inquiry" (p. 738). As Jennifer Robinson (2011) has suggested, in advocating comparative urban research, investigation "could draw both inspiration and method from the cities that form its objects of study" (p. 19) and generate a style of theorizing that escapes the convention of developing hypotheses "based on more or less parochi-ally generated theory" (p. 17). This chapter suggests the value of such comparative research by placing phenomena observed in Detroit against theories developed to account for processes in growing cities as well as theories that describe urbanization processes in the Global South.

Scholars in other disciplines can find other examples of ways to learn from Detroit and additional topics and theories they can enrich through Detroit-based research. Considerable potential exists to build further on what scholars can learn from Detroit. For instance, George Galster (2014) has argued that decline is distinctly different from growth in several ways. Research on Detroit has the potential to identify thresholds beyond which certain phenomena, for example, housing abandonment and residential change, slow or accelerate. Research inspired by disaster, especially in places such as New Orleans that were declining prior to disaster (for example, Lowe and Bates 2013; Ehrenfeucht and Nelson 2013), can offer additional insights in comparison with Detroit. Scholars in other fields will also be able to identify areas where research on Detroit shows the need for greater synthesis or an extension of received theory. The promise of such research on Detroit is considerable.

Note

1.   Because we puzzled over how we could learn from Detroit, we convened the two-year-long Detroit School Series hosted at the University of Michigan to address the following questions: Is it time to establish a Detroit School of Urban Studies? If so, what defines it? How does thinking about Detroit-like cities change the questions we ask and the answers we pursue in the many disciplines that contribute to urban studies? What do we gain by rallying a community of scholars under the Detroit School banner? What do we lose? The ideas in this chapter grew out of the lectures, seminars, and discussions in that series. See http://www.umich.edu/~detsch/.

References

Abrams, C. (1964). *Man's Struggle for Shelter in an Urbanizing World.* Cambridge, MA: M.I.T. Press.

Akers, J. (2013). "Making Markets: Think Tank Legislation and Private Property in Detroit." *Urban Geography*, 34 (8): 1070–1095.

Beauregard, R. A. (2011). "Radical Uniqueness and the Flight from Urban Theory." In D. R. Judd and D. Simpson (Eds.), *The City, Revisited* (pp. 186–202). Minneapolis: University of Minnesota Press.

Bockmeyer, J. L. (2000). "A Culture of Distrust." *Urban Studies,* 37 (13): 2417–40.

Bomey, N., and J. Gallagher. (2013). "How Detroit Went Broke." *Detroit Free Press* (Sept. 15) 1A.

Bowyer, W. W. (2014) "School of Public Health, Detroit Partners Aim to Improve City's Air Quality. *University Record* (Feb. 18). http://record.umich.edu/print/1663

Bratt, R. G. (2012). "Home Ownership Risk and Responsibility Before and After the U. S. Mortgage Crisis. In R. Ronald & M. Elsinga (Eds.), *Beyond Home Ownership*. New York: Routledge.

Brenner, N. (2003). "Stereotypes, Archetypes, and Prototypes." *City and Community*, 2 (3): 205–16.

Bright, E. (2003). *Reviving America's Forgotten Neighborhoods.* New York: Routledge.

Brophy, P. C., and J. S. Vey. (2002) "Seizing City Assets." (Oct.). Brookings Institution, Washington, DC.

Brown-Saracino, J., and C. Rumpf. (2011). "Diverse Imaginaries of Gentrification: Evidence from Newspaper Coverage in Seven U.S. Cities, 1986–2006." *Journal of Urban Affairs,* 33 (3): 289–315.

Colasanti, K. J. A., M. W. Hamm, and C. M. Litjens. (2012). "The City as an 'Agricultural Powerhouse'?" *Urban Geography*, 33 (3): 348–69.

Coulton, C., M. Schramm, and A. Hirsh (2010). "REO and Beyond: The Aftermath of the Foreclosure Crisis In Cuyahoga County, Ohio." In *REO and Vacant Properties: Strategies for Neighborhood Stabilization* (pp. 47–54). Washington, DC: The Federal Reserve Board and Federal Reserve Banks of Boston and Cleveland.

Darden J. T., R. C. Hill, J. Thomas, and R. Thomas. (1987). *Detroit: Race and Uneven Development.* (Philadelphia, PA: Temple University Press).

Data Driven Detroit. (2009). Detroit Residential Parcel Survey. Data file.

————.(2010). DetroitResidentialParcelSurvey.February. http://www.detroitparcelsurvey.org/pdf/
Detroit_Residential_Parcel_Survey_Presentation.pdf

Demsetz, H. (1967). "Toward a Theory of Property Rights." *The American Economic Review* 57 (2):
347–359.

Deng, L. (2013). "Building Affordable Housing in Cities After Abandonment." In M. Dewar and
J. M. Thomas (Eds.), *The City after Abandonment* (pp. 41–63). Philadelphia: University of Pennsylvania Press.

Detroit Blight Removal Task Force. (2014). *Every Neighborhood Has a Future. . . And It Doesn't Include
Blight*. Detroit: Detroit Blight Removal Task Force.

Detroit Works Project. (2012). *Detroit Future City*. Detroit, MI: Author. http://detroitfuturecity.com/wp-
content/uploads/2014/02/DFC_Full_2ndEd.pdf.

Dewar, M. (2006). "Selling Tax-Reverted Land." *Journal of the American Planning Association*, 72 (2):
167–80.

————. (2013). "What Helps or Hinders Nonprofit Developers in Reusing Vacant, Abandoned, and
Contaminated Property?" In M. Dewar and J. M. Thomas (Eds.), *The City after Abandonment*
(pp. 174–96). Philadelphia: University of Pennsylvania Press.

————. (Forthcoming). "Reuse of Abandoned Property in Detroit and Flint." *Journal of Planning Education and Research*.

————, E. Seymour, and O. Druță. (Forthcoming). "Disinvesting in the City." *Urban Affairs Review*.

————, and M. Weber. (2012). "City Abandonment." In R. Weber and R. Crane (Eds.), *Oxford Handbook
of Urban Planning* (pp. 563–86). Oxford: Oxford University Press.

Dixon, J. (2011, Aug. 15). "Fannie Mae and Freddie Mac's Fire Sales Dilute Metro Home Prices." *Detroit
Free Press*.

Draus, P. J., J. Roddy, and A. McDuffie. (2014). "'We don't have no neighborhood': Advanced Marginality
and Urban Agriculture in Detroit." *Urban Studies* 51 (12): 2523–38.

Ehrenfeucht, R., and M. Nelson. (2013). "Recovery in a Shrinking City." In M. Dewar and J. M. Thomas
(Eds.), *The City after Abandonment* (pp. 133–50). Philadelphia: University of Pennsylvania Press.

Eligon, J. (2014, July 7). "Testing Ground for a New Detroit." *New York Times*. 1A.

Elliott, M. (2012, Jan. 10). "Planning Appropriately for our Future." *Huffington Post Detroit*. Retrieved
January 10, 2012. http://www.huffingtonpost.com/meagan-elliott/detroitgentrification_b_1194534.
html.

Evans, C. (2013, July 22). "Fannie Mae Continues to Traffic in Zombie Properties." *Cleveland Plain Dealer*.

Farley, R., S. Danziger, and H. J. Holzer. (2000). *Detroit Divided*. New York: Russell Sage Foundation.

Frug, G. E. (1999). *City Making*. Princeton, NJ: Princeton University Press.

Galbincea, B., and R. L. Smith. (2007, Aug. 29). "Who Is Poor?" *Plain Dealer*. A6

Galster, G. (1987). *Homeownership and Neighborhood Reinvestment*. Durham, NC: Duke University Press.

————. (2001). "On the Nature of Neighbourhood." *Urban Studies*, 38 (12): 2111–24.

————. C. (2012). *Driving Detroit: The Quest for Respect in Motown*. Philadelphia: University of
Pennsylvania Press.

————. (2014). "Why Bother Learning from Declining Cities? Aren't They the Mirror Images of Growing
Cities?" Presentation at the Michigan Meeting "Learning from Detroit," May 30, 2014, University of
Michigan, Ann Arbor. http://www.youtube.com/watch?v=PSJjvg5cQ8.

Gittell, R. J. (1992). *Renewing Cities*. Princeton, NJ: Princeton University Press.

Hackworth, J. and K. Nowakowski. (2014). "Investment in Disinvestment: A critical examination of
forfeited land investors in Toledo, Ohio from 1993 to 2011." Unpublished paper.

Herscher, A. (2012). *The Unreal Estate Guide to Detroit*. Ann Arbor, MI.: University of Michigan Press.

Hwang, J., and R. J. Sampson. (2014). "Divergent Pathways of Gentrification." *American Sociological
Review*, 79 (4): 1–26.

Immergluck, D. (2009). *Foreclosed: High-risk lending, Deregulation, and the Undermining of America's
Mortgage Market*. Ithaca: Cornell University Press.

————. (2011). "The Local Wreckage of Global Capital." *International Journal of Urban and Regional
Research* 35 (): 130–46.

Jacobs, J. (1961). *The Death and Life of Great American Cities*. New York: Vintage.

Jindrich, J. (2010). "The Shantytowns of Central Park West." *Journal of Urban History*, 36 (5): 672–84.

Katz, D. S. W., B. T. C Barrie, and T. S. Carey. (2014). "Urban Ragweed in Vacant Lots." *Urban Forestry
and Urban Greening*. Available online: DOI: 10.1016/j.ufug.2014.06.001.

Keating, W. D., and N. Krumholz (Eds.) (1996). *Revitalizing Urban Neighborhoods*. Lawrence, KS:
University Press of Kansas.

Kinder, K. (2014). "Guerrilla-style Defensive Architecture in Detroit." *International Journal of Urban and Regional Research*. Available online: DOI/10.1111/1468-2427.12158.

King, R. J. (2001, Aug. 29). "MCA Exec Pleads Guilty to Fraud." *Detroit News*.

Logan, J. R., & Molotch, H. L. (1987). *Urban fortunes: The Political Economy of Place.* Berkeley, CA: University of California Press.

Logan, J. R., and B. Stults. (2011). "The Persistence of Segregation in the Metropolis: New Findings from the 2010 Census," Census Brief prepared for Project US2010. March 24. http://www.s4.brown.edu/us2010.

Los Angeles County Department of Public Health. (2013). *Air Quality Recommendations for Local Jurisdictions: Development of New Schools, Housing and Other Sensitive Land Uses in Proximity to Freeways.* https://www.publichealth.lacounty.gov/eh/docs/AQinFreeways.pdf.

Loveland Technologies. (2014). Why Don't We Own This? Wayne County Treasurer's auction, 1014. Whydontweownthis.org.

Lowe, J. S., and L. K. Bates. (2013). "Missing New Orleans." In M. Dewar and J. M. Thomas (Eds.), *The City after Abandonment* (pp. 151–73). Philadelphia: University of Pennsylvania Press.

Mallach, A. (2006). *Bringing Buildings Back.* Montclair, NJ: National Housing Institute.

Manaster, K. (1968). "Squatters and the Law." *Tulane Law Review,* 43: 94–127.

McFarlane, C. (2010). "The Comparative City: Knowledge, Learning, Urbanism." *International Journal of Urban and Regional Research*, 34 (4): 725–742.

Merrill, T. W. (2002). "The Demsetz Thesis and the Evolution of Property Rights." *Journal of Legal Studies,* 31 (June): 331–338.

Michigan Realtors. (2014). Residential sales statistics, March. http://www.mirealtors.com/Portals/0/Documents/Mar14stats-new%20logo.pdf.

Motor City Mapping. (2014). Property conditions [data file]. http://d3.d3.opendata.arcgis.com/.

Nassauer, J. (2014). "Improving Water Quality and Well-Being in Great Lakes Post-Industrial Cities." A proposal to the Water Center, Graham Institute of Sustainability, University of Michigan, Ann Arbor.

National Vacant Properties Campaign. (2005). *Vacant Properties.* http://www.vacantproperties.org/latestreports/True%20Costs_Aug05.pdf (accessed June 18, 2008).

Newman, K., and E. K. Wyly. (2005). "The Right to Stay Put, Revisited: Gentrification and Resistance to Displacement in New York City." *Urban Studies*. 43 (1): 23–57.

Olson, S., and M. L. Lachman. (1976). *Tax Delinquency in the Inner City: The Problem and its Possible Solutions.* Lexington, Mass.: Lexington Books.

Peck, J. (2012). "Austerity Urbanism: American Cities under Extreme Economy." *City*, 16 (6): 626–655.

———. (2014). "Pushing Austerity: State Failure, Municipal Bankruptcy and the Crises of Fiscal Federalism in the USA." *Cambridge Journal of Regions, Economy and Society*, 7: 17–44.

Peterson, J. D. (1991). "Squatters in the United States and Latin America." *Community Development Journal,* 26 (1): 28–34.

Platteau, J.-P. (1996). "The Evolutionary Theory of Land Rights as Applied to Sub-Saharan Africa." *Development and Change,* 27 (1): 29–86.

Rae, D. W. (2003). *City: Urbanism and its End.* New Haven: Yale University Press.

Raleigh, E., and G. Galster. (2014). "Neighborhood Disinvestment, Abandonment, and Crime Dynamics." *Journal of Urban Affairs.* doi: 10.1111/juaf.12102.

Robinson, J. (2011). "Cities in a world of cities." *International Journal of Urban and Regional Research,* 35 (1): 1–23.

Sands, G., & Skidmore, M. (2013). "Making ends meet: Options for property tax reform in Detroit." *Journal of Urban Affairs.* Available online: DOI: 10.1111/juaf.12069.

Seymour, E. (2014). *Federal financial institutions, foreclosure and the fortunes of Detroit's neighborhoods.* Unpublished paper.

Smith, N. (1979). "Toward a theory of gentrification." *Journal of the American Planning Association*, 45 (4): 538–48.

Smith, R. L. (2009, Sept. 29). "Ranks of the Near-Poor Grow in NE Ohio." *Plain Dealer.* A1.

——— and O. Perkins. (2008, Aug. 27). "Despite Higher Poverty, Cleveland Incomes Rise." *Plain Dealer.* A1.

——— and E. Starzyk. (2010, Sept. 29). "1 in 3 Living in Poverty in Cleveland." *Plain Dealer.* A1.

Sugrue, T. J. (1996). *The Origins of the Urban Crisis.* Princeton, NJ: Princeton University Press.

Stegman, M.A. (1972). *Housing Investment in the Inner City: The Dynamics of Decline; A Study of Baltimore, Maryland, 1968–1970.* Cambridge, Mass.: M.I.T. Press.

Sternlieb, G., and R.W. Burchell. (1973). *Residential Abandonment: The Tenement Landlord Revisited.* New Brunswick, NJ: Center for Urban Policy Research, Rutgers University.

————, R. W. Burchell, J.W. Hughes, and F.J. James. (1974). "Housing Abandonment in the Urban Core." *Journal of the American Planning Association*, 40 (5): 321–332.

————, and R. Lake. (1976). "The Dynamics of Real Estate Tax Delinquency." *National Tax Journal*, 29 (3): 262–271.

Thomas, J. M. (1990). "Planning and Industrial Decline: Lessons from Postwar Detroit." *Journal of the American Planning Association*, 56 (3): 297–310.

————. (1997). *Redevelopment and Race: Planning a Finer City in Postwar Detroit*. Baltimore: Johns Hopkins University Press.

Thomas, V. (2012). "Welfare recipients taking over foreclosed homes." WWJ/1270 Talk Radio, CBS Detroit. May 9. http://detroit.cbslocal.com/2012/05/09/welfare-recipients-taking-over-foreclosed-homes/.

United States Bureau of Labor Statistics. (2014). *Consumer Price Index Detailed Report*. Table 24. June. http://www.bls.gov/cpi/cpid1406.pdf.

United States Bureau of the Census. (1949). *Census of Manufactures*. Washington, DC: US Government Printing Office.

————. (1951). *Census of Business*: 1948. Retail Trade. Vol. III. Washington, DC: Government Printing Office.

————. (1952). *Census of Population: 1950*. Vol. II, Part 22 Michigan. Washington, DC: US Dept. of Commerce, Bureau of the Census.

————. (1962). *Census of Housing: 1960*. City Blocks, Detroit, Michigan. Series HC(3)–204. Washington, DC: US Government Printing Office.

————. (1963). *Census of Population: 1960*. Vol. 1, Part 24, Characteristics of the Population. Washington, DC: US Government Printing Office.

————. (1966). *Negro Population, by County, 1960 and 1950*. Washington, DC: US Bureau of the Census.

————. (1973). *1970 Census of Population*. Vol. 1: Characteristics of the Population. Part 24. Michigan. Washington, DC: US Department of Commerce, Bureau of the Census.

United States Census Bureau. (2007a). *Manufacturing: Geographic Area Series*. 2007 Economic Census of the United States. Accessed through American FactFinder. factfinder2.census.gov.

————. (2007b). *Retail Trade: Geographic Area Series*. 2007 Economic Census of the United States. Accessed through American FactFinder. factfinder2.census.gov.

————. (2010). *2010 Census*. SF 1-"Race and Hispanic or Latino Origin." "Housing Units." "Occupancy Status." Accessed through American FactFinder. factfinder2.census.gov.

————. (2012). *American Community Survey*. Selected economic characteristics, 1-year estimates. Accessed through American FactFinder. factfinder2.census.gov.

United States Environmental Protection Agency (2014). "What is Green Infrastructure?" http://water.epa.gov/infrastructure/greeninfrastructure/gi_what.cfm.

Van Vliet, W. (Ed.). (1998). "Gentrification." *The Encyclopedia of Housing* (p. 198). Thousand Oaks, CA: Sage.

Weber, M. (2014) "Informal Ownership and Shrinking Cities: The Role of Local Policies and Practices." Unpublished paper.

Whitehouse, M. (2007, May 30). "Debt bomb." *Wall Street Journal*, 1-A.

Yin, R. K. (2009). *Case Study Research*. 4th ed. Thousand Oaks, CA: Sage.

Part II

How We Got Here: Cities, the State, and Markets

4

National Urban Policy and the Fate of Detroit

William K. Tabb

For better, and in recent decades for worse, national urban policies[1] have influenced the development of Detroit over the last half-century. The choices made by policymakers were a product of economic and demographic developments in larger national, and indeed global, contexts that directly and indirectly affected Detroit. This essay describes how the New Deal and postwar liberalism that shaped national urban policy were dismantled and replaced by a very different set of presumptions and policies commonly known as neoliberalism. This neoliberal regulatory regime is now itself in crisis; new national trends including a big city progressive urbanism and the politics of the rising American electorate augur a more positive political environment for Detroit.

A key aspect of these transformations involves the ways that federalism—the relationship between cities and states and the federal government—has been understood over the past half-century. In the era of liberalism and Keynesian economics, Washington, whether under Democratic control or the leadership of centrist Republican presidents, favored redistributive policies of federal revenue sharing. Democrats preferred congressional guidelines and categorical grants in federally funded programs that were carried out by states and localities. In the tradition of states' rights and local control, Republicans preferred "no strings attached" assistance. However, there was general agreement that taxes were best raised centrally and resources transferred to subnational jurisdictions. In the current era of neoliberalism, the orientation and goals of federalism have been replaced by policies stressing individual liberty that specifically enhance exit options and privilege private choice. Michael Grieve, director of the American Enterprise Institute's Federalism Project, explained that in place of the liberal version of federalism, conservatives favor a "competitive federalism" that rather than empowering cities and states "seeks to discipline governments by forcing them to compete for citizens' business" (2000).

Liberal national urban policy prioritized a concern for reviving inner city economies and helping their low-income residents to a more productive relation to the economy and the larger society; neoliberal policy abandoned such goals, insisting instead on reliance on market tests of policy efficiency. Lurking behind this reliance on markets was the empowerment of dominant factions of capital, transnational corporations and internationalized finance. Because proponents of neoliberalism see the United States as just one among many profit centers, with capital often looking elsewhere to invest where market opportunities are better, they reject the Keynesian premise that an activist government should increase domestic spending. The successor public philosophy insists rather that cities essentially operate like businesses, in order to use market criteria in their own decision-making and to make efficient use of local resources. Federal funding has been cut. Moreover, neoliberal principles require that political jurisdictions live within their means, the rationale being that public choices should be made where people live; decisions on how to spend public funds are best closely tied to the taxes citizens are willing to pay for these services. The result has been an urban austerity that has proven destructive.

For a very long time the unemployment and poverty rates in Detroit have been accepted with resignation. However, the national pattern in the current period of presumed recovery from the Great Recession is seen as cause for alarm, with a continuation of high unemployment, especially long-term unemployment, stagnating or falling real wages, loss of retirement and other benefits, and even a fall in the labor force participation rate. *The Economist* warns, "America's labour market has suffered permanent harm" (2014: 63). Given disturbing data on the persistence of long-term national unemployment and a tendency toward more involuntary, contingent, part-time jobs and low-wage employment (National Employment Law Project 2014), Detroit's situation, while extreme, looks less unique; what has happened to the city offers a microcosm of what is occurring elsewhere in America.

This essay concludes by raising the question of whether once again the nation is at a turning point in terms of its dominant public philosophy, its attitude toward the responsibilities of government, and the rules properly imposed on the market. Is it possible that a commitment to undo the damage of austerity urbanism, and with it the marginalization of so many Americans, will be on the political agenda; if so it will be led by a large number of American cities that are beginning to set the example of alternative big-city urbanism supported by an ascendant bloc of voters whose numbers will grow and whose influence will be increasingly important. Such a development will prove important to Detroit's future. But let me add a spoiler alert: these long wave shifts in American politics happen over a long period, a matter of decades and not of years, just as the eclipse of national urban policy and the demise of the national Keynesian social structure of accumulation gave way to global neoliberalism over such an extended period (Tabb 2012: Chapter 2).

The Making and Unmaking of Liberal Urbanism, 1940–1980

A century ago the Republicans were the party of the Northern cities and urban-industrial elites, while the Democrats represented small towns and Protestant fundamentalism. This changed with the New Deal which won the support both of the largely immigrant urban proletariat, and also of the internationalist business community (Ferguson 1995). Further, the need for unity to win World War II prioritized the needs of ordinary people that Franklin Delano Roosevelt articulated in his Economic Bill Of Rights speech in 1944. It offered a vision of the welfare state responsibilities of government:

> The right to a useful and remunerative job in the industries or shops or farms or mines of the nation;
> The right to earn enough to provide adequate food and clothing and recreation. . . . The right of every

family to a decent home; The right to adequate medical care and the opportunity to achieve and enjoy good health; The right to adequate protection from the economic fears of old age, sickness, accident, and unemployment; The right to a good education. All of these rights spell security. . . . America's own rightful place in the world depends in large part upon how fully these and similar rights have been carried into practice for our citizens.

Certainly after the pain of the Great Depression, Americans needed such assurance. Moreover, given the need to win the war, it was important that the president's policies and pronouncements unify the country and build the sense that "we are all in this together." At the same time, the spatial impacts of wartime needs set the stage for new divisions based on the reorganization of where people lived and worked.

Building American capacity as the "Arsenal of Democracy" favored growth of the Great Lakes Industrial Belt, and especially for Detroit, which in 1950 was the country's fifth-largest city. The Northeast region was the employment center of the country, its manufacturing belt. It included over half of the nation's population and almost all of its major cities. The West was sparsely populated. The South had 44 million people, including 63 percent of the nation's black population, but no cities above a million people. During the next twenty years, however, factories moved from outmoded multistory plants in the Northeast's large cities to suburban and rural locations. Cities like Detroit, Buffalo, Pittsburgh, and St. Louis, among others, experienced falling average incomes and lost more than 20 percent of their population—even as the proportion of their black residents grew significantly. In contrast, the South, despite significant net black out-migration, gained over 30 percent in population (McDonald 2007).

In the postwar period, extensive federally sponsored income redistribution and social intervention promoted growth outside of the older industrial cities. Military spending financed many Southern and Western cities, from Charlestown and Cape Canaveral to San Diego and Seattle. This missile crescent was built by electronics and aerospace and by military base location. On the civilian side, the federal interstate highway program and the growth of suburban housing through Veterans Administration and Federal Housing Administration subsidies shaped postwar spatial development. At the same time, federal spending in older central cities increased as decentralization of industry and increased residential suburbanization took its toll.

In the 1940s and 1950s, many people remained innocent of these economic and spatial restructurings, focusing instead on changes in the racial order, symbolized by the US Supreme Court's 1954 Brown vs. the Board of Education integration decision, which many (especially white) Americans saw as a challenge to their status, and on the threat of Communism, for instance in the 1957 Soviet Sputnik launch, which created fear that America's preeminence had been challenged. Postwar liberalism no longer felt emotionally comfortable to many, especially white, Americans as they reacted to diminished dominance in the world and turbulence at home. Based on these factors and new spatial patterning the bottom-up liberal-labor coalition of the New Deal and post–World War II years unraveled, a new hegemonic bloc was solidified, one that captured the loyalty of many white working class Americans in a top-down alliance.

As African Americans grew to be an important constituency for the Democrats, liberals in that party presented the cause of black Americans as the unfinished business of American democracy. After passage of the Voting Rights Act in 1965, attention turned to the plight of blacks in Northern cities. Efforts were made to cast the issue in terms of the benefits to all Americans of an inclusive urbanism. In 1966 Robert F. Kennedy proclaimed, "To speak of the urban condition . . . is to speak of the condition of American life. To improve the cities means to improve the life of the American people" (Kennedy 1967[1966]). His comment, "To say that the city is a central problem of American life is simply to know that increasingly the cities are American life," would soon seem wide of the mark; and his statement "Within a very few years, 80 percent of all Americans will live in cities," ignored the reality that where a person lived in the expanding metropolitan regions mattered profoundly. Nor did Kennedy acknowledge the federal role in producing and reinforcing spatial racial segregation under Federal Housing Administration and Veterans Administration programs, or that America's postwar policy of highway building, funded by a dedicated gasoline tax, was one incentive for new construction to take place outside of central cities. Such programs were an economic growth strategy. They expanded the profit opportunities of auto producers, the construction industry, and sellers of white goods (refrigerators, stoves, and other appliances)—but they also produced a pattern of overwhelmingly white suburbs and minority inner cities. This spatial separation contributed to a new national politics in which attitudes toward race were a central factor.

Kennedy's premise, and that of postwar liberalism more generally, was that the poor are needlessly and wastefully excluded from what is basically a healthy, growing economy that can provide jobs for all those able and willing to work—whose contribution will add to the national income. This conclusion follows logically from the core assumption of Keynesianism: that the government, by cutting taxes and increasing spending, can raise aggregate demand for goods and services, which in turn will lead to new hiring that will absorb these potential employees. During these years the tax code was far more progressive than it is currently, and a greater share of increased government spending reached low-income Americans, although then as now, a full accounting would demonstrate that the special treatment of tax deductions dramatically favored the very wealthy (Congressional Budget Office 2013). Through better education and training programs, along with infrastructure modernization and maintenance, America could continue to grow; the "rising tide would lift all boats," as Robert Kennedy's brother President John F. Kennedy famously said. State spending, economic growth, and a commitment to social justice would thus combine to promote a fortuitous upward cycle.

This was perhaps the last hurrah of confident liberalism. These years saw deindustrialization and population shifts, the backlash to the Civil Rights movement in the South, the War on Poverty, and later the urban rioting in northern cities, which all contributed to a shift in voter allegiance. Political certainties were shaken. Many who had voted Democratic abandoned the party. In Michigan, Alabama Governor George Wallace, the symbol of opposition to the federal enforcement of integration and to Washington "meddling" in local affairs, won the 1972 Democratic presidential primary.

During the Kennedy-Johnson years there was an expansion of categorical grants to the states, with monies to be spent on education, Medicaid, manpower training, and economic development more generally which would be included as national urban policy programs. (There is extensive literature on how best to define national urban policy, and which federal assistance programs are included; see Wolman 1999, Cleaveland 1969.) Revenue sharing continued under Nixon and Ford; by the late 1970s there were more than five hundred such assistance programs, with 80 percent of the nation's local governments receiving some aid from Washington. During the 1970s, direct federal aid to cities more than quadrupled. By the end of the decade not only was Detroit to a considerable extent a ward of the federal government, but so also were other declining northern cities: Pittsburgh received ninety-one cents from the federal government for every dollar it raised locally, Newark sixty-four cents, and Cleveland sixty cents. As the fiscal situation of the cities of the North East-Industrial Midwest deteriorated, federal grants to state and local governments increased from less than 12 percent in 1950 to close to 17 percent in 1960, 23 percent in 1970, and almost 32 percent by 1980. In 1982, 60 percent of the city governments responding to Joint Economic Committee question-naires reported that current outlays including debt service exceeded current revenues (Joint Economic Committee 1984). The cost of city services rose significantly for the twenty-eight largest cities, tripling between 1962 and 1972, and as a proportion of the country's GDP, from 10.3 to 14.2 percent (Peterson 1976: 41). Detroit was hardly alone.

The era of global neoliberalism began during the stagflation of the 1970s, when the old formulas ceased working and the falling rate of profit invited a market-oriented alter-native to Keynesianism. The economic recession of 1974–5 led to a fall in revenues for states and cities. The Advisory Commission on Intergovernmental Relations (1984: 4) saw 1977 as the "watershed" year. Federal assistance to cities peaked in 1978. From the mid-1970s to the mid-1980s, city spending fell in absolute terms and declined substan-tially in inflation-adjusted terms. The level of real expenditures in both central cities and suburbs declined as voters at the state level rejected tax increases during a period of substantial inflation (Ladd and Yinger 1989, Reischauer 1990). Poor performance at the national level as international impacts were felt led to a change in the political climate and attitude toward government. By the late 1970s, ambitious interventions to change the life chances of the urban poor had been discredited.

In his second State of the Union message, President Jimmy Carter proclaimed that "government can't set our goals, it cannot define our vision. Government cannot eliminate poverty or provide a bountiful economy or reduce inflation or save our cities or cure illiteracy or provide energy." The administration's Urban Direct Action Grant Program (UDAG), part of Carter's "new partnership," focused on subsidizing private investment in "distressed" cities. Among other things, federal monies funded luxury hotels and upscale shopping complexes, two examples of trickle-down economics as an aspect of his national urban policy. President Carter's Commission on a National Agenda for the Eighties projected bleak prospects for urban revitalization; shrinkage and disinvestment were seen as inevitable. Efforts to revitalize communities were "ill-advised" and would conflict with the overarching goal of national economic com-petitiveness (O'Connor 2013: 24).

Declining cities and formerly powerful industrial states lost population and politi-cal influence to the point where Democratic politicians felt safe abandoning these constituencies. Between 1970 and 1980, the eleven largest Snowbelt cities lost 1.6 of their 2.7 million blue-collar jobs, a 63 percent loss. Diminished political influ-ence accompanied the drop of employment and population. There were calls for

Washington to rebuild the country's manufacturing base. *Business Week* declared, "The U.S. economy must undergo a fundamental change if it is to retain a measure of economic viability. . . . The goal must be nothing less than the reindustrialization of America" (1980: 58). Well-thought-out proposals existed that would have utilized the manufacturing talents and physical space available in Detroit (Luria and Russell 1984); however, political opposition to a strong government role precluded such revitalization initiatives.

Whereas Americans were ready to spend extensively for the military, allocating such expenditures to congressional districts based on political factors, there was a distaste for government-led industrial policy of the sort that had been so successful in producing manufacturing powerhouse economies in, for instance, East Asia. In these emerging-market economies, local capitalists sought an alliance with government to promote mutual interests. In the United States, globalized capital worked to prevent government from circumscribing its freedom to invest wherever it preferred, often to the abandonment of American workers. Barry Bluestone and Bennett Harrison, close students of deindustrialization, saw the process as "the outcome of a worldwide crisis in the economic system. The very success of the long postwar expansion generated conditions that ultimately turned the normal, and often healthy, disinvestment process into a torrent of capital flight and wholesale deindustrialization" (1982: 15). The pain in Detroit was considerable. But the city, once politically influential, was no longer able to muster support in Washington. It was to be far less successful decades later, under the control of an emergency financial manager imposed by a governor that more than 80 percent of the city's voters had rejected.

The Heyday of Neoliberal Dominance, 1980–2008

President Reagan successfully exploited middle-class discontent over the impact of stagflation in the late 1970s to urge lower taxes, the largest benefit of which went to the top 1 percent, who paid 30 percent less in taxes after the 1982 tax reduction. These revenue reductions were of course accompanied by reductions in spending, mostly in programs that had previously assisted poor Americans, with a disproportionate impact on older, deindustrialized cities. The Reagan Administration's 1982 Urban Policy Report argued that: "Greater self-reliance is essential to the long-run good health of our cities. Efficient and responsive local efforts will occur only if cities squarely shoulder the primary responsibility to shape their individual fates." Thus, cuts in federal aid, it was argued, could be offset by local governments, if they wished. With their declining tax base, however, this was unlikely; raising taxes would only insure the departure of businesses and individuals who could leave. A top-down coalition of elite interests and middle-class supporters, most living outside of, and many far from, the troubled declining cities, set the terms of urban policy making.

The economic theory driving the Reagan Revolution was premised on the assumption that a healthy urban economy, like economic development in general, is fostered by removing barriers to business investment—especially regulatory obstacles and burdensome taxation—so as to incentivize entrepreneurship and promote commercial growth. Efforts by government to mandate investment or inappropriately redistribute public funds from "makers to takers" explain why government was seen as the problem, not the solution. In his 1982 State of the Union address, Reagan spelled out his New Federalism. It relied on a strategy to shift responsibility from the federal government to the states and localities—many of these functions had been considered federal duties since the New Deal. His plan was that by 1987 the only remaining national human service programs would be Social Security and health care for the poor.

The Reagan program of withdrawal from issues of "purely local responsibility" essentially ended federal urban policy. Reagan cancelled five hundred separate funding programs, and assistance to cities of over three hundred thousand people was reduced by 35 percent. HUD funding plummeted from $57 billion in 1978 to $9 billion in 1989; total aid to cities fell from $5.2 billion in 1980 to $3.4 billion in 1989; and federal aid as a percentage of city revenue dropped from 23 percent in 1980 to 11.6 percent in 1986. His administration also proposed sizable reductions in federal spending for education, health, transportation, and urban aid. Congress complied, with tens of billions of dollars in cuts and the conversion of fifty-seven specific grant programs to nine broad block grants, giving states wide discretion on spending priorities (Parker 1995, de Rugy 2004). Total intergovernmental aid to cities was reduced from $14 billion in 1980 to $7 billion in 1988 (Sapoyichne 2010: 3). "Against the onslaught of Reaganism," as Heclo (1986: 48) wrote in the immediate aftermath of the Reagan strategy's implementation, "a great liberal silence prevailed." This urban policy remained consistent through the presidency of George H. W. Bush, after a brief flurry of excitement when his HUD Secretary Jack Kemp proposed a free-market approach to increase home ownership in distressed urban areas. The proposal produced little.

Some cities fared better than Detroit in adjusting to this abandonment by Washington. They tended to have a more educated workforce, a more diverse economic base (typically "eds and meds"—universities and hospital centers), and—it should not be overlooked—smaller proportions of black residents. The election of a Democratic president did not result in any substantive departure from neoliberal urbanism. Bill Clinton offered no new urban programs; his empowerment zones and enterprise communities were essentially based on the Republican program of tax incentives. Moreover, after the Republicans reclaimed the majority in the House of Representatives in 1994, they had a veto on policy directions.

The retreat of the Clinton presidency from the priorities of the Great Society was based on the now familiar argument that because Washington bureaucrats had failed in their social welfare policies for cities and states, spending authority should be removed from Washington through block grants to state and local governments—with minimal red tape and regulations—that is to those who best knew how to solve their own problems. Allowing such discretion negated the purpose of federal mandates, as many local governments demonstrated in their spending priorities a lack of regard for the poor. Moreover, the block grants were capped, as opposed to the open-ended spending that many federal programs had provided. Funding through block grants was no longer an entitlement, but a matter of local discretion. It was based on the following logic: why collect a tax nationally only to send it back to localities? Let the states and local governments raise the money themselves, and, answering to voters, ensure that all taxes be used efficiently.

From there it was merely one more step to advocate lowering taxes and letting people spend their own money, ignoring public funding altogether. Newt Gingrich, the speaker of the House when the Republicans reclaimed control after years of a Democratic majority, stated that "What we really want to do is devolve power all the way out of government and back to working American families. We want to leave choices and resources in the hands of individuals and let them decide if they prefer government, the profit-making sector, the nonprofit sector or even no solution at all to their problems" (1996: 104–5).

The public moved toward antigovernment attitudes as they watched their quality of life on average not improve from the 1960s into the 1990s, with family breakup, increased violence, and lack of opportunity (Blendon, et al. 1997). People blamed government, which is to say liberalism, for the ineffectiveness of government. Attitudes toward Social Security, the signature success of New Deal liberalism, demonstrate the deterioration of trust in government: in the mid-1990s only 23 percent of those surveyed said that federal programs had reduced the number of Americans over sixty-five who lived in poverty, compared to 32 percent who agreed that "the programs had made things worse," and 39 percent who said the programs had "not had much effect either way" (Edsall 1996: 12). This was remarkable, given how important Social Security has been in reducing poverty among those over age sixty-five. Antigovernment feelings may have been related to the widespread belief that the global economy was not working for most Americans, a belief that would grow. Community-based development, service provision, and organizing continue, but they have done so by "swimming against the tide," Alice O'Connor's title for her study of the long history of federal efforts to assist poor communities (2013).

Urban voters remained more committed to activist government than the population at large. In 2000, George W. Bush received relatively few votes in America's cities (35 percent to Gore's 61 percent), and his support among blacks was in the single digits. But cities cast only 29 percent of the total vote. Mr. Bush's most telling urban initiative was to redirect federal funds that had gone to social programs such as drug rehabilitation, food banks, and the homeless to faith-based organizations, effectively eviscerating public programs. It was his base—not the urban voters who had not supported him—that was of concern to the Bush policy makers. Moreover, the hallmark of his administration, the War on Terrorism, imposed costly mandates on cities, which were required to increase spending on a host of security measures that were not funded by Washington (Dreier 2004). The substantial loss of state and local tax revenues that resulted from the Great Recession was a far greater blow. Dramatic job losses for public workers and in-service provision heavily impacted the urban poor.

The diversity and rapid change that Americans identify with cities, and the awareness that by mid-twenty-first century the majority of Americans will be members of minority races and immigrant ethnic groups, have combined to produce a strong backlash against urban liberalism by older, white voters. Significantly, a larger proportion of them vote in non-presidential national elections than do young people and minority group voters (Craig and Richeson 2014, Wasserman 2013). The election of America's first black president did nothing to change this reality; indeed, Mr. Obama was watched carefully for signs that he favored African Americans (Tesler 2012). Since the 1960s the problems of large postindustrial cities have been linked in the popular mind not to the failure of government policies to remediate disinvestment problems produced by market forces, but rather to their large, poor, minority populations. Acceptance of neoliberal economic policies has combined with dominant American attitudes toward race to reinforce acceptance of disinvestment and abandonment. The changed voting map that gave less political clout to these cities, which are increasingly regarded as different from the rest of America, reinforced such policies.

The Obama Years: A Turning Point?

Barack Obama defeated John McCain by 65 to 35 percent in urban areas, offering the expectation that he would be the president who would bring the change many Americans saw as badly needed; Detroit desperately hoped Washington would endorse these changes under the new president's leadership. The Obama strategy was to "stop seeing cities as the problem and start seeing them as the solution," as places of opportunity (Benfield 2011). The administration developed a Partnership for Sustainable Communities that sought to bring elected officials together from throughout a metropolitan area to plan for the region's development and coordinate the programs of federal agencies and departments. While the program demonstrated the administration's recognition that metropolitan regions would function better if local governments worked together for the common good, this well-intentioned effort achieved little, since funding that might have encouraged cooperation was not forthcoming. Mr. Obama did create the first-ever White House Office of Urban Policy. But it was soon downgraded to "the Office of Urban Affairs." It never had high-profile leadership and soon fell relatively silent.

The major achievement of the administration in the area of urban policy was inclusion of provisions in the American Recovery and Reinvestment Act of 2009 that funneled large amounts of money to state and local jurisdictions, significantly reducing the austerity measures that would otherwise have resulted. The stimulus package set aside billions for highway construction, transit improvements, school modernization, and community development block grants. The Affordable Care Act also benefitted cities significantly.

Growth-oriented spending and social welfare policies that seek the improvement of the lives of ordinary citizens will, I suspect, replace dedicated urban policy. For example, the American Recovery and Reinvestment Act (2009) was designed as a stimulus for the economy to compensate for the damage caused by the Great Recession, but it was designed to help state and local governments meet basic functions, including, but not limited to, essential urban public services. It is to be expected that future programs to reinvest in America's human capital and infrastructure needs will fill part of the losses from the demise of national urban policy and will interact with, and help fund, local initiatives. Support for programs that have considerable redistributional impact are likely to evolve both from the examples of successful community and local government betterment activities and from blue-state initiatives prompted by concern over the impact of income inequality that is pushing poor and middle-class people out of their neighborhoods and beyond city limits. As they cumulatively influence national policy, such local efforts will also support less-favored cities like Detroit. Suburban areas and rural communities, feeling the impact of urban-style problems, will increasingly find their interests more congruent with city agendas.

By 2010, the fifteen Sunbelt states held 240 electoral votes compared to the four-teen Frostbelt states' share of only 164. For decades, such electoral mathematics had dismantled national urban policy. For decades it had been true that "Sunbelt suburban development has helped generate pro-growth 'boomburb' electorates who have little interest in federal programs to equalize regional development opportunities" (Kantor 2013: 838). But this math was based on a growth model that no longer obtains. Recently many of these boomburbs have themselves become depressed areas with unsold homes that are vacant, deteriorating, and a burden to local governments—problems exacer-bated by speculative overinvestment. Thus, the competition between city and suburb has given way to a more complex pattern in which older suburbs have problems, and needs, once thought to be restricted to inner city neighborhoods. A number of factors are converging; the politics of suburbanization are changing, and along with this, class-biased spatial appropriation accumulates, a neo-feudalism of the privileged becomes painfully visible. New urban struggles involve long-time residents, who have become increasingly angered by gentrification that now pits middle-class residents against the very affluent (Streitfeld and Wollan 2014).

The backlash against an urban entrepreneurialism that ignores the needs of the poor and the middle class reflects changes in the broader political economy. A new spatial politics is emerging in concert with responses to the way the financial crisis was "solved." But it is unlikely to transform politics at the national level, nor the dominant political philosophy of individual responsibility that has undermined efforts to help poor com-munities and their residents. An older, white voter base continues to focus anger down-ward, worried about status deprivation and translating a fear of an uncertain future into a nostalgia for the past that is easily inflamed by racial appeals in political campaigns (Banks and Bell 2013). For some time to come these voters will provide support for the gridlock that characterizes national partisan politics; in non-presidential year elections they threaten to increase the presence of Tea Party thinking in the halls of Congress.

On the other hand, two major developments are working in the opposite direction. The first is that in many of America's large cities there has been a turn to progressive action, importantly including the election of politicians supported by, and supportive of, neighborhood social movements. As this is written, New York City's progressive Mayor Bill de Blasio is receiving attention for his ambitious affordable housing program and for other measures designed to address the inequalities that characterize his city. Simi-lar projects are underway in major cities across the country, overseen by populist and reformist mayors in Pittsburgh, Minneapolis, Phoenix, and elsewhere. Seattle, whose mayor is Ed Murphy, is putting through a $15 minimum wage. As Harold Meyerson reports, the mayors and city councils elected in 2013 may be charting a new course for American liberalism (2014: 33).

The second trend is that nationally, resentment is growing over rising inequality, stagnant or falling income for the vast majority of Americans, and the ability of the rich to resist taxation, even as they increase the economic rents they extract at the expense of what Occupy Wall Street termed "the 99 percent." Adjusting for inflation, between 2009 (the official end of the Great Recession) and 2012, the top 5 percent of earners saw income gains of 17 percent, compared to 1 percent for the other 95 percent of Americans (Cynamon and Fazzari 2013). Economists, including researchers at the

International Monetary Fund, find that increased inequality is producing more frequent and deeper crises and that greater redistribution would not in fact hurt growth as has been widely asserted. IMF researchers support what they call "the tentative consensus in the literature" that "inequality can undermine progress in health and education, cause investment-reducing political and economic instability, and undercut the social consensus required to adjust in the face of shocks, and thus that it tends to reduce the pace and durability of growth" (Ostry, Berg and Tsangarides 2014: 4). Rising inequality is indeed stifling growth, and monopoly rents now contribute substantially to this rising inequality (Stiglitz 2012). The question is how Americans, and indeed others, will understand what needs to be done to improve things. That Thomas Piketty's 655-page academic tome *Capital in the Twenty-First Century* (2014) became a best seller is perhaps the clearest indication that a large part of the public was interested in, and concerned about, the growing inequality of wealth in their country.

As global neoliberalism has grown more destructive, both expert opinion and popular awareness have evolved. In early 2014, five years after the economy officially emerged from recession, most Americans (57 percent) thought the economy was still in recession (O'Connor 2014). They may not have known that 95 percent of the income gain from 2009 to 2012 went to the top 1 percent of earners (Saez 2013); however, there is widespread suspicion that the rising tide is not lifting all boats, only the yachts. The share of income going to labor fell from 51 percent in the late 1960s to 42 percent in the most recent data. The share of income going to the 1 percent in the United States, which has doubled since 1980, is higher than in any other developed country. Most of this goes to the richest one-tenth of one percent whose share of total US income rose from 2.6 percent to 10.4 percent between 1980 and 2012 (Organization for Economic Cooperation and Development 2014). These OECD researchers suggest that a more equitable distribution may provide a net benefit to growth. Can a political movement be built on an awareness that it is not just inner city Detroit, but most of America that is penalized by such lopsided distribution?

According to the OECD, the United States has the highest share of pretax income going to the top 1 percent of earners of all thirty-four members of this organization of wealthy nations. Its comparative studies note that because the forces of globalization and technological change are felt everywhere, they cannot explain the extreme and growing inequality in the United States. Before government taxation and spending, the United States has less inequality than countries like Finland and Germany and about the same as Denmark, Norway, and Sweden. These countries have markedly less inequality than the United States does *only after* we account for taxation and government spending. It is because the rich pay far lower taxes, and the US government spends less in ways that reduce inequality, that the United States so definitively leads its rich peers in inequality.

While it is true that Americans show a far greater tolerance for inequality than Europeans, the issue of public attitudes is complex (Clark and D'Ambrosio 2013). The response to these trends has generally been increasingly widespread anger at their unfairness. Reenergized social movements are addressing inequality, demanding the reorientation of government priorities. A backlash has also occurred at the local level against strategies of urban renewal that favor the affluent and ignore other urban residents; examples that have received widespread media attention include campaigns by low-paid workers at big box stores like Wal-Mart and fast-food chains like McDonald's (Strauss 2013), along with resistance by middle-class residents under pressure from gentrification, as illustrated for instance in the protests against the private transportation system of buses for high-tech workers in San Francisco (Streitfeld and Wollanjan 2014). Outrages such as the killing of an unarmed black man by a white policeman who fired six shots into him in Ferguson, Missouri, a city two-thirds black with an almost all-white police force in 2014, now lead to national, indeed, international protests. The urban terrain is once again the site of significant social activism.

Social movements are spearheaded by members of particular class fractions: the Populists in the 1890s led by angry farmers who had been squeezed by the railroads and the bankers and by mortgage burdens that rose with deflation even as their incomes fell; the Progressives at the start of the twentieth century, led by a rising professional class fighting the corruption of ethnic urban political machine politics on the one hand, and on the other, the abuses of monopolies; the industrial working class during the 1930s, which was in turn pushed by radical organizers to support the New Deal (Piven and Cloward 1993 [1971]). In the present historical moment, the millennials are hostile to the institutions of social control and reject the bromides accepted—or at least not challenged—by their elders. This generational group has been most affected by the destructive features of the contemporary neoliberal economy. Composing a large part of what has been described as "the rising American electorate" (Judis and Teixeira 2002), they will change the nation's political "common sense" (Edsall 2012).

Millennials represent a generational rather than a traditional class-based force, composed as they are of young folks from middle-class and aspirational social positions who share the experience of frustrated expectations. The cohesion of youth culture and this generation's acceptance of inclusion of racial, gender and other divisions that prevent unity of outlook among many of their elders resonates with the class proxy shorthand of the 99 percent and the 1 percent. Pew researchers find that millennials are "forging a distinctive path into adulthood"; propelled by changed economic conditions of the early twenty-first century, they question the conventional neoliberal agenda and its rationale (Pew Research Social & Demographic Trends 2014). Peter Beinart (2014) writes,

> Since the 1970s, the conservative movement has used the myth of a classless America to redistribute wealth upward, thus hardening class divisions, at least relative to other nations. It's no surprise that the young, having no memory of the more equal, more mobile America of popular legend, see this reality more clearly. And because they do, they are more eager to change it.

This cohort will comprise a third of voters and up to two-fifths of the electorate over the next decade. They "stand out" for their liberal views on many political and social issues (Pew Research Social and Demographic Trends 2014). Pew researchers find that millennials are the most diverse generation in American history (43 percent of millennial adults are nonwhite). Seventy-one percent of nonwhite millennials prefer that big government provide more services; only 21 percent of them support smaller government. While white millennials prefer a smaller government that provides fewer services (52 percent compared to the 39 percent who prefer bigger government and more service), they are more liberal than whites of older generations. The reasons are clear enough. As Pew explains, millennials are the first age cohort in the modern era to have higher levels of student loan debt, poverty and unemployment, and lower levels of wealth and personal income, than their two immediate predecessor generations at the same stage of their life cycles.

Their difficult economic circumstances in part reflect the impact of the Great Recession (2007–2009) and in part the longer-term effects of globalization and rapid technological change on the American workforce. Median household income in the United States today remains below its 1999 peak, the longest stretch of stagnation in the modern era, and during that time income and wealth gaps have widened (Pew 2013).

The views of millennials have thus been shaped by larger, ongoing economic change, and in some ways are thus reflective of the larger society. Whether we will see a functional equivalent of 1960s-style national urban policy on a national basis will depend on the balance between the political awareness of this rising electorate and that of older, conservative white voters working hard to hold back a future they do not want. The question is whether millennials will become politically activist, organize for the long haul, and bring the kind of meaningful change they favor to America. A related question is what political lessons the country as a whole takes from slower growth, greater inequality, and widespread insecurity.

As the economy disappoints, the alliance that has reigned politically in the neoliberal period comes under pressure. A movement to *re-embed* markets in a moral economy matrix, as has happened in periods of social protest in the past, could reverse decades of attacks on the postwar social contract that have been discussed here in the context of national urban policy. The good news for the residents of cities like Detroit is that the rising electorate is quite different in composition and politics than the coalition of economic and social conservatives who have dominated American politics during the decades of neoliberal hegemony. More substantial resources flowing to local governments will provide resources that communities can claim.

But such a change will not take place quickly. Partisan antipathy is deep and extensive. 'Ideological silos' are more common on right and left than they have been in past decades, and those most resistant to progressive urban policy, the base of the Republican Party, have 'veered sharply to the right' on issues related to government and the economy (Pew 2014). For the country to reorient will not happen speedily or smoothly even as it grows substantially more urban.

This larger perspective frames another relevant question: "Is it 'cities' that have a crisis?" As awareness grows of the larger context within which an urban crisis happens, we may come to question the habit of seeing the city as the actor responsible for the fate of its residents. Perhaps we may move to a perspective closer to that which inspired national urban policy over half a century ago. As Peter Marcuse writes:

> Each city has a history, a particular demographic profile, a particular set of economic relations, etc. But what is meant is city as a place, a place where certain actions have taken place, certain things have happened, particular things have been done by particular people and to other particular people. But a city in this sense is not an actor; a city does not compete, pass this legislation, treat those people that way. . . . [S]peaking of them as if they described an active entity implicitly steers away from examining who in the city is acting, in whose interests, against whose interests, who is in power, who is oppressed (Marcuse 2014: 9).

To ask such questions is also to ask how a larger society should act to improve the fate of fellow citizens trapped in places where they lack power and face serious life challenges.

In broadening the perspective on Detroit's future, the argument made in this essay is that it is not only local events, community organizing, and Michigan politics that determine the health and wealth of the city, but national, and even global developments, which can initiate broad movements for policy change. After decades of dominance, neoliberalism has proven a costly public philosophy and set of economic policies. Whether the pendulum swings toward a more inclusive set of social relations and programs that would benefit the majority of citizens, most assuredly including those in Detroit, depends on the character of popular agency in the coming period. The possibility of such a positive outcome is not a prediction. Austerity politics continues not only at the level of many large American cities from Los Angeles, to Chicago and to Philadelphia, and of course Detroit, but at the national level, and on both sides of the Atlantic. Existing policy measures are widely contractionary. It is to be seen whether solidaristic organization can overcome such barriers.

Note

1. For more extensive discussions and definitions of national urban policy (Wolman,1999, Cleaveland 1969, Sapotichne 2010).

References

Advisory Commission on Intergovernmental Relations. (1984). *Fiscal Disparities: Central Cities & Suburbs, 1981*. Washington DC: ACIR.

Banks, A. J. and M. A. Bell. (2013). "Racialized Campaign Ads: The Emotional Content in Implicit Racial Appeals Primes White Racial Attitudes." *Public Opinion Quarterly*, 77 (2): 549–560.

Beinart, P. (2014). "The End of American Exceptionalism." *National Journal*. February 3.

Benfield, K. (2011). "Seeing Cities as the Environmental Solution, Not The Problem." http://www.sustainablecommunities.gov.

Blendon R. J., J. M. Benson, R. Morin, D. E. Altman, M. Brodie, and M. Brossard. (1997). "Changing Attitudes in America." In J. Nye, P. Zelikow, and D. King (Eds.). *Why Americans Mistrust Government*. Cambridge, MA: Harvard University Press.

Bluestone, B. and B. Harrison. (1982). *The Deindustrialization of America: Plant Closings, Community Abandonment, and the Dismantling of Basic Industry*. New York: Basic Books.

Business Week. (1980). "The Reindistrialization of America." June 30.

Clark, A. E. and C. D'Ambrosio. (2013). "Attitudes to Income Inequality: Experimental and Survey Evidence." In A. B. Atkinson and F. Bourguignon (Eds.). *Handbook of Income Distribution*, Volume 2A. Amsterdam: Elsevier.

Cleaveland, F. N. and Associates. (1969). *Congress and Urban Problems*. Washington, DC: The Brookings Institution.

Congressional Budget Office. (2013). *The Distribution of Major Tax Expenditures in the Individual IncomeTaxSystem.h*ttp://www.cbo.gov/sites/default/files/cbofiles/attachments/43768_Distribution-TaxExpenditures.pdf.

Craig, M. A. and J. A. Richeson. (2014). On the Precipice of a "Majority-Minority" America: Perceived Status Threat From the Racial Demographic Shift Affects White Americans' Political Ideology. *Psychological Science* doi: 10.1177/0956797614527113.

Cynamon, B. Z. and S. M. Fazzari. (2013). "Inequality, the Great Recession, and a Stagnant Recovery." http://papers.ssrn.com/sol3/papers.cfm?abstract_id=2205524.

Dreier, P. (2004). "Urban Neglect: George W. Bush and the Cities." National Housing Institute. http://www.nhi.org/online/issues/137/urbanneglect.html.

Economist. (2014). "Closing the Gap; America's Labour Market Has Suffered Permanent Harm." February 15.

Edsall, T. B. (1996). "The GOP Gains Ground as Trust in Government Erodes." *Washington Post National Weekly Edition*, February 12–18.

Edsall, T. B. (2012). *The Age of Austerity: How Scarcity Will Remake American Politics.* New York: Random House.

Ferguson, T. (1995). "From 'Normalcy' to the New Deal: Industrial Structure, Party Competition, and American Public Policy in the Great Depression." In T. Ferguson, *Golden Rule: The Investment Theory of Party Competition and the Logic of Money-Driven Political Systems.* Chicago: University of Chicago Press.

Gingrich, N. (1995). *To Renew America.* New York: Harper Collins.

Greve, M. S. (2000). "The AEI Federalism Project." AEI Online, June 1, 2000. http://www.aei.org/article/economics/the-aei-federalism-project/.

Hill, R. C. (1984). "Economic Crisis and Political Response in the Motor City." In L. Sawers and Tabb, W.K. (Eds.), *Sunbelt/Snowbelt: Urban Development and Regional Restructuring.* New York: Oxford University Press.

Joint Economic Committee, United States Congress. (1984). *Trends in the Fiscal Conditions of Cities: 1982–1983.* Washington, DC. Government Printing Office.

Judis, J. B. and R. Teixeira. (2002). *The Emerging Democratic Majority.* New York: Simon & Schuster.

Kantor, P. (2013). "The Two Faces of American Urban Policy." *Urban Affairs Review,* 49 (6): 821–850.

Katznelson, I. (1976). "The Crisis of the Capitalist State: Urban Politics and Social Control." In D. Hawley (Ed.). *Theoretical Perspectives on Urban Politics.* Englewood Cliffs, NJ: Prentice Hall.

Kennedy, R. F. (1967[1966]). "Statement Before the Subcommittee on Executive Reorganization of the Senate Committee on Government Operations, August 15." *Pratt Planning Papers,* 4 (4).

Ladd, H. F. and J. Yinger. (1989). *America's Ailing Cities: Fiscal Health and the Design of Urban Policy.* Baltimore: Johns Hopkins Press.

Levine, M. v. (2007). "Downtown Redevelopment as an Urban Growth Strategy: A Critical Appraisal of the Baltimore Renaissance." *Journal of Urban Affairs,* 9 (2): 103–123.

Luria, D. and J. Russell (1984). "Motor City Changeover." In L. Sawers and W.K. Tabb (Eds.), *Sunbelt/Snowbelt: Urban Development and Regional Restructuring.* New York: Oxford University Press.

Marcuse, P. (2014). "The one-dimensional language of urban policy," forthcoming in *Cities—The International Journal of Urban Policy and Planning.*

McDonald, J. F. (2007). *Urban America: Growth, Crisis and Rebirth.* New York: M. E. Sharpe.

Meyerson, H. (2014). "The Revolt of the Cities." *The American Prospect,* May/June.

National Employment Law Project. (2014). *The Low-Wage Recovery: Industry Employment and Wages Four Years into the Recovery.* http://www.nelp.org/page/-/reports/low-wage-recovery-industry-employment-wages-2014-report.pdf?nocdn=1.

O'Connor, A. (2013). "Swimming Against the Tide: A Brief History of Federal Policy in Poor Communities." In J. DeFilippis and S. Saegert (Eds.). *The Community Development Reader, Second Edition* (pp. 11–29). New York: Routledge.

Organization for Economic Cooperation and Development. (2014). *Crisis Squeezes Income and Puts Pressure on Inequality and Poverty; New Results From the OECD Income Distribution Database.* Paris: OECD.

Ostry, Jonathan D., Andrew Berg, Charalambos G. Tsangarides. (2014). "Redistribution, Inequality, and Growth." Research Department, International Monetary Fund.

Palmer, J. L. (Ed.). (1986). *Perspectives on the Reagan Revolution.* Washington, DC: Urban Institute Press.

Parker, R. A. (1995). "Patterns of Federal Urban Spending: Central Cities and their Suburbs, 1983–1992," *Urban Affairs Review,* 31 (2): 184–205.

Peterson, P. E. (1981). *City Limits.* Chicago: University of Chicago Press.

Pew Charitable Trusts. (2013). *The Great Recession Accelerated Detroit's Downward Trajectory.* http://www.pewstates.org/uploadedFiles/PCS_Assets/State_Factsheet_Graphics /detroit_profile.pdf.

Pew Research Center for the People & the Press. (2014). *Political Polarization in the American Public.* http://www.people-press.org/2014/06/12/political-polarization-in-the-american-public/.

Phelps, N. A. and A. M. Wood. (2011). "The New Post-Suburban Politics?" *Urban Studies,* 48 (12): 2591–2610.

Piketty, T. (2014) *Capital in the Twenty-First Century.* Cambridge: Harvard University Press.

Piven, F. F. and R. Cloward. (1993 [1971]). *Regulating the Poor: The Functions of Public Welfare.* New York: Random House.

Reinhold, R. (1977). "Carter Aides Focus on Jobs In Shaping Policy for Cities." *New York Times,* September 19.

Reischauer, R. (1990). "The Rise and Fall of National Urban Policy: The Fiscal Dimensions." In M. Kaplan and F. James (Eds.) *The Future of National Urban Policy*. Durham: Duke University Press.

deRugy, V. (2004). "President Reagan, Champion Budget-Cutter." http://www.aei.org/papers/economics/fiscal-policy/president-reagan-champion-budget-cutter/.

Saez, E. (2013). "Striking it Richer: The Evolution of Top Incomes in the United States (Updated with 2012 estimates)." *real-world economics review*, Number 65, September 27, 120–128.

Sapotichne, J. (2010). "The Evolution of National Urban Policy: Congressional Agendas, Presidential Power, and Public Opinion," Paper prepared for a Congress Project-Comparative Urban Studies Project Seminar, http://www.wilsoncenter.org/sites/default/files/Sapotichne.pdf.

State Budget Crisis Task Force. (2014). *Final Report: Report of the State Budget Crisis Task Force*. http://www.statebudgetcrisis.org/wpcms/wp-ontent/images/SBCTF_FINALREPORT.pdf.

Stiglitz, J. (2012). *The Price of Inequality: How Today's Divided Society Endangers Our Future*. New York: W. W. Norton.

Strauss, G. (2013). "Fast-Food Workers Strike for Higher Pay." *USA Today,* August 30.

Streitfeld, D. and M. Wollan. (2014). "Tech Rides Are Focus of Hostility in Bay Area." *New York Times*, January 31.

Tabb, W.K. (2012). *The Restructuring of Capitalism in Our Time*. New York: Columbia University Press.

Tesler, M. (2012). "The Spillover of Racialization into Health Care: How President Obama Polarized Public Opinion by Racial Attitudes and Race." *American Journal of Political Science*, 56:3, 690–704.

Wasserman, D. (2013). "The GOP's Built-In Midterm Turnout Advantage," http://cookpolitical.com/story/5776.

Wolman, H. (1999). "Urban Policy Processes at the National Level: The Hidden World of Urban Politics," In Nagel, S (ed.) *The Policy Process*. Hauppauge, NY: Nova Science: 25–46.

5

The Normalization of Market Fundamentalism in Detroit: The Case of Land Abandonment[1]

Jason Hackworth

When financial markets collapsed in 2007/8, a political and intellectual void was created. Critical scholars openly pondered about how this might mark the end of neoliberalism—an idea that has gone virtually unchallenged in policy circles since President Reagan famously christened government as *the problem* in his 1981 inauguration speech. A variety of social movements also emerged to protest the capitalist system at a broad level—Arab Spring, Occupy, even the Tea Party in some of its forms. Some began to ponder whether these constituted a nascent social challenge to re-embed markets à la Polanyi's (1944) double movement (see Burawoy 2010, Dale 2012). Some scholars were particularly interested in what urban social movements represented (Harvey 2012). Within the American context in particular, municipal government has been pushed to conform to market dictates by neoliberal think tanks, bond-rating agencies, and sympathetic elected officials for over forty years (Harvey 1989, Hackworth 2007). The Keynesian-managerial state has not only been replaced by the entrepreneurial state; the latter has become thoroughly normalized. Once debatable policy interventions like creating more public housing, or raising taxes to blunt inequality are now rarely discussed (openly) as policy options. Asking whether there will be a social movement built on different logics is thus an interesting intellectual pursuit. A focus on Detroit is particularly apt for questions of this sort. Detroit is a city where the collision between state, market, and race have a long and bloody history (Sugrue 2005, Thomas, 2013a). It is a place whose policies have been overdetermined by forces external to, and often hostile to, people living in the city.

Unfortunately, however, I think that the double-movement read of history, and the optimism underlying it, is misplaced within the urban policy context. There are two particularly salient dimensions to this. First, there is a notable asymmetry of policy making (and policy influencing) capacity within the urban political realm. The think tanks, banks, corporations, and advocacy groups attempting to advance a disembedded market agenda are far more organized, funded, numerous, and established than the forces seeking to advance a postcapitalist solution or even a return to the Keynesian-managerial state. The anticapitalist Left has nothing even approaching this in institutional strength and capacity.

Market-logic forces are able to acquire just enough electoral legitimacy—or in the case of Detroit, work around it through emergency management—to sow serious doubt on the efficacy of real alternatives. Second, and related, though neoliberalism has rolled back many gains made during the Keynesian period (Peck and Tickell 2002), there are still important relics from that moment from which people still benefit, and on which they desperately depend. Public pensions, social housing, infrastructure, parks, and the like that were created when government was deployed differently may have been cut, but they still exist in some measure, and have constituencies that benefit from them. There is often thus a divided potential opposition, with certain constituencies seeking to protect the (Keynesian relic) gains from which they continue to personally benefit.[2]

The impact of forces impeding a wider countermovement at the urban scale become clearer when focusing on a particular policy realm. With that goal in mind, this chapter focuses on land abandonment in Detroit. Land abandonment is arguably the most visible symbol of urban decline, and Detroit's version of it is both widespread and highly publicized. My general argument is as follows. The land abandonment regime—the totality of policies and practices that govern property ownership in a particular city—in Detroit (and elsewhere) is not on the precipice of a great countermovement, but rather fits more neatly into a policy framework in which market logics have been normalized. The most significant tension within this model is not between market society seeking to disembed, and other forces seeking to embed, but rather between forces seeking a market-only paradigm (the full removal of state oversight) against those seeking a market-first paradigm (using statecraft exclusively to promote markets). The chapter begins with a conceptual discussion of the broader transition away from managerial (and non-market) land abandonment techniques to those dominated by market logics. It then considers the more proximate, and recent battle against the managerial tendencies of newly formed land banks to give this picture some contextual grounding. The land abandonment regime in Detroit is then described and placed within this context. Finally, the chapter concludes with some thoughts about the relevance of this particular policy realm to the wider question of postcapitalist social movements.

The Normalization of Market-Oriented Urban Policy

Harvey (1989) classically identified a shift from "managerial" to "entrepreneurial" governance over twenty-five years ago. The postwar period, he argued, was characterized by an activist Keynesian state whose primary role was to serve as referee for capital, and to guide growth. It was never *anti*capitalist, but this form of governance served in some forms to blunt the force of capital accumulation by facilitating moderate redistribution, labor laws, housing, and regulation. The local corollary of this state involved a strong managerial role in distributing funds from higher levels of government, and enforcing zoning to force development to conform to certain social mores. With the onset of crisis in the 1970s, however, the regulatory and redistributive roles of the local state were increasingly replaced by an entrepreneurial focus. The nature of this varied somewhat from place to place, but often involved some mixture of deregulation, the facilitation of consumption, the lowering of taxes, and the assumption of greater levels of debt for economic development (Hackworth 2002, Davidson and Ward 2014). The entrepreneurial city thesis was a path-breaking observation at the time. It provoked a conversation about the role of planning and the state that lives on today. But in the twenty-five years since that thesis was devised, I argue, a further shift has occurred. The Overton Window has shifted considerably to the right—so much so that the entrepreneurial state has become normalized and is now being challenged on the Right by an array of forces dedicated to removing the state almost entirely from urban affairs. The Overton Window is fittingly named after the former vice president of the Mackinac Center for Public Policy, Joseph Overton. The Mackinac Center is a Michigan-based neoliberal policy think tank that has been instrumental in shifting the range of acceptable policy options for Detroit to the right. The Overton Window is a metaphor for the current politically acceptable range of policy options available to elected officials (Mackinac Center for Public Policy 2014). Think tanks like Mackinac see it as their purpose to shift the window to the right to make once unrealistic policy ideas possible, or if they are really successful, inevitable. In part because of their work, the urban policy window has shifted considerably to the right in the last forty years. The practical bookends for what remains of urban policy are market-first efforts on the one hand and market-only efforts on the other (Hackworth 2014a). Market-first efforts are essentially the entrepreneurial city that Harvey identified in his original essay. This is the notion that statecraft should be deployed to facilitate economic development, brand cities, assemble land, and maintain a business-friendly environment. Market-only efforts are an extreme (largely imaginary) view that argues that the state should be reduced to almost nothing. Channeling the classic Ayn Rand (1962: B3) desire to have a "complete separation of state and economics," market-only policy seeks to create a fully disembedded market. There are real debates to be had about the practicality of such a goal, but I wish to simply point out that whatever its efficacy as an actual policy goal, it resonates strongly as a discursive goal that continues to successfully frame any (even market-first) deployment of the state as "an assault on freedom."

The market-first/market-only continuum has narrowed the range of acceptable social policy options considerably, particularly in the United States. Neither model challenges the primacy of capitalism—they simply differ in the imagined (and real) role that the state should have in it. Neither acts as a referee, as was the case during the Keynesian-managerial moment. Social housing, rent control, tax increases, and meaningful regulation have been increasingly backgrounded (or eliminated) in many urban-policy conversations. The remaining discourse revolves around a much narrower set of concerns. The contours of this shift become clearer when we focus on a particular sector. The remainder of this chapter will focus on land abandonment and the changing policies designed to deal with it in Detroit and cities like it.

To adapt Harvey's (1989) thesis to the realm of land abandonment, however, several qualifiers and alterations are needed. First, the original thesis was designed to assess a broad turn away from the Keynesian-managerial to the present entrepreneurial one. This was immensely useful at provoking a conversation, but I conceptualize "managerialism" and "entrepreneurialism" a bit differently here. At the local state level, there is a range of techniques that are simultaneously present but variably important that can be categorized under these headings. A city might, for example, engage in a managerial zoning or code enforcement exercise, while also entrepreneurially subsidizing a developer to build a casino downtown. This is particularly the case for land

Table 5.1. Land-abandonment techniques for declining cities.

Type	Logic	Examples
Non-Market	To remove land from the private ownership for various social or environmental purposes.	Social housing on tax reverted properties; publicly managed green space
Managerial	To penalize property owners who are not achieving certain legal or social expectations.	Building code enforcement; health code enforcement; property registration laws; tax delinquency enforcement
Market-First	To partner with private investors who will achieve certain legal or social expectations.	Side lot programs; buyer assistance; developer subsidies
Market-Only	To remove state oversight from property ownership so that capital is interested in investing.	Unregulated tax auctions; lack of building, health and tax delinquency enforcement; lower property taxes

abandonment, so I use these terms as adjectives for techniques rather than a period per se. The totality of these techniques is what I deem a land-abandonment regime. Second, given the actualized range of techniques used in most land-abandonment regimes, I feel it is useful to subdivide Harvey's "managerialism" and "entrepreneurialism" into two further categories. The following typology is built on four types of techniques: non-market, managerial, market-first, and market-only. These categories are schematically summarized in Table 5.1 and spelled out in the text below. Finally, techniques should not be conflated with laws in this typology. Tax-reversion laws, for example, provide the basic parameters that counties (and cities) must follow in the foreclosure process. Questions such as whether to aggressively pursue tax delinquent properties, or whether to utilize an unregulated auction to recover tax liens are subject to some local autonomy. Few laws are thus intrinsically "managerial" or "market first," but all such strategies are framed by legal parameters. Thus, the argument here is not that we have entered a rigidly bound market-only era, but rather that market-only and market-first techniques dominate the policy window in Detroit and elsewhere in the world of declining cities.

Non-Market Techniques

Non-market techniques include policies that seek, or function, to decommodify land that is currently available for private consumption. Harvey (1989) originally placed such practices (e.g., building public housing) within managerialism, because while they are superficially about removing land from the market, they are ultimately part and parcel of reproducing capitalism (see also Harvey 1985: Chapter 7). I do not disagree with this larger analysis but feel it is useful to distinguish between policy forms in a land-abandonment (rather than -growth) context. Fining a slumlord for a building-code violation is a qualitatively different deployment of the state than, say, building a park, even if both have the same effect of legitimating the state as a counterbalance to unvarnished capitalism.

With that in mind, the first category of policy forms might be deemed non-market. The most common variation of this occurs through the tax reversion process. Often, declining cities either have a land bank (or a similarly functioning office) that takes in more land (from unsuccessful auction sales) than it is able to sell to private investors. Some then attempt to sell or give the land to nonprofit housing providers to build non-market (or, more precisely, limited-market) housing. In Toledo, Ohio, for example, roughly 5 percent of the 4,487 parcels that went to discount auction for tax delinquency between 1993 and 2012 were then eventually transferred to a community-development corporation (see Hackworth and Nowakowski 2014).[3] If subsidized housing is success-fully built on these sites, the land thus converts from private to limited-market, that is, from something that can be bought and sold easily to something that has significant resale restrictions.

Though subsidized housing is the most commonly practiced version of this technique, planning scholars have recently discussed the possibility of converting large sections of declining cities into untended parkland or green corridors as part of "right-sizing" initiatives (see Schilling and Logan 2008) or simply to generate scarcity by remov-ing the glut of surplus housing currently on the market (Mallach 2011). In theory, such land would then be publicly owned and thus adhere to an even more complete decommodification as the housing example explained earlier. But in practice, most cities interested in right sizing are not unveiling plans that follow this arc (Hackworth 2014b). Perhaps because of the cost that it entails (to maintain publicly held park-land) or perhaps because legal scholars have argued that such a "downzoning" could constitute a "taking" to current and future land owners (see LaCroix 2011), most cities have suggested a private outcome for "greened" land. A careful look at right-sizing plans in five cities (including Detroit) suggests that while environmental benefits are emphasized, most plans aim to return land to the market (rather than conserve it as green space) (Hackworth 2014b). Thus, greening and right sizing are not intrinsically or exclusively non-market activities. In fact, most actualized plans of this sort fall under the market-first activities. In general, while these techniques are technically possible in many cities, the actual removal of land from the market is seldom used.

Managerial Techniques

Managerial land-abandonment policy techniques function to regulate investment and penalize delinquent forms of ownership. The basic logic is that land abandonment is less a binary condition than a process that begins with property neglect and ends with literal abandonment. Some cities feel that by arresting the process at an earlier stage they might limit its damage and encourage more responsible ownership. A number of techniques and policy forms can be classified under the managerial umbrella. First, some cities responding to land abandonment have begun to strengthen their existing blight legislation so they can penalize, and if necessary acquire and demolish, property that has been purchased and left to rot (Alexander 2011). Some cities are also using programs of this sort to predict which properties might eventually become formally abandoned, allowing the city an earlier intervention (Hillier et al. 2003). Others have established or strengthened property registration systems, "spot blight" capabilities, or building codes to pursue negligent slumlords. The logic of these programs is that property purchases by speculators who do not perform normal levels of upkeep cre-ate a negative externality, or "neighborhood effect," that suppresses nearby property values. The nature of managerial programs vary, but they typically consist of legal mechanisms allowing the city to inspect properties and then warn owners who are in violation. If the property owners refuse to comply with city orders, such laws enable the city to perform maintenance against a lien on the property.

In short, a number of managerial land-abandonment techniques still exist and are sometimes used to penalize property owners who fail to live up to community mores or safety requirements. But the willingness to deploy such measures consistently and evenly is undermined by fiscal desperation, ideology, and the enshrinement of property rights (which enable slumlords to contest such measures in court). Thus, while there is discussion of these measures in academic policy circles and symbolic enforcement at key locales, the frequency of their actual deployment is uneven, and less prevalent that before.

Market-First Techniques

Market-first techniques emphasize partnerships with (rather than penalties for) private investment. These partnerships vary considerably in size and method, but they all involve a private land-ownership outcome. The scale can range from land assembly for massive private developments (Fainstein 2001) to piecemeal side-lot programs designed to incentivize a city's remaining owner-occupiers to absorb surplus land by making it part of their property (Schilling and Mallach 2012). Declining cities, almost by definition, lack fiscal resources, so the most common partnership form tends to be tax subsidies or financing (rather than direct outlays from the general fund). Again, the scale can range considerably, from special-purpose districts whose municipal property taxes are diverted so that they can leverage the stream for private real-estate development (Weber 2002) to individual property tax breaks designed to dissuade owner-occupiers from joining the exodus from the city. Though there are important differences in the scope of enabling legislation (see Alexander 2011), many land banks (particularly recently formed ones) have emerged from within the market-first paradigm. Most, for example, absorb certain properties from the tax-reversion process and then partner with "good" buyers (owner-occupiers with a clean property tax record) by providing financing and maintenance assistance. Because most (new) land banks are required to be fiscally self-sustaining, the emphasis on profitable sales is an important part of their activities and impels them to adhere to a market logic. In general, market-first techniques deploy the state to partner with, rather than penalize, investors. The partnerships can range in scale from subsidies to large commercial developers to small house-rehabilitation loans for inner-city owner-occupiers. For many declining cities, this approach marks the interventionist extreme, increasingly seen as the government-oriented counter-policy to market-only techniques.

Market-Only Techniques

Almost by definition, market-only is a difficult category to identify as a policy form. In its purest sense, market-only is the absence of government-led policy. The basic market-only logic is that cities experience decline because of regulation, managerial-ism, and other "misguided" efforts to embed markets (Glaeser 2011). Accordingly, the most desirable path forward is to deregulate, to lower (or eliminate) taxes, to shrink government, and to allow property owners virtual sovereignty over their holdings.

Within significantly abandoned cities, the market argument has been that registration laws, land banks, and any other mechanisms meant to limit or select certain buyers over others are fundamentally unfair or even "socialistic" (Harding 2010, Spalding 2012a, Spalding 2012b). The accompanying belief is that investors will eventually return to the city, as they have in other heavily abandoned places, only if it is priced properly and devoid of regulation.[4] Governmental authorities should lower taxes to a point where tax delinquency is rarer, and when delinquency does occur, should hold no-minimum-bid auctions with no participation by governmental entities like land banks (see Spalding 2012c). While this fantasy remains prevalent among neoliberal activists, municipal government is present in some form, so it is impossible to identify pure ideal-type examples.

There are, however, certain conditions that increase the likelihood of acquiescence to capital, and strengthen the gravitational pull of market-only ideals. The most basic of these conditions is fiscal crisis that can lead to staffing cutbacks and in turn morph into a lack of enforcement capacity for taxes and building-code issues. In Detroit, for instance, Wayne County refused to foreclose on forty thousand delinquent properties in 2012 alone because they were "overwhelmed" by the number of owners not paying their bill (MacDonald 2013). There are doubtless thousands more that do not meet nominal building or safety code thresholds. Though the numbers are inflated because of the scale of the problem in Detroit, the lack of enforcement capacity is not uncommon in declining cities in general. Existing policies are likely to go unenforced, creating a de facto space of legal impunity for property investors trying to milk properties of their value. A related condition that can open a similar legal space is a lack of cooperation between governmental entities, usually county and city governments. Some counties are more willing, for example, to hold no-minimum-bid auctions or to discount foreclosed property against the wishes of the affected city. A further condition that can facilitate the emphasis of market-only planning exists when the balance of power in a state tilts rural or if there is one large city that serves as a political "other" in the state. Detroit is a classic case. Still the state's largest city, Detroit looms large in Lansing as a political symbol. Many outstate politicians (in both parties) openly run on a platform that is unhelpful, if not hostile to the interests of Detroit. Rural state legislators in such environments must tread lightly with legislation that might "benefit" Detroit, or Cleveland, or New York City and so on (see Brachman 2012b for a discussion of this in Ohio). Creating a more regulatory environment for property ownership for a large, prominent, declining city, is politically treacherous since such places are widely seen by rural voters as being overregulated. In total, these forces align (more acutely in some contexts, like Detroit, than others) not only to marginalize managerial policy techniques but also to inevitabilize market-only solutions. Some of this is an accident of political geography, but much of it is designed and strenuously supported by an array of market-only think tanks and allies.

The Movement against Managerial Land-Abandonment Policy

Since 2003, when Michigan reformed its tax-reversion and land-banking laws, other major Rust Belt states (Ohio, Pennsylvania, New York, and Missouri) have followed suit. Most are mild reforms that allow land banks to proactively participate in the tax-reversion process and attempt to find owner-occupier buyers that might be more community minded than speculators who dominate at unregulated auctions. And yet even these gentle reforms have inspired an organized backlash. For realtor associations, neoliberal think tanks, slumlords, and financial interests, such reforms are government overreach, and they have spent copious resources fighting the land-bank movement and softening related legislation in recent years. Resistance has come in a variety of forms and has had different levels of success. In some instances, it has been sufficient to derail land-banking efforts. In almost all cases, resistance has been sufficient to affect policy outcomes—in particular by weakening land banks and regulations to make them more property friendly (see Hackworth 2014a).

Real-estate associations have objected to the proposals in every state in which land banking has been considered, and were particularly influential in derailing plans in Illinois and delaying them in Pennsylvania (*Pittsburgh Today* 2011, Illinois Association of Realtors 2012, Spalding 2012c). They object to government intervention that might impede the number of property sales (Illinois Association of Realtors 2012). Anything that might inhibit or prohibit the repetitive transfer of properties in cities or other jurisdictions—no matter how deleterious to planning efforts in that city—would likely reduce opportunities for association members. Similarly, financial interests have resisted reform efforts in a number of states as part of an almost reflexive inclination to resist government oversight of the economy (Brachman 2012a 2012b).

Political momentum induced by the anti-eminent domain wave that occurred in the wake of the 2006 Supreme Court case *Kelo versus New London, Connecticut* has also made it difficult to enact any regulations that enhance the power of government over property. The Kelo case affirmed the right of cities in the United States to use eminent domain for commercial redevelopment purposes—essentially using expropriation laws to take property (with compensation) from one private owner, assemble it, and then give it to another, with the goal of enhancing tax revenue. Libertarian activists, especially the Castle Group (the firm that represented Kelo in the case) and their think-tank offshoot, the Institute for Justice, were outraged by the decision and mobilized political efforts to pressure state legislatures to limit the basis on which cities could exercise eminent domain. The legal impact of these specific resistance measures has been debatable (Jacobs and Bassett 2010), but the political impact has been more prominent. Enacting legislation designed to enhance the power of government, even if not technically in the area of eminent domain, has been resisted by legislators under pressure from the Institute for Justice and other conservative groups. In the Michigan/Detroit context, the Poletown Case had an earlier and similar effect on legislation pertaining to government involvement in land-based economic development. The highly charged atmosphere has made it even more challenging to create legislation that might give local government the tools needed to proactively deal with land abandonment.

Finally, the most systematic, if not always most influential, source of opposition to land abandonment reforms in recent years has been from market-oriented think tanks including but not limited to the aforementioned Mackinac Center. Because their opposition is articulated comprehensively in report form, it is possible to explore their arguments in detail. Though there are regional and ideological differences in think-tank arguments, their objections can be summarized as follows. Above all, they argue that land banks in particular, and managerialism in general, have failed in the past, so it is foolish to try this approach again. Stahl and Spalding (2012, Spalding 2012c) and other critics, for example, argue that land banks like those in Cleveland, Saint Louis, and Atlanta have existed for decades, and abandonment in those cities is as bad as if not worse than in other shrinking American cities. They single out the ineffectiveness of acquiring and assembling land in anticipation of future development (Spalding 2012a, 2012c) and argue that land banks fail as a reinvestment strategy (Harding 2010). They suggest that land banks create advantages for (pernicious) government over (benevolent) investors (Harding 2010) and view official mandates about "returning land to private productive use" as disingenuous (Spalding 2012a). In their view, land banks, more often than not, hold land and never really return it to private investors (Spalding 2012b). They argue that it is unfair to investors, developers, and citizens when government is allowed to participate as an investor in this way (Spalding 2012b). The alliance of market-oriented think tanks and real estate associations desires a policy regime that is as market only as possible. They believe that property acquired through tax fore-closure should be returned to investors as quickly and inexpensively as possible, and unencumbered by regulation and title problems. Existing nuisance regulations that allow for "spot condemnation" or even fines for lack of upkeep should be loosened or eliminated (Spalding 2012b). Within this worldview, investors and the market in general will correct the problems facing cities—governments will only worsen them.

In short, there is an organized effort—somewhat ideological, somewhat self-interested—to oppose land banking in particular, managerial-land and market-first techniques in general. In Michigan, this has been led by an array of groups like the Mackinac and Hudson Institutes, and supported by sympathetic Republicans in Lansing. This opposition taps into deep-seated assumptions about the role of government in general and urban planning in particular. Within this perspective, the notion of government assistance or regulation is framed as misguided at best, malevolent at worst. Advocates of even modest managerial or market-first reform struggle to gain traction because ideological resistance is so deeply entrenched and well funded. Resulting legislation in Michigan, Ohio, and Pennsylvania thus emphasizes self-sufficiency and the sale of land, and contains loopholes that protect certain investors and limit government overreach.

Detroit's Land-Abandonment Regime

Detroit's land abandonment regime is notable in a number of respects. First, the scale of the problem is larger than in any city in the United States, certainly in absolute terms, and arguably in relative terms. The recently released *Every Neighborhood Has a Future* found that over 30 percent of the city already consists of vacant lots that were once the site of houses, factories, and institutions (Detroit Blight Removal Task Force 2014). According to estimates by the US Census American Community Survey (2008–2012), a mere 71.3 percent of its housing units are currently occupied. The staggering 28.7 percent of units that are unoccupied do not include the 10,000-plus units that the Census does not even count because they are uninhabitable. The majority of new real estate investors are not owner-occupiers and pay cash for abandoned units at various public and private auctions (Hackworth 2014b). As outward population flows have accelerated in recent years, so has the abandonment of housing. For this reason, the Detroit Blight Removal Task Force (DBRTF) (2014) identified 78,504 structures that they feel are in need of demolition. To put this number in perspective, the second-largest city in Michigan, Grand Rapids, has roughly the same number of total housing units (80,619) that Detroit is seeking to demolish. The geography of this is uneven to be sure. Some neighborhoods in the city are relatively dense and intact, while others are highly abandoned, but there is no other city in the United States facing an abandonment problem of the scale that exists in Detroit.

A second distinguishing characteristic of Detroit's land-abandonment regime is the degree of authorship and influence by outside, particularly neoliberal forces. The broad parameters of land-abandonment law were set with a 2003 state law that changed the way that tax reversion worked and allowed counties to establish land banks. The law was written by the American Legislative Exchange Council (ALEC)-funded Hudson Institute and pushed by state legislators, who are generally indifferent, if not hostile to Detroit (Akers 2013). The chief problem it sought to address was how to allow for a more expeditious government foreclosure of tax-delinquent properties and how to assure that the titles were cleared of past liens so that investors would be interested in purchasing them at auction. In a sense, then, it set up the machinery for a market-oriented urban policy—using statecraft to facilitate and organize investment.

But there was considerable local autonomy, particularly with the design and reach of the land banks that were created so counties (and cities, to a lesser extent) could decide whether to gravitate toward a market-first or market-only pathway. A recent lawsuit by investors in Grand Rapids brings this distinction into relief. In 2013, a group of real-estate investors who are connected to state-level Republican officials sued Kent County (Grand Rapids), essentially for being too market-first and not market-only enough (Gryczan 2014). Specifically, the investors felt that the county was poaching properties from them and denying "their right" to profit from them. The suit was dismissed (and is currently on appeal), but it was sufficiently influential to prompt the governor to introduce legislation to curb the power of land banks. This matter is ongoing, and the outcome far from determined, but I raise it here to highlight the issue at hand. The 2003 legislation did indeed allow county-level land banks to have some autonomy in how they approach abandonment. But the parameters have been set by the market logic of the initial bill, and are continually challenged by forces on the Right who feel that it allows the local state to be too interventionist. The emphasis on attracting investment, the legal necessity that land banks be self-sustaining, and the larger reality of austerity have narrowed the practical range of this autonomy considerably. So while, for example, the Genesee County Land Bank is considered a national model for, among other things, denying access to some predatory speculators, it is not empowered or inclined to de-privatize large swaths of land or vigorously penalize slumlords. Its emphasis (and the basis on which it is judged) is on acquiring tax-reverted property, demolishing the hopeless cases, and renovating the better properties for prescreened buyers. Its track record at creating better housing conditions than slumlords who reigned in the previous system is difficult to deny. But it is equally difficult to argue that this represents a return of interventionist-managerial governance (or that this practice is sufficient to put a meaningful dent in the overall abandonment problem there). The land-bank model in Michigan and elsewhere is set up to be more benevolent than speculators would be in a market-only model, but it is still centered on market promotion. Genesee County has become a national best-practice model in this respect. And yet, this is the interventionist extreme for government allowed by the state law.[5] Other localities, either out of necessity for revenue, poor county-city relations, ideology, or all of the above, have chosen to emphasize the auction, and thus have adopted what amounts to a market-only path. The Wayne County version of this legal framework has adopted the auction-first model—encourage investment at almost no cost, and little to no screening of buyers. Foreclosed property that goes unsold during the first auction migrates to a $500-minimum-bid second auction where there are few restrictions on who can buy it, including parties with known delinquency records (MacDonald 2011). Investors need not even be present at the auction to bid on properties. The auction itself occurs online and is managed by a private firm, Bid4Assets. Much of the property goes unsold through the first auction, but more speculators become interested during the second (Bailey et al. 2006). *The Detroit News* (MacDonald 2011; MacDonald & Wilkinson 2011a, 2011b) recently published an exposé on speculators who have purchased hundreds of properties this way. Some, like Michael Kelly, the city's most notorious speculator, have hundreds of code violations and copious tax delinquency elsewhere in the city but are able to buy property freely. The City of Detroit—which has its own land bank and itself owns over forty thousand parcels—is generally very displeased with the lax nature of the Wayne County structure and often refuses to take possession of the virtual archipelago of troubled properties that results after this process is complete. Thus, while the 2003 state law outlining the pathway for tax delinquency allows some autonomy, it is premised on a market logic. It requires that land banks be self-sustaining and that they emphasize sale over other goals. Some city-county combinations have adopted a more interventionist market-first approach to this, while others (Wayne-Detroit) have adopted a de facto market-only system—open to the highest bidder with few restrictions on what they do with the property afterward.

Though some of this policy emphasis is homegrown, much of it has been imposed by outside forces—by the think tanks who wrote the legislation and state-level Republicans who pushed it through. The recent bankruptcy-emergency management regime has only intensified this dynamic. There are several dimensions to this. First, the practical collapse of governance capacity has created a policy vacuum that has been filled by well-intended foundations like Kresge, market-oriented investors like Dan Gilbert, and state-backed government liquidators like Kevyn Orr. They have successfully pushed through policy frameworks that might not have been as possible if Detroit had a functioning city government with local representation. Most relevant to the question at hand has been the ongoing effort to "right size" Detroit by engaging in blight removal and potentially deurbanizing certain areas of the city (Kirkpatrick 2014). This effort has intensified both the external governance dimension to Detroit's land abandonment regime, but also the overwhelmingly market-only nature of it.

Detroit's right-sizing vision is spelled out with two ostensibly unofficial but influential documents: *Detroit Future City* (Detroit Works 2012) (hereafter *DFC*) and *Every Neighborhood Has a Future* (DBRTF 2014). Within the current context of Detroit—a city under "emergency management" and if the bankruptcy deal is approved, under state supervision for at least thirteen years—it is likely that such documents have more influence on the city's future than ostensibly official ones. Released in December 2012, *DFC* was the culmination of a two-year process financed and managed by a number of local foundations (in particular the Kresge Foundation), and assisted by nonprofits like Data Driven Detroit. It involved participation by city officials but is not an official master-planning document. One particular emphasis of *DFC* is on the cost of maintaining street, sewer, and utility infrastructures that sprawl across the city's vast landscape for a population that is less than half its mid-twentieth-century size. *Detroit Future City* outlines a number of right-sizing land use ideas, none more provocative than the proposed ruralization of vast sections of the city through two new land-use categories, "innovation productive" and "innovation ecological." Innovation-productive landscapes will be used for large-scale commercial farming, while innovation ecological will be areas that will be allowed to return to untended urban forests and prairies. Approximately 20 percent of the city's land area has been mapped in *Detroit Future City* as innovation ecological, and one estimate suggests that as many as 88,000 people still live in the areas affected (Kirkpatrick 2014). *DFC* contains promises that every resident who wants to stay can, but as some have argued, it is difficult to understand how the goal of infrastructure downsizing might be achieved without displacement or forced removal (Hackworth 2014b, Kirkpatrick 2014). If, for example, the city were able to demolish seven of ten remaining houses on a given street, the city's utilities would still have to serve the same length of pipe, wire, and road for the remaining three houses. Without moving the remaining three off of the grid or inducing (or forcing) them to move, it is difficult to understand where the infrastructure cost savings would be realized. *DFC* is light on details of how this would be possible and what options might exist for the displaced.

Detroit Future City has been (and remains) immensely important since its release, but the city's subsequent bankruptcy has ratcheted up the urgency to achieve certain land abandonment policy goals and the degree of control exercised by non-Detroit authorities. One outgrowth of this context is the release of *Every Neighborhood Has a Future* (DBRTF 2014).[6] The Report's name derives from the campaign slogan of the current Mayor Mike Duggan, who wanted to distance himself from the perception (provoked by the previous Mayor Dave Bing) that certain neighborhoods would simply be erased.[7] Though the scope is different, in many ways *Every Neighborhood* picks up where *Detroit Future City* left off. In fact, the authors of *Every Neighborhood* devote an entire chapter to spelling out how cohesive and integral their vision is with *DFC* and the mayor's own plan to tackle land abandonment. Whatever their similarities, however, *Every Neighborhood* is different in a number of respects, most pertinently that it is solely focused on demolition, and that it specifies how this will be paid for.

The DBRTF (2014) openly invokes the language of "triage" (p. 101, among others) and specifies certain neighborhoods where current efforts to demolish would be best focused (p. 94). The DBRTF (2014: 235) estimates that the task will cost approximately $850 million and that they already have about half of this at their disposal. *Every Neighborhood* lacks the environmental sentimentality of the *DFC* and the other reports. It is also more specific about what should happen to the parcels after the structures are demolished. The DBRTF is explicit that a market-only pathway should be pursued. Namely, properties should be auctioned with clear title as soon as possible and it is confident that once "cancerous blight" (p. iii) has been removed such interest will exist.

In short, whatever its legal possibilities, Detroit's actualized land-abandonment regime largely vacillates between market first and market only. If the *Every Neighborhood* is followed, massive demolition will be followed by nearly unfettered access to property. But even if a more "moderate" market-first path is chosen (e.g., *DFC*), it will still result in little resources for the social economy or non-market initiatives. Detroit's land-abandonment regime is shaped by powerful extra-local forces, and has been for decades. The potential for a post-market or even managerial land-abandonment policy is severely limited within this framework.

Countermovements, Urban Policy, and Bad Choices

There is considerable scholarly conversation about whether decades of attempts by neoliberal activists, politicians, and think tanks to institute a disembedded market society has (or will) inspire a countermovement to re-embed markets within a wider socio-moral context. On the one hand, it is difficult to think of a place in the United States that is more exposed to the rawness of the market than Detroit. What remains of its social economy is currently being dissolved by emergency management, under the banner of fiscal necessity. Repeated experiments to "free the market" in Detroit have failed and done much damage to community in the process. But yet, it is not a socializing countermovement that has emerged in the Detroit context; it is a much narrower market-reinforcing one. The policy spectrum is increasingly defined at one end by the entrepreneurial city—the use of statecraft to help markets—and at the other by a colder puritanical neoliberalism that seeks fully disembedded markets.

The machinery of neoliberalism is pervasive, adaptable, organized, and well funded. Think tanks wrote the underlying legislation for the land-abandonment regime, and neoliberal notions of profligacy are driving the current austerity budget that will be imposed after bankruptcy. And if that is not puritanically neoliberal enough, there are self-interested forces with impressive machinery to contest these measures as being too interventionist. In part for this reason, constituencies that might have once clung to a non-market political strategy begrudgingly stand behind the market-first camp, because well-funded extremists at the Hudson Institute and Americans for Prosperity have so successfully moved the Overton Window to the right that a plausible left-leaning alternative largely does not exist. Thus, for example, there have been lopsided votes in the summer of 2014 by City Council to cede the Detroit Institute of Art to a suburban-controlled nonprofit (Guillen 2014a) votes agreeing to at least thirteen years of state oversight (Helms 2014), and former employees voting to accept deep pension cuts (Guillen 2014b) because the putative alternative is not only palpably worse, but imminently possible. This extends to the realm of land abandonment as well. Many community members are more receptive to *Every Neighborhood* and *Detroit Future City* than similar earlier schemes,[8] in part because the alternative (continued benign neglect) is worse and because many might personally benefit from its vision (no matter what its impact on the wider community). The alternatives created by the market-first/market-only tension thus create a sort of prisoner's dilemma for those affected. If for example, they choose an abstract option like an equitable, limited-market renewal of Detroit, they might lose the chance to remove the vacant house across the street that is a drain on their own house value. A potentially re-embedding community response is thus complicated by self-interest—by the knowledge that an equitable wave of market-embedded policy forms are unlikely (and perhaps not even desirable), but the ability to solve more limited problems (like "blight") might just be attainable.

The machinery and will to create an alternative to the current land-abandonment regime does not currently exist. Non-market ideas like permanently conserved community gardens, social housing clustered near one of the development cores, or permanently conserved green space are more influential among planning scholars than they are at affecting policy outcomes. Nothing about the future is rigidly predetermined, and social conditions in Detroit could indeed change, but the recent past and current institutional structure suggest a near future that is dominated by market logics. This emphasis is particularly pronounced within Detroit's land-abandonment regime, which is largely contained by market-first techniques at one end and market-only techniques at the other.

Notes

1. Sections from this chapter initially appeared in Hackworth (2014a). The author gratefully acknowledges both Elsevier and the editors of this volume for permission to reprint them.
2. For a similar argument in relation to public housing in the United States, see Hackworth (2005). Briefly, public housing tenant opposition to HOPE VI—a program that sought to demolish as much public housing as possible—was deeply divided in part because some tenants thought that remaining apolitical would allow them to gain access to a better housing unit in a redeveloped community (even if it meant that some of their neighbors would be displaced).
3. In Detroit, polluted titles and bureaucracy inhibit more CDCs from pursuing this path, but there are projects built in this way using Low Income Housing Tax Credits (Deng 2013, Thomas 2013b).
4. New York City is the frequently used example to illustrate this argument. Though in the 1970s officials were discussing the possibility of "planned shrinkage," New York (and other East Coast "gateway cities") partially or fully reversed this population flow. Rust Belt "legacy" cities have not shown credible signs of following this trajectory.
5. Moreover, it is continually challenged by market-oriented think tanks. Mackinac recently deemed the Genesee model a "threat to private property rights" (Harding 2010).
6. The Task Force was co-chaired by Dan Gilbert, owner of Quicken Loans and numerous commercial buildings in downtown Detroit, Glenda Rice of the Detroit Public Schools Foundation, and Linda Smith of U-SNAP-BAC. U-SNAP-BAC is a consortium of community organizations in the city's east side. The acronym stands for "United Streets Networking and Planning; Building A Community."
7. Which is ironic because the *Every Neighborhood* proposes to do just that.
8. The suggestion, for example, that sections of the city be "moth-balled" in 1993 was met with public ridicule (Worthington, 1993).

References

Akers, J. (2013). "Making markets: Think tank legislation and private property in Detroit," *Urban Geography*, 34 (8), 1070–1095.

Alexander, F. (2011). *Land Banks and Land Banking*. Retrieved from http://www.communityprogress. net/filebin/pdf/new_resrcs/LB_Book_2011_F.pdf.

Bailey, S., S. Fisher, C. Hoss, M. Khanna, M. Ledford, B. Lutenegger, & K. Maurer. (2006). *Planning for Detroit's Tax-Reverted Properties: Possibilities for the Wayne County Land Bank*. Urban and Regional Planning Program, University of Michigan, Ann Arbor. Retrieved July17,2014,fromhttp:// taubmancollege.umich.edu/planning/pdfs/planning_for_detroit_s_tax_reverted_propertiescomp.pdf.

Brachman, L. (2012a). "New State and Federal Policy Agendas: Realizing the potential of America's legacy cities and their regions," In A. Mallach (Ed.), *Rebuilding America's Legacy Cities: New directions for the industrial heartland* (pp. 265–290). New York: The American Assembly/ Columbia University Press.

Brachman, L. (2012b). "Case study: Building a coalition to pass a state land bank." In A. Mallach (Ed.), *Rebuilding America's Legacy Cities: New directions for the industrial heartland* (pp. 291–294). New York: The American Assembly/ Columbia University Press.

Burawoy, M. (2010). "From Polanyi to Pollyanna: The false optimism of global labor studies." *Global Labour Journal*, 1 (2), 301–313.

Dale, G. (2012). "Double movements and pendular forces: Polanyian perspectives on the neoliberal age." *Current Sociology*, 60 (1), 3–27.

Davidson, M., and K. Ward. (2014). "'Picking up the pieces': austerity urbanism, California, and fiscal crisis." *Cambridge Journal of Regions, Economy and Society*, 7 (1), 81–97.

Deng, L. (2013). "Building affordable housing in cities after abandonment: The case of lower income housing tax credit developments in Detroit." In M. Dewar and J. M. Thomas (Eds.), *The City After Abandonment* (pp. 41–63). Philadelphia: University of Pennsylvania Press.

Detroit Blight Removal Task Force (DBRTF). (2014, May). *Every Neighborhood Has a Future. . . And it Doesn't Include Blight: Detroit Blight Removal Task Force Plan.* Detroit: Detroit Blight Removal Task Force. Retrieved July 17, 2014, from http://report.timetoendblight.org/.

Detroit Works. (2012). *Detroit Future City: Detroit strategic framework plan.* Detroit: Detroit Works. Retrieved July 17, 2014, from http://detroitworksproject.com/the-framework/.

Fainstein, S. (2001). *City Builders: Property development in New York and London, 1980–2000.* (Second Edition). Lawrence KS: University of Kansas Press.

Glaeser, E. (2011). *Triumph of the City: How our greatest invention makes us richer, smarter, greener, and happier.* New York: Penguin Press.

Gryczan, M. (2014, January 12). "Land bank . . . or land grab? Experiment in Kent County has some raising roof." *Crain's Detroit Business.* Retrieved July 17, 2014, from http://www.crainsdetroit.com/article/20140112/NEWS/301129999/land-bank-or-land-grab-experiment-in-kent-county-has-some-raising.

Guillen, J. (2014a, June 16). "Detroit City Council seconds transfer of DIA art to charitable trust." *Detroit Free Press.* Retrieved July 17, 2014, from http://www.freep.com/article/20140616/NEWS01/306160135/Detroit-council-DIA-art.

———. (2014b, June 19). "Police and Fire pension board vote 'yes' on proposed cuts." *Detroit Free Press.* Retrieved July 17, 2014, from http://www.freep.com/article/20140619/NEWS01/306190182/Detroit-fire-police-pension-vote.

Hackworth, J. (2002). "Local autonomy, bond-rating agencies and neoliberal urbanism in the US." *International Journal of Urban and Regional Research,* 26, 707–725.

———. (2005). "Progressive activism in a neoliberal context: the case of efforts to retain public housing in the US." *Studies in Political Economy,* 75, 29–51.

———. (2007). *The Neoliberal City: Governance, ideology, and development in American urbanism.* Ithaca, NY: Cornell University Press.

———. (2014a). "The limits to market-based strategies for addressing land abandonment in shrinking American cities." *Progress in Planning,* 90, 1–37.

———. (2014b). "Right-sizing as spatial austerity in the American Rust Belt." Unpublished Manuscript, available online at: http://individual.utoronto.ca/hackworth/Right_Sizing.pdf.

———, and K. Nowakowski. (2014). "Tax foreclosure, land-banking, and urban shrinkage in Toledo, OH" Unpublished Manuscript, available online at: http://individual.utoronto.ca/hackworth/toledo.html.

Harding, R. (2010, July 1). "Genesee County Land Bank threatens private property rights." Retrieved July 17, 2014, from http://www.mackinac.org/13090.

Harvey, D. (1985). *The Urbanization of Capital: Studies in the history and theory of capitalist urbanization.* Baltimore, MD: Johns Hopkins University Press.

———. (1989). "From managerialism to entrepreneurialism: The transformation of urban governance in late capitalism." *Geografiska Annaler,* 71, 3–17.

———. (2012). *Rebel Cities: From the right to the city to the urban revolution.* New York: Verso.

Helms, M. (2014, July 13). "Orr: Duggan, City Council are ready to run Detroit." *Detroit Free Press.* RetrievedJuly17,2014,fromhttp://www.freep.com/article/20140713/NEWS01/307130093/detroit-bankruptcy-orr-duggan-jones.

Hillier, A., D. Culhane, T. Smith, and C. Tomlin. (2003). "Predicting housing abandonment with the Philadelphia neighborhood information system." *Journal of Urban Affairs*, 25(1), 91–105.

Illinois Association of Realtors. (2012). "Illinois realtors oppose land bank authority." Press Release. Retrieved July 17, 2014 from http://www.illinoisrealtor.org/member/landbanking.

Jacobs, H., and E. Bassett. (2010). "After 'Kelo': Political rhetoric and policy responses." *Land Lines* 22(2), 14–20.

Kirkpatrick, L.O. (2015). "Urban triage, city systems, and the remnants of community: some 'sticky' complications in the greening of Detroit." *Journal of Urban History* (forthcoming)

LaCroix, C. (2011) "Urban green uses: the new renewal." *Planning and Environmental Law* 63: 3–13.

MacDonald, C. (2011, February 3). "Private landowners complicate reshaping of Detroit." *The Detroit News.* Retrieved July 17, 2014, from http://www.detroitnews.com/article/20110203/METRO01/102030395.

———. (2013, February 21). "Overwhelmed Wayne County ignores thousands of possible Detroit foreclosures." *The Detroit News.* Retrieved July 22, 2014 from: http://www.detroitnews.com/article/20130221/METRO01/302210394.

———, and M. Wilkinson. (2011a February 3). "Interactive Map: Who owns the most private property in Detroit?" *The Detroit News.* Retrieved July 17, 2014, from http://www.detroitnews.com/article/20110203/SPECIAL01/110202002.

———, and M. Wilkinson. (2011b, February 4). Detroit's Real Estate Bazaar: Reforms urged to deter land speculators. *The Detroit News.* Retrieved July 17, 2014, from http://www.detroitnews.com/article/20110204/METRO01/102040358.

Mackinac Center for Public Policy. (2014). "A model of policy change." Retrieved July 17, 2014, from http://www.mackinac.org/OvertonWindow.

Mallach, A. (2011). "Demolition and preservation in shrinking U.S. industrial cities." *Building Research and Information*, 39(4), 380–394.

Peck, J., and A. Tickell. (2002). "Neoliberalizing space." *Antipode*, 34 (3), 380–404.

Pittsburgh Today. (2011). "Pittsburgh seeking new ways to keep up with number of vacant properties." Retrieved July 17, 2014, from http://www.communityprogress.net/news-pages-9.php?id=238.

Polanyi, K. (1944). *The Great Transformation.* Boston: Beacon Press.

Rand, A. (1962, June 17). "Ayn Rand ties her beliefs to today's world." *Los Angeles Times*, B3.

Schilling, J., and J. Logan. (2008). "Greening the rust belt: a green infrastructure model for right-sizing America's shrinking cities." *Journal of the American Planning Association*, 74: 451–66.

———, and A. Mallach. (2012). *Cities in Transition: A guide for practicing planners* (PAS report number 568). Chicago: American Planning Association.

Spalding, A. (2012a, February 8). "Legislators Should Seriously Consider the Failings of the Saint Louis Land Bank before Creating a Kansas City Land Bank." Retrieved July 17, 2014, from http://showmeinstitute.org/publications/testimony/red-tape/702-land-bank-faillings.html.

———. (2012b, February 28). "Land bank recommendations." Retrieved July 17, 2014, from http://showmeinstitute.org/landbank.html.

———. (2012c, March 26). "Land banking: an old idea with a poor track record." Retrieved July 17, 2014, from http://showmeinstitute.org/publications/commentary/red-tape/732-land-banking-old-idea.html.

Stahl, B. and Spalding, A. (2012, April 2). "Don't Bank On It: When it comes to vacant property, learn from Saint Louis' failures." Retrieved July 17, 2014, from http://showmeinstitute.org/publications/commentary/red-tape/739-dont-bank-on-it.html.

Sugrue, T. (2005). *The Origins of the Urban Crisis: Race and inequality in postwar Detroit.* (Princeton Classic Edition). Princeton, NJ: Princeton University Press.

Thomas, J.M. (2013a). *Redevelopment and Race: Planning a finer city in postwar Detroit.* Detroit: Wayne State University Press.

———. (2013b). "Targeting strategies of three Detroit CDCs." In M. Dewar and J.M. Thomas (Eds.), *The City After Abandonment* (pp. 197–224). Philadelphia: University of Pennsylvania Press.

Weber, R. (2002). "Extracting value from the city: Neoliberalism and urban redevelopment." *Antipode*, 34 (3), 519–540.

Worthington, R. (1993, May 5). "What to do with vacant city lots? Mothball them, city official says." *Chicago Tribune.* Retrieved July 17, 2014, from http://articles.chicagotribune.com/1993-05-05/news/9305050086_1_east-side-city-hall-common-counc.

Part III

Where We Are: Fiscal Crisis, Local Democracy, and Neoliberal Austerity

6

Detroit in Bankruptcy

Reynolds Farley

In July 2013, Detroit Emergency Manager Kevyn Orr requested Chapter 9 bankruptcy for the City of Detroit. Federal bankruptcy Judge Steven Rhodes presided over the hearings and in October granted the request.[1] Detroit became the largest city to enter bankruptcy. This essay first describes why Detroit ran out of funds to pay its obligations; then it describes the contentious bankruptcy process that may end in late 2014. The final section discusses the future of the city after bankruptcy.

Why Is Detroit Bankrupt?

Collapse of the Tax Base

Municipal governments are supported primarily by taxes they levy upon property owners, residents, and those who do business in the city. By 2013, the City of Detroit was at risk of being unable to pay its police and fire officers and its other employees, or to provide basic services because its tax base declined greatly in the years after World War II.

Thanks to the emergence of the vehicle industry, no large US city grew faster than Detroit between 1900 and 1930. After a pause during the Depression, population and economic growth resumed in the 1940s, as Detroit became the true "Arsenal of Democracy." The nation's economy continued to grow rapidly for a quarter century after World War II, and, for a few years, the City of Detroit shared in that growth. By 1950, the incomes of men in Detroit were higher than those of men in any other large city—higher than wages in New York, San Francisco, or Washington.[2] By that time, however, almost all the land area within the city was filled with homes, factories, stores, schools, and office buildings. The decline of Detroit's tax base started in the 1950s. Numerous vehicle-assembly and parts plants were in the city. Indeed, the 1947 Census of Manufacturers counted 3,300 manufacturing plants in the city (US Bureau of the Census 1952). Many of them were antiquated, since they dated from the early 1900s. As manufacturing output soared, firms built modern, one-story plants on tracts of empty land available in the suburban ring but not in the city. The federal government's housing policies stimulated a tremendous amount of new construction by keeping down payments and mortgage rates low. For three years after the end of World War II, about as many new homes were built in Detroit as in the suburban ring, but after that new housing construction was overwhelmingly in the ring. City residents found they could readily purchase a more modern, spacious, and attractive home in the suburbs. Thus began the demographic process that reduced the city's population from almost two million residents in 1950 to fewer than seven hundred thousand at present. Detroit was once a major center for wholesaling. But with the development of the interstate highway system in the late 1950s, trucks became competitive with trains, and wholesalers, seeking modern low-rise buildings, moved from the city to the ring. In every city, retail stores are major employers, but as the population shifted from Detroit to the suburbs, retailers moved out.

The collapse of Detroit's tax base may be easily summarized:

- From 1950 to 2013, the population fell by 63 percent
- From 1950 to 2013, the number of occupied homes and apartments fell by 51 percent
- From 1950 to 2013, the number of Detroit residents holding a job declined by 74 percent
- From 1947 to 2007, the number of manufacturing firms fell by 86 percent
- From 1947 to 2007, the number of manufacturing workers in the city fell by 93 percent
- From 1947 to 2007, the number of retail stores fell by 88 percent
- From 1947 to 2007, the number of wholesale firms fell by 88 percent

The recession that began in 2008 explains the timing of the bankruptcy. Between 2007 and 2012, per capita income in the city dropped by 14 percent in constant dollars, the number of employed residents fell by 18 percent, the assessed value of residential property by 47 percent, while the poverty rate increased from 34 percent to 41 percent. By 2011, property taxes were being paid on only 53 percent of taxable properties (Citizens Research Council of Michigan 2013, MacDonald and Wilkinson 2013). In addition, the Census 2010 census count and a change by the legislature in how sales taxes receipts were distributed to local governments reduced Detroit's revenue by $69 million annually (Oosting 2014). The disappearance of its tax base is the key reason for the bankruptcy of Detroit, but three other issues accelerated the city's bankruptcy:

Michigan's System for Supporting Local Government

In 1909 Michigan adopted a system of local government that was appropriate for the pre-automobile era when many people lived, worked, and shopped in their own municipality. But that system is not suitable for the modern era. And it is not a system that can adjust to population stagnation and decline. The Michigan Home Rule Law made it easy for townships, villages, and other population clusters to form their own highly independent governments. It gave them great power to tax, assume debts, and manage their own responsibilities, such as zoning, policing, fire protection, and economic development. It provided localities with no incentives to cooperate with neighboring governments. With few exceptions, the Home Rule Law made annexations and mergers difficult.

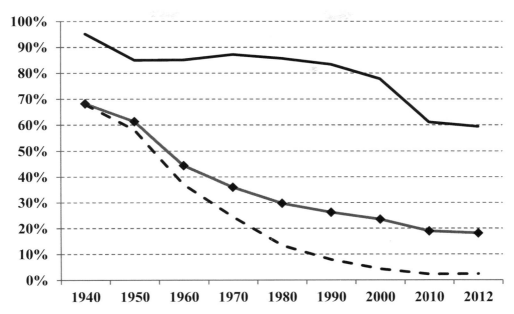

Figure 6.1. Percent of Metropolitan Detroit Population Living in the City of Detroit: 1940 to 2012.

Figure 6.1 considers the three-county Detroit metropolis: Macomb, Oakland, and Wayne counties. It reports the percent of the metropolitan population living in the City of Detroit. At the outset of World War II, the suburban population was substantial, but two-thirds of metropolitan residents resided in the city. By 1955, the suburban population was as large as the city's. By 2012, only 18 percent of metropolitan residents had a Detroit home address.

Local governance became a metropolitan issue in the years after World War II. By the 1960s, Detroit was surrounded by 124 suburban governments. No longer were municipalities local places where people worked, shopped, lived, worshiped, and raised their children. Most residents traveled throughout the metropolis daily with little attention to corporate limits. A public transportation system, you might think, would be designed to serve city and suburban residents. Parks in one part of the metropolis might attract visitors from a wide area. Economic development, land use, and environment are certainly dealt with best at the metropolitan or regional level, but that seldom happens in Michigan. School districts would be more efficient and less costly if they served more than one small suburb where the district enrollment might be less than one thousand. But Michigan's Home Rule Law precludes regional solutions to regional problems. Instead, great competition emerged in metropolitan Detroit: the suburbs against the city and individual suburbs against each other. When it came to offering incentives to residential developers or offering sites for new factories and warehouses, Detroit did not fare well in competition with the suburbs, where land was much more available.

By the 1950s, urban officials and planners across the nation understood the rapid growth of the suburbs and the diminishing resources of older cities. In numerous states, legislatures allowed cities to annex outlying land so that their tax base could increase. Detroit annexed no land since 1926, so the city missed out on the tremendous

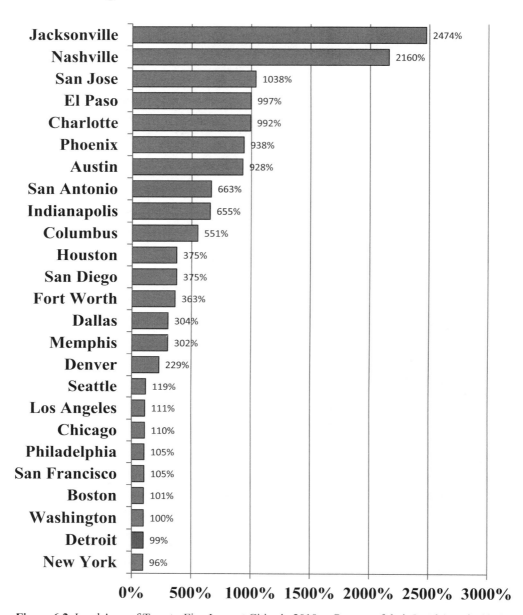

Figure 6.2. Land Area of Twenty-Five Largest Cities in 2010 as Percent of their Land Area in 1950.

population and economic growth that occurred in southeast Michigan from the 1940s through the 1970s.

Figure 6.2 presents information about the land area of the twenty-five largest cities. It shows the city's land area in 2010 as a percent of its land area in 1950. Detroit, the fourth-largest city in 1950, fell to rank eighteen in 2010, now surpassed by seven Southern, four Western, and three Midwestern cities. A major reason is that Detroit did not annex any outlying land. Jacksonville, at present, is twenty-five times bigger than it was in 1950; Nashville twenty-two times bigger in land area, and San Jose ten times bigger. If the City of Detroit had annexed as much outlying area as Columbus or Indianapolis, its population would probably be close to two million rather than the 688,000 estimated for 2013, and the city would not be bankrupt. Similarly, if the state government, in the 1950s, had realized that economic development, transportation, environmental protection, education, and parks were regional issues and established authorities whose scope spanned metropolitan Detroit, the city would not be in bankruptcy court.

The Continuing Legacy of Racial Conflict and Racial Disparities

No city has been as riven by race as Detroit. It is the only place where federal troops have been dispatched to the streets four times to stop blacks and whites from killing each other: twice in the nineteenth century (Frost 2007, Katzman 1973) and twice in the twentieth (Shogan and Craig 1964, Fine 1989). During World War I—for the first time—thousands of southern African Americans migrated to Detroit for defense-industry jobs. Jim Crow had not been the rule in Detroit, but such policies quickly developed and were strictly enforced (Zunz 1982, Boyle 2005). Residential segregation—and the school segregation that followed—were major issues. In Detroit, intimidation, real-estate marketing practices, and restrictive covenants restricted blacks to specific neighborhoods: one on the East Side and another on the West Side.

World War II greatly heightened racial conflict. The first major racial confrontation of World War II—in February 1942—involved the Sojourner Truth Housing Complex in northern Detroit, a project built for blacks. Whites forcefully prevented blacks from living there for several months (Jenkins 1991). President Roosevelt's 1941 Executive Order #8802 mandated that blacks and whites be treated similarly in defense industry employment, an order that triggered a series of bitter racial hate strikes in Detroit's factories—white workers struck if blacks were promoted and blacks workers struck if they were not (Meier and Rudwick 1979). This was one of many factors leading to the bloodiest racial confrontation of World War II: the June 1943 violence that was put down when President Roosevelt dispatched the Fifth Army—but 34 Detroit residents lost their lives (Shogan and Craig 1964).

No city experienced as much and as prolonged racial conflict in the post-World War II years as did Detroit. Many whites feared that the arrival of blacks in their neighborhoods would decimate the value of the property, increase crime, destroy the quality of schools, and put wives and daughters at risk of violence. As Thomas Sugrue (1996) vividly describes, whites sought to preserve the racial homogeneity of their neighborhoods using a variety of strategies to make sure no blacks entered. But the full employment and high wages of World War II meant that many African Americans had the resources to secure more attractive housing than in the neighborhoods where they were confined. Detroit became a center for block busting: real estate brokers frightening whites to sell their properties for low prices, then marketing the same property to African Americans for a higher price. Many whites grew tired of their struggle to maintain neighborhood homogeneity and learned that federal housing policies provided them with an opportunity: higher quality homes in the suburbs, where real estate practices and other techniques ensured that all their neighbors would be whites (Jackson 1985).

Thus began the biggest demographic change in Michigan's recent history. The white population of the City of Detroit fell by 360,000 in the 1950s, by 340,000 in the 1960s and by 425,000 in the 1970s. More than 1.5 million whites lived in Detroit in 1950; the Census Bureau estimates that in 2013 only 62,000 whites resided in the city. Orville Hubbard, who served as mayor of Dearborn from 1942 to 1978, became a national symbol of suburban hostility to the entry of blacks (Good 1989, Freund 2007). L. Brooks Patterson, who became Oakland's County Prosecutor in 1976 and has served as the county's chief executive since 1992, articulately and forcefully argued that the interests of the suburban ring not only differed from those of the city but often conflicted sharply with those of the black dominated city (Williams 2014).

The soul music radio stations of the 1960s played the tune "Chocolate City, Vanilla Suburbs," one that celebrated blacks taking control of the nation's biggest cities. No city illustrated that divide more clearly than Detroit. By 2000, African Americans made up 83 percent of the population of the city, but only 7 percent of the suburban ring. The city-suburban divide in the Detroit area was largely a black-white divide. Michigan's Home Rule Law combined with the area's long legacy of racial hostility to prevent the city and suburbs from cooperating to solve metropolitan challenges.

The Misjudgments and Corruption of Detroit's Leaders

Detroit officials made many decisions that eventually hastened bankruptcy. Recognizing the disappearance of the tax base, they initiated new taxes and raised traditional ones, making the city a less attractive place to live or do business. Detroit was the first Michigan city to impose an income tax: 3 percent in 1963. It is the only city with a 5 percent tax on all utility bills. Property-tax rates were raised to the highest levels permitted by state law. Also, it is the only Michigan city to gain a large fraction of its general funds revenue from casino gambling.

Given the financial crisis, city leaders reduced municipal services. And, unable to offer city workers wage increases, they promised extensive retirement and fringe benefits. Bankruptcy proved that those promises could not be kept. As the tax base shrunk in recent years, the city has borrowed tremendous amounts of funds to sustain its operation using traditional and innovative financial instruments. Once again, it turned out that the city lacked the resources to pay these obligations. The city gained a reputation for poorly administering its basic functions due, at least in part, to the absence of tax revenues. The water and sewerage system, unable to satisfy environmental regulations, was superintended by federal judges from 1977 through 2013. The police department had a reputation for the excessive use of force and civil rights violations. The Department of Justice began an investigation in 2000 and then took over supervision of the department in 2003, supervision that continues. Because of financial mismanagement, the federal Department of Housing and Urban Development took control of city's Housing Commission in 2005. The State of Michigan took over control of the city's schools in 1999, returned them to local control in 2005, and then took them over again in 2008.

Quite a few elected and appointed officials have gone to jail. Phillip Hart, chief of police while Coleman Young served as mayor, was convicted of stealing $2.6 million from the city and sentenced to ten years. Kwame Kilpatrick, mayor from 2003 to 2008, briefly benefited from a "Pay to Play" scheme. After six years of litigation, thirty-four were convicted—eighteen city officials and sixteen private individuals. Mayor Kilpatrick is now serving a twenty-eight-year sentence (Schaffer 2013, Yaccino 2013). Monica Conyers, who served as president pro-tem of Detroit's Common Council in 2008 and 2009, was sentenced to thirty-seven months for her role in steering municipal contracts (White 2010). Building inspectors and officials from the school district, the water and sewerage system, and the city's pension funds have recently been convicted of white-collar crimes.

And yet, Detroit's bankruptcy is not the result of the venal behavior of its officials. Given the collapse of the tax base, perhaps no mayor could have worked the miracle needed to prevent bankruptcy. But, from the perspective of 2014, it is clear that many Detroit officials contributed to the image that the city could not manage its own finances and that state and federal funds flowing to Detroit were often poorly managed.

The Bankruptcy Process in Detroit

Municipalities and school district are chartered by the State of Michigan. Thus the state, in some sense, is responsible for their operation, but the Home Rule Law gives them great autonomy. Michigan's population and economic base grew rapidly from the end of the Depression until the 1970s. While rates of growth varied from one place to another, most municipalities could count on annual increases in tax revenue so even if their infrastructures were antiquated and their bureaucracies inefficient, the city remained solvent.

The OPEC oil boycott of 1973 marked an important turning point in the history of the state. Since then, the population and the number of jobs have grown slowly. As the nation shifted from an industrial to a knowledge-based economy, Michigan fell behind. For instance, from 1970 to 2013, the nation population increased by 56 percent; Michigan's by only 11 percent. Across the nation, the number of jobs nationally rose by 90 percent from 1970 to 2013; in Michigan, only 34 percent. Michigan's cities and school districts—especially those whose tax base was closely linked to manufacturing—faced dire financial straits for the first time since the Depression.

Hamtramck—a small municipality surrounded by Detroit—approached insolvency in 1988, leading the state legislature to enact an Emergency Financial Manager law. The state treasurer was obligated to assess the financial status of Michigan cities and school districts. If the city or district seemed destined to soon run out of funds, the treasurer brought the crisis to the attention of the governor. If the governor concurred that there was a problem, the treasurer was to negotiate a consent agreement with the elected officials of the city or school district. Presumably, they would agree to drastically cut spending to bring expenditures in line with revenues primarily by laying off employees, cutting salaries, reducing services, and delaying payments to creditors. If the troubled city or school district complied with the consent decree and balanced its books, state supervision ended. If the state treasurer determined that, after six months, little or no progress was made by the city or school district, he or she was to consult with the governor. If the governor agreed, he or she could appoint an emergency financial manager who would take over operation of the city or school district. Mayors, city councils, and school boards had only such power as those delegated to them by the governor's emergency manager. The emergency manager had the authority to abrogate almost all contracts and to sell assets in order to pay debts and keep the city or school district in operation. However, the emergency manager was obligated to pay bonded indebtedness and could not, on his or her own, impose new taxes. When the emergency manager and governor agreed that the city or school district was financially secure, the manager's appointment would end (www.michigan. gov/treasury/0,1607,7-121-1751_51556-201116--,00.html).

In the fifteen years before Detroit's bankruptcy, emergency managers were appointed for eight cities and three school districts. Interestingly, all but one of them were either majority black locations or had proportions of African American residents far about the state's average. After the recession of 2008, this led to a decrease of employment in Michigan that was greater than any other state, local governments and school districts faced the challenge of sharply reducing their budgets, a task that officials find challenging since it means laying off police officers and firefighters, or closing schools and increasing class sizes. Local governments adapted to the loss of tax revenue and the number of their workers in Michigan fell by 30 percent from 2005 to 2012—a loss of 98,000 jobs. In 2012, State Treasurer Dillon reported to Governor Snyder that the City of Detroit would likely soon run out of funds to pay its employees and debts because of the sharp drop in the city's tax receipts. A consent agreement was worked out and Common Council took the traditional steps in such circumstance. For example, wages of city workers were cut 10 percent and then frozen, capital expenditures were deferred and public services curtailed. The city, however, continued to pay debt service.

In Michigan, it is relatively easy for citizens to put propositions on the ballot for statewide votes, such as a proposition to overturn a law enacted by the legislature. Many municipal workers, teachers and school administrators questioned the wisdom of the Emergency Manager Law since such managers, typically, began by terminating employees, reducing wages, and eliminating fringe benefits. Others raised the issue of democratic representation since an emergency financial manager supplanted the officials that local voters had chosen. Civil rights activists were aware that the emergency financial manager law had been, almost exclusively, applied to cities and school districts with many African Americans and that if Detroit were to have such a manager, the majority of Michigan blacks would have no say over their local government.

In November 2012, Michigan voters—by a 53 percent to 47 percent margin—removed the Emergency Manager Law (ballotpedia.org/). That did not, however, address the problem of local government insolvency. A lame-duck legislature in December 2012 enacted a new emergency manager law that closely resembled the one the voters rejected. This one contained provisions making it somewhat more difficult for an emergency manager to sell assets and included a provision that, after eighteen months, a city council or school board could, by a two-thirds vote, oust the governor's emergency manager. Presumably, the governor would then appoint a new manager. A city or school district was also given the option of bankruptcy rather than an emergency manager. The new law was passed as an appropriations bill, which meant that Michigan voters could not vote it off the books. Both the former and new Emergency Manager Law focus exclusively on fiscal issues. They do not specify any minimum level of city or school-district services.

In early 2013, the state treasurer reported to the governor that Detroit was not making satisfactory progress with its consent decree. Mayor Bing and the Common Council failed to reduce wages or cut services rapidly enough nor did they restructure debt. Governor Snyder agreed and appointed Kevyn Orr to take over the City of Detroit less than a week after the new law went into effect. Orr is a bankruptcy lawyer who played important roles in the federal government's support of the bankrupt Chrysler Corporation and its subsequent sale to Fiat. He holds degrees from the University of Michigan and attended their law school, where Governor Snyder was a classmate.

Kevyn Orr examined the revenues, expenses, and obligations of Detroit and concluded that there was no way to solve the financial problems. Governor Snyder concurred that the city should file for bankruptcy so that it could be freed from its obligations, including those to bond holders and pensioners. Kevyn Orr requested Chapter 9 bankruptcy protection from the federal bankruptcy court in July. Judge Steven Rhodes held hearings about the city's eligibility for bankruptcy. Orr stressed the city's lack of resources, its indebtedness, and its inability to pay for requisite city services. Creditors—especially bond holders and pensioners—stressed that Orr was greatly overestimating debts and underestimating city-owned assets that might be sold, particularly art works in the Detroit Institute of Art. Others challenged the figures Orr presented and stressed the importance of the state cut in revenue sharing payments to Detroit (Turbeville 2013). In October 2013, Judge Rhodes approved the bankruptcy.

Chapter 9 bankruptcy is designed for cities. It is unlike Chapter 11 bankruptcy, in which a potentially profitable corporation is freed of its debts and then reorganized so that it might continue to operate. It is also unlike Chapter 7 bankruptcy, in which a firm goes out of business and its assets are sold. Chapter 9 assumes that the municipality will continue to function during and after the bankruptcy. The specified process calls for the bankrupt city to negotiate with debtors to reach a mutually agreeable solution. Both assets and revenue streams are to be maintained so that the city can function both during and after the bankruptcy process. Bankruptcy Judge Rhodes appointed Gerald Rosen, senior federal judge for the Eastern District of Michigan, as the lead negotiator. Emergency Manager Orr was obligated to draft what is known as a Plan of Adjustment, which might or might not be approved by the bankruptcy judge. This is a document that specifies what amounts will be paid to debtors, what are the assets and revenues of the city and how post-bankruptcy financial stability will be assured.

Kevyn Orr found city debts approaching twenty billion dollars and enumerated them, roughly, as follows:

- $ 6.4 billion in obligations backed by city revenue generating enterprises, primarily the Detroit Department of Water and Sewerage;
- $6 billion approximately for other post-employment benefits for city employees (Scorsone 2013);
- $3.5 billion in underfunded liability for the city's two pension funds, one for uniformed employees and one for other city employees;
- $1.4 billion for bonds issued to fund the city's pension funds;
- $650 million in unsecured municipal debt;
- $480 million in secured municipal debt;
- $345 million derivative and SWAP debts owed to banks results from a 2005 attempt to support pension funds.
- $300 million other unsecured debts to local firms, individuals and other debtors.

At the start of the negotiations process in 2013, many assumed that Detroit had numerous valuable assets that might be sold to pay debts and pension obligations: a water and sewerage system that served most of southeast Michigan, a system for distributing electricity in the downtown area, three museums other than the art gallery, an incinerator that generated power, numerous large parks, a municipal airport and thousands of parcels throughout the city, many of them obtained as a result of foreclosure for nonpayment of property taxes. Kevyn Orr took the city's most attractive park, Belle Isle, off the table by renting it to the state for thirty years. Other city-owned assets such as the Zoo, the Cobo Hall Convention Center, and the Eastern Market had, in previous years, been transferred to public-private nonprofits, freeing the city from making capital investments in them.

It became clear that the only city asset that could be sold quickly to raise funds were the artworks in the Detroit Institute of Art. That organization faced a financial crisis in 1919. Detroit, at that time, was prospering so the trustees of the art gallery gave their holdings to the city in return for a generous annual stipend, monies that were paid until the early 1970s. The most vocal parties in the early discussion were spokespersons for the two major funds that provided pensions for city workers and those who wished to preserve the city's art. Spokespersons for current and retired employees asserted that a clause in Michigan's constitutions meant that pensions must be paid even if a city or school district were bankrupt. Kevyn Orr, Judge Rhodes, and Governor Snyder did not strongly endorse that idea but suggested that cutting pensions to current retirees should be a last resort.

Kevyn Orr had the art auction firm Christies assess that portion of the art unambiguously owned by the city. They estimated that it had a current retail value of between $454 million and $867 million (Stryker 2013). Orr—apparently with the concurrence of the bankruptcy judge—argued that there was no provision in the bankruptcy law that required the sale of a city's assets. At this point, the lead negotiator, Judge Rosen, orchestrated a "Grand Bargain" that would simultaneously protect pensions and save the art. Using his influence, he got an agreement where prosperous foundations linked to Detroit—Ford, Kellogg, Kresge, Mott, and Skillman—would provide $366 million, the State of Michigan, $350 million, while the Detroit Institute of Art would raise $100 million over twenty years. These monies would be transferred to the pension trust funds, while the art and the Gallery would be transferred to a nonprofit organization. If this Grand Bargain is approved in the bankruptcy proceedings, the pensions of uniformed officers will be paid at 100 percent for the next ten years, with 1 percent annual increments. The pensions of other city workers will be paid at 95 percent with no cost-of-living adjustments. Current and future pensioners voted on this and overwhelmingly accepted it. This settlement appears to put off litigation about whether or not the Michigan constitution protects civil service pensions.

Emergency manager Orr's final Plan of Adjustment calls for reducing the city's debt to $7 billion while reserving $1.4 billion for investments in the city in the next decade. These investments will largely be devoted to three expenditures: higher wages and more resources, including personnel for the fire and police departments; new computers and information technology; and the demolishment or deconstruction of some of Detroit's 85,000 blighted structures. A summary of the proposed debt resolution is shown below:

Kevyn Orr's Revised Plan for City of Detroit Unsecured Debts

	Pre-Bankruptcy	Post-Bankruptcy
Unfunded Pensions	4.3 billion	1.4 billion
Other Post-employment	4.3 billion	450 million
Certificate Debt for Pensions	1.5 billion	162 million
General Obligation Bonds	552 million	397 million
SWAPS	290 million	85 million
Misc. Unsecured Debt	184 million	21 million
Total	8.9 billion	2.6 billion

This Plan of Adjustment was submitted to Bankruptcy Judge Rhodes and, on September 2, 2014, the bankruptcy trial began. Judge Rhodes must decide whether the Plan of Adjustment Kevyn Orr submitted is equitable to those debtors who did not negotiate a settlement and whether it reserves sufficient funds for Detroit to function well after bankruptcy. Presumably, this trial will reach its conclusion late in November 2014. Judge Rhodes has the authority to "cram down" any settlements that he thinks are needed and are consistent with federal law. He may also reduce settlements to reserve more funds for the city's future operations.

Most debtors settled with Detroit before the start of the trial. But not all did so. Many of Detroit's bonds were sold to hedge funds and to German banks. Those banks and funds bought insurance on their bonds so the two most adversarial parties at the bankruptcy trial were Snycora and Financial Guarantee Insurance Company, two firms that might lose as much as about $1.7 billion since Kevyn Orr originally proposed to settle with bond holders for about six cents on the dollar. After the trial began, Snycora negotiated a settlement. They will have a profitable contract to operate—but not own—the Detroit-Windsor tunnel, will operate a major downtown parking facility and will have the option to purchase—at a discount—valuable city-owned real estate, including some on the riverfront. It seems likely that the other insurance firm will work out a similar deal in which some city-owned assets, including land, will be transferred to them so that they may be developed for commercial purposes.

Detroit's Bankruptcy: Who Won and Who Lost

Winners

- Michigan taxpayers. After Orange County went into bankruptcy in 1993, California municipalities found they had to pay much higher interest rates in the bond market. A messy and prolonged Detroit bankruptcy would, likely, have raised debt service rates for Michigan cities and school districts.
- Detroit pensioners. Many feared there would be drastic cuts in pensions. Kevyn Orr mentioned a figure of 30 percent early in the proceedings.
- Detroit and Michigan residents who will be able to continue to visit the Detroit Institute of Art.

- Detroit residents and those who do business or work in the city. If the Plan of Adjustment provides $140 million per year for improvements in the city, the quality of life may improve and Detroit may once again provide adequate municipal services.

Losers

- Retired city employees. While pensions are protected, other retirement benefits will be paid about ten cents on the dollar. The city promised to provide health insurance for early retirees and their families, supplemental insurance for Medicare, life insurance as well as vision and dental coverage. It also supported a generous annuity program. The Plan of Adjustment established a Trust Fund with about 10 percent of what would be needed to fund what was promised.
- Persons and firms in debt to the city. The negotiated settlements were small, most of them, I believe, about twenty cents on the dollar.
- Some bond holders.
- The insurance companies that guaranteed bond payment, although they may receive control of assets from the city, assets that may have sharply increasing value if Detroit is revitalized.
- City residents, who have lost, not ownership, but control of the city's revenue generating assets.
- Elected officials of Detroit since the State of Michigan established a Financial Stabilization Board that will superintend city budgets well into the indefinite future.
- Past and current city employees who either lost their jobs or saw their pay and benefits reduced.

Detroit after Bankruptcy

Detroit became the country's most negatively stereotyped city after the 1967 riots. Coffee-table "ruin porn" books were published with glossy photographs of abandoned homes, derelict parks filled with litter, and dilapidated factories that once produced thousands of cars every day (Moore 2010, Taubman 2011). Detroit became known for its high crime rates, especially murder. Since the city approached bankruptcy, its boosters—with considerable success—promoted a different image. They stressed the many restored buildings in downtown Detroit, the expansion of major hospitals, the rise of information technology employment, and the modest influx of population to a few increasingly upscale locations. Kurt Metzger, who ran the Data Driven Detroit organization, describes a "Tale of Two Cities." Downtown, Midtown, and the east waterfront are thriving and may compare favorably to other redeveloping areas in Rust Belt cities. And then there is the other Detroit: many neighborhoods characterized by urban decadence and disinvestment. The most informative way to think about the post-bankruptcy period is to focus on the following three topics.

Jobs and Capital Investments in Detroit

The future of Michigan, metropolitan Detroit, and the city depend, more than anything else, upon employment trends. Employers pay property taxes on their businesses, and their workers pay city income taxes. In recent years, those two sources accounted for more than 60 percent of the city's General Fund Revenues (Citizens Research Council 2013: Chart 18). Employment in the city reached a recent peak of 368,000 in 1999, fell to a low of 274,000 in 2011, and then rebounded a bit to 285,000 in summer 2014 (US Bureau of Labor Statistics 2014a).

There are optimistic signs. Marathon Oil invested $2.2 million to modernize their refinery in southwest Detroit and is now the largest payer of property taxes. The vehicle manufacturers invested substantially in modernizing their plants in and around Detroit. General Motors, since its bankruptcy, spent more than $350 million on its Hamtramck plant that straddles the city's border. Ford Motor has updated their Dearborn Assembly plant (where F-150s are assembled), as well as their nearby Flat Rock plant and Wayne assembly plants. In Detroit, Fiat-Chrysler made major investments in their Mack Avenue engine plants and their Jefferson North plant, where 35,000 Jeep Cherokees and Dodge Durango are assembled every month. The share of North American vehicle production occurring in the Detroit area is growing. The two basic steel mills in the Detroit area have both been modernized and are now more efficient and environmentally acceptable than in the past.

Meanwhile, Detroit Medical Center, in 2010, announced an $800 million dollar expansion of its huge medical campus near downtown and, two weeks later, Henry Ford Medical Center announced an expenditure of $500 million to build a new hospital campus just across Grand Boulevard from their present campus. Similarly, Wayne State University, home of the nation's largest medical school, continues to build new structures near their campus. Blue Cross-Blue Shield transferred several thousand employees from suburban offices to the Renaissance Center, and, in 2012, for the first time, that complex was fully utilized.

Dan Gilbert, chief officer of the Quicken Loans firm, also shifted his employees from the suburbs to the central business district of Detroit. He then purchased or took options on sixty downtown buildings containing more than eight million square feet of space: offices, commercial buildings, a casino, parking decks and a hotel (Gallagher 2014). He aims to attract firms and entrepreneurs developing the information technologies and computers that will make our vehicles safer and more efficient. In 2014, he began construction of a server farm near downtown. Now, more so than in the past, numerous programs in Detroit promote innovation and entrepreneurship. Space and the requisite support is available for innovative people, be they creative artists, software developers, or people working to develop strategies to deconstruct—rather than demolish—homes. The area between Midtown and New Center has been branded as Techtown since it provides space and assistance to start-up companies, primarily those linked to the vehicle industry. The Pony Ride and The Green Garage are smaller-scale efforts to promote local entrepreneurship.

Despite signs of progress, there is a clear recognition that there is a skills mismatch in Detroit. Very many of the rapidly growing occupations require specialized skills and advanced training. One way to summarize the problem is to compare the education attainment of Detroit's current adult population to that of other large cities. (See Figure 6.3.)

In Washington and San Francisco, the majority of adults have four-year college degrees. Austin, Denver, and Boston are not far behind. Detroit is distinctive for the

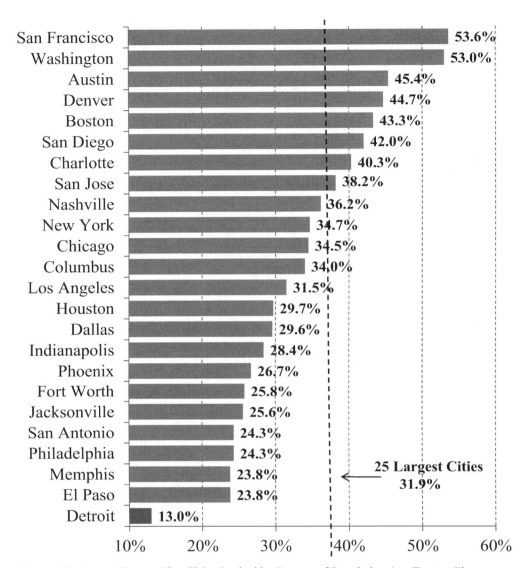

Figure 6.3. Largest Twenty-Five Cities Ranked by Percent of Population Age Twenty-Five and Over with a Four-Year College Degree in 2012.

low proportion of residents with college credentials—just 13 percent or far below the national average of 31 percent. But efforts are being made to improve the city's schools. The state has taken them over twice recently and there are now more state supported charter schools in Detroit than traditional public schools. Detroit parents have a wide array of choices. The New Economic Initiative for Southeast Michigan—an organization funded at $100 million by contributions from the Fisher, Ford, Kellogg, Kresge, Mott, Skillman, and other foundations—aims to reawaken and leverage creative entrepreneurial activities in the Detroit area to produce a diverse economy that will benefit all residents. One of its major aims is the training of more

local residents for the jobs that are becoming available in the increasingly sophisticated vehicle industry.

Perhaps Detroit and the suburbs are now poised for employment growth. The aging
of the Michigan population ensures the growth of medical sector jobs. Downtown
Detroit could become an important international center for the application of information technology to manufacturing. But it is much less certain that there will be a
rapid growth of the traditional blue-collar jobs. In the vehicle and steel industries,
labor force productivity has increased by an average of 4 percent per year for several
decades (US Bureau of Labor Statistics 2014b). This means that, year after year, a
fixed number of workers can produce 4 percent more vehicles. The number of vehicles
assembled in metropolitan Detroit is likely to increase substantially, but the number
of workers may not.

Population Trends and Neighborhoods

The city's revenues depend upon the number of residents and their ability to pay taxes.
Shortly after Mike Duggan became mayor in early 2014, he asked Detroit residents to
stay and suggested that they should judge his administration by whether his policies
stabilized the population. Within six months of taking office, he suggested he would
not run for reelection if the population continued to decline (Dolan 2014). Will the
long-standing pattern of migration away from Detroit continue? The number of white
residents fell 96 percent in the two-generation span from 1950 to 2013; from 1,546,000
to 62,000. Until the 1990s, most communities in the suburban ring were firmly closed
to black residents but the Open Housing Law of 1968 and whites changing attitudes
about integration have had an effect (Farley 2011). The black population of Detroit,
in 2013, is 229,000 smaller than it was in 2000, a decline of 30 percent. Although a
few suburban communities are predominantly black, African Americans are widely
distributed throughout the suburban ring, even in those places that once had reputations
for hostility to blacks including Dearborn and Warren. Suburbs have strong motiva-
tions to maintain their population size since it is linked to Michigan's revenue sharing.

Retaining current residents and attracting new ones depends upon having appealing neighborhoods. There are elegant upscale neighborhoods in Detroit—the Berry
Subdivision, Indian Village, North Rosedale Park, Palmer Woods, Sherwood Forest,
and the University District—where extremely attractive homes may be purchased
for reasonable sums. Presumably, their future is secure. Other neighborhoods with
architecturally appealing homes were once on the cusp of sliding into decline but their
residents and investors made great efforts and turned around their trajectory. They are
now charming neighborhoods appealing, perhaps, to the younger professionals who
prefer city living. This includes the Corktown, East Canfield, East Kirby, West Village, and Woodbridge Historic Districts. Some other neighborhoods with a potentially
attractive housing stock may join this list such as Detroit's North End, the Atkinson
Avenue Historic District, and Palmer Park Apartment House Historic District.

Those neighborhoods are exceptions. Most of Detroit's current housing stock was
built to serve as the homes of workingmen and their families. Many homes were
located close to rail lines and factories. They are small structures on tiny plots and

lack the amenities that most middle-class people seek: a bedroom for each family member, many bathrooms, a modern, spacious kitchen, a two-car garage, efficient heating and cooling, and enough green space around the home so that you do not hear your neighbors. The quality of life in such neighborhoods will be crucial in determining whether their populations stabilize (Helms and Guillen 2014). There are signs of improvement. In 2013, just over one-half of the city's streetlights worked. Shortly after taking their offices, Kevyn Orr and Mayor Duggan collaborated upon a program whereby the city's utility tax will fund bonds to pay for improvements in lights. By the fall of 2014, many neighborhoods once again had streetlights. A similar story can be told with respect to law enforcement. The City of Detroit had seven different police chiefs in the five years before the arrival of the Emergency Manager. Lacking resources to purchase new equipment, local entrepreneurs Dan Gilbert and Roger Penske raised funds in 2013 to purchase 100 new patrol cars and twenty-three EMS vehicles that were loaned to the city. Kevyn Orr recruited a former Detroit police officer who had been laid off in 1980 but then went on to become chief of police in Portland, Maine, and Cincinnati. The new chief adopted new strategies of policing and reported, in the fall of 2014, that violent crimes had fallen 8 percent and property crime by 21 percent since 2013 (City of Detroit 2014). Murders in Detroit peaked at 714 in 1974 but there may be fewer than 300 in 2014.

To maintain tax revenue, Detroit maintained assessed values on many or most residences that were unrealistically high. Mayor Duggan instituted a review of assessments that will likely reduce property taxes by about 15 percent—a cut to city revenues but an incentive for residents to remain in the city. More importantly, the city instituted new Detroit Land Bank policies. The city, as a result of foreclosures, owns approximately thirty thousand residential properties. Traditionally, they had been sold to the highest bidder, often a speculator who made no investments in the property and held on to it for three years without paying property taxes (Lynch and MacDonald 2014). The Detroit Land Bank developed a modern website to feature foreclosed properties in neighborhoods that have potential for renovation. This includes East English Village and the North End districts. Importantly, bidding is done online, and speculators are excluded, since a purchaser must make a down payment immediately, obtain a mortgage within thirty days, and bring the property up to code within months. Assistance is provided to winning bidders by linking them to banks that will make loans on such properties (Haimerl 2014).

An effort is underway to remove blight in Detroit. In 2013, the city—with assistance from the federal government—contracted local information tech entrepreneurs to visit and take pictures of all 378,000 land parcels with their 264,000 structures in the city. Seventy-eight thousand structures were categorized as blight. The report suggested that about 85 to 90 percent of those structures needed to be demolished or deconstructed at a cost of about $800 million (Detroit Blight Removal Task Force Plan 2014). The federal government made $152 million available to begin the process.

There are many active groups and individuals with innovative ideas about how to revitalized troubled neighborhoods (Gallagher 2010, 2013). Detroit financier John Hantz secured title to several hundred parcels on the East Side and planted what will become the nation's largest urban forest. In the Morningside and Hubbard Richard neighborhoods, Habitat for Humanity is constructing several hundred moderately priced homes. A number of artists, urban farm advocates and imaginative young people are seeking to improve the quality of life in the remote Morningside neighborhood. The Write-a-House endeavor is purchasing foreclosed homes, rehabbing them and making them available to poets and writers who win a competition to spend a year in Detroit creating. The Marathon Oil Company offered above-market prices to about three hundred homeowners in the Oakman Heights neighborhood that was contiguous to their refinery. More than 85 percent accepted the offer so a large green space replaced a working class neighborhood. More homes in southwest Detroit will be razed when the New International Trade Crossing Bridge is built, a project that may bring warehouses and a truck-train transfer terminal to southwest Detroit. Peruvian investor Fernando Palazuelo purchased the nation's iconic industrial ruin in 2013: the former Packard Plant on East Grand Boulevard that once included almost three million square feet of space in forty-five buildings. He intends to invest $500 million in the next decade to renovate the buildings for a variety of uses (Muller 2014). Perhaps these many endeavors will lead to the renewal of neighborhoods throughout the city to complement the growth now occurring in Downtown, Midtown, and the East Waterfront.

Governance

Along with the population, the city's government has been greatly downsized in recent decades. Facilities that the city once supported have been transferred to nonprofits or other governmental agencies. Other city services that have been contracted to for profit or nonprofit groups include the collection of trash, public health, and city-planning activities. Following bankruptcy, city revenues may be directly focused upon basic services. The Plan of Adjustment, if it is approved by Bankruptcy Judge Rhodes, will provide substantial funds to improve city services and remove blight.

Will the city's General Fund Tax revenues increase sufficiently in the future to support governmental services for a population of 688,000 spread across 138 square miles? Property-tax revenues may decline as assessments are made realistic, or they could increase if there is an influx of population and commercial activity. In recent years, Detroit has obtained as much as one-quarter of its revenue from gambling taxes (Citizens Research Council 2013: Chart 18). This revenue source appears to be slowly declining. Income tax is another major revenue generator. Detroit is one of twenty-one Michigan cities with such a tax, and some Detroit residents who work in the suburbs apparently avoid paying this tax, costing the city about $35 million annually. Governor Snyder proposed merging municipal income-tax collecting with the state income tax, presumably leading to increased revenue for Detroit. It is difficult to imagine new sources of tax revenue for the city, any increases in their already elevated tax levels, or a large new flow of state funds to the city.

Detroit is still surrounded by more than a hundred independent and competitive suburbs. But changing attitudes and, perhaps, the demographic shift such that many metropolitan blacks now live in the ring may have beneficial consequences. In 2012, suburban voters approved a 0.2 mill property tax increase to support the Detroit Institute of Art (Cohen 2012). After twenty-six attempts to enact laws that would create a Regional Transit Agency, the Michigan Legislature did so in 2013. The bankruptcy means that, unlike the past, the city and suburbs will have to cooperate on water and sewerage issues.

There are many optimistic developments. Efforts to portray Detroit positively as a place of opportunity for creative innovators may be succeeding. A realist, nevertheless, will stress two fundamental issues that confront the city's revival: one is governmental and the other racial. The system of financing local government remains inappropriate. Since Detroit entered bankruptcy, three suburbs—Inkster, Lincoln Park, and Royal Oak Township—have either had emergency managers appointed or signed consent agreement to avoid one. As populations and tax bases contract, more cities will be unable to pay their bills. In March 1993, public schools in Kalkaska County ran out of funds and closed. The state promptly switched away from supporting local schools by taxing local property. Instead, funds collected at the state level—sales taxes, property transfer fees, and an assessment on commercial properties—are distributed to school districts on the basis of enrollment. These state-generated funds pay for the operation of local public schools (Courant and Loeb 1997). A similar system to support local governments should be considered. Collecting tax revenue at the state level and distributing it to municipalities on their basis of their population and other needs would be much more equitable and efficiently than the present system. And, it would likely reduce many local property taxes and prevent more bankruptcies.

The Civil Rights Revolution has had beneficial effects in Michigan. Detroit's suburban ring has been peacefully integrated and if middle-class blacks continue to leave Detroit for the suburbs at current rates, it is possible that the majority of metropolitan Detroit's African Americans will be suburbanites at the next census date. Interracial marriages are more common than in the past and blacks are now represented at all levels of the occupational hierarchy. Detroit, where the electorate was 82 percent black, elected a white man as their mayor in 2013.

There has been the emergence, among blacks, of a middle class and a small economic elite since the Civil Rights Revolution. But the economic status of blacks as a group vis-à-vis whites has deteriorated in recent decades. Manufacturing industries once provided the jobs that sustained a reasonably secure and large black middle class. In 1970, 76,000 black men in metropolitan Detroit worked in manufacturing and they had average earnings (in 2012 dollars) of $49,700. By 2012, that was down to 26,000 working in manufacturing and their average earnings had fallen to $44,700. Few new economic opportunities opened up for those who assembled vehicles. As a result, the economic status of African Americans deteriorated. In metropolitan Detroit in 1970, blacks had median household incomes 60 percent those of whites. By 2012, it had declined to 51 percent. In 1970, the black poverty rate of 22 percent was 17 points higher than that of whites. By 2012, poverty in the black community had increased to 34 percent, a rate 24 points higher than the one for whites. To be sure, whites have suffered substantially in the era of industrial restructuring as earnings fell and poverty increased, but they have not suffered as much as African Americans for two reasons. First, the white middle class was less dependent than the black upon the blue-collar industrial jobs that disappeared rapidly. Second, college enrollment rates of young whites ascended much more rapidly than college enrollment rates of blacks.

Detroit remains an overwhelmingly black and impoverished city. If the many innovative efforts to bring jobs to Detroit are successful, if the new training programs can effectively provide skills to Detroit's residents who lack educational credentials, and if the efforts to reform the city's public and charter schools succeed, they may begin to narrow the increasingly wide black-white gaps in educational attainment, earnings and occupational achievement, leading to a more prosperous city.

On June 11, 1805, winds fanned unattended fires of baker John Harvey and a conflagration turned the village into ashes. Local curate Gabriel Richard uttered the words that have served as the city's motto for two centuries: *Speramus meliora, resurgent cineribus.* ("We hope for better things. May they arise from ashes.") Detroit was rebuilt, and in 1950, was, arguably, the most prosperous city in the nation. Perhaps many of the ideas about urban reinvention will prove fruitful and Detroit, one day, may be recognized as the Rust Belt city that most successfully returned to vitality.

Notes

1. The emergency manager has posted all documents pertinent to Detroit's bankruptcy, including the Plans of Adjustment, on the following site: http://www.detroitmi.gov/EmergencyManager.aspx.
2. In 1950, the per capita income of men twenty-one to sixty-four living in Detroit was $31,800 in 2013 dollars; in Washington, $28,900; in San Francisco, $28,800 and in New York, $28,600. Unless otherwise noted, demographic data are from the Public Use Microdata Files from the American Community Survey, the decennial censuses and the Current Population Survey available from the University of Minnesota Population Center (Ruggles, et al. 2010).

References

Boyle, K. (2005). *Arc of Justice: A Saga of Race, Civil Rights and Murder in the Jazz Age*. New York: Henry Holt and Company.

Citizens Research Council of Michigan. (2013). *Detroit City Government Revenues*. Report #382 (April), Lansing: Citizens Research Council of Michigan.

City of Detroit. *Police Department, Crime Statistics*. http://www.detroitmi.gov/DepartmentsandAgencies/PoliceDepartment/CrimeStatistics.aspx.

Cohen, P. (2012). "Suburban Taxpayers Vote to Support Detroit Museum," *New York Times* (August 8).

Courant, P. and S. Loeb. (1997). "Centralization of School Finance in Michigan." *Journal of Policy Analysis and Management* Vol. 16, No. 1, Fall, Pp. 114–136.

Detroit Blight Removal Task Force Plan. (2014). *Every Neighborhood Has a Future . . . and It Doesn't Include Blight*. Detroit.

Dolan, M. (2014). "Mayor Aims to Reverse Detroit Exodus." *Wall Street Journal* (June 22).

Farley, R. (2011). "Black-White Residential Segregation: The Waning of American Apartheid." *Context* Vol. 10, No. 3: Pp. 36–43.

Fine, S. (1989). *Violence in the Model City: The Cavanagh Administration, Race Relations and the Detroit Riot of 1967*. Ann Arbor: University of Michigan Press.

Freund, D. M. P. (2007). *Colored Property: State Policy & White Racial Politics in Suburban America*. Chicago: University of Chicago Press.

Frost, K. S. (2007). *I've Got a Home in Glory Land*. New York: Farrar, Straus and Giroux.

Gallagher, J. (2010). *Reimaging Detroit: Opportunities for Redefining an American City*. Detroit, Wayne State University Press.

———. (2013). *Revolution Detroit: Strategies for Urban Reinvention*. Detroit, Wayne State University Press.

———. (2014). "One Downtown, Two Empires," *Detroit Free Press* (July 27).

Good, D. L (1989). *Orvie: The Dictator of Dearborn: The Rise and Reign of Orville L. Hubbard*. Detroit, Wayne State University Press.

Haimerl, A. (2014). "Will Detroit's Land Bank Auction Build Value for Housing*?*" *Crain's Business Detroit* (June 15).

Helms, M. and J. Guillen. (2014). "'The Change in Detroit is Real': Mayor Mike Duggan Promises Better Parks, Cheaper Insurance in State of City." *Detroit Free Press* (February 26).

Jackson, K. (1985). *Crabgrass Frontier: The Suburbanization of the United States.* New York: Oxford University Press.

Jenkins, B. S. (1991). "Sojourner Truth Housing Riots." In W. W. Hendrickson, ed., *Detroit Perspectives: Crossroads and Turning Points.* Detroit: Wayne State University Press.

Katzman, D. (1973). *Before the Ghetto: Black Detroit in the Nineteenth Century.* Urbana: University of Illinois Press.

Lynch, J. and C. MacDonald. (2014). "$3M bid on bundled Detroit lots." *Detroit News* (October 22).

MacDonald, C. and M. Wilkinson. (2013). "Half of Detroit Property Owners Don't Pay Taxes." *Detroit News* (February 21).

Meier, A. and E. Rudwick. (1979). *Black Detroit and the Rise of the UAW.* New York: Oxford University Press.

Moore, A. (2010). *Detroit Disassembled.* Akron, Oh: Akron Art Museum.

Muller, D. (2014). "Packard Plant project manager: Half Billion Dollar Detroit Redevelopment in Happening" M-Live, http://www.mlive.com/business/detroit/, (October 8).

Oosting, J. (2014). "How Michigan's Revenue Sharing 'Raid" Cost Communities Billions for Local Services," MLIVE (www.mlive.com), (March 30).

Ruggles, S. J., T. Alexander, K. Genadek, R. Goeken, M. B. Schroeder, and M. Sobek. (2010). *Integrated Public Use Microdata Series: Version 5.0* [Machine-readable database]. Minneapolis: University of Minnesota.

Scorsone, E. A. (2013). "Funding the Legacy" The Cost of Municipal Workers' Retirement Benefits to Michigan Communities." (March 14). East Lansing: Michigan State University Extension.

Schaefer, J. (2013). "Kwame Kilpatrick Public Corruption Trial Evidence Revealed." *Detroit Free Press* (March 12).

Shogan, R. and T. Craig. (1964). *The Detroit Race Riot: A Study in Violence.* Philadelphia: Chilton Books.

Stryker, M. (2013). "Did Christie's Put the Right Appraisal on DIA's Art Treasures?" *Detroit Free Press* (December 20).

Sugrue, T. (1996). *The Origins of the Urban Crisis: Race and Inequality in Postwar Detroit.* Princeton: Princeton University Press.

Taubman, J. R. (2011). *Detroit: 138 Square Miles.* Detroit: Museum of Contemporary Art.

Tuberville, W. C. (2013). "The Detroit Bankruptcy," *Demos* (November).

US Bureau of the Census. (1952). *City-County Data Book.* Washington, DC:

US Bureau of Labor Statistics (2014a). Local Area Employment Data, http://www.bls.gov/lau/.

———. (2014b). Productivity Data for Manufacturing Industries, http://data.bls.gov/cgi-bin/dsrv?ip.

White, E. (2010). "Monica Conyers, Wife to John Conyers, Sentenced to 3 Years In Prison for Detroit Bribes." *The Huffington Post* (May 25).

Williams, P. (2014). "Drop Dead Detroit! The suburban kingpin who is thriving off the city's decline." *New Yorker* (January 27).

Yaccino, S. (2013). "Kwame M. Kilpatrick, Former Detroit Mayor, Sentenced to 28 Years in Corruption Case," *The New York Times* (October 10).

Zunz, O. (1982). *The Changing Face of Inequality: Urbanization, Industrial Development, and Immigrants to Detroit: 1880–1920.* Chicago: University of Chicago Press.

7

Democracy vs. Efficiency in Detroit

John Gallagher

In his pre-World War II heyday, the fascist dictator Benito Mussolini boasted (falsely, as it turned out) that he had made the notoriously inefficient Italian trains run on schedule. Few were impressed. Even if true, critics scoffed, efficiency of operations is at best just one test of a free society and not the most important one. Democracy, critics then and now said, means more than making the trains run on time.

The notion that improved efficiency of municipal operations never trumps the imperatives of democracy has been put to the test in recent years in the city of Detroit. This chronically underperforming city has seen remarkable improvements in efficiency of its municipal operations in recent years, but these have come only with a diminishing of local democratic oversight and control. The city's woefully debt-burdened balance sheet was being scrubbed clean in a municipal bankruptcy court overseen by a federal judge. Chronically inefficient city departments are posting better performances, but only after being taken over by an emergency manager appointed by the governor over the strenuous opposition of local Detroit officials. Multiple other city operations, from the city's convention center to its farmers market, are showing remarkable turnarounds in their efficiency and performances, but only after being spun off into a series of nonprofit public authorities and conservancies away from direct daily city control.

It is the purpose of this paper to examine the trade-offs involved and to draw some conclusions about when, if ever, it is acceptable to silence the peoples' voice as a cost of delivering better services. Ultimately, this paper finds that sometimes it is indeed necessary to bypass locally elected officials who are unable or unwilling to deliver the services that citizens deserve. However, bypassing locally elected officials can and should only be done within the confines of clear state or federal laws that are themselves democratically enacted, and the loss of local control ought to continue no longer than is absolutely necessary.

The Crisis

Since the year 2000 or so, Detroit could lay claim to the title of the most dysfunctional large city in America.[1] Running chronic budget deficits, the city sank hopelessly into debt, owing current and long-term obligations to the tune of about $18 billion by the time the city filed for Chapter 9 municipal bankruptcy in July 2013—the largest American city to ever file for bankruptcy. In a June 2013 report by Kevyn Orr, the city's emergency manager (a financial dictator created by state law and appointed by the Michigan governor), the city's inefficiencies were laid bare: the city carried unfunded municipal pension obligations of more than $3 billion, unfunded retiree health care commitments running billions of dollars more, a police department with the slowest response times to 911 calls in the nation, a fire department with barely enough operational manpower and equipment to keep fires in check, a public lighting system so broken that nearly half the streetlights in Detroit were dark on any given night.

Under Orr's bankruptcy reorganization plan, worked out in painful negotiations with multiple groups in ensuing months following the July 2013 filing, the city would renege on its promises to pay bondholders all they were owed and also trim municipal pensions to some degree. The savings would allow the city to spend more on needed services and to minimize the pain to municipal retirees. Orr's plan would trim those pensions slightly but not cut them dramatically, as many at first feared. But these improvements hardly pleased all. Even the emergence of a so-called "grand bargain" in which foundations, the State of Michigan, leading companies including General Motors, Ford, and Chrysler, and others would contribute hundreds of millions of dollars to shore up city pensions did not still the protests that democracy had been usurped.

These protests over the Orr/Snyder emergency manager effort were long, loud, and unrelenting. Then-Mayor Dave Bing, the members of City Council, and virtually all of the candidates for city offices in the November 2013 elections, including the winner of the mayoral race, corporate turnaround expert Mike Duggan, ran more or less against the Snyder/Orr emergency management protocol, vowing to take back democratic control as soon as Orr's statutory eighteen-month term was up. Typical of the street protests that greeted Snyder's appointment of Orr was that voiced by Helen Moore of the Keep the Vote No Takeover Coalition, founded in 1999 to fight the state's takeover of the Detroit Public Schools system, who told an anti-Orr rally on July 4, 2013, "There is no reason to celebrate the Fourth of July, because Detroit is not free. We have no democracy. Our school system has been practically destroyed by state takeovers. We are crying out today for freedom for our people, black, white and Latino. We don't do second-class citizenship very well."[2]

And in June 2014, Detroit Mayor Duggan, seemingly speaking for many, said, "There is nothing more important to Detroiters than earning our right to self- determination back."[3]

The Emergence of Quasi-Democracy in Detroit

In the broadest sense, Detroiters began to see a diminishing of their democratic voice as early as the 1950s. That was the decade when the city began to bleed residents, jobs, and tax base to the new suburbs to the north and west. Since population equates to political power in the American system, Detroit's voice in government circles grew fainter and fainter as time went by. In the 1950s, fully one-third of Michiganders lived in the City of Detroit. By 2010, that percentage had diminished to 15 percent. Nor was this shrinking of Detroit's role in state governance taking place in isolation. At the same time, Michigan was losing clout nationally as American population growth slowed in the industrial heartland and swelled dramatically in the South and Southwest. In 1950 Michigan sent nineteen elected representatives to Congress; by 2010, that number had dwindled to fifteen. Detroiters were suffering a double loss—a diminished level of influence in a state that was itself losing its clout.[4]

Yet this ongoing loss of political power did not by itself raise the conflict of democracy vs. efficiency. Detroiters remained firmly in control of their municipal apparatus even if they were powerless to stop the forces of suburbanization and de-industrialization that were hollowing out their city. The issue of local control was especially acute for Detroit's growing African American population, whose leaders often complained that white suburbanites had fled the city only to try to exert control in a variety of ways from north of the city's border at 8 Mile Road. Longtime mayor Coleman A. Young, in office from the mid-70s to the mid-90s, worked furiously to maintain the city's credit rating, fearing a loss of control to state officials or other outsiders if the city's finances got out of hand. And he stoutly resisted the notion of spinning off municipal operations to private contractors or other levels of government, famously declaring that Detroit wouldn't sell its jewels for the price of the polish.

But such spinning off of underfunded, inefficient city operations did begin to take place in the late 1990s, a trend that set in motion a debate over democracy versus efficiency that continues to this day.[5] Among those operations spun off:

— The city-owned and -operated Eastern Market departed from direct city control in 2006, spun off into the new nonprofit Eastern Market Corp. With professional management, a nonprofit board, and newly gained foundation funding, the Market showed an immediate improvement in its lackluster performance. Market stalls that were only half leased became fully rented out; a new array of specialty food vendors were recruited to sell locally produced pickles, cheeses, meats, and breads; the Saturday-only market expanded to Tuesdays and, recently, to Sundays.

— Also in 2006, the Detroit Historical Museum was spun off from direct city control to the nonprofit Detroit Historical Society. Almost immediately, the museum began to gain savings from operations. The museum now operates with fewer than half the employees it had in 2006 when it left direct city control. Savings were gained in the building operations department, which was reduced by 75 percent. During this same period the museum has undergone a renovation and mounted well-received public exhibits.

— Cobo Center, Detroit's downtown convention center, was the subject of years of fierce debate over taking it away from the city and giving control to a regional authority. At the height of this debate, the city's signature annual auto show threatened to leave Cobo for Chicago unless something was done to improve the overpriced, underperforming operations at Cobo. The situation grew so absurd that when Cobo's roof leaked rainwater onto the show floor, Monica Conyers, then a City Council member who later went to prison for corruption, suggested that Cobo's managers were just seeking sympathy by complaining about the leak. When a regional authority finally took control in 2009, the operational efficiency improved almost immediately. Cobo launched a $277 million expansion and upgrade, a program that saw the creation of a new riverside ballroom that immediately became one of Detroit's premier venues for public events. Loading docks were improved, work rules streamlined, and marketing updated. The annual auto show renewed its contract with Cobo for several more years.

In addition to these examples, the city's two new downtown parks, the jewel-like Campus Martius in the heart of downtown and the waterfront promenade known as the RiverWalk, were both built by nonprofit conservancies rather than the city's recreation department. The city still owns the parks, but the separate conservancies make all day-to-day decisions, including fundraising, booking of events, and dealing with personnel matters. When the RiverWalk construction was launched in 2002 with a $50 million challenge grant from the Kresge Foundation, matched by General Motors, then-Mayor Kwame Kilpatrick was the lead voice taking credit at the press conference, but the unspoken narrative was that Kresge and GM would never have put their money into the project had they had to go through the normal city department channels. Only an outside independent conservancy structure would be acceptable to them.

In 2014, during the Orr emergency-management era and the bankruptcy case, two more significant cases of spinning off municipal functions occurred. The inept and inefficient streetlight system was taken over by a new public lighting authority, and, most significantly, the city agreed to place ownership of the municipal water system—which served not only Detroit but large portions of the suburbs—into a new regional water authority. Detroit leaders had long vowed never to let that happen; but the millions of dollars suburban counties would have to pay to Detroit and significant control remaining with city leaders on the authority made the deal more palatable.

Resisting the Quasi-Democratic Model

The spinning-off of operations like Eastern Market and Cobo Center happened only in the face of grumbling and some opposition from city unions over the loss of direct oversight and control by the city administration and City Council. Yet these episodes, divisive as they proved, were as nothing compared to the storm that erupted once Michigan Governor Snyder opted to appoint an emergency manager to serve as a virtual financial dictator over the city in 2013. More than a year after Orr's appointment, protesters still picketed speaking events by Snyder and Orr; they filled the Internet blogs with vituperative screeds against a white Republican governor denying democratic control to a mostly black city. Critics complained that Snyder and Orr were part of a cabal aimed at breaking unions, selling off Detroit's assets, and putting black residents of Detroit in their place.

It didn't soothe feelings that Orr's appointment had been clouded by old-fashioned power politics in the state capitol. Michigan, like many states, had an emergency manager statute on its books, but in 2011 a Republican-controlled state government with majorities in both houses passed a much stricter version that gave emergency managers all but unlimited powers to displace elected local city officials. That the legislature was dominated by conservative white Republicans, many elected with the support of Tea Party enthusiasts, and who tended to cast a cold eye on the largely black Detroit, did not sit well with residents of Detroit and other fiscally troubled cities such as Flint and Saginaw, likely to get emergency managers. Voters responded with a statewide referendum in 2012 that repealed the law, but the state legislature immediately passed a new version that was only slightly modified and just as tough. Snyder used that law to appoint Orr in Detroit.

Why Quasi-Democracy Worked

Supporters of these moves cited the improved efficiencies that came with the quasi-privatization of the operations and with Orr's appointment. As mentioned above, the city's street-lighting system was spun off into a new public lighting authority during Orr's tenure; able to borrow new funds in the bond market and cut better deals with suppliers, the new authority said the city's chronically broken street-lighting system would dramatically improve its performance even as the cost of running it dropped by about 75 percent. At Cobo Center, operating expenses have been reduced by 28 percent, from an estimated $20 million in the year prior to the authority's assumption of control to $14.5 million by 2012. Over that time, Cobo's utility costs dropped from about $4.8 million in 2010 to about $2.8 million in 2012, a reduction of nearly 42 percent. Cobo operates with roughly the same number of employees today as before, even though the authority picked up several new functions that were based elsewhere in city government, including finance and accounting, payroll, human resources, marketing, and sales.[6]

Sheila Cockrel, a former City Council member who now teaches at Wayne State University, supported the moves. "Moving to these authority models has made it possible to see some real improvements," she told the *Detroit Free Press*. "These new authorities are able to create more flexibility in job descriptions and setting standards for acceptable performance, and I think that has had an impact." She added, "The spinoffs are able to procure faster with less bureaucracy, get better prices. These institutions aren't bogged down with the financial chaos that has impeded efficient operation in Detroit for so long. People get paid on time."[7]

Even city insiders had long complained about the tiresome requirements built into getting any contract, development deal, or operational change through the city's bureaucracy. Even simple contracts often had to be approved by multiple departments, a process that could bog down for months. Those requirements vanished as an operation was spun off into its own independently managed entity, with the result that improvements took place sometimes in weeks instead of months or years.

Adding to the inefficiency of city operations were the bleak facts of life in a shrinking city. Detroit's city hall had suffered declining revenues since the 1970s, despite adding a city income tax and casino gaming tax to its shrinking property tax base. The city's municipal workforce dwindled from more than twenty thousand in the 1960s to about ten thousand by the time of Orr's appointment, adding to the inefficiency.

In addition to these problems, the city government's computer systems were notoriously out of date. Beth Niblock, a former information technology chief for the city of Louisville, Kentucky, who was recruited in early 2013 by Mayor Duggan, testified during the bankruptcy trial in September 2014 that the city's information technology was "generations behind" current standards. About nine in ten of the city's computers were operating on the decade-old Windows XP operating system or something older. "They're atrocious," she said. "Depending on what luck of the draw you have, your desktop can take almost ten minutes to boot up." Sometimes, she said, city workers would send emails that never arrived in the recipient's inbox. The city's systems are also extremely susceptible to cybersecurity attacks. The antiquated systems made it more difficult for the city to issue paychecks, collect taxes, communicate internally, and dispatch police and firefighters, city officials have said. "It is fundamentally broken or beyond fundamentally broken," Niblock testified. "In some cases fundamentally broken would be good." In one notorious example, it emerged that some firefighters would position empty soft drink cans on their fax machines so that when a fax came in alerting them to a fire, the paper sliding through would knock over the pop cans, an arrangement necessary because the bells on the fax machines no longer worked.[8]

Unnecessary layers of bureaucracy, broken technology, short staffing, dwindling revenues—all pieces of the puzzle that explained why the normal democratic processes no longer produced efficient government in Detroit. And all were cited as among the reasons behind the appointment of an emergency manager and the spinning off of so many municipal operations.

Dale Thomson, a professor of political science at the University of Michigan-Dearborn who has studied the new management structures, generally supports the trend, but with reservations, saying certain conditions must be met for a spinoff to be successful. There needs to be a discreet mission with relatively clear boundaries, such as operating Cobo Center, a museum, or building the RiverWalk. It helps if there is a dedicated revenue stream to support the new management structure. It also helps if the tasks involved are technical rather than those that involve solving social problems. In an interview with the *Detroit Free Press*, Thomson added that authorities "need to balance the potential for service improvement with the potential for diminished accountability or democratic control."[9]

Justifying Quasi-Democracy

One justification for the usurpation of democratic control is that the new decision-makers were in fact themselves either elected by the people on a statewide basis—the governor who appointed Orr and the state legislators who created the emergency manager law—or directly appointed by elected leaders. The Cobo regional authority, for example, had its five members appointed one each by the governor, the mayor of Detroit, and the three regional county executives. The City Council and the mayor can similarly exercise some measure of control over, say, Eastern Market or the RiverWalk through a variety of means, including zoning and planning decisions that impact those operations. Then, too, when Orr proposed that the State of Michigan take over and manage Detroit's famed Belle Isle Park as a state park on a long-term lease (citing the city's inability to even keep restrooms on the island open for lack of funds), storms of protest were followed eventually by a reluctant approval from City Council.

So democracy, while diminished, could be said to not exactly disappear. Rather, it receded somewhat into the background while duly elected leaders and their appointees made tough decisions on behalf of the city.

An intriguing incident in September 2014 illustrates the complexity of this question. Decades earlier, the city had created a set of entities called Citizens District Councils. These were neighborhood boards set up to advise city leaders on any project backed by the city taking place in a given neighborhood. The CDCs (not to be confused with community development corporations, also known as CDCs) added a layer of bureaucracy to the already cumbersome development process, but it also injected more voices into the system, and these were voices at the local level that often went ignored. Over time, the citizens district councils tended to operate well or poorly, depending on the membership, and few thought they added much essential to the redevelopment efforts. Yet a measure of outrage flared in early autumn 2014 when Orr, as one of his final acts as the city's emergency manager, abolished the citizens district councils in the name of smoothing out the redevelopment bureaucracy. Orr spokesman Bill Nowling told the media that the CDCs hampered growth. "It was felt that the CDCs created an unnecessary level of bureaucracy that was hindering future development and revitalization efforts," he said.[10] Critics lamented yet another loss of democracy in the name of efficiency; yet the more informed questioned whether Orr, at the end of his statutory tenure and within days of turning control of the city back over to the mayor and City Council, would have abolished the CDCs without at least the tacit consent of Mayor Duggan. Unlike the strained relationship between Orr and former Mayor Dave Bing, Duggan and Orr had met daily for months; they had already arranged a power-sharing arrangement, with Orr giving some of the powers of control back to the mayor; and Duggan, a corporate turnaround expert, had long since shown that he expected to rule as an activist mayor with control over all aspects of his administration. Some insiders wondered if Orr abolished citizen district councils at the private behest of the mayor. If so, it would demonstrate that the extent of democracy in Detroit could ebb and flow even as locally elected officials took control once again. And it would confirm what many insiders said privately, that the mayor and council would miss Orr when he was gone for his ability to act quickly and decisively.

Of course, the argument that quasi-democracy is the same as genuine local democracy goes only so far. Nobody pretended that emergency manager Kevyn Orr was anything but a dictator in Detroit. The weighing of democracy versus efficiency in Detroit cannot be settled by any niceties or parsing of the terms of Orr's tenure. Pure and simple, the question boils down to this: Is the loss of democratic control, which everyone including Orr and Snyder admits took place in Detroit, worth it because of gains in efficiency?

Two Perspectives on the Crisis

Perhaps one way to answer that question is to consider it first from afar, from the cool perch of a dispassionate observer, and, second, from the view of a citizen of a deeply troubled city. It may be easy for an outsider to say, as critics of Mussolini did, that making the trains run on time is never enough, that once a little bit of democratic control is lost, so one by one are a host of citizen protections—free speech, a free press, the right to assemble, the right to critique government actions freely and openly, perhaps even eventually the right to vote. The loss of democracy little by little is not so much a slippery slope as it is a greased chute, where rights disappear with headlong speed once basic democracy is usurped.

This has proven particularly problematic to city workers, city government retirees, and others more likely to be burdened directly by the "efficiency" dictates of someone like Orr. As it turned out, the settlement reached in the bankruptcy case involved only minor cuts to city pensions, far less than originally feared; pensioners themselves voted to accept the settlement, albeit under the gun that something much worse would be coming if the deal was scuttled. And if city workers and their union leaders had complained so strongly about spinning off city operations to conservancies and authorities, it was because some city workers would in fact lose their jobs in those spinoffs; these losses were usually cushioned by giving workers a chance to transfer back into the city or accept some other form of compensation. And the losses inherent in a streamlining of city government, whether by Orr's dictates or by the bankruptcy court, would come only after many years of job cuts, furloughs, and occasional payless paydays for city workers.

But as Orr argued over and over, his role demanded that he place priority on the seven hundred thousand citizens of Detroit rather than the ten thousand municipal workers and twenty thousand city retirees. And he would tell city workers and pensioners that he wasn't the guy who had done this to them; decades of city leaders had betrayed them and produced the crisis.

And crisis it was. A beleaguered citizen of Detroit in 2013 might sigh and say that arguments over democracy were irrelevant in a city where the buses were not only late but often didn't run at all; where calls to 911 sometimes went unanswered; where a previous mayor, Kwame Kilpatrick, and a couple of dozen of his aides were on their way to prison for corruption; where services had collapsed to an astonishing degree, and virtually every department—from public lighting to code enforcement to parks and recreation—operated so inefficiently that parts of the city could be said to remain virtually ungoverned. When Detroit voters elected Michael Duggan as their mayor in late 2013, choosing a former county prosecutor and CEO of the Detroit Medical Center with a reputation as a tough turnaround expert, they gave executive powers to Detroit's first white mayor in forty years—a fact widely interpreted as proof the voters so desperately wanted change that they would ignore concerns like race. Of course, Duggan had only so much power until Orr's tenure as emergency manager expired in the fall of 2014, but nonetheless his election sent a signal about the need for change.

Conclusion

So perhaps the debate devolves to the difficult question of which parts of a democratic system we can put on hold for a time while outsiders enact needed radical change. Had elected statewide officials ignored the realities of a broken city, a city where municipal services had collapsed to a degree perhaps unknown in twenty-first-century America, they would have been guilty of governmental misconduct. (Indeed, the fact that Michigan's leaders did so little for so long during Detroit's decades-long slide into defeat could itself be interpreted as almost criminally negligent.) Cities, after all, are creatures of state invention, not sovereign entities in their own right. Under the federal constitution, states create cities and other local municipalities and the rules under which they operate. State officials operate entirely within their powers and responsibilities to change the rules from time to time as needed—albeit with a weather eye to the political realities of their actions. One might hope that state leaders would exercise their powers as gently as possible when depriving local elected officials of their powers; but sometimes surgery is necessary with or without balm.

In the decades to come, when the temporary loss of democracy in Detroit appears as no more than a disturbing episode in history's rearview mirror, these years may be classified as a textbook illustration of Bismarck's "laws and sausages" remark—that ugly things must happen now and then to keep government on track. Just as Lincoln suspended habeas corpus during the Civil War, and just as the nation has imposed a military draft on unwilling citizens from time to time, these breaches of democratic practice have been more or less justified in the long view of history. And so it may be again in Detroit—a case of a temporary loss of local democratic control during the worst fiscal emergency in the city's history. As the great British editor Walter Bagehot wrote in his *English Constitution*: "In such constitutions there are two parts . . . first, those which excite and preserve the reverence of the population—the *dignified* parts . . . and next, the *efficient* parts—those by which it, in fact, works and rules."

Notes

1. Detroit Emergency Manager Kevyn Orr described the city's dysfunction at length in his Proposal for Creditors, June 14, 2013, available at http://www.detroitmi.gov/EmergencyManager/Reports. See also "How Detroit Went Broke," by Nathan Bomey and John Gallagher, *Detroit Free Press*, Sept. 15, 2013. Cited hereafter as Bomey & Gallagher.
2. Quoted in "Detroit Residents on Bankruptcy - We Have No Democracy!" by David Bacon, Truthout, Aug. 15, 2013, available at http://truth-out.org/news/item/18196-detroit-residents-on-bankruptcy-we-have-no-democracy.
3. See Twitter post by Rick Pluta, WDET radio, quoted in "Detroit Bankruptcy and Beyond," available at https://storify.com/fuzzytek/detroit-bankruptcy-and-beyond.
4. Bomey & Gallagher.
5. "City Jewels Shine with a Bit of Help," by John Gallagher, *Detroit Free Press*, April 3, 2013. Cited hereafter as Gallagher, "City Jewels Shine."
6. Gallagher, "City Jewels Shine."
7. Gallagher, "City Jewels Shine."
8. "City computers 'beyond' broken, expert testifies," by Nathan Bomey and Joe Guillen, *Detroit Free Press*, Sept. 9, 2014.
9. Gallagher, "City Jewels Shine."
10. Nowling quoted in "Before relinquishing control of Detroit, EM Kevyn Orr abolished Citizens' District Councils," *Motor City Muckraker*, Oct. 2, 2014, available at http://motorcitymuckraker.com/2014/09/29/before-relinquishing-control-of-detroit-em-kevyn-orr-abolished-citizens-district-councils/. See also Nancy Kaffir, "Duggan must find a way to give citizens a voice," *Detroit Free Press*, Oct. 2, 2014.

8

Ritual and Redistribution in De-democratized Detroit

L. Owen Kirkpatrick

On November 5, 2013, the City of Detroit, Michigan, held an off-year general election. With no national or state races on the ballot, residents focused their attention on local offices—the mayor and city council chief among them. For casual or uninitiated observers of this civic exercise, nothing would appear amiss: candidates ran predictably spirited campaigns, and contested results were resolved through well-established institutional protocols. If there were lingering doubts as to the procedural integrity of the exercise, officials from the Department of Justice were on hand (for purposes related to the Voting Rights Act), further insuring electoral transparency. In some respects, the election was a veritable picture of local procedural democracy. One need only scratch the surface of things, however, before the image of normalcy is cracked open, revealing something quite peculiar.

Conventionally, local elections determine—by way of more-or-less rational public deliberation—which individuals and parties will wield political power in a municipality. As a practical matter, therefore, an election is an instrumental process. In Detroit, however, those elected to local office have no formal power. Authority over the city currently resides wholly in the office of an "emergency manager" (EM). Appointed by the governor of Michigan for purposes of fiscal crisis management, the pseudo-dictatorial EM controls the gears of city government in a manner unconstrained by the checks and balances traditionally associated with urban democracy. Emergency managers are free to make unilateral decisions concerning (among many other things) privatizing public assets, restructuring or voiding collectively bargained public contracts, disbursing incoming funds, dismissing elected officials, and dissolving entire departments and agencies. The mayor and city council, legally powerless, serve at his or her pleasure. In short, the appointment of an EM directly negates the instrumentality of the local electoral process. And yet, local elections continue to be re-enacted as elaborate political rituals.

Purveyors of conventional wisdom maintain that local elections in Detroit faithfully retain their utilitarian functions, though such functions have been briefly suspended while the city is under EM control. This interpretation views emergency management as a harmless cloud, which momentarily obscures the democratic sun of popular sovereignty and

123

local self-rule. Thus, as we will see, Detroit residents were still vigorously urged to vote on the basis that the EM's reign would be inevitably short and the transfer of power clean and definitive; soon every vote would fully and faithfully "count." If true, the city's democratic, sovereign autonomy would be quickly and unambiguously restored, and local elections would retain their fundamental instrumentality. But there is reason to doubt this interpretation of events. Far from a momentary aberration, the EM is quite likely to have long-term, structural effects on the local democratic efficacy of Detroit residents. The following case study of the local electoral process in EM-controlled Detroit generates several observations that bolster this conclusion.

First, the expressed raison d'être of the EM is to oversee the process of municipal restructuring in a manner that conforms to the urban austerity model (see Peck, this volume). This process is crucial because it permanently shapes the long-term form and functions of the city. Yet it is precisely this process from which citizens and their elected representatives are prohibited from taking part. Thus, when weighted by their strategic importance and long-term structural impact, the decisions made by the EM will tend to outweigh those made through traditional democratic mechanisms after the EM's departure (or doled out to local officials during the EM's tenure). Second, conventional wisdom does not acknowledge the capacity of emergency managers to imbue a position, office, or mechanism with EM-like powers. Here again, the permanent establishment of a pseudo-dictatorial municipal apparatus significantly diminishes the instrumentality of the electoral process. Third, the history of fiscal crisis management in Michigan suggests that the duration of direct EM control will not be particularly brief. Additionally, it is not uncommon for emergency management to become a recurrent pattern of urban governance, whereby EMs return to the same cities multiple times in quick succession.

My primary thesis, therefore, is that the appointment of an EM significantly decreases the instrumental utility of municipal elections, while significantly increasing their ritualistic and symbolic content. This is not to say that all instrumentality has been completely wrung out of the practice. There are several ways the election may retain some of its original utility. For one, while frequently overstated, sovereign autonomy may in fact be restored to local elected officials—in whole or in part—after the departure of the EM. Further, the EM may engage in limited power-sharing arrangements during his/her tenure. Also of note is the functional utility of incumbency vis-à-vis future re-election efforts. On balance, however, local elections in EM-controlled cities have ceased being essentially rational and functionally utilitarian and are now, instead, essentially performative and functionally symbolic.

This ritualization of the electoral process in Detroit poses formidable analytic problems for popular theories of political ritual. To begin, theoretical explanations of modern political ritual tend to emphasize the capacity of symbols and ceremony to generate social cohesion and value consensus. But as we will see, this model is supported by a set of assumptions that are highly tenuous in the case of Detroit. Second, there is a common presumption that symbols and discrete rituals and ceremonies exist within otherwise utilitarian political systems and are attendant to the practical political functionalities of those systems. But this interpretation is not viable in Detroit, where the pivotal issue is no longer the role of ritual *in* politics, but rather the role of ritual *as* politics.

The following analysis thus proposes an alternate theoretical framework that defines local democratic process in Detroit (and other EM-controlled cities) in terms of strategic institutional ritualization. According to the proposed model, the stage was set for electoral ritualization when the intensifying demands of finance markets came to stand in direct and fundamental opposition to the norms, institutions, and practices traditionally associated with urban democracy. Drawing on the work of Janusz Mucha (1991), the model posits that in situations where two powerful societal forces are mutually opposed in the political sphere, the more powerful entity may attempt to "ritualize" the weaker by decreasing its instrumental content while increasing its symbolic impact. The model becomes more precise when we tailor it to the sphere of municipal politics. Scholars of local fiscal crisis have noted that the urban political arena is organized such that the demands of investment capital are structurally segregated from the demands of the electorate (Piven and Friedland 1984). While the former channel of governance handles the technical requirements associated with capital accumulation and value extraction, the latter handles the social requirements associated with popular legitimacy. While the power typically exercised by citizens via the latter channel is limited, it is real.

In the postcrisis period, however, the financial imperatives associated with value extraction have intensified and can no longer be relegated to the back channels of municipal governance. Today, extractive demands hinge on the massive leverage derived from municipal debt service and the threat of large-scale financial repossession—including the wholesale transfer of public assets to private hands. For deeply indebted cities, value extraction is presented as an absolute financial imperative that will be achieved via appropriation and/or repossession, if necessary (Kirkpatrick and Breznau 2014). This is a profound shift that brings the demands of finance capital into direct opposition with the demands of urban democracy. One way this tension can be resolved is through the ritualization of local democratic practices. The analysis begins by setting the historical stage.

Setting the Stage: The Economic Decline and Political Fall of the Motor City

Detroit long served as the undisputed epicenter of the auto industry, a crucial national hub of Fordist production, and a triumphant worldwide symbol of industrial urbanism. But if Detroit once personified the glorious acme of the industrial metropolis, it now represents its painful nadir.

The Decline of Detroit

Once the fifth-largest city in the country (1.85 million residents in 1950), the Motor City was brought to its knees by unrelenting economic pressures related to decentralization, deindustrialization, and globalization.[1] Today, Detroit's population stands at less than seven hundred thousand, a stark sign of chronic socioeconomic decline fueled by the coterminous flight of (blue-collar) jobs and (white) residents away from the metropolitan core (Sugrue 1996). By 2010, Detroit had the nation's highest unemployment and violent crime rates, 20 percent of the city lay vacant and abandoned, and officials struggled with a budget that had cratered in the aftermath of the financial crisis (Clement 2013). Hollowed of its industrial and residential foundations, Detroit now grapples with a radically eroded tax base and long-term structural budget deficits, ultimately leaving officials without the revenues to adequately fund welfare programs, schools and other basic public infrastructures and services (Kirkpatrick 2015b).

Detroit is not only much poorer than it once was; it is also much blacker. The racially exclusionary nature of the mass urban exodus ("white flight") of the postwar years had a profound impact on the social geography of the region. As upper- and middle-class whites fled to the suburbs, the proportion of black Detroit residents soared—from 16 percent in 1950 to 83 percent in 2010 (US Census). Despite talk of recent desegregation (ostensibly due to an influx of young members of the "creative class"), racial segregation continues its stubborn advance. Between 2000 and 2010, for instance, Detroit's white population dropped from almost 100,000 to 55,000, or 7.8 percent of the city's population (Sugrue 2013: 118), and the area remains (one of) the most racially segregated metropolitan regions in the United States (Logan and Stults 2011). When white flight occurs alongside economic decentralization, it creates a spatial mismatch between where jobs are located and where the people who need them live. In this manner, the city has become a site of concentrated black poverty and advanced socio-spatial marginality.

The Financialization of Detroit

Despite its industrial and residential evisceration, Detroit remains an important site of real and potential (financial) value extraction. Extractive demands of this sort are now largely satisfied through or facilitated by urban financialization, the process whereby urban economies are shaped by expanding financial markets and municipal budgets become infused with "financial accounting innovations" (Pacewicz 2012). This was certainly true before the global crisis, and it remains true in its wake.

In the *pre-crisis period*, banks and investment firms profited handsomely from Detroit and its residents in two ways. First, there were the high fees the city paid on complex debt instruments designed to lower borrowing costs on variable-rate debt (such as interest rate swaps and derivatives). For a time this allowed the city to escape the consequences of running continuous, year-over-year budget deficits. Banks including JP Morgan and Bank of America "enabled about $3.7 billion in bond issues to cover deficits, pension shortfalls and debt payments since 2005." All told, these deals "cost Detroit $474 million, including underwriting expenses, bond-insurance premiums and fees for wrong way bets on swaps, [which] almost equals the city's 2013 budget for police and fire protection" (Preston and Christoff 2013). Second, and simultaneously, many of the same banks were also extracting value from Detroit residents via subprime consumer lending. Variable rate municipal debt thus found a corollary in variable rate mortgage debt. "As banks were collecting fees from the bonds," notes the aforementioned Bloomberg report, "some [also] targeted homeowners with subprime loans that led to foreclosures, depressing real-estate values and tax revenues" (Ibid.).

In *the postcrisis period* there remains a financial imperative to extract value from formerly industrial cities. This can occur in two general ways. First, banks can and do reap sizable rewards by way of penalties and accelerated fee schedules triggered by crisis conditions. For instance, in the Detroit case, a key pension swap deal contained several benchmarks (a missed payment, the appointment of an EM, a credit rating downgrade) that would trigger exorbitant termination penalties, including the immediate payment of all "projected future profits" to the deal's counterparties. Rather remarkably, each and every one of the early termination benchmarks was met (Turbeville 2013: 27–32), leading a Bloomberg report to bluntly conclude, "[t]he only winners in the financial crisis that brought Detroit to the brink of state takeover are Wall Street bankers" (Preston and Christoff 2013). Second, cities retain valuable assets that can be claimed by extralocal entities via financial repossession. In its efforts to pay off favored financial creditors, Detroit is expected to sacrifice collective assets when needed—public pensions, infrastructure and service systems, natural resources and amenities, cultural artifacts, and the like, are at risk of appropriation in this manner. In Detroit we are thus witness to a form of urban extraction based on financial leverage (contra financial investment) and value appropriation (contra value production). In the Motor City, industrial productive forms of value extraction have largely been abandoned in favor of a set of methods more akin to *financial redistribution*, whereby public assets (both collectively held and collectively bargained) are monetized and/or modified in order to better meet the city's financial obligations. Here again, while the Detroit case is extreme in its particulars, it is not anomalous in its contours. "The main substantive achievement of neoliberalization," notes Harvey, "has been to redistribute, rather than to generate, wealth and income" (2005: 159).

The Emergency Management of Detroit

A financial strategy of urban value extraction based on appropriation and repossession is unlikely to win popular democratic support in those communities being targeted by such measures. Thus, in the post-crisis period, we see new techniques of urban governance gain traction that are designed to enforce market discipline on recalcitrant communities (Kirkpatrick and Breznau 2014). For Michigan officials the preferred mechanism for this task is the emergency manager (EM), and in May 2013, the Governor appointed Kevyn Orr as emergency manager of the City of Detroit.

While the de facto deployment of EMs began in 1986, the practice was codified through a series of legislative initiatives known loosely as the Fiscal Responsibility Acts (FRA). These laws provide a pseudo-legal framework for extra-constitutional, emergency-based intervention (Citizens Research Council 2010). All along, Michigan's system of fiscal crisis management stood in direct contradiction to the right of citizens to local "home rule." Successive iterations of the law (passed in 1988, 1990, 1992, 2002, 2003, and 2009) expanded the powers of the EM, broadened the universe of potential targets, and made the triggers for intervention more plentiful and sensitive. In 2011, the gradual ramping up of the law accelerated with the passage of Public Act (PA) 4, which significantly expanded the purview of EM authority (Citizens Research Council 2011). In November 2012, Michigan citizens responded by repealing the law via popular referendum.[2] Unchastened, legislators immediately went to work replacing PA 4 with a version made all the more stringent due to the inclusion of appropriations, rendering the law immune to future electoral challenges (Oosting 2012).

Today, state officials enjoy near total discretion in calling for fiscal reviews, declaring local fiscal emergencies, and (in the figure of the EM) managing local affairs in times of crisis. Once appointed, the EM assumes vast, pseudo-dictatorial powers, effectively supplanting elected and appointed local officials without legal due process (House Judiciary Committee 2012). Once in place, the EM operates outside of the formal boundaries of democratic governance and thus evades traditional constraints on political activity (e.g., institutional checks and balances, the electoral process). Powers currently at the disposal of the EM include, but are not limited to, rewriting public contracts, engaging in collective bargaining on behalf of the city, privatizing public assets, determining who receives incoming funds, dismissing local officials or dissolving entire agencies or departments, and, in the case of school districts, a host of additional curricular powers (Peck, this volume; Citizens Research Council 2011, Abowd 2012). Until the EM deems the fiscal emergency resolved and the city on solid footing, the state of emergency continues and the normal workings of local democratic rule are suspended.

In the interim, Detroiters (and residents of similarly designated cities) face the stark reality that their citizenship rights are deeply abridged (Conyers and Peters 2013). The curtailment of rights in EM-controlled cities proceeds along four dimensions (Kirkpatrick 2015a). First, and as noted, the appointment of an EM radically impinges on the right of local home rule. Second, collective bargaining rights are suspended for municipal employees during the tenure of the EM. Third, the legal-juridical rights of Detroit residents are in a state of flux. Finally, and most importantly for our purposes, the special juridical status of Detroiters is marked by their sharply attenuated electoral rights. Emergency managers (and their executive orders) are immune to local electoral challenge, and duly elected officials and democratically established policies are rendered moot. Put differently, the appointment of an EM serves to directly diminish the functional instrumentality of local democratic practices. In order to more fully explore the nature and extent of this diminishment, the analysis turns to a case study of the 2013 Detroit election.

The Election

The following case study of Detroit's 2013 election is organized in three parts. First, the analysis considers what the election was: what it consisted of, how it was structured, and what it produced. The second section of the study considers what the election was not: what it prevented, what it lacked, and what it negated. Lastly, we consider political negotiations in the aftermath of the election, specifically a power-sharing agreement struck by the EM and the new Mayor several months after the election, an episode of strategic ritualization in microcosm.

What the Election Was

The 2013 Detroit election had the procedural appearance of a normally functioning election. One common marker of contemporary electoral normalcy—the "get-out-the-vote" campaign—was certainly in evidence. Indeed, an interesting aspect of the election—given its diminished instrumentality—was the diverse and widespread efforts to increase voter turnout. These efforts originated from across the political spectrum and employed a variety of arguments. To begin, some argued that the state takeover served to alienate the electorate and decrease the political interest of voters. According to these analysts, voters were more concerned about candidates' plans for fixing public services than limitations on democratic rule under emergency management (Ferretti 2013a). Voter turnout was expected to be normal, but for reasons relating to streetlights and water pipes. Many others believed (including many area activists) that strenuous objections to emergency management would (or should) fuel both increased voter turnout and greater participation in local governance. For instance, Nabih Ayad, an attorney for the Arab-American Civil Rights League, argued that voting would send a clear message that Detroiters want their voting rights back (Nichols and Ramirez 2013).

Overwhelmingly, however, the get-out-the-vote messaging was based on the assumption, expressed either implicitly or explicitly, that the tenure of the EM would be short and clearly defined; people's votes would ultimately "count"—fully and unambiguously. For instance, outgoing Mayor Dave Bing (who opted not to seek re-election) urged residents to vote because elected officials would soon recover political power. "You've got to come out in numbers and vote," he implored. "Your voice is important" (Bing, quoted in Nichols 2013a). As the *Detroit News* reported, "Public and private officials outside the mayoral campaigns have urged residents in the predominantly African-American city to remember the struggle of blacks to win voting rights and exercise those rights because the city's elected officials eventually will operate the city again" (Nichols and Ramirez 2013). Others stressed variants of the same theme. The president of the Detroit branch of the NAACP, for example, argued that voting is the fundamental method for improving life and exercising local political power (regardless of EM status), and residents concerned with the direction of the city, or with protecting their democratic rights, should vote "like your life depends upon it because quite frankly it does" (Nichols 2013a). There were warnings not to use the emergency management of the city as an excuse not to participate. Malik Shabazz, an area minister, associated voting with the restoration of democratic norms, and opined that Detroiters "are the last people who should have a laissez-faire, nonchalant attitude about voting" (Nichols and Ramirez 2013).

Importantly, efforts to increase electoral turnout may have overstated the instrumental utility of the votes being drummed up. As noted, underlying most of the appeals was the assumption (expressed implicitly or explicitly) that the EM's control would be short and clearly delineated, immediately followed by the full and complete restoration of local popular sovereignty and democratic self-rule. But an analysis of other EM cases across Michigan casts doubt on this assumption (Kirkpatrick and Breznau 2014). First, EMs have the capacity, and demonstrate the tendency, to create a permanent pseudo-dictatorial municipal apparatus before their departure. In this scenario, while formal power is transferred back to local officials, substantive power remains invested in some extra-constitutional position or office that remains insulated from popular democratic control. For example, Pontiac's departing EM created a new position ("city administrator") with EM-like powers, leaving local residents in a prolonged state of political limbo long after the originating fiscal crisis has been resolved (Ibid.; Laitner 2013). Similar arrangements also currently exist in the cities of Ecorse, Benton

Harbor, and Allen Park, and many expect Detroit's EM to take similar steps. Kenneth Schneider, a bankruptcy attorney in the city, has argued that those elected will not regain authority over city finances when Mr. Orr vacates his position as Detroit EM because a Financial Control Board will be indefinitely put in place. Hence, he reasons, city officials will have to work with the state in exercising authority over city finances in perpetuity (Williams 2013a).

There are additional reasons to question the idea that the tenure of Detroit's EM will be brief and well defined. An analysis of the fifteen Michigan cities and school districts assigned an EM between 2000–2013 reveals that the average length of a continuous EM assignment is 3.33 years, or only eight months shy of an entire (four-year) election cycle. However, this figure is conservative, perhaps significantly so, due to the fact that several cases of local emergency management (including Detroit) are still ongoing. Also of note is the recurrent nature of local emergency intervention. It is not uncommon for a local jurisdiction to be subjected to several rounds of emergency management in quick succession. For instance, the cities of Pontiac and Hamtramck have each had three EMs in the span of a decade (Kirkpatrick and Breznau 2014). When we calculate the length of emergency management as experienced by cities and school districts, including non-continuous EM appointments, the average length swells to 3.85 years. (And here again this is a conservative estimate.)

Despite the questionable assumptions underlying various get-out-the-vote campaigns, the collective effort was a success: over 25 percent of the city's registered voters participated, up from 22.6 percent for the last mayoral/city council election cycle in 2009 (Wilkinson, Nichols, and Pardo 2013). Indeed, voter turnout was in line with what we would expect given twenty-first-century trends in the city. And, as always, the votes cast needed to be counted, a task handled via the comforting dictates of procedural democracy.

Despite the exceptional circumstances in which it was held, the election largely followed the customary legal-juridical protocols associated with local procedural democracy. Consider, for example, the mayoral primary. Detroit holds a nonpartisan primary, with the top two finishers, regardless of party affiliation, meeting in the general election. In 2013, the primary saw business executive Mike Duggan come in first with 46 percent of the vote, while Wayne County Sheriff Benny Napoleon come in second with 30 percent of the vote. Despite the seemingly decisive nature of the result, the ballots were subject to recount on no less than four separate occasions due primarily to irregularities arising from Duggan's status as a write-in candidate. (Because of a residency issue, Duggan's name did not appear on the ballot.) According to candidate Tom Barrow, a review revealed thousands of "clearly fraudulent ballots" had been cast for Duggan in the same handwriting (Barrow, quoted in Walker 2013b). In response to this charge, the Wayne County Board of Canvassers brought in fifty full-time staffers to conduct the recounts and forensics experts to examine handwriting samples. Ultimately, at a cost of nearly $500,000, the primary result was certified (Neavling 2013, Wischusen 2013). Whatever the status of the election's functional utility, its procedural sanctity was strictly honored.

In November of 2013, Mike Duggan secured 55 percent of the general vote, becoming the seventy-fifth mayor of Detroit (Wilkinson, Nichols, and Pardo 2013). While in many ways, the general appearance of the election followed procedural norms, the results of the election were highly out of the ordinary. Most dramatically, Mike Duggan, a Democrat, is Detroit's first white mayor in forty years (Williams 2013b). He was also the more conservative, business-friendly candidate, and struck the more conciliatory posture with respect to the EM prior to and during the mayoral race. Duggan's victory (and the election of like-minded council members)[3] may thus be taken as evidence that the appointment of an EM has an implicitly conservatizing impact on local elections, though this implication requires elaboration.

I have argued that the appointment of an EM directly diminishes the instrumental utility of the local electoral process. But the precise level of this diminishment is a variable decided in no small measure by the outcome of the election itself. Put differently, the postelection relationship between the EM and elected officials is largely determined by the stance of those newly elected officials toward the austerity agenda. For the most part, this logic was communicated to voters in the lead-up to the election. For instance, Duggan walked a fine line between denouncing the disenfranchisement entailed by emergency management, while also signaling that he was the candidate best equipped to work with the EM in moving the city past bankruptcy. Duggan stressed that his "restructuring expertise" would help the city's postcrisis transition (Nichols and Pardo 2013a), and spoke of his intentions to "shorten Kevyn Orr's stay" (quoted in Williams 2013a). Meanwhile, several candidates charged that Duggan himself had been previously offered the EM position. To the extent that residents were voting in a practical, strategic manner, the election of Duggan could signal the begrudging acknowledgement that the quickest way to regain local democratic autonomy is with the real and symbolic acceptance of the more conservative candidate. In this manner, the appointment of an EM may have a conservatizing impact on the electoral process. But elections held in EM-controlled cities also effect political discourse in the negative sense—by what they prevent and preclude.

What the Election Wasn't

While the election provided the proper procedural shell for local democracy, it did not provide a substantive opportunity for the community to meaningfully engage with the process of municipal restructuring. Indeed, Michigan's system of fiscal crisis management is consciously designed to preclude precisely such democratic engagement. When democratic practices no longer function as an authentic platform for local participation, they must play a different role in the process of systematic municipal restructuring and the quest for financial value extraction. In such a context, as Lukes observes, elections may, instead, merely "express a hegemonic ideology." Political ritual, he continues,

> [H]elps to define as authoritative certain ways of seeing society: it serves to specify what in society is of special significance, it draws people's attention to certain forms of relationships and activity—and at the same time, therefore, it deflects their attention from other forms, since every way of seeing is also a way of not seeing (1975: 301).

As ritual, the election shapes how people see (and fail to see) local political possibilities. It negates and precludes certain ways of seeing the social world and acting within it by placing boundaries around acceptable forms of political discourse and engagement. This has important implications for the realpolitik of postcrisis Detroit.

In the context of urban austerity (Peck 2012, 2014), cities struggle to trim budgets quickly enough to match declining revenue streams (i.e., cratered tax receipts and dried-up funding from federal and state governments). This squeeze is compounded in shrinking, formerly industrial cities such as Detroit, where public infrastructure networks, service systems, natural amenities, and cultural artifacts have all been threatened with monetization and/or privatization. Similarly, public union pensions and health benefits—as well as current, collectively bargained contracts—are being restructured so as to lower the legacy costs borne by the city. These assets are dispensed so that the city can better meet the demands of financial markets. Financial value extraction of this sort pits the interests of local actors (residents and workers) against those of extra-local financial interests (municipal bondholders and Wall Street firms). Emergency managers will systematically favor the latter set of interests in their attempt to settle the financial accounts of the city in full and faithful fashion. This tendency is not due to the personal predilections of individual EMs, but is rather a structural imperative of the position as cities are now heavily dependent on access to financial markets to pay for the things their residents need. In practice, this means putting financial interests at "the head of the line" in bankruptcy negotiations (Preston and Church 2013).[4] Financial obligations are prioritized because financial markets must be placated in order to insure future access to them.

Ultimately, therefore, the election did not and could not challenge a key objective of emergency management—namely, the enforcement of market discipline. Recalcitrant communities, it is argued, need the firm hand of an EM to make good on their financial obligations, and so preserve the integrity of municipal debt and municipal debt markets. The figure of the EM is uniquely equipped to play this role, as it exists outside the boundaries of local democracy, and can thus enforce market discipline even in the face of popular, democratically expressed opposition. Given the disciplinary functions of the EM, it goes to reason that the critical decisions with respect to municipal restructuring and financial value extraction will not be open to public discussion or political negotiation. When democratic norms are eventually reestablished, it will be to deliberate on matters of peripheral importance to the austerity agenda. To explore this charge in more detail, we briefly consider post-election power sharing arrangements in Detroit.

After the Election: The Power-Sharing Agreement

Michigan's emergency manager law establishes broad limits to the amount of power and autonomy a given EM can restore to local officials during his/her tenure. As noted, however, the precise degree of political utility enjoyed by newly elected officials is determined at the discretion of the EM. This determination is presumably based on several factors, not least being the stance of the winning candidates toward the twin projects of municipal restructuring and financial value extraction.

In Detroit, as we have seen, voters elected the more business-friendly candidate(s) that had taken the more conciliatory position with respect to emergency management. There were very early signs of compatibility. EM Orr and Mayor Duggan immediately began discussions concerning how much, if any, authority the new mayor would yield. Just two days after the election, they held a meeting that an Orr spokesman defined as "positive, productive, and collaborative" (Daniels and Nichols 2013). Members of both Governor Snyder's and EM Orr's administrations wasted little time indicating that Duggan's "turnaround experience" makes him a good candidate to take responsibility for certain limited city functions (Nichols 2013b). During a forum held at Wayne State University, Duggan reported he hoped to gain control of some city services, especially the police force (Nichols and Ferretti 2013b). In a conciliatory gesture of his own, Orr gave Duggan $275,000 to assemble a "transition team." Duggan was optimistic during this period, telling reporters he was preparing for an expanded role under Orr. He expected significant economic improvement to take at least two or three years, longer than he felt Orr would oversee the city (Hijazi 2013).

According to reports, Duggan and Orr met at least weekly throughout November and the better part of December. On December 19, they announced a power-sharing deal. In broad strokes, Orr granted Duggan control over some city services, including the fire department, lighting, and blight removal; he can also make appointments with EM approval. But Orr stayed in control of the police department, bankruptcy restructuring, and dispersal of federal grants. Orr reported that the deal is in the best interest of Detroiters and allows the restructuring of city finances to move forward. Newly elected council members Scott Benson and Mary Sheffield described the deal as a movement toward "normal" government (Nichols 2013c).

Orr made the power sharing agreement official by signing an executive order on December 30 (Order #20), which states that, "[t]he EM has determined that the Mayor will play a vital role in the collaborative process of ensuring the continuity of essential services and restoring financial stability." The protocols put in place by the order allow Orr to delegate authority to Duggan without violating Michigan's EM law. Orr and Duggan may attend each other's departmental meetings, and the mayor may attend meetings between the EM and governor at the request of either the EM or the mayor. Duggan cannot do anything to interfere with the bankruptcy proceedings but will be involved in negotiations with labor where they involve city operations. Any departmental restructuring, outsourcing of governmental functions, or public/private partnership, as well as hirings that cost over $50,000/year and investments over $50,000, require EM approval. The mayor and department heads may make changes to the EM's "restructuring initiatives" only when: 1) Orr consents to the changes, and 2) the financial outcomes are similar to those of the original initiative (Emergency Manager City of Detroit 2013).

The duties delegated to Mayor Duggan include certain important public works and high visibility agencies, to be sure. However, they are not pivotal vis-à-vis restructuring and financial value extraction. Indeed, even if he happened to feel so inclined, Duggan would be categorically unable to influence, much less prevent or significantly alter any of the key initiatives currently being undertaken or explored by Orr. The mayor is incapable of shoring up the precarious position of public pensions. He cannot protect public infrastructure networks, such as Detroit's Water and Sewer Department, from being regionalized or privatized. Indeed, Duggan can do nary a thing about the many community assets currently at risk of appropriation. And even within

Duggan's limited sphere of influence, the EM retains veto control. We see that even within purported power sharing arrangements, the EM retains unconditional control, rendering the political utility of elected officials greatly diminished and its symbolic content greatly enhanced.

Ritual Theory

The historical persistence of political rituals in liberal democracies would come as something of a surprise to canonical sociologists such as Max Weber and Emile Durkheim, who predicted that ritual and symbolism would fade from importance in modern public life, replaced with rational, purposeful action.[5] For Durkheim—whose work casts a long shadow on subsequent ritual research—the world of the "sacred" was being slowly eroded by the world of the "profane" (1976). This transformation was viewed poignantly because symbolic systems, such as religion, fulfill key social functions. In the modern world, such systems provide the cognitive tools for making sense of complex social systems, while expressing "the interdependency of the members of societies in a particular symbolic idiom" (Baringhorst 2001: 291). From Durkheim, we are left with the foundational insight that even in modern industrial societies, rituals can and will function to "strengthen the bonds attaching the individual to the society of which he is a member" (1976: 226). Furthermore, despite his predictions concerning an inevitable historical arc toward public disenchantment and de-sacralization, rituals have proven to be remarkably resilient and remain a key part of the sociopolitical landscape. "Contrary to Durkheim's assumption", observes Baringhorst, "many social scientists have highlighted *the ubiquity of ritual behavior* in the realm of the profane: not only concerning everyday life practices, but also the crucial function of rituals *in modern liberal democracies*" (2001: 292; emphasis added). On the whole, scholars who broadly share Durkheim's emphasis on the integrative functions of rituals have tended to dominate this body of research.

Edward Shils and Michael Young (1953) provide an early example of a neo-Durkheimian tack in their study of British coronations. The masses faithfully celebrate coronations with religious-like intensity, the authors note, though for reasons they often cannot fully articulate. ("The heart has its reasons which the mind does not suspect.") On this question, "political science and philosophy too are silent" (Shils and Young 1953: 63). In explaining the mass appeal of coronations (as well as their integrative social functions), the authors highlight their mythical and symbolic elements.

> A society is held together by its internal agreement about the sacredness of certain fundamental moral standards. In an inchoate, dimly perceived, and seldom explicit manner, the central authority of an orderly society. . . is acknowledged to be the avenue of communication with the realm of sacred values. Within [British] society, popular constitutional monarchy enjoys almost universal recognition in this capacity [. . .]. Intermittent rituals bring the society . . . repeatedly into contact with the vessel of the sacred values. The Coronation provided at one time and for practically the entire society such an intensive contact with the sacred that we believe we are justified in interpreting it . . . as a great act of national communion" (Ibid.: 80).

Two decades later, Blumler (et al., 1971) developed a similar analysis of the investiture of the Prince of Wales in 1969 (nationally broadcast on live television), which is seen as a ritual event that generated a "profound emotional commitment to the

Monarchy," while reaffirming "fundamental social values (family solidarity, national pride)" (Ibid.: 170).

Scholars have developed similar analyses of political rituals in the United States. For instance, in his study of the ceremonial significance of national celebrations such as Armistice Day and Veteran's Day, Lloyd Warner emphasizes "the unifying and integrative character" of public ceremonies "in which the many become the one" (Warner 1962: 16). In a representative treatment, the Memorial Day rites witnessed in "hundreds of . . . American towns . . . are a modern cult of the dead and conform to Durkheim's definition of sacred collective representations" (Warner 1959: 278). Functionalist themes are also taken up by political scientist Sydney Verba, who studied the role of the mass media in the dissemination of political symbols and ceremonies.[6] Based on his analysis of the Kennedy assassination, he argues that a central symbolic-integrative force in modern industrial society is now "political symbols that stand on the highest level for the society—in the American case by the Presidency above all." This "central commitment to the symbols of nationhood" is generated via "periodic ceremonies and collective events that allow the members of the society mutually to reinforce each other's commitment" (Verba 1965: 353–354).[7] In a complementary analysis of Kennedy's inaugural address, Robert Bellah posits the event functioned as an important ceremony in "the American civil religion," serving to ritually reaffirm "the religious legitimation of the highest political authority" (Bellah 1968: 6). "What we have," he concludes, "is a collection of beliefs, symbols, and rituals with respect to sacred things and institutionalized in a collectivity. This [is a] religion—there seems no other word for it" (Bellah 1967: 8). While Bellah concedes that America's "civil religion has not always been invoked in favor of worthy causes" (Ibid.: 14), he ultimately finds, in true Durkheimian fashion, that inaugural ceremonies are "powerful symbols of national solidarity" that are able "to mobilize deep levels of personal motivation for the attainment of national goals" (1968: 15).

At first blush, we can see how the Durkheimian model might provide an attractive explanation for electoral ritualization in EM-controlled Detroit. From this perspective, holding the election despite its diminished instrumental capacity could serve to minimize political disruption in a time of crisis by maintaining established patterns of social integration. While no longer functional in the traditional, utilitarian sense, the election remains the expression of collectively held values and thus retains deep symbolic and ceremonial significance. In a way, this is a comforting thought: the symbolic representation of noble ideals (democracy, popular sovereignty), authentically held by the populace, is ritually performed so as to increase social cohesion and political stability. On further inspection, however, the Detroit case poses several fundamental analytic and interpretive challenges that the Durkheimian model is ill equipped to address.

First, the preeminent position afforded the positive structural functions of political rituals—namely value cohesion and social integration—seems misplaced in the Detroit case. Steven Lukes provides a useful critical blueprint for this point. To begin, the Durkheimian model tends to overstate the level of value consensus in modern society and its importance in securing social integration. Such scholars, complains Lukes, "never even consider the possibility that there might be divergences in the interpretation of such values within a society" (1975: 297). Further, once we allow for value pluralism, we must also consider that the "compliance of subordinate classes" is not necessarily the product of "shared value commitments." Societies can and do develop "functional alternatives to value consensus" (Ibid.: 298), such as in societies where social order is attained through separation and coercion (or the threat thereof). This would appear to be the case, for instance, in Northern Ireland and apartheid South Africa. As noted, a similar form of socio-spatial separation can be observed in the Detroit area, which was one of the most racially segregated metropolitan regions in the United States "for the entire twentieth century" and remains so now well into the twenty-first (Sugrue 2006: 234, Logan and Stults 2011). As Detroit became a poorer, blacker city, the suburbs and exurbs were arcing in the opposite (whiter and wealthier) direction. It is not unreasonable to consider that uneven and exclusionary settlement patterns of this sort could contribute to a fundamental divergence in the ways in which widely disseminated political symbols and ceremonies are received.

Second, analysts tend to emphasize the role of symbols *within* functionally operational (i.e., instrumental) political systems. This is as true for the neo-Durkheimian camp (the structural functionalists) as it is for their conflict-oriented critics. For instance, Lukes notes that the ritual dimension of a given political event or practice "may be more or less indirect" relative to its utilitarian dimension. Thus, "instrumentally oriented activities in general, may have their symbolic or ritual aspect, and . . . to identify this is not *eo ipso* to deny or debunk their non-symbolic aspect. To see them as rituals is to tell half the story" (Ibid.: 299). In Detroit, however, the key questions do not concern the role of ritual *in* politics, but rather, the role of ritual *as* politics. In EM-controlled cities, the local electoral process has been so thoroughly ritualized that it now stands as a singular dramaturgical meta-performance (within which discrete symbols and ceremonies continue to be deployed). While, typically, instrumentality coexists with symbolism in the electoral process, in Detroit the former has been almost entirely (if temporarily) subsumed by the latter. If, as I have suggested, existing models inadequately explain this process, we are left with the task of developing an alternative theoretical model.

Electoral Ritualization in Detroit: An Alternative Model

A more useful approach begins with Janusz Mucha's theory of "ritual substitution" (1991). At the heart of the theory lie two decisive societal acts. The first act is the cleaving of a given political arena into two component camps representing contradictory "sacred concepts of social order." Political ritualization occurs when these two "incompatible supreme values", connected to two different sources of social power, are positioned in opposition to one another. In such cases, the stronger political power may "ritualize" the weaker by increasing the symbolic content of its actions while decreasing its instrumental influence. This act of substitution (*of* the symbolic *for* the instrumental) is the second decisive act in Mucha's theory. England is taken as an example. To begin, the sovereignty of the people, a supreme value, bestows the representative parliament with "real political power" (Ibid.: 221). At the same time, the monarchy is seen "as a symbol representing a continuity of historical tradition that the society does not want to give up"—a second and competing supreme value. This creates "tensions between the two political institutions," which is resolved through the "ritualization of the monarch's political activities. The same rituals that in the past highlighted the monarch's real power *now only replace it*" (Ibid.; emphasis added). As they are central to an accurate accounting of the Detroit case, a closer analysis of these dual foundational acts is warranted.

The Cleaving of the Local Political Arena

For Mucha, a necessary precondition for ritual substitution is "a tension between the declared sovereignty of the people and the actual state of affairs" (Mucha 1991: 224). In Detroit, this disjuncture pits democratic principles and practices against financial markets—a competing pole of power and contradictory supreme value. "We are dealing," notes Mucha, "with, on the one hand, the sacralization of democracy, that is, the sovereignty of the people and only of the people, and on the other hand the sacralization of another centre of political power" (Ibid.). This foundational social contradiction between competing sacred value systems (in this case democratic versus financial) must be managed or resolved in some manner (relieved, sublimated, redirected, or forestalled). While Mucha identifies this tension in the abstract ("incompatible supreme values") and highlights how it can be resolved symbolically (via the process of ritualization), other scholars have grappled with the tension in its particulars, and have demonstrated how it can be managed institutionally and politically on the level of municipal governance.

For our purposes, we can fill in the political particulars of Mucha's theory by looking at the literature on the fiscal crisis of the state. According to James O'Connor (1973), the state faces structural tensions stemming from the intersection of two contradictory functions. First, the state must attend to the requirements of *capital accumulation*. This means it is pressured to socialize the cost of economic development, such as the social and infrastructural preconditions for private enterprise. Second, the state must also maintain *popular legitimacy* by way of social safety nets and progressive patterns of resource redistribution. Both of these functions generate pressure for increased expenditures. However, the profits generated with the help of state activity are invariably privatized, creating structural fiscal imbalances—over time, expenditure demands will outpace revenue flows. On the scale of the urban, the structural contradiction identified by O'Connor is manifest in a fundamental tension between the economic (revenue and expenditure dynamics) and the democratic (popular demands for municipal services). On one hand, cities must "support urban economic processes" by being responsive to the infrastructural, service, and subsidy "requirements of capital accumulation, and to changes in these requirements generated by economic growth [and decline]." On the other, cities must "promote the political integration of the urban population," which entails managing "political participation among the masses of the urban population who do not control capital accumulation and may not benefit from it either" (Friedland, Piven, and Alford 1977: 447, 449). More recently, researchers have emphasized how such pressures are exacerbated under conditions of advanced neoliberal austerity (Peck 2014, Peck 2012, Kirkpatrick and Smith 2011, Hackworth 1998).

While we might expect that this arrangement would produce "extraordinary convulsions" and widespread "popular discontent" in municipal politics, "such convulsions are not frequent" (Friedland, Piven, and Alford 1977: 349). One of the ways that resistance is tamped down and political disruption minimized is via the "structural segregation" of contradictory municipal functions. Specifically, "[t]he devices by which [structural segregation] is accomplished include locating potentially contradictory functions in different agencies; structuring these agencies so that access to economically important decisions is difficult while access to integrative ones is relatively easy; and locating these different functions at different levels of government" (Ibid.: 457). As a practical matter, this means that agencies whose primary function is securing conditions suitable to capital accumulation are insulated from electoral politics. Instead, such agencies "tend to be controlled by those groups who have production interests in their services. Local banks dominate finance boards, developers the zoning boards, downtown corporations the urban renewal agencies . . . and so on" (Piven and Friedland 1984: 396).

Scholars of local fiscal crisis have provided important insights about how a fundamental societal tension between two "sacred value systems" (accumulation vs. legitimation) is mediated through the dualistic structure of urban governance. This structural perspective is usefully married to the theory of ritual substitution with which we began. With respect to US cities, theories of local fiscal crisis highlight the structural-institutional framework (e.g., structural segregation) within which the clash between "incompatible value systems" unfolds.

The Act of Ritual Substitution

One way in which the tension between incompatible social paradigms can be reconciled is for the political power of one system to be neutralized through the process of ritualization, or the substitution of symbolic substance for instrumental substance. Thus, the second decisive event in Mucha's account is the act of "ritual replacement" that the more powerful entity forces upon the weaker. "My thesis," summarizes Mucha, "is that the ritualization of collective behaviour may serve not only to highlight . . . its instrumental aspects in a symbolic way, but also to substitute them after eliminating them or altering their traditional meaning" (1991: 220). While ritual substitution can occur in a range of sociopolitical contexts, the electoral process is a particularly ripe target. Elections possess several special qualities—important symbolic and social characteristics—that make them susceptible to ritual substitution. "[I]t is, undoubtedly, elections which are the most important form of political ritual in liberal democratic societies," notes Lukes, "partly because of their central place in the official ideology of such societies, [and] partly because of the high degree of mass participation they involve" (Ibid.: 304). The election process is already pregnant with symbolism (though typically their symbolic function is secondary to their utilitarian function in liberal democracies), which can be enhanced and exploited should the need arise.

The nature of ritual itself is also of crucial importance here. When we dispense with assumptions related to value consensus, it becomes theoretically possible for political rituals to be used in ways that differentially impact various subpopulations. In highly stratified and exclusionary social formations, for instance, "[political] rituals can be seen as modes of exercising, or seeking to exercise, power along the cognitive dimension" (Lukes 1975: 301). This is no small matter. Rituals can be strategically deployed precisely because of their capacity to "reinforce and perpetuate dominant and official models of social structure and social change, [. . .] of political order and political conflict, and indeed of the very nature and boundaries of 'politics'" (Ibid.: 302). In this manner, one social group could conceivably deploy ritual substitution against another, less powerful group for purposes of sociopolitical manipulation and strategic control.

In Detroit, the ritual substitution of the electoral process has been sudden, overt, and comprehensive. With the assignment of an EM, the instrumentality of the election was greatly diminished, while its symbolic dimension was enhanced. The scale of ritualization in Detroit invites unexpected historical comparisons. For instance, there are revealing parallels with local elections in communist societies. In both cases the ultimate outcome of a given election was effectively controlled, keeping the instrumental purpose of the exercise at a minimum and ritualizing popular sovereignty, such that participation itself becomes a tacit sign of support for the existing regime. "[Elections] have had no less important role in the U.S.S.R.," reports Lukes, "where the extremely high voting figures evidently have considerable symbolic significance. Participation in elections can plausibly be interpreted as the symbolic affirmation of the voters' acceptance of the political system and their role within it" (1975: 304). Similarly in Communist Poland, authorities "attached unusual significance to the proper performance of the [local] election ritual. For them a turnout very close to 100 percent meant their total legitimation" (Mucha 226). Likewise in Detroit, we observe what might be considered a disproportionate amount of energy and resources expended on get-out-the-vote campaigns and (multiple) recounts, while the city was (and remains) under the complete control of an EM. But these efforts and expenses make more sense when we consider the value of the election as a ceremony signifying the legitimacy of the system.

As Mucha demonstrates, the "legitimating role . . . elections ha[ve] for the political system and the ruling group" can be observed in both liberal democracies and Communist societies (1991). Scholars of the fiscal crisis of the state have further shown how, in liberal democracies, the legitimation function of local government (determined via democratically accessible channels) is typically separated from its accumulation and extraction functions. Structurally segregated, the door is opened for the more powerful system to ritualize the weaker. In the normal course of events, this does not happen as elections retain a certain level of democratic efficacy, though this utility is limited to the realm of social expenditures. Extractive demands, safely insulated from democratic mediation, are also typically satisfied by this arrangement. In the postcrisis period, however, financial imperatives related to value extraction have become so great (relative to some cities' ability to meet them) that they can no longer be reliably satisfied in this segregated, "back channel" manner. New structural arrangements must be devised. In Detroit, this tension has been resolved through the process of ritual substitution. The arm of the local state related to legitimacy is emptied of utility and infused with symbolism. "[T]he electoral process," Mucha laments, "turns out to have been an activity that replaced the sovereignty of the people, not expressed it" (Mucha 1991: 227).

Conclusion: Substitution Abrupt and Subtle

The emergency management of Detroit is a form of urban governance that precludes authentic democratic engagement and meaningful participation. With the appointment of an EM, depoliticization through ritualization is both sudden and comprehensive. But the model of political ritualization suggests that the structural preconditions for ritual substitution exist in all US cities. The core underlying tension between two competing and (potentially) incompatible "sacred concepts of social order" (financial demands vs. democratic demands) exerts pressure on all governance structures in the postcrisis period. Many cities, most of the time, may successfully manage this tension without resorting to wholesale ritualization. "Whether or not these dual functions of urban government [the economic and the democratic] are . . . inherently and consistently contradictory," observe Friedland, Piven, and Alford, "they are clearly contradictory at certain junctures in the process of capitalist economic development—for example during extreme downturns in the business cycle" (1977: 349).

At those junctures where this tension is "clearly contradictory" we might expect the process of ritual substitution to be sudden and comprehensive. At other junctures, however, the tension may produce a gradual process of substitution that slowly erodes the instrumental utility of local democratic practices and institutions. The process of incremental ritualization may also function to provide a symbolic and ceremonial cover for the strict demands of financial value extraction. As more responsibilities are gradually shifted to private and public-private entities, local democratic norms are chipped away. As more decisions are made by unelected and unaccountable experts and technicians, democratic efficacy is further eroded. And as more of the city is managed by shadow governments and quasi-public institutions, the ideal of local autonomy and self-rule fades. In this manner, Detroit may be representative of a broader trend in which the instrumental functionality of municipal/elected authorities is diminished—and its symbolic and ritualistic elements enhanced—in the face of urban austerity.

Notes

1. Thomas Sugrue has demonstrated how the city's economic decline began, somewhat counter-intuitively, in the heyday of Fordist expansion. "Between 1947 and 1963—during a period of remarkable national economic prosperity in the United States—Detroit lost over 137,000 manufacturing jobs" (Sugrue 2006: 233). This trend continued through the twentieth century; between 1960–2002, the city lost 165,000 of its 230,00 (remaining) industrial jobs, while adding only 30,000 in the service sector. Over the same period, the whiter, wealthier suburbs gained a net total of 50,000 industrial jobs as well as 600,000 jobs in the service sector (Oswalt 2006: 230).
2. Officially, 2.37 million Michigan residents (53 percent) voted to repeal it, while 2.13 million (47 percent)—only eight of the state's eighty-three counties—voted to retain it (Michigan Secretary of State 2013).
3. New council members Scott Benson, Raquel Castaneda-Lopez, and Gabe Leland profess the necessity of working with the EM and that they expect certain council members to lead the council toward productive cooperation with the EM. Mary Sheffield, also newly elected, says she hopes the council will be able to lead democratically once Orr is gone (Ferretti 2013).
4. The "head of the line" principle was codified in the most recent iteration of Michigan's EM law (Public Act 436, Section 11(1)(b)), guaranteeing that banks and firms handling municipal debt issuance or restructuring for distressed cities will receive "payment in full" (Kirkpatrick and Breznau 2014).
5. For his part, Weber bemoaned the gradual entrapment of western society in an "iron cage" of rationality and utilitarian efficiency (Weber 2998).

6. For Verba, the mass media (especially television) plays a key role in this equation by providing a platform that ensures "almost total [ceremonial] participation" based on a "universality of information" (Verba 2965, p. 353). Others have also focused on the role of the mass media in enhancing the integrative capacity of political rituals. For example, Dayan and Katz (1992) examine the unifying capacity of various types of political media events (i.e., contests, conquests, and coronations), while Carey (1998) explores the role of the media in public rituals of shame, degradation, and excommunication. Carey accords special attention to the ritual form of the quasi-judicial "hearing" (e.g., the McCarthy hearings, Iran-contra hearings, Watergate hearings, etc.), which serves to establish important socio-symbolic group boundaries.

7. Verba continues, "In the relatively simple societies of which Durkheim wrote, this was accomplished by periodic reunions and ceremonials. In a complex and widely extended society like the United States, a society without the ceremonies of royalty, such reunions and common observances are somewhat rarer, though national elections and some national holidays may be examples of such events. The assassination crisis is important here because it is probably the nearest equivalent in a large modern nation-state to the kind of intense mutual rededication ceremony that is possible in a smaller, simpler society" (1965: 354).

References

Abowd, P. (2012). "Michigan's Hostile Takeover." *Mother Jones*, (February 15).

Arnhart, L. (1985). "Murray Edelman, Political Symbolism, and the Incoherence of Political Science." *The Political Science Reviewer* 15: 185–213.

Baringhorst, S. (2001). "Political Ritual," in K. Nash and A. Scott (eds.) *The Blackwell Companion to Political Sociology*. Oxford: Blackwell Publishing: 291–301.

Bell, C. (1992). *Ritual Theory, Ritual Practice*. Oxford: Oxford University Press.

Bellah, R. N. (1967). "Civil Religion in America." *Daedalus* 96 (1): 1–21.

———. (1968). "Civil Religion in America," in W. G. McLoughlin and R. N. Bellah (eds.), *Religion in America*. Boston: Houghton Mifflin.

Blumler, J. G., Brown, J. R., Ewbank, A. J. and Nossiter, T. J. (1971). "Attitudes to the Monarchy: Their Structure and Development during a Ceremonial Occasion." *Political Studies* 19: 149–171.

Carey, W. J. (1998). "Political Ritual on Television: Episodes in the history of shame, degradation and excommunication," in T. Liebes and J. Curran (eds.), *Media, Ritual and Identity*. London and New York: Routledge: 42–70.

Citizens Research Council of Michigan. (2010). "Financial Emergencies in Local Governments." White Paper, Report 362.

———. (2011). "The Local Government and School District Fiscal Accountability Act: Public Act 4 of 2011." White Paper, Report 368.

Clement, D. (2013). "The Spatial Injustice of Crisis-Driven Neoliberal Urban Restructuring in Detroit." *Open Access Thesis*. Paper 406.

Conyers, J. and G. Peters, US House of Representatives. (2013). Letter to Comptroller General Dodaro (General Accountability Office). (March 21).

Daniels, S. M. and D. A. Nichols. (2013). "Snyder touts city, state on cable shows- Gov. says Detroit's comeback 'has been going on for years.'" *The Detroit News*. (November 9): A5.

Dayan, D. and E. Katz. (1992). *Media Events: The Live Broadcasting of History*. Cambridge, MA: Harvard University Press.

Durkheim, E. (1976). *The Elementary Forms of the Religious Life*, translated by J. W. Swain, with an Introduction by R. Nesbit. 2d ed. New York, London: George Allan & Unwin Ltd.

Edelman, M. (1971). *Politics as Symbolic Action: Mass Arousal and Quiescence*. Chicago: Markham Publishing Company.

———. (1985). *The Symbolic Uses of Politics*. Urbana: University of Illinois Press.

Emergency Manager City of Detroit. (2013). *Order Restoring the Salary and Benefits of the Mayor and Adopting the Agreement Between the Emergency Manager and Mayor Duggan Concerning Delegation of Authority and Transition Protocols*. Emergency Manager Order No. 20, December 30. Retrieved October 1, 2014 (http://www.detroitmi.gov/EmergencyManager/Orders.aspx).

Ferretti, C. (2013). "Officials have high hopes for Detroit Council election despite apathy over EM." *The Detroit News: Web Edition Articles*. October 24 (Retrieved from NewsBank on September 23, 2014).

Friedland, R., F. F. Piven and R. R. Alford. (1977). "Political Conflict, Urban Structure, and the Fiscal Crisis," *International Journal of Urban and Regional Research* 1.1–4, 447–71.

Hackworth, J. (2007). *The neoliberal city: governance, ideology, and development in American urbanism.* Ithaca, NY: Cornell University Press.

Harvey, D. (2005). *A Brief History of Neoliberalism.* Oxford: Oxford University Press.

Hijazi, S. (2013). "Duggan announces transition team, holds public forum at WSU." *The Arab American News.* (November 22). Retrieved September 27, 2014 (http://www.arabamericannews.com/news/news/id_7850).

House Judiciary Committee Democratic Staff. (2012). "Democracy for Sale: Subverting Voting Rights, Collective Bargaining and Accountability under Michigan's Emergency Manager Law" (n.p., Feb 21).

Kirkpatrick, L. O. (2015a). "Graduated Sovereignty and the Fragmented City: Mapping the Political Geography of Citizenship in Detroit." In Cherstin Lyon (ed.), *Place, (Dis)Place, and Citizenship.* Wayne State University Press (Forthcoming).

———. (2015b). "Urban Triage, City Systems & the Remnants of Community: Some "Sticky" Complications in the Greening of Detroit." *The Journal of Urban History* (Forthcoming).

———, and N. Breznau. (2014). "The (Non)Politics of Emergency Intervention: Exploring the Racial Geography of Urban Crisis Management in Michigan." Unpublished Working Paper.

———, and M. P. Smith. (2011). "The Infrastructural Limits to Growth: Rethinking the Urban Growth Machine in Times of Fiscal Crisis." *International Journal of Urban & Regional Research* 35(3): 477–503.

Laitner, B. (2013). "Pontiac's no longer under an emergency manager but leader want the last word." *Detroit Free Press* (August 26).

Logan, J. R. and B. Stults (2011). "The Persistence of Segregation in the Metropolis: New Findings from the 2010 Census." Census Brief prepared for *Project US2010.*

Lukes, S. (1975). "Political Ritual and Social Integration." *Sociology* 9(2): 289–308.

Michigan Secretary of State (Ruth Johnson), General Election Results (Final Count, Jan. 4, 2013), State Proposal 12-1: Referendum The Emergency Manager Law. Last Accessed: Web. 15 Oct. 2013. At: http://miboecfr.nictusa.com/election/results/12GEN/90000001.html.

Mucha, J. (1991). "Ritualization as Substitution." *Journal of the Anthropological Society at Oxford* 22(3): 219–234.

Neavling, S. (2013). "Recount changes primary election by just 9 votes." *Motor City Muckraker* (September 27).

Nesbit, R. (1976). Introduction," in *The Elementary Forms of the Religious Life*, translated by J. W. Swain, with an Introduction by R. Nesbit. 2d ed. New York, London: George Allan & Unwin Ltd.

Nichols, D. A. (2013a). "Bing, NAACP branch urges Detroiters to vote on Tuesday." *The Detroit News: Web Edition Articles.* November 1 (Retrieved from NewsBank on September 27, 2014).

———. (2013b). "Duggan names 4 to transition team—He is talking with Orr about how much power he will have." *The Detroit News.* November 14, pp. A4.

———. (2013c). "Duggan's duties detailed—Mayor-elect names top aides, will oversee Detroit's lighting, fire dept., blight removal." *The Detroit News.* December 20, pp. A4.

——— and C. Ferretti. (2013b). "Duggan unsure when he'll take on bigger role—Mayor-elect in talks with Orr; wants to oversee police, services." *The Detroit News.* November 20, pp. A1.

——— and S. Pardo. (2013a). "Mayoral hopefuls differ on role with EM—Duggan to plan for transition from state control; Napoleon won't be 'do-nothing' city leader." *The Detroit News.* October 10, pp. A1.

——— and C. E. Ramirez. (2013). "Rivals race to rev up turnout at polls." *The Detroit News.* November 4, pp. A6.

O'Connor, J. (1973). *The fiscal crisis of the state.* New York, NY: St. Martin's Press.

Oosting, J. (2012). "Michigan Emergency Manager Law: What's next after Public Act 4 repeal?" *MLive.com.* N.p., 11 Nov. 2012. Last Accessed: Web. 15 Oct. 2014. At: http://www.mlive.com/politics/index.ssf/2012/11/michigan_emergency_manager_law.html.

Oswalt, P., ed. (2006). *Shrinking Cities, Vol. 1: International Research.* Ostfildern-Ruit, Germany: Hatje Cantz.

Pacewicz, J. (2013). "Tax increment financing, economic development professionals, and the fnancialization of urban politics." *Socio-Economic Review* 11(3): 413–440.

Peck, J. (2012). "Austerity Urbanism: American Cities Under Extreme Economy." *City* 16(6): 626–655.

———. (2014). "Pushing Austerity: State Failure, Municipal Bankruptcy and the Crises of Fiscal Federalism in the USA." *Cambridge Journal of Regions, Economy and Society* 7(1): 17–44.

Piven, F. F. and R. Friedland. (1984). Public choice and private power: a theory of fiscal crisis. In A. Kirby, P. Knox and S. Pinch, *Public service provision and urban development.* New York, NY: St. Martin's Press.

Preston, D. and S. Church. (2013). "Detroit swap banks go first as bankruptcy looms." *Bloomberg News* (June 20).

Preston, D. and C. Christoff. (2013). "Only Wall Street Wins in Detroit Crisis Reaping $474 Million Fee." *Bloomberg News* (March 13).

Shils, E. and M. Young. (1953). "The Meaning of the Coronation." *Sociological Review* 1(2): 63–81.

Sugrue, T. J. (1996). *The Origins of the Urban Crisis: Race and Inequality in Postwar Detroit*. Princeton, NJ: Princeton University Press.

———. (2006). "Racism and Urban Decline," in P. Oswalt (ed.), *Shrinking Cities, Vol .1: International Research*. Ostfildern-Ruit, Germany: Hatje Cantz.

———. (2013). "Notown." *Democracy Journal*. Spring 2013.

Turbeville, W. C. (2013). *The Detroit Bankruptcy*. White Paper. Demos.

Verba, S. (1965). "The Kennedy Assassination and Nature of Political Commitment," in B.S. Greenburg and E.B. Parker (eds.), *The Kennedy Assassination and the American Public: Social Communication in Crisis*. Stanford: Stanford University Press.

Wacquant, L. (2008). *Urban Outcasts: a comparative sociology of advanced marginality*. Cambridge: Polity.

Walker, M. A. (2013b). "Detroit mayoral ballot recount meets challenges right off the bat." *Detroit Free Press* (September 10).

Warner, W. L. (1959). *The Living and the Dead: A Study of the Symbolic Life of Americans*. New Haven: Yale University Press.

———. (1962). *American Life: Dream and Reality*. Revised Edition. Chicago: University of Chicago Press.

Weber, M. (1998). *The Protestant Ethic and the Spirit of Capitalism*, translated by T. Parsons, with a foreword by R. Collins. 2d ed. Los Angeles: Roxbury.

Wilkinson, M., D. A. Nichols, and S. Pardo. (2013). "Detroit picks Duggan—Candidate who touted turnaround expertise says he'll work with EM." *The Detroit News*. (November 6): A2.

Williams, C. (2013a). "Bankruptcy shadows Detroit 's mayoral election." *Associated Press State and Local Wire*. November 4 (Retrieved from NewsBank September 27, 2014).

———. (2013b). "Detroit voters elect 1st white mayor in 4 decades." *Associated Press State and Local Wire*. November 6 (Retrieved from NewsBank September 20, 2014).

Wischusen, P. (2013). "Barrow believes write-in votes are fraudulent." *The Michigan Citizen*, September 19, 2013.

9

Framing Detroit

Jamie Peck

This chapter sets out to explore how Detroit has been framed—legally, fiscally, politically, and discursively—as the architect of its own misfortune. Dominant narrations of the Detroit bankruptcy displace both the blame and the burden of economic adjustment, dumping the costs and risks onto the city itself, and onto the most socioeconomically marginalized. Under the hegemony of the model of neoliberal devolution known as fiscal federalism, the underlying causes of municipal financial crisis have been localized, endogenized, and pathologized. And the remedies must also be found locally, as under no circumstances must cities be "bailed out." This framing speaks to the way in which the banking crisis of 2008 has been translated into a state crisis, an urban crisis, and a social crisis, an improbable feat that Mark Blyth has characterized as "the greatest bait and switch in human history" (2013: 13, Peck 2013). This ideological offensive has been pursued in the context of the ongoing financialization of the American urban system, exacerbating its still-unfolding contradictions. The effect has been to lock in a regime of "austerity urbanism" in which an adverse bundle of financial and political pressures work in a downward direction—in both social and scalar terms.

Imagining "New Detroit"

The resulting form of trickle-down fiscal discipline goes further than merely blaming the (local) victims; the victims are also sent the bill. Or, as the founder of the conservative Heritage Foundation, Ed Feulner (2013: 3), prefers to put it, "It's bad enough that a bailout would be patently unfair to taxpayers who aren't at fault in Detroit's failure to govern itself, but the city itself would learn nothing. The bad behavior that led it to this point would go uncorrected." More than a mere change of course is implied by the word "correction," needless to say; there are penal undertones too. Detroit is seen to be largely at fault in its own default, an undeserving subject of austerity. Peddlers of what have become new urban orthodoxies take the view that the bankruptcy represents a long-postponed opportunity for Detroit to atone for past political sins, and to embrace a privatized, more market-friendly future. Prominent amongst these, Harvard's Edward Glaeser, a senior fellow at the Manhattan Institute, apparently shares the conservative think

145

tank's assessment that "the city's problems are mostly self-inflicted" (Malanga 2009: 9). Since this is a city saddled with the dual burden of "public-sector irresponsibility" and a crippling deficit of "entrepreneurial inclination," Glaeser (2010: 1, 2013: A11) believes that Detroit's best hope is to "shrink its way back to greatness," fashioning a new mode of deregulated growth, duly cognizant of the continuing constraints of its inhospitable climate and depleted tax base.

Not surprisingly, Detroit represents a target-rich environment for Tea Party activists like Judson Phillips, whose "Cold, hard truth" column in the *Washington Times* spins a now-familiar combination of free-market reason and partisan bile. Here, Detroit's bankruptcy presented an opportunity to amputate the dead hand of US-style municipal socialism. Conveniently, the full array of the usual suspects were right there at the scene of the crime—corrupt local politicians, superannuated bureaucrats, belligerent public-sector unions, surrounded by a workless and racialized underclass—together wallowing in this "open sewer of the Midwest," whose predictable encounter with "fiscal Armageddon" was a premonition of the fate awaiting other Democratically controlled cities (Phillips 2013: 1). "Dissolving" Detroit would make way for a New Detroit, constructed as a small-government demonstration project:

> The plan is simple: Dissolve Detroit, then replace it, or at least part of it, with the city of New Detroit [where] there would be no taxes. None. People whose primary residence is in New Detroit would pay no federal, state or local income taxes. Corporations with their primary offices in New Detroit would also pay no taxes, federal, state or local. Those who moved to New Detroit would not have to file a tax return that said anything more than, "My primary residence is New Detroit" (2013: 2).

The appeal of this scorched-earth scheme for a tax-free makeover is that Old Detroit, its defenders and dependents would at a stroke be gone, wiping the social and fiscal slate clean and opening a deregulated space for a new "land rush." A bothersome wrinkle in this deceptively simple plan, however, was that at least until the extreme tax cut worked its magic the State of Michigan "would have to pick up the tab for certain things that are traditionally funded by the city," like schools and emergency systems for policing and firefighting, but surely these services could be kept out of the hands of "bloated unions" by outsourcing to private contractors (Phillips 2013: 2). At least one reader spotted the glaring contradiction in Phillips's myopic plan, *FLTransplant* asking how it could be that "dumping the costs of Detroit upon Michigan is capitalism at its finest while dumping the costs on a greater number of people—the citizens of the USA—is socialism" (comment, Phillips 2013: 3).

The political economy of sociospatial redistribution is, inescapably, the central issue when it comes to the fiscal fate of Detroit, or for that matter any American city. Phillips's faltering logic is really nothing other than a cavalier over-interpretation of the conservative legal doctrine of fiscal federalism, where not only "each level of government," but in effect each *unit* of government, is expected (or required) to "internalize both the costs and the benefits of its activities" (Gillette 2012: 287). As the antithesis of Keynesian redistribution, and its panoply of fiscal transfers and automatic stabilizers, the doctrine of fiscal federalism holds that cities, suburbs, and local-government entities must always be free to opt out (of revenue and responsibility sharing), but they must never be bailed out. This disaggregated state of go-it-alone, beggar-thy-neighbor competition is a world ruled by fiscal discipline, both between tiers of government and between jurisdictions; (in)solvency is a local matter, or a problem for that place down the road. And it is an economizing world increasingly divided between free-riding, low-tax suburbs and debt-ridden cities. In the morality plays of austerity urbanism, "irresponsibility" is perversely conferred on the latter, not the former.

As a place that allegedly "emblematizes un-entrepreneurial America" (Glaeser 2011: 36), Detroit has only itself to blame; a "victim of its own political vices," it would now be a poster child for a new generation of "deadbeat cities" (Wall Street Journal 2013e: A14). Detroit's curse (and in the circumstances that may not be too strong a word) is to have become practically synonymous with bankruptcy, not just as a passing legal status but as an entrenched urban condition. The cold, hard logic of fiscal federalism dictates that the accompanying pain is regressively redistributed; it must be both localized and compressed—hence the singular intensity of Detroit's court-administered structural adjustment, under the control of a state-appointed emergency manager as well as under the surveillance of the bankruptcy court.

New narratives of urban crisis are being fabricated around the profoundly stressed circumstances of cities like Detroit, but the incessant conservative chorus should not distract from an underlying pattern of causality of a much more structural kind, one that is marked by deep historical roots as well as by extralocal drivers. According to Steven Rattner, architect of the auto industry's corporate bailout, the city's bankruptcy was the financial equivalent of a hurricane (Rattner 2013), even if this particular extreme-weather event may have been more predictable than most. A wide range of similarly exposed cities are also finding themselves confronted by elevated environmental risks, courtesy of the financial version of climate change characterized here as austerity urbanism. Detroit has been hit by the perfect storm, but the clouds have been gathering around other cities as well—hence the need to deal with how Detroit is being framed (in all senses of the word). Localized explanations play into localized narratives of culpability, which already have a close-to hegemonic grip. The horizons of critical analysis must be much wider—as must the horizons of any credible response to the multiscalar urban crises of which Detroit's bankruptcy is symptomatic.

As a contribution to this critical project, the chapter begins by positioning Detroit in fiscal terms, in relation to the long but hitherto rather sparse history of municipal bankruptcies, prelude to the technocratic takeover that has been executed in the name of "emergency management." This is followed by a critique of the post hoc reconstruction of Detroit's bankruptcy as a product of a bloated public sector, manifest in the form of a pensions crisis. Against this legitimizing narrative, the chapter makes the argument that Detroit's bankruptcy should be understood as an "ordinary crisis" of a faltering regime of municipal financialization and devolved institutional risk. The implications of this, needless to say, are also more than local in scope and scale.

Everyday Emergencies

> **Emergency**, *n.* A state of things unexpectedly arising, and urgently demanding immediate action
>
> **Manager**, *n.* A person who organizes, directs, or plots something; a person who regulates or deploys resources (*Oxford English Dictionary*)

Municipal bankruptcies have generally been quite rare financial events. Since local government units were included in the federal bankruptcy code—in 1937, under what are known as Chapter 9 provisions—they have numbered fewer than a dozen per year on average, the vast majority of which have not been cities as such, but special tax districts, public utilities, and other local-government entities precluded from issuing public debt. Full-scale municipal bankruptcies, in this context, are something of a post-Keynesian phenomenon, the modern history of which begins with the Orange County default of 1994—for some time the largest on record until the Wall Street crash of 2008 and its protracted aftermath. Since then, the rash of municipal filings has included Vallejo, CA (2008), Harrisburg, PA and Jefferson County, AL (both in 2011, the latter setting a new record, at $4.2 billion), and San Bernardino, CA and Stockton, CA (both 2012, the latter being, at the time, the largest city to file), before Detroit's bankruptcy in 2013 established a new mark in terms of scale, depth, and public attention, combining a revenue collapse with up to $18 billion in long-term debt (see Baldassare 1998, Peck 2014b). If New York City's near-bankruptcy in 1975 symbolized the birth of neoliberal urbanism (Harvey 2005, Phillips-Fein 2013), Detroit's default represents the most explicit manifestation yet of a systemic crisis in the ensuing regime of crisis management—a structural failure in the debt-loaded model of financialized entrepreneurialism (Peck 2012, 2014a; Tabb 2014).

Conventional wisdom has it that, with the notable exception of Detroit, most of the recent wave of municipal bankruptcies can be put down to "a single identifiable cause," a "one-time blow," or in some cases "a structural problem that worsened over time" (Pew Charitable Trusts 2013a: 7, 13). Some of these, of course, are truly contingent events. In 2013, the Los Angeles suburb of Bell was taken to the brink of bankruptcy by what investigative reporters at the *Los Angeles Times* portrayed, in a Pulitzer Prize–winning exposé, as "corruption on steroids." The township of Westfall, PA filed for bankruptcy in 2009 when it was slapped with a $20 million lawsuit from a local developer, the roots of which probably had more to do with a history of racketeering than with the pitfalls of municipal entrepreneurialism. And the High Sierra resort of Mammoth Lakes, CA may also have been at fault when revised plans for an airport expansion violated a long-term agreement with a local developer, who was then awarded a $43 million breach-of-contract judgment against the town. Elements of corruption and incompetence figure in other municipal bankruptcy stories too, but these also reveal underlying patterns—speaking as they do to the recurring theme of financialization-too-far. Jefferson County, AL and Harrisburg, PA both fell foul of creditors on the basis of unfavorably structured infrastructure projects, which in the Alabama case involved JP Morgan Chase in an interest-rates swap deal to fund the sewer system of the struggling city of Birmingham, later dubbed "Bankrupt, USA" (Walsh 2012). And in both Vallejo, CA and Central Falls, RI, the prelude to bankruptcy was an unsustainable combination of long-term economic decline, a property slump amplified by the subprime mortgage crisis, and a collapse of municipal tax revenues, culminating in an inability to meet either payroll or pension-fund obligations.

The argument that municipal bankruptcy is precipitated by a particular economic event or political act is hardly plausible in the case of Detroit, the cumulative crises of which are intergenerational in depth and not only national but international in reach. Undeniably, the city has had its share of corruption scandals and episodes of local-government mismanagement, but as drivers of systemic financial stress these pale into insignificance alongside long-run pressures associated with the structural decline of the North American auto industry, a race- and class-driven pattern of extreme suburban flight, the chronic underfunding of public services and basic infrastructure, and a history of dysfunctional and conflictual relations with state and federal governments. The fact, however, that these structural pressures find their contemporary expression in the form of public-service failures, notably in education and policing, in crumbling city infrastructures, and in a public-sector pay and pensions crisis, has set the stage for classically conservative attacks on labor unions, on state bureaucracies and their racialized and pathologized "dependents," and on Democratic Party office holders. It also provides an unprecedented opportunity to rationalize, and then to pursue with accelerated, imperative force, distinctively neoliberal restructuring strategies, which together define the framing conditions of austerity urbanism. These include privatization, asset stripping, deunionization, government downsizing, social scapegoating, and the joint imposition, often by technocratic means, of financial and political discipline.

Step forth Mr. Kevyn D. Orr, the emergency manager for the City of Detroit, whose charge, in the language of his state contract, is to "remedy the financial distress of the City by requiring, within available resources, prudent fiscal management and efficient provision of municipal services by exercising the necessary authority conferred herein" (State of Michigan 2013: 1). Mr. Orr's powers, which effectively override those of Detroit's elected officials, including the mayor, extend to the privatization or termination of city services, the voiding of contracts with unions and creditors, and the hiring and firing of staff (one of his early appointees being a new police chief). His job description has been summarized as "Urban planner, numbers cruncher, city spokesman, negotiator, politician, good cop, bad cop" (Davey and Vlasic 2013: A1). A veteran of the corporate bankruptcy world, including the 2009 restructuring of Chrysler, Mr. Orr established two offices in Detroit, one down the corridor from the mayor in the municipal building and one in premises formerly used by General Motors. Here, he keeps a collection of characteristically gritty photographs of New York City during its financial crisis in the 1970s, as a reminder of the self-actualizing potential for a fiscally assisted turnaround.

Emergency management is about more than balancing the books. It is also about governing the city differently, if not governing a different city. As a self-styled "restructuring professional" (and allegedly, by the same token, no "political animal"), Orr pledged to govern the city according to the "rule of reason" (quoted in Vlasic and Yaccino 2013: A17). The inexorable logic of finance is duly raised above the earthly domain of "politics." By implication, Detroit before the time of emergency management was a place of unreason, a politicized city, in contrast to the financially rationalized city in which politics-as-usual is suspended. A future beckons in which financial order begets social and political order—and eventually the "earned" resumption of home rule. Either implicitly or explicitly, the past is pathologized. (That is where the culprits lived.)

There are pragmatic observers who now take the view that, to coin an apt phrase, Detroit was left with "no alternative" but to surrender to a period of accelerated purging and restructuring, under emergency management and then bankruptcy protection. Fiscal conservatives, on the other hand, tend to see the crisis as a pattern-breaking opportunity to be maximized. Here, Mr. Orr has the support of financial rationalist, Charles Ortel (2013)—"most impressive" was the summary verdict on the emergency manager in his *Washington Times* column, Brass Tacks. The *Wall Street Journal*'s editorial board likewise greeted the appointment of Mr. Orr as "Motown's best hope."

> Mr. Orr correctly diagnoses the causes of the city's collapse: fiscal mismanagement, unaffordable labor agreements, lack of public safety and high tax rates. [He] points out that Detroit's property and income tax rates are the highest in the state. Many residents can't afford to pay their tax bills, which then go delinquent. Others leave, further depressing revenues. Laffer curve, Q.E.D. His refreshing antidote? Growth: "The City cannot stabilize or pay creditors meaningful recoveries if it continues to shrink." . . . Unions are protesting Mr. Orr's plan as a Wall Street bailout, which is ironic since capital market creditors who helped finance worker pensions will receive some of the roughest treatment. If Mr. Orr can't get the unions to swallow his medicine, bankruptcy is Detroit's only recourse (Wall Street Journal 2013b: A16).

While Orr publicly stated that he did not want the job, a sense of duty and the call of a once-in-a-lifetime opportunity prevailed. And he evidently shared the view that the city had truly hit the bottom—in the form of a compounded fiscal, institutional, and democratic deficit—such that surely the only way to go was up. City leaders had labored through several months of a consent agreement (the singularly inapt, if not purposefully misleading, name for a negotiating framework "agreed" with the State of Michigan as a means of staving off the need for a financial takeover). Now that the City had an emergency manager, the restructuring would (have to) continue until some kind of "resolution" was found.

Mr. Orr's first significant task as the Manager of Detroit's Emergency was to prepare a proposal for the City's creditors, in principle as a means to avert a bankruptcy filing but in practice as its prelude. This first-cut financial plan (since much revised) took the form of an extended litany of structural problems, depicting a broken-down place with a local-government system already shrunk to the point of incapacitation: even as the City's operating costs had been slashed (in large measure thanks to headcount reductions, wage cuts, and mandatory furloughs secured under the consent agreement), revenues were falling still faster, and would continue to do so as accumulated deficits ballooned to "unprecedented levels," possibly quadrupling the debt burden by FY2017 in the face of "strong economic headwinds" (City of Detroit 2013: 6, 37). Technically insolvent, the City had been deferring capital outlays and contributions to its (underfunded) pension fund; two-thirds of its parks had been closed; some 78,000 buildings within the city limits were considered abandoned, half of these in a dangerous state, while an additional 66,000 structures were either vacant or (deemed) blighted; the fire department was found wanting for standard-issue equipment; the fleet of police patrol cars was "extremely old" and poorly maintained; barely one-third of the city's ambulances were in service, while some of the emergency-medical service's other vehicles had been running over potholed streets for more than 250,000 miles, "break[ing] down frequently" (City of Detroit 2013: 12–14). In Orr's plan, alongside the proposed downsizing of municipal government, modest provision was made for essential items of "new" spending (on emergency services, blight remediation, an

IT upgrade, and urgent maintenance on the city's dilapidated electricity and sewer system), but it transpired that the City's creditors were not prepared to countenance the necessary "haircuts," in the order of twenty cents on the dollar. The plan was doomed, and Orr would file for bankruptcy protection the following month. Worse was to come.

In a protracted hearing, required to determine the City's legal eligibility for bankruptcy "protections," Mr. Orr was later chided by Judge Steven W. Rhodes for having failed to bargain in good faith with the City's creditors, although it was conceded that dealing equitably with around one hundred thousand interested parties would have been practically impossible. Orr was repeatedly accused of rattling the municipal-bonds market, to which his stock reply was that an emergency manager's only obligation is to the city, not to bond holders or to "the markets" (see Cherney, Nolan, and Glazer 2013; Finley 2013). This said, Detroit's travails are reported to have driven up borrowing costs elsewhere in Michigan, and in some cases beyond (Nolan 2013), while the five biggest bond insurers that together hold around $6.5 billion of the city's debt were exerting intense pressure to settle on (relatively) favorable terms (Wirz and Glazer 2013).[1] Bondholders were seeking to avoid a court-administered haircut—likely yet more severe than would have been conceded in a negotiated deal. Instead, they favored tax hikes, asset sales, and further workforce rollbacks, a "resolution" diametrically opposed to the position (and interests) of the municipal unions, and for that matter local residents.

Making a Pensions Crisis

During the period of Detroit's consent agreement, the unions were also determined to avoid a bankruptcy filing, calculating that a unilaterally imposed restructuring package would not only be brutal, but that it would likely breach into the hitherto protected domain of public-sector pensions. The unions petitioned the court on the grounds that pension rights were protected under Michigan's constitution. Detroit's eligibility hearing duly become the test case for public-sector pension "reform," which in the years since the Wall Street crash had been framed by conservative forces as a primary cause of the municipal funding crisis, an assertion that quickly acquired mainstream currency (see Malanga 2013a, cf. Harrington 2013, Taibbi 2013, Turbeville 2013). More accurately, pension rights and public-sector unions, both irresistibly exposed, had become strategic targets for conservative forces, while the more of the costs of restructuring could be loaded onto retirees, the less that Wall Street investors would have to bear.

Judge Rhodes's December 2013 ruling, which cleared the way for the restructuring of the City of Detroit under the federal bankruptcy code, fatefully went against labor-union petitioners and the defenders of pension rights. This precedent-setting decision meant not only that federal bankruptcy law trumped social rights written into the Michigan constitution, but that pensions were no different to any other contract subject to "impairment" under Chapter 9. Asked about an earlier statement, made at a town-hall meeting in Detroit, that pensions were "sacrosanct," Kevyn Orr resorted to a lawyerly response: "I would say rights are subject to the supremacy clause in the US Constitution" (quoted in Davey and Vlasic 2013: A1).

For their part, editorialists at the *Wall Street Journal* and their conservative allies hailed the decision, and not just because it would avert a "creditor brawl" in Detroit (which "would have turned into a legal Game of Thrones"); Judge Rhodes was praised for putting the "union conceit" of pension protection to the sword: "he may have done an even larger public service for cities nationwide by ruling that the pensions of local government employees can be impaired under Chapter 9 of the federal bankruptcy code" (*Wall Street Journal* 2013a: A16). Predictably, the advocates of municipal downsizing and public-asset stripping have been monitoring these and other cases for not only legal but for policy precedents—for neoliberal demonstration effects.

The opportunistic exploitation of a moral panic around what is now presented as a state and local government pensions *crisis* has duly become a strategic goal. "In state after state," Matt Taibbi (2013: 35) writes, conservative politicians, think tanks, and media organizations have been "using scare tactics and lavishly funded PR campaigns to cast teachers, firefighters and cops—not bankers—as the budget-devouring boogeymen responsible for the mounting fiscal problems of America's states and cities," which in light of the radical disjuncture between the downstream social costs and the actual pattern of culpability, represents "a scam of almost unmatchable balls and cruelty." While there were some localized problems, the state and local government pension system was broadly in balance prior to the crash of 2008, and would have remained in a healthy condition, long term, had it been more prudently managed, instead of being (over)exposed to the mortgage-backed securities market and to other Wall Street machinations of its ilk (Baker 2011). Even the City of Detroit's pension scheme, one of the more stressed parts of the system, was 92 percent funded as recently as 2010, albeit on shaky foundations (Pew Charitable Trusts 2013b).

What took Detroit over the edge, ultimately, was the unprecedented depth and duration of the Great Recession, which was hardly made in Motown but stripped out a large share of the remaining employment base and cratered revenue flows (Pew Charitable Trusts 2013; Turbeville 2013), coupled with the localized consequences of the failure of the subprime mortgage market (Wyly, Moos, Hammel, and Kabahizi 2009). And if there was a cluster of events that sealed Detroit's fate, it was the antics in the bond market by the crisis-prone Kilpatrick administration and its Wall Street enablers. A calamitously misjudged refinancing scheme had been hatched by the City and its bond-market partners in 2005, involving an elaborate (and barely legal, perhaps illegal) system of certificates of participation (known as COPs) and interest-rate swaps. It had been a deal designed to cover the City's "unfunded pension obligations and [to] attract investor interest," engineered with the assistance of "fortunate market timing," avant-garde interpretations of the law, and the "expertise of a host of bond professionals"—all of which notoriously earned Mayor Kilpatrick a Deal of the Year Award at a black-tie dinner organized by *Bond Buyer* magazine (Carvlin 2005: A28). The unraveling of this singular financial wheeze would itself generate "crippling debt" for Detroit, as the largest single contributor to the City's "legacy costs" spike since 2008 (Bomey and Gallagher 2013; Turbeville 2013).

Notably, the original deal had been awarded investment-grade status by the major ratings agencies, with a moderate credit risk of BBB, on the (ultimately mistaken) grounds that even though "the city had a constitutional requirement to pay its pension obligations," the responsibility to creditors would always come first: "no matter what, the city has to pay its obligations on the COPs" (Carvlin 2005: A28; Weyl, Xue, and Zhang 2013).

The subsequent breach of the constitutional protection of pension rights, courtesy of the federal bankruptcy court's Detroit ruling, means that municipal retirees will also have to bear the burden of "adjustment." The protracted legal maneuvering that has taken place in order to position Detroit's pension-fund obligations on an equal (legal) footing with the city's other creditor liabilities, which has been accompanied by an intensifying moral panic around supposedly "skyrocketing employee benefits" (Bomey and Gallagher 2013: 4), must not be allowed to conceal the social suffering that has been visited on the city. The combined legal and media attack on pensioners, pensions, and pensions rights has been strangely abstracted from, if not callously detached from, the very material reality that the average City of Detroit retiree lives on the poverty line, on an annual income of $19,000. Turbeville's (2013: 4–5) meticulous analysis of the city's finances, conducted for Demos, concludes that pension contributions "did not play a role" in pushing Detroit into bankruptcy, because the main drivers were not benefit costs, but nationwide increases in the healthcare inflation rate, coupled with the fallout of the "complex financial deals Wall Street banks urged on the city over the last several years."

Cities like Detroit are not going bust because their pensioners are dragging them down. Their remaining assets are being ransacked by the same class of financial experts that engineered the debt-dodging schemes, and similarly "creative" workarounds, at a time when the fiscal options of US cities were running out, courtesy of reduced intergovernmental revenue sharing, heightened exposure to (cyclical) property-tax revenues, and long-run infrastructure shortfalls. Cities entered the most recent phase of austerity urbanism in a lean and fragile state, with pension funds one of their few remaining "assets." The fiscal disarray created by the Great Recession duly set the scene for what Dean Baker (2013) bluntly calls "pension theft."

Malfinancialization Goes to Town

Beyond the specificities of Detroit's particularly toxic conjuncture, what is at stake here is the entrenched financialization of the American urban system. The historical pattern, dating back to the Nixon Administration, has been for the cumulative defunding and dismantlement of intergovernmental fiscal transfers and revenue-sharing machinery (draining funding for cities from both the state and federal levels), coupled with the erosion of automatic stabilizers linking financial support to demonstrated need and cyclical stress. There has, furthermore, been a structural shortfall in infrastructure investment for transportation, utilities, and social services, driving an increased reliance on competitive sources of financing from both the public and private sectors, on speculative development, and on debt financing via the bond market (see Clavel, Forester, and Goldsmith 1980;

Burchell and Listokin 1981; Sbragia 1996; Kirkpatrick and Smith 2011; Peck 2014b; Tabb 2014). In what resembles, to all intents and purposes, the autumn of this financialized regime (cf. Braudel 1984: 246), in which crisis tendencies have been displaced and rescheduled rather than resolved, conditions of instability and insecurity are showing signs of becoming systemic in scope and severity. The practical hegemony of fiscal federalism, in this context, effectively "hardwire[s] . . . cyclical financial distress" (Levitin 2012: 1404), especially at the urban scale, normalizing small-state modes of local administration and triaged service delivery. Hence the important of models like the "downsize[d] Detroit," where straitened financial circumstances have impelled a singular focus on the bottom-line and on an increasingly narrow repertoire of minimalist-state functions, like "crime-fighting and redevelopment efforts," areas where the city can "do the most good" (Malanga 2009: 8). This begins to resemble, to all intents and purposes, a neoliberal version of the "nightwatchman" state.

In this respect, the Obama Administration's stimulus package (the American Recovery and Reinvestment Act of 2009) can be seen as a partial exception that proves the more general rule. Its sub-Keynesian boost probably did avert a complete failure of the state and local government system, albeit at the cost of a massive political backlash across the country, under the sway of which stimulus became equated with "socialism." In practical terms, the stimulus package only served to ameliorate what was the worst revenue collapse on record, partially backfilling subnational budget deficits for a two-year period (Olif, Mai, and Palacios 2012; Pew Charitable Trusts 2013a; Peck 2014b). It is not simply that countercyclical policies are weaker than they once were, that needs-based spending priorities have been superseded by calculations of competitive potential and the search for "investment-grade" returns, or that infrastructure investment and even maintenance have become more sporadic, or postponed indefinitely; much that remained of the old Keynesian impulses has been repudiated, if not reversed, under the influence of neoliberal ideologies.

For a host of reasons, cities have been particularly exposed to the accompanying fiscal rollbacks and ideological assaults. First, they have been the principal delivery agents for a wide range of welfare and social services, the focus of sustained political attacks since the 1970s, which have since been increasingly privatized, outsourced to "shadow state" or faith-based providers, and then under-resourced or incrementally defunded. Second, cities are infrastructure-intensive places, fundamentally dependent on a (now crumbling) network of water and sewerage systems, public-transportation networks, and once-public utilities, for which debt-based financing (based on projected revenue streams or returns on speculative development) is often the only option. Third, American cities occupy a constitutionally weak position within the framework of federal governance, as creatures of the states, subject to varying degrees of control and discipline from above, often subject to taxation and spending caps, and increasingly dependent on (volatile) local revenues, particularly from property taxes. And fourth, urban regions have been an often fertile and occasionally febrile source of oppositional politics during the long neoliberal ascendancy, as basing points for labor unions (especially in the public-sector) and for alternative social movements of many kinds, which has positioned cities variously as defenders of the New Deal social contract, as the site of signature struggles around gentrification, immigrant rights, workfare, environmental justice, and (increasingly) social inequality, but also (and not least) as *targets* for public-sector disinvestment, political counterattacks, and market-oriented demonstration projects.

These macropolitical conditions—combining cumulative neoliberalization, waves of defensive and offensive entrepreneurialism, and deepening financialization—establish what is effectively a new operating environment for American cities. In the wake of the Wall Street crash and the Great Recession, the resulting landscape has been reconfigured according to the (il)logics of austerity urbanism. The new generation of bankrupt cities occupy distinctive, but not wholly exceptional, positions on this unevenly developed financial terrain. It is a terrain in which, not by accident but by design, "fiscal stress rolls downhill" (SBCTF 2012: 17), to borrow a phrase from the report of the blue-ribbon state budget crisis taskforce co-chaired by Paul Volcker and Richard Ravitch. The majority of states now impose tax and spending limitations on cities, not only precluding deficit budgeting but legally constraining expenditure growth and tax-raising powers, while at the same time "continu[ing] to pass their own problems down to local government" (SBCTF 2012: 17; Bae, Moon, and Changhoon Jung 2012). Under these conditions, the notion that cyclical recessions should serve to purge and purify the (state) system is translated from a Hayekian abstraction into a fiscal fact of life.

A Pew Charitable Trusts investigation found that fluctuations in aid to cities from state and local government, far from compensating for the vicissitudes of the market, have become the "leading factor" in the volatility of urban financing, while "[f]ederal spending limits currently pose the most direct threat as states and city governments work to absorb the cuts" (2013a: 3, 20). And here, it is the State of Michigan, as opposed to the City of Detroit, which defines the boundary case. Michigan's powers of local-government "intervention," epitomized by its especially draconian emergency-management law, are the most extensive in the nation—winning praise (somewhat perversely) as a "model" of proactive fiscal governance well suited to these straitened times (SBCTF 2012: 26; Pew Charitable Trusts 2013c). The origins of Michigan's heavy-handed fiscal interventionism, in fact, date back to the late 1980s, and emergency-manager laws have been used by both Democratic and Republican governors, albeit never more aggressively than by the Snyder Administration.[2] (For recent declarations of fiscal emergency in Michigan, see Table 9.1.) Notably, this tightening of external fiscal control has been accompanied by a significant *reduction* in state aid to Michigan's cities, and especially to Detroit, since the early 2000s (Maynard 2013; Turbeville 2013). This alone has been enough to push some localities into the red, exposing the hypocrisy behind the state's declarations of local financial "emergencies." As the Michigan Municipal League plainly states, the State has "balanced its own budget on the backs of local communities," gutting the local government revenue-sharing budget by more than 70 percent and withholding over $700 million from Detroit alone between 2003 and 2014 (Minghine 2014: 2).

Table 9.1. Financial emergencies in Michigan.

Local entity	Financial status	Date	Emergency management (appointees at January 2014)
City of Allen Park	Financial emergency	Declared by Governor Rick Snyder, October 24, 2012	Emergency manager: Joyce A Parker [formerly president, The Municipal Group, LLC and city manager for several municipalities]
City of Benton Harbor	Financial emergency	Declared by Governor Jennifer M Granholm, March 25, 2010	Emergency manager: Tony Saunders II [formerly partner, WYLD Marketing Group and political appointee at the City of Detroit]
City of Detroit	Financial emergency	Declared by Governor Rick Snyder, March 1, 2013	Emergency manager: Kevyn D Orr [formerly partner and bankruptcy specialist at Jones Day, a Washington, DC-based international law firm]
City of Ecorse	Financial emergency, followed by receivership	Declared by Governor Jennifer M Granholm, October 26, 2009; receivership commenced April 30, 2013	Emergency manager: Joyce A Parker [formerly president, The Municipal Group, LLC and city manager for several municipalities]; superseded by Receivership Transition Advisory Board
City of Flint	Financial emergency	Declared by Governor Rick Snyder, November 8, 2011	Emergency manager: Darnell Earley [formerly city administrator for City of Flint]
City of Hamtramck	Financial emergency	Declared by Governor Rick Snyder, June 11, 2013	Emergency manager: Cathy L Square [formerly city administrator for City of Pontiac]
City of Highland Park	Preliminary review	Commenced September 9, 2013	
City of Inkster	Consent agreementa	Signed February 28, 2012	
City of Lincoln Park	Preliminary review	Commenced October 14, 2013	
City of Pontiac	Financial emergency, followed by receivership	Declared by Governor Jennifer M Granholm February 20, 2009; receivership commenced August 19, 2013	Emergency manager: Louis H Schimmel Jr [former entrepreneur and director of municipal finance at the Mackinac Center, a conservative think tank]; superseded by Receivership Transition Advisory Board
City of River Rouge	Consent agreementb	Signed December 15, 2009	
Benton Harbor Area Schools	Financial emergency	Declared August 1, 2014	

Detroit Public Schools	Financial emergency	Declared by Superintendent Michael P Flannagan, December 3, 2008	Emergency manager: Jack Martin [formerly chief financial officer, City of Detroit]
Highland Park School District	Financial emergency	Declared by Governor Rick Snyder, March 2, 2012	Emergency manager: Gregory D Weatherspoon [formerly school principal and education consultant]
Muskegon Heights School District	Financial emergency	Declared by Lt Governor Brian Callan, April 19, 2012	Emergency manager: Gregory D Weatherspoon [formerly school principal and education consultant]
Pontiac Public Schools	Content agreement[c]	Signed September 18, 2013	

[a] Consent agreement states: "The City shall pursue alternative means of providing services [including] negotiations with other units of local government concerning the consolidation of public services including, but not limited to tax collection, financial services, sanitation, garbage collection, street maintenance, police protection, fire protection, and public works, and the city shall investigate other options including privatization of the foregoing services, or no longer providing certain services."

[b] Consent agreement states: " [T]he Mayor and Councilmembers shall commence discussions with the Emergency Manager . . . concerning the consolidation of services . . . to include but not limited to police protection, fire protection, financial and accounting, legal, sanitation, garbage collection, street maintenance, and public works."

[c] Consent agreement states: "Service Alternatives may, without limitation, be implemented through agreements or cooperative arrangements with other entities, public or private."

Source: State of Michigan, Department of Treasury, http://www.michigan.gov/treasury/0,1607,7-121-1751_51556-201116--,00.html, accessed September 28, 2014

The effect of these efforts has been to normalize, by dint of fiscal discipline and legal interventions, the small-state conditions, together with the rolling privatization-cum-cannibalization of both assets and services. And then there are the favored "models" of reform. Take the City of Ecorse, Michigan, a tiny municipality just outside Detroit, which has long been celebrated in conservative circles as "the city that privatized everything" (Barnes 1989, *Wall Street Journal* 1990). The handiwork of court-appointed receiver, Louis Schimmel, Jr., the restructuring of Ecorse illustrates the perversity of localized fiscal retrenchment. In the wake of deindustrialization, the city had been forced to raise taxes, the growth-impeding effects of which were interpreted in the *Wall Street Journal* as an(other) affirmation of the Laffer-curve gospel. Post-bankruptcy, Schimmel balanced the municipal books by selling off assets and privatizing to the point of public-sector incapacitation ("I wanted to make sure it would never come back," he said of the Department of Public Works); and while the receiver expressed some misgivings over the closure of the public library, residents could always take advantage of the tax-funded services of their neighbors, since at the time there was "no shortage of libraries in nearby cities" (Barnes 1989: A18).

The City of Ecorse has since become a staple point of reference for the Mackinac Center's *Michigan Privatization Report,* a defining policy product of the state's most prominent free-market think tank, where Mr. Schimmel resurfaced as director of municipal finance and a member of the "board of scholars." Known for its ideologically inflexible stance, the Mackinac Center promotes a predictable package of privatization proposals, tax cuts, and public-sector rollbacks. Detroit is a recurring target. Amongst Mackinac's *101 Recommendations to Revitalize Michigan*, for example, are the following (re)statements of the neoliberal logic of fiscal federalism:

- ✓ Let Detroit save itself by fundamentally reforming the city's government and business climate, rather than pursuing further rounds of flashy, government-subsidized projects.
- ✓ Let Detroit save itself and better serve its residents through a comprehensive program of privatizing city services.
- ✓ Let Detroit save itself by repealing the city's income tax, downsizing the city's bureaucracy and rolling back the regulatory burden on city businesses to a level similar to cities of comparable size (Mackinac Center for Public Policy 2011: 12–13).

On his retirement, at the age of seventy-six, the indefatigable Mr. Schimmel had been serving as the third emergency manager of the City of Pontiac, Michigan, on the heels of an earlier stint in the same role at the City of Hamtramck, in the Detroit suburbs. By this time many more of Michigan's libraries had been closed for budgetary reasons, including several branches in Detroit, although some were saved after public protests—including symbolic threats of book burning in the streets of the city of Troy (see Jaffe 2012).

Episodic efforts to "save" Michigan libraries are in many ways emblematic of the politics of austerity urbanism. Resistance to what has (d)evolved into a systematic, strategic, and coordinated effort to reconstruct the fiscal conditions of existence for cities, and to lock in norms of lean local government, has tended to be sporadic, defensive, and localized, having little option but to operate within the necessitarian frame of budgetary stringency and its practical counterpart, zero-sum struggles over an inexorably shrinking financial pie. To be sure, these constrained oppositional politics reflect entrenched (and scaled) power asymmetries, organizational and funding limitations, and the bundle of *strategic* advantages that austerity conditions deliver to conservative, small-state forces (Edsall 2012, Peck 2012, Blyth 2013, Tabb 2014), rather than some structural deficit in political will or imagination. The recurring pattern has been one of principled and focused, but sporadic and specific, eruptions of protest. These may aspire to, but have yet to realize, a more transformative form of progressive counter-politics—one that might begin, first, to augment, stabilize, and (perhaps) institutionalize robust bulwarks against austerity urbanism, and then from these bases to foster systemic alternatives, including noncompetitive regimes of socio-spatial redistribution. If fiscal devolution tends, for the right, to lock in the condition of municipal restraint while incentivizing small-state experimentation, it seems to have the effect of isolating, limiting, and incapacitating the progressive localisms of the left (Peck 2014a). The recent leftward tilt in Democratic Party leadership in cities like New York and Boston may be indicative of a turning of the tides, but it is notable that Detroit's mayor and the majority of the city's council members chose to stand down in the same November 2013 election cycle in which Bill de Blasio and Marty Walsh came to office on the East Coast. A former hospital executive known for his budgetary acumen, Mayor Mike Duggan was elected on a 25 percent turnout in Detroit, with a pledge to negotiate a "power sharing" arrangement with Kevyn Orr.

Meanwhile, there are signs that the neoliberal position on urban fiscal crises—as articulated by the closely aligned forces of the conservative media, the free-market think thanks, right-wing policy shops like the American Legislative Exchange Council (ALEC), and the billionaire bankrollers of ideologically filtered causes and candidates (see Akers 2013, Caldwell 2013, Center for Media and Democracy 2013, Clark 2013, Gold 2014)—has been effectively mainstreamed. The argument is that municipal stress is a local problem. It is seen to derive from endogenous causes and as a result must be subject to locally ring-fenced forms of structural adjustment, combining technocratic management with new rounds of privatization, asset selloffs, and the gutting of public-sector employment, workplace rights, and pension funds.

The doctrine of fiscal federalism, based on the axiom of competitive self-sufficiency, holds that each and every jurisdiction must live within its budget-determined means, all of the time—irrespective of structural pressures, strategic imperatives, extreme events, or localized crises—consequently finds its politically demobilizing but deeply politicized expression. This logic of fiscal Darwinism has been gradually melded with mainstream definitions of political "reality" and budgetary "responsibility" (see Taibbi 2013, Peck 2014b). Spending commitments must be recalibrated to the bottom of the business cycle, and in Detroit's case to the bottom of a structural trough. Investment plans, where they are not preapproved by the (bond) markets, are branded in the debilitating language of "debt." Any suggestion of fiscal transfers, or indeed of shared responsibility, is met with reflexive cries of "bailout." This would be tantamount to a restoration of what the Manhattan Institute pointedly calls "tin-cup urbanism" (Malanga 2008, 2013a); so any form of federal assistance to Detroit is branded as a "back-door bailout," and no solution to the problems of "debt, crime, failing schools and public-union dominance [which] are endemic to urban America" (*Wall Street Journal* 2013d: A14).[3]

This resembles a metropolitan-scale reiteration of racialized "dependency culture" narratives. In Detroit, educational and entrepreneurial deficits had metastasized with political dysfunction, degenerating into a citywide form of "dependency," a culture of entitlement that a "bailout" (read: handout) would merely enable rather than cure (Malanga 2010, Glaeser 2011, Powell 2013, Schneider 2013). This is an interpretation that Kevyn Orr, who usually chooses his words more carefully, rather crassly endorsed in an observation that,

> For a long time the city was dumb, lazy, happy and rich. . . . Detroit has been the center of more change in the 20th century than I dare say virtually any other city, but that wealth allowed us to have a covenant [that held] if you had an eighth grade education, you'll get 30 years of a good job and a pension and great health care, but you don't have to worry about what's going to come (quoted in Finley 2013: A11).

While Mr. Orr later tried to walk back these comments, they spoke a deeper truth. Those that have long awaited Detroit's bankruptcy, as a fiscal day of reckoning, always understood that the "welfare state dies hard," and that it would come from a thousand cuts, not one (Bray 2005: A17). For a "dependent" city like Detroit, the *Wall Street Journal* (2013e: A14) explains, "a bailout would merely forestall the necessary rehab;" its bankruptcy should be an occasion to learn the hard lesson that, "There is no such thing as a free pension." Those that quaintly hold on to the notion that pension rights represent a social contract (see Stiglitz 2013), it follows, are living in an irresponsible past detached from fiscal reality. Under the (revised) terms of the federal bankruptcy code, pension obligations are no more than contracts, and as such are subject to "impairment." Welcoming this development, the Manhattan Institute's Steven Malanga (2013b: 1) remarked, "Only when a government goes bankrupt are municipal workers likely to share in the pain."

In this way, Detroit's bankruptcy—aptly characterized by Kirkpatrick and Breznau (2014) as a fiscal state of exception—becomes folded back into a new normal. Locally, such states of exception—extending to the suspension of democratic procedures and the unilateral imposition of technocratic control—have been justified on the grounds that these are sites of aggravated local-state failure, where social order itself has been compromised. Having "revert[ed] to a wild state," Detroit has spun out of control—apparently licensing comparisons of its "feral" residents to "domesticated animals that [have been] abandoned and must survive on their own" (Malanga 2009: 8). In the special case of "feral Detroit," not only is poisonous rhetoric rendered somehow acceptable, martial measures are deemed necessary for the restoration of order, since the city must now be "saved from itself" (Malanga 2009, Schneider 2013). This might prove to be a painful and protracted process, but the local pain would surely secure an extralocal gain. By way of a new kind of urban spectacle, the fiscal demonstration effect of Detroit's bankruptcy-assisted restructuring would stand as a stark lesson for other cities.

Detroit's bankruptcy consequently represents a moment of opportunity—to entrench and deepen the neoliberal "reform" of municipal government. The path is (relatively) clear, because defensive and oppositional forces have been delegitimized (if not incapacitated), while indulgent local electorates are seen to have invited their own disenfranchisement. Conservative policy advocates like Steven Malanga (2103a: 6) consequently know exactly where to apportion the blame for the fiscal crisis of the local state: "Politicians consistently made bad deals for constituents, while union leaders regularly sued for plusher benefits, thoughtless about how city governments could pay for them. And voters persisted in electing those governing in this irresponsible way." The day of reckoning, however, has now arrived. "Politicians and unions have been emboldened in resisting reform because they expect that the federal government won't let big cities or their major pension systems fail" (Malanga 2013a: 8). Detroit's test case demonstrates the new political-economic reality: banks and corporations may be bailed out, but cities will not. Malanga's colleague, Nicole Gelinas, pressed home the point on the occasion of Detroit's bankruptcy declaration:

> What a difference a few decades makes. In the mid-seventies, New York City's looming bankruptcy was a horror that the state, feds, and city ultimately avoided. Last week, Detroit declared bankruptcy because Michigan thought it was the best choice available—and Washington stayed out of it. . . . Back in the seventies, the specter of bankruptcy prophesied urban death. New York could never recover from such a cataclysm, many believed. Now, Detroit is pushing bankruptcy as the catalyst for a turnaround, telling locals that City Hall can do everything from fixing street lights to hiring police with the money that taxpayers save by stiffing creditors. Detroit should stand as a warning: New York's bondholders and public-sector workers can never look upon their city as "too big to fail" again (2013: 1).

The investor class evidently shares this view of the catalytic potential of Detroit's widely watched bankruptcy, at least in as far as it will enable the state-assisted but privately led makeover of parts of the downtown core, with arterial connections to a penumbra of hipster enclaves. (This is not quite Judson Phillips's New Detroit, but it is not far off.) The slash-and-burn strategies of blight removal, fiscal cleansing, and municipal-government austerity have been preparing the ground for the (selective) return of private capital. At the forefront of these developments, billionaire financier Dan Gilbert has annexed more than forty downtown buildings, amounting to some eight million square feet of real estate primed for gentrified redevelopment; meanwhile, transnational investors like DDI take the view, from their Shanghai offices, that the "bankruptcy is a terrible thing to a certain extent [but] there is a good feeling about the next move to a new direction" (Peter Wood, DDI, quoted in Dolan 2013: C8).

Conclusion: Liquidated City

Detroit has been framed, in the pejorative sense of the word, as the author of a self-inflicted crisis. Conservative narratives of the city's failure make this argument explicitly, and it is one that reverberates extensively through mainstream commentary. Structural adjustment by way of the combined and intensified processes of emergency management and the municipal bankruptcy code duly concentrate the costs and the burden of recovery onto the city itself, and onto its residents. In turn, this framing also operates to shape (and limit) the discursive and administrative parameters of plans for the recuperation-cum-reconstruction of Detroit. Conventionally, these accord with the principles of debt ring fencing, in the form of attempts to contain the costs of adjustment within the city limits without resort to "bailouts"; demonization of the local political class (and often local residents too) for what is portrayed as irresponsible or corrupt behavior; and downsizing and deregulation, as the proper path toward free-market salvation. This calls attention to a different kind of framing—the structural and ideological frame established by the prevailing form of fiscal federalism. Antithetical to notions of revenue sharing and sociospatial redistribution, the credo of fiscal federalism holds that risk and responsibility must be devolved to, and contained at, the local scale. As a result, fiscal stress tends to trickle down, in a material way, justified by political attacks on local government inefficiency and corruption. The encompassing ideology of austerity urbanism displaces the burdens of economic stagnation onto cities, translating failures of financial-class autoregulation into (social) state failures, and outsourcing the responsibility for managing both the fallout and the recovery to the local scale. In the wake of the Great Recession, these downloaded fiscal disciplines have been generating "ordinary crises" across the local-government system while propagating (and legitimating) new forms of technocratic governance.

If cities refuse to apply the austerity leeches themselves, as in Michigan-style "consent agreements," then the money doctors must do it for them. So, the declaration from Michigan Governor Snyder of a state of financial emergency in Detroit was prelude to his appointee Kevyn Orr's declaration of the "rule of reason" in what has been portrayed—in familiar, but in ever more vehement, terms—as an unruly, almost ungovernable, place. Operating in an electoral vacuum, Detroit's emergency manager immediately went to work on a program of fiscal purging, promptly declaring bankruptcy as a means to implement a "plan of restructuring" designed to drive the downsized city in the direction of solvency. Such have been the challenges of this task, the emergency manager was later persuaded to hand back responsibility for some of the city's day-to-day operations to the newly elected mayor, Mike Duggan, even as the resumption of limited democratic control was deemed to involve, by the (new) standard that is technocratically managed structural adjustment, a "risk element" (Kevyn Orr, quoted in Finley 2013: A11).

There is further irony in the fact that speculators in the municipal bond markets made the calculation that their risks were socially insured. Now, bankruptcies in Detroit and elsewhere are undoing not only these implicit creditor contracts, but also the social contracts previously established with City employees, pensioners, and residents. In states of fiscal exception, even the right to have rights is subject to question (Kirkpatrick and Breznau 2014). The prevailing neoliberal narrative has it that municipal financial crises are the outcome, fundamentally, of local profligacy, the causes of which are in turn traced to an alleged compact between public-sector unions and Democratic Party politicians—what Michael Bloomberg has called the "labor-electoral complex" (see *New York Post* 2013). Attacks on municipal unions, on pension rights, and on a wide range of city services, are now justified by this fiscal imperative. Once again, there is no alternative but to downsize the social state, and the remaining residents must bear the consequences. Against this view, there are relatively few mainstream voices that will defend the position that, "the 700,000 remaining residents of the Motor City are no more responsible for Detroit's problems than were the victims of Hurricane Sandy for theirs" (Rattner 2013: A19).

The Detroit bankruptcy represents an extreme but nevertheless "ordinary" crisis of the unforgiving regime of fiscal federalism, inviting the unilateral imposition of the same tired repertoire of neoliberal "cures," of which even more is being expected, despite a track record that is checkered at best. As such, Detroit's fiscal and social crisis is symptomatic of the perverse logic (and deepening contradictions) of austerity urbanism, which is predicated on the expedient reapportionment of political accountability, enabling regressive financial redistribution, "downward" in both social and scalar terms, together with the localized concentration of the short-term costs of "adjustment," not to mention the long-term price that must be paid for living under minimalist municipal government, where the flipside of privatized opportunity is social triage. These are not stable or sustainable conditions. This is not a "solution" for the city as a whole. Even though a narrow class of elites and property owners look set to benefit from the city's "restructuring," the underlying plan for market-led reconstruction and small-state reform is scarcely any more viable than Judson Phillips's zero-tax vision for a New Detroit. Far from inaugurating some utopian state of small-state equilibrium, Detroit's fiscal emergency represents a crisis of crisis management itself, under which "lean state failure" is much more of a symptom than a cure. It speaks to the effective limits of the devolved, neoliberal form of fiscal federalism. As such, this has been, and will remain, much more than a local event.

Acknowledgments

I am most grateful, without assigning any responsibility, to Josh Akers, Lucas Kirkpatrick, Michael Peter Smith, Heather Whiteside, and Elvin Wyly for their comments and suggestions on an earlier version of this chapter.

Notes

1. At least one of these bond insurers, Syncora, was reported to be sufficiently exposed that its own financial viability was in question. During Detroit's bankruptcy negotiations, Syncora has been one of the City's most aggressive creditors.
2. Snyder's extension of the emergency-manager law (Public Act 4 of 2011) was later rejected in a statewide referendum, only to be reenacted (as Public Act 436 of 2012), in a form insulated from the "threat" of referendum challenge, in a lame-duck session of the Republican-controlled legislature.
3. Senator Rand Paul has declared that a bailout of Detroit would occur only "over my dead body" (quoted in Boyle 2013: 1).

References

Akers, J. M. (2013). "Making Markets: Think Tank Legislation and Private Property in Detroit." *Urban Geography,* 34 (8): 1070–95.

Bae, S., S. Moon, and C. Changhoon Jung. (2012). "Economic Effects of State-Level Tax and Expenditure Limitations." *Public Administration Review*, 72 (5): 649–58.

Baker, D. (2011). *The Origins and Severity of the Public Pension Crisis*, Washington, DC: Center for Economic and Policy Research.

———. (2013). "Pension Theft: Class War Goes to the Next Stage." *Huffington Post,* December 5, accessed at http://www.huffingtonpost.com/dean-baker/pension-theft-class-war-g_b_4394375.html.

Baldassare, M. (1998). *When Government Fails*. Berkeley, CA: University of California Press.

Barnes, J. A. (1989). "The City That Privatized Everything." *Wall Street Journal,* May 17: A18.

Blyth, M. (2013) *Austerity*. New York: Oxford University Press.

Bomey, N., and J. Gallagher. (2013). "How Detroit Went Broke." *Detroit Free Press,* September 15, accessed at http://www.freep.com/interactive/article/20130915/NEWS01/130801004/Detroit-Bankruptcy-history-1950-debt-pension-revenue.

Boyle, M. (2013). "Rand Paul: Obama Will Bail Out Detroit 'Over My Dead Body'." *Breitbart News Network,* July 19, accessed at http://www.breitbart.com/Big-Government/2013/07/19/Exclusive-Rand-Paul-Obama-bails-out-Detroit-over-my-dead-body.

Braudel, F. (1984). *The Perspective of the World*. New York: Harper & Row.

Bray, T. (2005). "Motown Loses Its Mojo." *Wall Street Journal*, December 8: A17.

Burchell, R. W., and D. Listokin (Eds.) (1981). *Cities Under Stress*. New Brunswick, NJ: Center for Policy Research.

Caldwell, P. (2013). "Outmatched." *American Prospect*, 24 (2): 7–9.

Carvlin, E. (2005). "Detroit Uses COPs to Shift Pension Burden and Set a Few Records." *Bond Buyer*, December 29: A28.

Center for Media and Democracy. (2013). *ALEC at 40*. Madison, WI: Center for Media and Democracy.

Cherney, M., K. Nolan and E. Glazer. (2013). "Detroit Rattles Muni Market." *Wall Street Journal,* August 8: C1.

City of Detroit, Office of the Emergency Manager. (2013). *Proposal for Creditors*. Detroit, MI: City of Detroit.

Clark, A. (2013). "Michigan's 'Free-Market' Media Machine." *Columbia Journalism Review,* July 16, accessed at http://www.cjr.org/united_states_project/mackinac_center_for_public_policy_is_major_player_in_state_media.php?page=all.

Clavel, P., J. Forester, and W. W. Goldsmith. (Eds.) (1980). *Urban Planning in an Age of Austerity*. New York: Pergamon Press.

Davey, M., and B. Vlasic. (2013). "The Man Hired To Save Detroit (Not by Detroit)." *New York Times,* December 9: A1.

Dolan, M. (2013). "Billionaire's Detroit Buying Spree Starts to Spread." *Wall Street Journal* December 17: C8.

Edsall, T. B. (2012). *The Age of Austerity*. New York: Doubleday.

Feulner, E. (2013). "It's a bankruptcy, not a bailout." *Washington Times*, July 30: 3.

Finley, A. (2013). "The Weekend Interview with Kevyn Orr: How Detroit Can Rise Again." *Wall Street Journal*, August 3: A11.

Gelinas, N. (2013). "What New York Should Learn from Detroit." *City Journal,* July 23, accessed at http://www.city-journal.org/2013/eon0723ng.html.

Gillette, C. P. (2012). "Fiscal Federalism, Political Will, and Strategic Use of Municipal Bankruptcy." *University of Chicago Law Review* 79 (1): 281–330.

Glaeser, E. L. (2010). "Shrinking Detroit Back to Greatness." *New York Times Economix*, March 16, accessed at http://economix.blogs.nytimes.com/2010/03/16/shrinking-detroit-back-to-greatness/.

Glaeser, E. L. (2011). "Unleash the Entrepreneurs." *City Journal*, 21 (4): 34–41.

———. (2013). "Bad Policies Bear Bitter Fruit." *Boston Globe,* July 23: A11.

Gold, M. (2014). "A Koch-Tied Labyrinth of Political Spending." *Washington Post*, January 6: A1.

Harrington, C. (2013). "Fox Ignores Facts To Blame Pensions For Detroit Bankruptcy." *Media Matters,* December 4, accessed at http://mediamatters.org/research/2013/12/04/fox-ignores-facts-to-blame-pensions-for-detroit/197137.

Harvey, D. (2005). *A Brief History of Neoliberalism*. Oxford: Oxford University Press.

Jaffe, E. (2012). "The Book-Burning Campaign That Saved a Public Library." *Atlantic Cities,* June 29, accessed at http://www.theatlanticcities.com/politics/2012/06/book-burning-campaign-saved-public-library/2412/.

Kirkpatrick, L. O., and N. Breznau. (2014). "Emergency Management and the (Non)Politics of Urban Crisis: Exploring the Racial Geography of Fiscal Intervention." *Mimeo*, University of Michigan.

Kirkpatrick, L. O., and M. P. Smith. (2011). "The Infrastructural Limits to Growth: Rethinking the Urban Growth Machine in Times of Fiscal Crisis." *International Journal of Urban and Regional Research,* 35 (3): 477–503.

LaFaive, M. D. (2014). "Don't Bail Out Detroit With State Tax Dollars." *Capitol Confidential,* January 15, accessed at http://www.mackinac.org/19559.

Levitin, A. J. (2012). "Bankrupt Politics and the Politics of Bankruptcy." *Cornell Law Review,* 97 (6): 1399–1459.

Mackinac Center for Public Policy. (2011). *101 Recommendations to Revitalize Michigan*. Midland, MI: Mackinac Center for Public Policy.

Malanga, S. (2008). "We Don't Need Another War on Poverty." *City Journal*, 18 (4): 34–41.

———. (2009). "Feral Detroit." *City Journal,* 19 (4): 6–8.

———. (2010). "The Next Wave of Urban Reform." *City Journal,* 20 (4): 14–25.

———. (2013a). "Bailouts for Cities?" *City Journal* 23 (4): 6–8.

———. (2013b). "Who Really Betrayed Detroit?" *City Journal*, December 4, accessed at http://www.city-journal.org/2013/eon1204sm.html.

Maynard, M. (2013). "Michigan and Detroit: A Troubled Relationship." *Stateline,* July 31, accessed at http://www.pewstates.org/projects/stateline/headlines/michigan-and-detroit-a-troubled-relationship-85899493926.

Minghine, A. (2014). "The Great Revenue Sharing Heist." *Michigan Municipal League Review*, March/April, accessed at http://www.mml.org/advocacy/great-revenue-sharing-heist.html.

New York Post. (2013). "The Labor-Electoral Complex." *New York Post,* December 20: 34.

Nolan, K. (2013). "Muni Investors Make Michigan Pay." *Wall Street Journal*, August 15: C1.

Oliff, P., C. Mai, and V. Palacios. (2012). *States Continue to Feel Recession's Impact*. Washington, DC: Center on Budget and Policy Priorities.

Ortel, C. (2013). "President Obama: Don't Saddle America's Babies with Detroit's Debt." *Washington Times,* July 24, accessed at http://communities.washingtontimes.com/neighborhood/brass-tacks/2013/jul/24/mr-president-do-not-punish-americas-babies-bailing/.

Peck, J. (2010). *Constructions of Neoliberal Reason*. Oxford: Oxford University Press

———. (2011). "Neoliberal Suburbanism: Frontier Space." *Urban Geography,* 32 (6): 884–919.

———. (2012). "Austerity Urbanism: American Cities Under Extreme Economy." *City,* 16 (6): 621–50.

———. (2013). "Austere Reason, and the Eschatology of Neoliberalism's End Times." *Comparative European Politics*, 11 (6): 713–21.

———. (2014a). "Entrepreneurial Urbanism: Between Uncommon Sense and Dull Compulsion." *Geografiska Annaler,* forthcoming.

———. (2014b). "Pushing Austerity: State Failure, Municipal Bankruptcy and the Crises of Fiscal Federalism in the USA." *Cambridge Journal of Regions, Economy and Society,* 7 (1): 17–44.

Pew Charitable Trusts. (2013a). *America's Big Cities in Volatile Times*. Washington, DC: Pew Charitable Trusts.

Pew Charitable Trusts. (2013b). *Detroit*. Washington, DC: Pew Charitable Trusts.

Pew Charitable Trusts. (2013c). *The State Role in Local Government Financial Distress*. Washington, DC: Pew Charitable Trusts.

Phillips, J. (2013). "Defeat Socialism and Save Detroit, All in One Move." *Washington Times,* July 28, accessed at http://communities.washingtontimes.com/neighborhood/judson-phillips-cold-hard-truth/2013/jul/28/defeat-socialism-and-save-detroit-all-one-move/.

Phillips-Fein, K. (2013). "Biting the Bullet, 37 years later." *The Nation,* May 6: 24–27.

Powell, J. (2013). "What are the Most Likely Outcomes of State and Municipal Financial Crises?" *Forbes,* August 20, accessed at http://www.forbes.com/sites/jimpowell/2013/08/20/what-are-the-most-likely-outcomes-of-state-and-municipal-financial-crises/.

Rattner, S. (2013). "We Have to Step In and Save Detroit." *New York Times,* July 20: A19.

SBCTF [State Budget Crisis Task Force]. (2012). *Report of the State Budget Crisis Task Force*. New York: SBCTF.

Sbragia, A. M. (1996). *Debt Wish*. Pittsburgh, PA: Pittsburgh University Press.

Schneider, C. (2013). "Can Governor Snyder Save the Motor City From Itself?" *City Journal*, 23 (2): 16–17.

State of Michigan, Department of Treasury. (2013). *Contract for Emergency Manager Services*. Lansing, MI: State of Michigan.

Stiglitz, J. (2013). "The Wrong Lesson from Detroit's Bankruptcy." *New York Times Opinionator,* August 11, accessed at http://opinionator.blogs.nytimes.com/2013/08/11/the-wrong-lesson-from-detroits-bankruptcy/?_r=0.

Tabb, W. K. (2014) "The Wider Context of Austerity Urbanism." *City,* 18 (2): 87–100.

Taibbi, M. (2013). "Looting the Pension Funds." *Rolling Stone,* October 10: 34–39.

Turbeville, W. C. (2013). *The Detroit Bankruptcy*. New York: Demos.

Vlasic, B., and S. Yaccino. (2013). "Detroit Waits, Apprehensive, for Manager to Take Over." *New York Times,* March 24: A17.

Wall Street Journal. (1990). "The Public Fat Cats." *Wall Street Journal*, December 28: 6.

Wall Street Journal. (2013a). "Detroit's Bankruptcy Breakthrough." *Wall Street Journal*, December 4: A16.

Wall Street Journal. (2013b). "Motown's Best Hope." *Wall Street Journal*, June 17: A16.

Wall Street Journal. (2013c). "Motown's Pension Showdown." *Wall Street Journal*, August 6: A12.

Wall Street Journal. (2013d). "Obama's Detroit Bailout." *Wall Street Journal*, October 1: A14.

Wall Street Journal. (2013e). "Saving Detroit From Itself." *Wall Street Journal,* July 27: A14.

Walsh, M. W. (2012). "When a County Runs Off the Cliff." *New York Times,* February 19: BU1.

Weyl, T., S. Xue, and M. Zhang. (2013). *Detroit: Chapter 9 Begins*. New York: Barclays Municipal Credit Research.

Wirz, M., and E. Glazer. (2013). "Fight for Detroit's Assets: Round 1." *Wall Street Journal*, September 17: C1.

Wyly, E., M. Moos, D. Hammel, and E. Kabahizi. (2009). "Cartographies of Race and Class: Mapping the Class-Monopoly Rents of American Subprime Mortgage Capital." *International Journal of Urban and Regional Research* 33 (2): 332–54.

Part IV

Where We Are Going: Pitfalls and Possibilities

10

Detroit Prospects: Why Recovery is Elusive

Peter Eisinger

It is difficult these days to write about Detroit without resorting to the language of morbidity and death. One recent book purports to offer an "autopsy" of the city (LeDuff 2013), and another sets out to chronicle the city's "afterlife" (Binelli 2013). Brent Ryan (2013), an urban planner, proposes "palliative" strategies for a city in "hospice," and George Galster (2013), an urban economist, ends his account of the city's troubles by writing its epitaph.

The case that Detroit is at least a dying city, if perhaps not yet dead, is based not simply on its extraordinary population loss since the late 1950s (from 1.85 million to a current estimate of approximately 688,000 in 2013) or its concomitant loss of jobs and employers (80 percent of its manufacturing establishments and 78 percent of its retail stores). Although such decline is a necessary condition of urban death, it is not sufficient. Other cities, after all, have experienced huge losses of population and jobs, then stabilized as smaller places and eventually revived: Pittsburgh and Boston are examples. The case for Detroit's situation rests ultimately on an analysis of its vital governance and economic stewardship functions. In their healthy state these functions may be understood as those sets of political, economic and social processes that provide a democratic arena for collective decision-making, a robust array of effective public services, a rewarding labor market for both employers and local and in-migrant job seekers, a fertile site for business formation, and a safe and cosmopolitan setting for daily life. In a vital city these functions are maintained by the combined efforts of a robust local government, an array of market actors, and society, a category that includes civic associations and a population that for the most part shares community identity and a common set of social norms. The effective maintenance of these functions makes a large place a city in the Aristotelian sense rather than simply a large population concentration. In the Detroit case, however, these vital functions exhibit high levels of morbidity.

The roots of this condition in Detroit are complex. They may be traced to the city's singular reliance on the automobile industry (Galster 2013), the rapid disinvestment of that industry following World War II (Sugrue 2005), and the hypersegregation of the metropolitan housing market, enabled by federal housing policy and maintained for decades by bitter white suburban resistance both to housing desegregation and to metropolitan cooperation to address regional issues (Farley, Danziger, and Holzer 2002; Williams 2014). Racial tensions, embedded in the city's history (Martelle 2012), emerged in full force when African Americans migrated in huge numbers to the city to take advantage of Henry Ford's willingness to employ them in his auto plants and later to compete with white workers, many from the South and Appalachia, for work in the war industries. Add to these factors the failure to build an alternative economy to replace auto manufacturing and the eventual out-migration of the black middle class as housing discrimination abated that left the city to deal with an inner city poverty distillate unmatched in any other large city.

Despite professions of optimism and resolve by politicians, community groups, and business leaders, it is not at all clear that the city will ever recover its vitality. This essay lays out the key challenges to any successful effort at revival and suggests that the odds of recovery are long.

Detroit Optimists

By any metric Detroit is the prime example in the United States of big-city decline. It either leads the nation's largest cities or is close to the top in its poverty rate, unemployment rate, and murder rate. Of its roughly 380,000 properties, fully 84,641 or 22 percent are blighted and in need of demolition, according to a recent survey (Detroit Blight Removal Task Force 2014). The city ranks ninety-fourth out of the top one hundred cities in percentage of adults with a college degree; a majority of high school students fail to graduate in any given year; and its labor-force participation rate is the lowest among the top forty-one largest cities. Most of its streetlights don't work, and neither does much of its ambulance fleet. The city has been governed for a year and a half by an outside emergency manager, to see it through bankruptcy, but even as it emerges from that condition, it will likely face financial oversight by a state-appointed commission at least until 2027 (Gray and Guillen 2014).

In the midst of this sea of dysfunction, Detroit nevertheless has its boosters and visionary planners, people who have not given up. Mayor Mike Duggan, elected in 2013, followed in a long tradition of Detroit mayors by proclaiming in his first state of the city speech that the city was "turning around": "The change in Detroit has started, and the change in Detroit is real" (*Detroit Free Press* 2014; on prior mayors' optimism, see Eisinger 2003).

A consortium of greater downtown business organizations, with support from the Hudson-Webber Foundation, compiled and published a report on the state of greater downtown that, while acknowledging "challenges," offers a "celebration of progress" (Detroit 7.2 2013). Most of the report is a compendium of downtown assets: the number of retail shops, jobs, miles of bike lanes, cultural institutions, housing units, and grocery stores. The report seeks to show "the momentum of today and the promise of tomorrow" inherent in the commercial real estate investment and central city housing development of the last decade. The report may be read as an assertion of the city's vitality, based on developments in the 7.2-square-mile greater downtown, which, it must be noted, accounts for a shade over 5 percent of the city's total 139 square miles.

A far more substantial statement of faith in the city is the Detroit strategic framework plan, *Detroit Future City* (2013). Contained in a 347-page volume, this is the product of a two-year effort begun under Mayor Dave Bing. It involved hundreds of community meetings, a nationally recruited planning team, numerous working groups, widespread support from a range of public and private institutions, and foundation funding. Its drafters call the plan "aspirational." The report is not easily summarized: it "articulates a shared vision" for the city's future and recommends a host of specific actions ranging from revitalizing selected residential neighborhoods to focusing resources on designated employment districts and sectors to building green and blue (water) infrastructure on the city's abundant vacant land. The plan projects education reform, doubled job growth in a diverse array of industries, neighborhood rehabilitation, the creation of landscapes for recreation and environmental protection, upgrades to water, energy, and telecommunications infrastructure, and a regionally integrated public transit system.

The plan finally offers a grand, or perhaps grandiose, vision: by 2050, the report says, "Detroit regains its position as one of the most competitive cities in the nation, the top employment center of the region, and a global leader in technology and innovation . . ." (Detroit Future City: 31). Almost nothing is said, however, about the possible impediments or challenges on the road to this future. Neither does the report dwell on how these things will be paid for nor whether the city can aggregate the capacity to achieve these goals.

Challenges to the Detroit Optimists

Even if Detroiters managed to form a political and community consensus about a revival strategy, at least five serious structural challenges promise to undercut its success. These are: 1) a long-term mismatch of resources and problems; 2) a deep institutional and human capacity deficit; 3) market marginalization; 4) the dismantling of municipal government institutions; and 5) spreading privatization.

The Resource/Problem Mismatch

The problem/resource mismatch problem is simple to state: the problems are too big, the city must pay its new debts (some incurred during bankruptcy), and it must pay for the municipal services that remain its responsibility. But its revenue stream, far from stabilized, will continue to languish or decline for many years. These projections are laid out to 2023 in the city's Plan for the Adjustment of Debts (City of Detroit 2014: 39–42).

* From 2000 to 2008 income tax revenues declined from $378 million to $276 million. They then plunged to a low of $217 million in 2010. Although there has been a slight increase in revenues since that low point, revenues are not expected to reach even 2008 levels by 2023.
* Detroit relies on a utility users' tax, which in 2012 accounted for $39.8 million in revenue. It is projected to remain flat for the next decade, generating only $40.4 million by 2023.
* Casino taxes have provided approximately $180 million a year to the city, but the opening of new casinos in Ohio has cut into Detroit casinos' market share. Revenue projections are currently falling and are not expected to recover to current levels until at least 2023.

* State aid is tied to population, but as population continues to fall, revenue-sharing payments are projected to decline by 20 percent from 2011 levels and remain there "for the foreseeable future" (40).
* Despite well-publicized recent downtown real estate investments, Detroit's total assessed property value actually declined by $1.6 billion between 2008 and 2013. Not only have housing prices in Detroit fallen more precipitously than in any other large city, according to a study by Michigan United, a housing advocacy organization. Detroit homeowners, predominantly African American, lost $1.3 billion in value through housing foreclosures in 2012 alone (Muller 2013). Not surprisingly, property tax revenues fell to a modern low in 2013 and are projected to continue to decline at least until 2020.

Although the city has received several hundred million dollars of federal aid during the bankruptcy period, nearly all the money has come from existing federal programs: $150 million to clear blighted property; $140 million in transportation aid to upgrade the deteriorated bus system; $58 million for police and fire services. No federal funds are to be used to reduce the city's debt. These are onetime federal grants, and they are modest sums compared to the problems they are designed to address.

The only realistic conclusion is that Detroit faces years of fiscal penury, no matter how the bankruptcy is resolved. Revenue projections do not point to a time in the future when the city will have the fiscal cushion that not only allows it to provide good public services but also makes possible innovative problem-solving or recovery initiatives of the sort that Detroit Future City envisions.

The Capacity Deficit

Detroit municipal government lacks the technology systems necessary to perform modern, efficient public administration. Furthermore, many key departments are understaffed, compromising the city's ability to meet its service responsibilities. Both of these problems constitute a severe public institutional capacity problem. In addition, the city's population is characterized by unusually low educational achievement, a human-capacity problem that bears in large part on the resource pool that both public and private employers can draw on. Both institutional and human capacity problems are not only costly to address, but make the city less attractive to investors, businesses, and job seekers.

In the summer of 2013 the *Huffington Post* reported that the city had misplaced a $1 million check, a routine payment from the Detroit School District. It was found a month later in a desk drawer. The story was not so much about carelessness as it was about a city that still uses paper checks (Abbey-Lambert 2013). Much of the work of city government is indeed done manually, and where computer technology is used, the IT systems are so outmoded in some departments (police, fire, EMS) that the vendors no longer supply technical assistance (City of Detroit 2014: 51). The Plan for Adjustment enumerates the technology problems, department by department. From the public safety departments to the payroll division and from the tax-collection office to the budget and accounting system, computerization relies on obsolete operating systems. In the tax division, computer-tracking technology is so inadequate that the city has had to rely on Wayne County to pursue property-tax delinquents. Furthermore, each department seems to have its own system and cannot interface with other departments. This is even true *within* departments: police precincts have not been able to share information with each other across their respective IT systems. The cost of upgrading these various IT systems is put at $83 million over the next decade (Guillen 2013).

Detroit's public agencies are often understaffed, and their employees face a range of challenges, not the least of which is whether they will have a decent pension when they retire. Among other problems, absenteeism rates in some departments are high. The Plan for Adjustment reports that in January 2013, more than a third of all bus drivers in the Department of Transportation were absent, an unusually high rate (City of Detroit 2014: 50). Despite rising crime rates, police ranks are down 40 percent since 2003, and thus the department "lacks the manpower to adequately respond to the more than 700,000 calls for service it receives annually" (City of Detroit 2014: 45). Of the approximately 2,900 police department employees, including both sworn officers and about 300 civilians, over 40 percent are eligible for retirement through 2019. Replacing them with qualified officers will not be easy: morale is reportedly low in this agency (Maynard 2013), a function of having to deal with five police chiefs in the five years leading to bankruptcy, layoffs, obsolete and shoddy equipment, and pay cuts. Morale is also low in the Fire Department, where "the stations, equipment and vehicle fleet [as of the date of the bankruptcy plan of adjustment] were old and in states of disrepair" (City of Detroit 2014: 49; see also Le Duff on firefighter morale 2013: 49–55).

Not every city agency is understaffed compared to other cities, but personnel are often deployed inefficiently. For example, the Fire Department is able to assign only one mechanic for every thirty-nine vehicles it has, making both repairs and preventive maintenance slow and difficult (City of Detroit 2014: 50). And because the city's payroll system is so reliant on manual data entry and check cutting, the city assigns an unusually high number of employees to these payroll tasks. Indeed, fifty-one uniformed police officers, who could be assigned to patrol duties, are instead working in clerical positions in the police payroll division.

Detroit has a human capacity problem to go along with its institutional capacity deficit: only 12.5 percent of its adult population has a college education, a figure that puts the city ninety-fourth among the one hundred largest cities in the United States (Eisinger 2014). For all the movement of employers into the core in the last few years, most of the workers who qualify for the jobs in those companies are still suburban commuters. An analysis of 2011 data by the Chicago Federal Reserve shows that despite the relocation of white-collar companies like Blue Cross Blue Shield, Quicken Loans, and Compuware to downtown locations, 72 percent of all workers in the city still do not live in Detroit. This figure is comparable to those of some other older manufacturing cities (Pittsburgh, 75 percent; Baltimore, 66 percent), but it compares unfavorably to many places in the Midwest such as Chicago (46 percent), Indianapolis (55 percent), and Milwaukee (57 percent) (Lavelle and Ogbonna 2013). Although workers commuting from suburban communities to Detroit pay a local income tax to the city, set at 1.4 percent, this is lower than resident workers pay (2.4 percent). About half of workers resident in the city commute to jobs in suburbs, and they do not pay any income tax to Detroit (Maciag 2014).

Among people in the labor force who still live in the city, Bureau of Labor Statistics data show that the unemployment rate is the highest among the top fifty cities in the United States (BLS 2013). Most white-collar employers who choose to move to Detroit bring their own workforce, some of whom have populated downtown condo developments; such firms do little for those workers long resident in the city.

Market Marginalization

Except for its downtown core and few scattered neighborhoods, Detroit is a city that the market has all but abandoned. Until the very recent past, most business firms and workers, the preponderance associated with the automobile industry, had left the city, confident that they would be better off elsewhere. Galster (2013) calls the city's historic reliance on the carmakers a "Faustian bargain": for decades that industry created a prosperous middle class of skilled workers and a complacent city. But when the industry struggled in the face of foreign competition, and assembly plants and suppliers moved to other states to follow their markets, Detroit had done little to prepare for the possibility that it would ever face such losses.

Today the city is hoping to rebuild its local economy in large part through small business start-ups and downtown corporate office development. The heart of the small business effort is Wayne State University's Research and Technology Park, called Techtown, established in 2000 to incubate small technology-based businesses that spun off from the remnants of the auto industry and the large medical school. The research park did not host its first business until 2007, but it claims to have incubated more than three hundred companies since then (Carter 2012). Many of these turned out to be what *Crain's Detroit* calls "lifestyle" or service and retail businesses. This was enough of a concern that the board replaced its leadership in 2013 to refocus the incubator's efforts on tech and science-based businesses, thought to promise higher job multipliers (Henderson 2013).

Nevertheless, taken at face value, these numbers indicate some sparks of economic life. Compared to other cities, however, Detroit still appears to lag behind on measures of entrepreneurial activity. There is even evidence that its business start-up rate has actually gone down in recent years, although data are based not on the city alone but on a regional base. Nevertheless, the picture is suggestive. The Kauffman Index of Entrepreneurial Activity, which uses data from the Census Bureau's Current Population Survey, ranks the top largest fifteen metropolitan areas on a measure based on the percentage of the adult non-business population that starts a business each month, averaged over a year. In 2012 the Detroit-Livonia-Warren metropolitan area ranked last with an index score of .10. This score was actually lower than in 2011, when the metropolitan area tied for last with Chicago at .185 (Fairlie 2012).

Although Detroit has attracted a few small venture-capital firms, the city does not appear on Richard Florida's list of the top twenty metropolitan areas measured in terms of venture dollars invested (Florida 2013). Many places smaller than Detroit appear on the list, including Provo, Boulder, Raleigh, Santa Barbara, and even one small older industrial city that remade itself, Pittsburgh. There may be the beginnings of a start-up market in Detroit, but it has neither produced any blockbuster business take-offs, nor has it yet achieved a scale commensurate with the city's size.

The market for housing and office space is also modest at best. Although downtown condo and rental housing stock increased by 5 percent in the decade after 2000, the share of vacant units downtown also increased in that period from 18 percent to 24 percent, suggesting that supply had outpaced demand (Detroit 7.2: 63). Housing subsidy incentives provided by some employers, particularly among healthcare providers, encouraged some people to seek downtown housing, and more recent data suggest that demand has picked up. The *Detroit Free Press* reported in 2012 that rentals in the immediate downtown area were at 97 percent occupancy (Gallagher 2012). In the single-family home market, which characterizes the bulk of the city's housing stock, however, there is little evidence of growing demand: according to data gathered in the American Community Survey, Detroit had the lowest median house value ($48,000) among the top largest fifty cities in the 2010–2012 period, down considerably from its $81,000 value in 2007–2009 (Block 2013).

Office vacancy rates remain unusually high. Dan Gilbert, the founder of Quicken Loans and the CEO of Rock Ventures, an umbrella of various business enterprises, has purchased more than sixty office and commercial properties in the downtown, most of them vacant, at the cost of $1.3 billion (Dolan 2013). But Gilbert's buying spree is not a response to high demand: 26.5 percent of developed office space is vacant, compared to a national average of 15.2 percent (Detroit 7.2 2013). Most of what Gilbert has purchased is filled with employees of his own companies. Although other companies, including Blue Cross/Blue Shield and Compuware, have moved their operations from suburban locations into their own properties in the downtown, a reporter for the *New York Times* observed on a visit to the city that the city is "now so sparsely populated that it doesn't have a rush hour" as employees drive from their offices to the freeways (Segal 2013).

Finally, the city is not a magnet for would-be workers seeking opportunity. This is particularly true for foreign immigrants, who cluster instead in communities in the suburban ring. Detroit, the eighteenth-largest city in the United States, ranks 138th among US cities in the proportion of immigrants in its population (Global Detroit 2014).

Dismantling of Municipal Government

As the city comes to terms with its bankruptcy, the municipal government has gradually been dismantled, divested of many of its responsibilities. Various functions have been shifted to nonprofit providers, special authorities, or other governmental entities, and the process is likely to continue, leaving the city itself with a skeletal set of public responsibilities. While these governmental changes tend to relieve the city of some of its fiscal and managerial burdens and will potentially increase government efficiency, they diminish local democracy and impede local initiative. To complicate matters, there is an acute racial dimension to many of these changes: authority and responsibility are being shifted from the black city to entities where African Americans are a minority.

The process of dismantling began not with the municipal government itself but with the state takeover of the public school system from 1999–2005, during which time the governance of the schools was stripped from the elected school board. Although local control was briefly reestablished in 2005, Michigan Governor Jennifer Granholm (D) appointed an emergency manager in 2009 to administer the school district's finances.

In 2011 Governor Rick Snyder (R) appointed an emergency manager to assume control of all aspects of the school system, and the legislature created a new State Education Achievement Authority to take over selected "failing schools" in Detroit.

Since the initial school takeover, the state has created or proposed other regional entities or special authorities to manage what were once municipal responsibilities. The Detroit Regional Convention Facility Authority, created in 2009, removed Cobo Convention Center, site of the annual International Auto Show, from the city's control. In 2012 the state created the Detroit Public Lighting Authority to try to restore street lighting, and in the same year it established the Regional Transit Authority of Southeast Michigan to plan for an integrated metropolitan transportation system. In 2014, after much resistance, the city leased its Olmstead-designed Belle Isle Park to the state for the next thirty years. The next target for divestment is the water and sewer system, a city-owned treatment and distribution facility for both the city and 127 suburban municipalities. Water system bonds account for a significant portion of the city's unpayable debt, yet the city has resisted relinquishing ownership of this service.

Some of the dismantling process was initiated by the city itself during the last year of the Bing administration. Most of this effort involved contracting out services for the poor and low- income population. The 2013 budget eliminated own-source funding entirely for the Department of Health and Wellness Promotion, transferring most of its functions, including WIC and Medicaid enrollment, to a nonprofit contractor called the Institute of Population Health and paying for them with state and federal financial aid. Similarly, the functions of the Department of Human Services, including food assistance, shelters, Headstart, and weatherization, were all contracted out to the Wayne Metropolitan Community Action Agency and the Community Development Institute, again relying on government grants.

Because it will be difficult to maintain effective public services without a steady and adequate revenue flow, it is not unreasonable to predict that there will be additional pressures to regionalize public functions, even if both city and suburban interests resist. Low police response and clearance rates and poor law enforcement infrastructure (police cars, crime labs) make this public safety function a target for assignment to the county sheriff's department, and so are public health and economic development functions candidates for county or regional control.

Historically, metropolitan reform movements have advocated regionalization in the interests of greater planning capability and fiscal efficiency. Furthermore—and this is an important consideration in the Detroit case—regionalization may broaden the tax base on which services are financed. In 2012 after the city withdrew its funding from the Detroit Institute of Arts, voters in the three-county metropolitan region approved a ten-year property tax millage to finance the museum, thus establishing a metropolitan financial base for the museum for the first time. This was a rare instance of metropolitan cooperation in a region marked more characteristically by great suburban hostility toward the city. (See Paige 2014.) But many have observed that there are tradeoffs in regionalization, not only in local democratic control and accountability but also in governmental responsiveness to citizen desires. Furthermore, regionalization forces central city interests to compete for attention and resources with outer metropolitan interests. Would a regional transportation authority devote resources to a central city bike-sharing program? Would regionalized social services be assiduous in addressing the needs of the inner city poverty population? Finally there are the costs of racial humiliation in dismantling the government of a black city, no matter how fiscally compromised, and assigning its functions to bodies that serve predominantly white constituencies.

It is true that a city is more than its government. But local government institutions are the heart of a city's capacity to manage and orchestrate its public responsibilities. City government in most cities is a key facilitator or enabler and sometimes initiator and dealmaker in the nexus of problem solvers and city builders, even if many of the players are from the private sphere. A mayor of a robust city government can, for example, mobilize and integrate cross-agency initiatives, but a government stripped of its functions lacks not only resources but legal and moral authority.

Privatization

The dying city is a stage for playing out all sorts of private interests, sometimes for the purpose of maintaining the community, other times in pursuit of private moral obligations, ambitions, or projects. A common theme is that in the absence of effective public authority the city is increasingly reliant on, served by, and being shaped by private action. On one end of the privatization process is the assignment of what has been a traditionally public function to a private entity, an orthodox strategy in modern public administration and another example of the dismantling process discussed above. For example, in early 2014 the city council privatized trash collection in the city, approving a five-year contract with a private disposal company. And if the Detroit Water and Sewer Department is not eventually taken over a by a public regional body, one alternative proposal is to sell it to a private company (Dolan 2014).

But privatization in Detroit has many other dimensions. These include the growing reliance on foundation and corporate funding for the operating expenses and capital upgrades of standard public services; the growth of grassroots private solutions to problems once dealt with by the public sector; and the unconstrained reimagination of the city's downtown by a small number of unaccountable private real estate investors.

A rich array of Detroit- and Michigan-based foundations has historically supported social service, planning, and economic development projects in the city. But recently many of these foundations, as well as some based outside of Michigan, have provided or offered to provide huge one-time grants for the support of standard municipal functions. For example, in the spring of 2013 the mayor announced that the city would have to close half the public parks that summer for lack of funding. But a combination of foundation and corporate donors stepped forward with $14 million that allowed the city to keep all of its parks operating for the summer. In the same year the city had to rely on a charitable donation to pay for the inspection of ladders on its fire trucks because the Fire Department did not have the funds to pay for the required inspections.

Private philanthropy has supported other municipal services: in 2013 corporate donors provided grants to the city sufficient to purchase twenty-three new ambulances and one hundred new police cars. The most substantial foundation initiative came early in 2014 when a consortium of foundations pledged $330 million to offset some of the public pension shortfall (estimated at around $3.5 billion), if the bankruptcy court would take the potential sale of the Detroit Institute of Arts collection off the table. This arrangement, part of what was called the "Grand Bargain," was subject to the approval of the bankruptcy court. Another large grant was announced in the late spring of 2014 when JP Morgan Chase Bank gave the city a combination of grants and loans worth $100 million over five years, targeted to blight removal, small business loans, and workforce training.

Foundation and corporate funding of operations or debt is a high-risk proposition for a city. Such funding may or may not accord with the city's priorities established through the political process. These private institutions are not accountable to the people of the city. Nor is foundation or corporate funding sustainable on a long-term basis, and in the best of circumstances it is unpredictable. It opens the way for other cities to make similar claims on foundations, and it raises the issue of the extent to which foundations can make demands on the city to act or conform in certain ways (Perry 2014).

Another form of privatization taking shape in Detroit is the widespread resort to volunteer citizen-initiated projects that substitute for or supplement public services. A group called the Mower Gang brings its members' personal riding mowers to a different park or vacant lot each weekend to mow the grass, and various neighborhood groups have taken it upon themselves to board up vacant houses. Binelli calls Detroit a "DIY city" (Do It Yourself), pointing to the citizen safety patrols that have formed in some high-crime neighborhoods, the volunteer anti-arson squads that circulate on Halloween (a night famous in Detroit for its rampant arson, though now much diminished), the shared private jitneys that replace unreliable bus service, and the growth of community gardens and guerilla park spaces fashioned from abandoned public and private lots.

The most dramatic evidence of privatization lies in the investments and grand plans of a small number of extremely wealthy businesspeople. These are people with their own private visions of how to remake the city, and they have proceeded unconstrained by any public urban plan or formal public debate. Unlike the classic growth machine coalitions that first appeared in the postwar years, where the city is often a proactive partner, planner, or broker (Richard Lee of New Haven, Mike Bloomberg of New York), Detroit has for the most part simply been a willing enabler. "My job," said Dave Bing, then Detroit mayor, "is to knock down as many barriers as possible and get out of the way" (quoted in Segal 2013). Ironically, as Stephen Henderson of the *Detroit Free Press* points out, the city rarely gets community benefits such as guaranteed jobs or affordable housing from enabling or subsidizing these projects (Henderson 2014).

Dan Gilbert is the most prominent of these developers. Many of the downtown properties he has purchased were abandoned office towers, some of which are now occupied by the 3,800 employees of Gilbert-owned companies. Along with his business investments, Gilbert has plans for street improvements, retail strips, and entertainment amenities in the downtown, and he has installed a state-of-the-art street surveillance system to supplement the antiquated Detroit Police Department cameras. Gilbert's projects are so big and so numerous that the *National Journal* calls him "Detroit's de facto CEO" (Alberta 2014). Indeed, his plans, according to Brent Ryan, "amount to one of the most ambitious privately financed urban reclamation projects in American history" (quoted in Segal 2013). Notably, Gilbert's decision to move his Quicken Loans operation downtown was subsidized by a $47 million state tax credit, and his plans to redevelop a major downtown vacant property will be subsidized by a fifteen-year city tax credit from bankrupt Detroit.

Another wealthy figure reshaping Detroit is Mike Ilitch, owner of the Detroit Red Wings professional hockey team, the Detroit Tigers baseball team, and various entertainment venues in the downtown. Ilitch has won approval for the construction of a new hockey arena just north of the downtown, designed to anchor an expanded entertainment district that already includes many of Ilitch's other properties, including the Fox Theater, Comerica baseball park, the Motor City Casino Hotel, and the Hockeytown Café. The city has agreed to sell thirty-nine parcels of city-owned land to the Detroit Development Authority (DDA), the action arm of the city's nonprofit economic development agency, for $1. The DDA would then enter a partnership with Ilitch allowing him to lease the land rent free for ninety-five years. The DDA will capture some local school property tax revenues to pay off public bonds that will cover 58 percent of the cost of the construction of the arena. Although no municipal tax revenues are involved in the financing of the construction, the city will lose approximately $7 million a year on its share of ticket and concession sales from its old arrangement with the hockey team when it played in Joe Louis Arena.

This is a classic "bread and circuses" approach to urban economic development, relying on building entertainment amenities such as stadiums and concert venues to create jobs, attract retail and leisure businesses, and generate tax revenues. But these projects often cost more in public subsidies than they pay in taxes. They rarely anchor vibrant retail investment or create well-paying permanent jobs or affordable housing, and they generally do not have discernible spillover effects on desolate contiguous neighborhoods (Eisinger 2000).

The grand projects of developers like Gilbert and Ilitch raise several issues. One is that the tax incentives cost the city—this *bankrupt* city, it must be remembered—real dollars in foregone tax revenues. But more important, perhaps, is that they permit single, unaccountable individuals to impose their visions on significant portions of the city. Detroit is blank slate: "It's a dream," Gilbert told a journalist recently. "Down here, it's like in basketball, you can create your own shot" (Austen 2014: 25). Developers have always shaped American cities with their big projects, of course, but such projects in most cities—think Atlantic Yards in Brooklyn or Boston's Harbor and Waterfront development—are contested, constrained by affordable housing or minority contracting set-asides, subject to larger city plans, or planned in conjunction with or even initiated by city government actors. Few are as comprehensive, grandiose, unregulated, and unchallenged as those in Detroit.

Another issue becomes clear on inspecting a map of Gilbert's and Ilitch's holdings: these nearly all cluster tightly along the lower Woodward Avenue corridor, a small downtown speck in the huge territory of the city. These projects embody a "tale of two cities" strategy: build the downtown for middle class workers, resident urban cosmopolitans, and visiting sports fans, but do nothing for the crumbling neighborhoods that stretch from the edge of downtown into the distance.

The Prospects for the Patient

Prospects for recovery to the sort of prosperity envisioned by Detroit Future City and other professional optimists are slim. A downtown business core is not a city. A handful of artisanal manufacturing ventures (Shinola bikes and watches) or barbecue and bakery ventures (Slow's BBQ, Avalon Bakery) may improve daily life for the young middle-class residents in Midtown, but they are exceedingly modest business initiatives given the scale of economic devastation. The rest of the city—its hundreds of thousands of poor people, its vast supply of empty houses, its crumbling strip malls, its shabby parks, its acres of weedy prairie, its abandoned industrial hulks—is not going to disappear, of course. For many residents, there is nowhere else to go, and others will choose to stay or come for the challenge and adventure of trying to help. But Detroit is not likely to function in the near or midrange future like a fully viable city. Its municipal government, facing chronic impoverishment even as it emerges from bankruptcy, already has much-diminished power as functions have been reassigned to other governmental and nonprofit bodies. Its revenue stream, dependent on population, employment numbers, and property values, is on a steadily downward trajectory. Outside foundation, corporate and federal financial aid, much of it doled out over a five- or ten-year schedule, does not come to much more than one year's operating budget.

The forces of privatization, while certainly gritty evidence of people's energy, self-reliance, and innovativeness, nevertheless all encourage in one way or another social fragmentation: the alienating effects of lack of accountability in the decisions of foundation and corporate donors, the atomizing effects of beleaguered neighborhood volunteer efforts, and the exclusivity of grand downtown projects for the middle classes in an overwhelmingly poor city all work to weaken the sense of shared purpose and destiny.

So for now Detroit may not yet be dead, but in its dying state it increasingly resembles a refugee camp with an uncertain future, a fragmented, poorly organized, and poorly served concentration of people, many living in squalid condition and deprived of full rights of democratic self-determination. Most people in a refugee camp want to leave. (Indeed, fully one-third of Detroiters say they would like to leave if they could [Detroit Future City Executive Summary 15]). As with most refugee camps, no one in the outside world—not Washington, not the State of Michigan—is willing to take responsibility. A refugee camp has little effective internal public authority, and it is typically dependent on none-too-reliable outside aid, ranging from foundation and charitable monies to faith-based organizations to members of the helping professions. Refugee camps, like Detroit, are fertile ground for a few ambitious entrepreneurs and operators, for there is always money to be made even in the most inhospitable circumstances. Few share in their good fortune. Nothing in this sorry story suggests that the city will ever become, as Detroit Future City predicts, "one of the most competitive cities in the nation" or "a global leader in technology and innovation."

References

Abbey-Lambert, K. (2013). "Detroit Lost $1 Million in a Desk Drawer for a Month, Just One Example of City's Inefficiencies." *The Huffington Post*. Posted online August 8.

Alberta, T. (2014). "Is Dan Gilbert Detroit's New Superhero?" *National Journal*. Posted online Feb. 27.

Austen, B. (2014). "Buy Low." *New York Times Magazine*. July 13.

Binelli, M. (2013). *Detroit City is the Place to Be: The Afterlife of an American Metropolis*. NY: Metropolitan Books.

Block, D. (2013). "Detroit ranks last among Top 50 US cities in median home value, survey finds" mlive. com. Nov. 16.

Carter, N. (2012). "Detroit's Education Edge" Inc. Posted online March 1.

City of Detroit. (2014). *Disclosure Statement with Respect to Plan for the Adjustment of Debts of the City of Detroit*. Feb. 21.

Detroit Blight Removal Task Force. (2014). *Motor City Mapping*.

Detroit Free Press. (2014). "Duggan In State Of The City: 'The Change In Detroit Is Real'" (February 26).

Detroit Future City. (2013). *Detroit Future City: Detroit Strategic Framework Plan*.

Detroit 7.2. (2013). *7.2 Square Miles: A Report on Greater Downtown Detroit*.

Dolan, M. (2013). "Billionaire's Detroit Buying Spree Starts to Spread." *Wall Street Journal*. Posted online Dec. 17.

———. (2014). "Detroit Seeks Proposals to Privatize Its Water System." *Wall Street Journal*. March 25.

Eisinger, P. (2000). "The Politics of Bread and Circuses: Building the City for the Visitor Class." *Urban Affairs Review*. (January): 316–333.

———. (2003). "Reimagining Detroit." *City and Community*, 2 (June): 81–99.

———. (2014). "Is Detroit Dead?" *Journal of Urban Affairs*: 1–12.

Fairlie, R. (2012). *Kauffman Index of Entrepreneurial Activity, 1996–2011*. Kauffman Foundation, March.

Farley, R., S. Danziger, and H. Holzer. (2000). *Detroit Divided*. New York: Russell Sage.

Flanagan, C. and E. Wilson. (2013). *Home Value and Home Ownership Rates: Recession and Post-Recession Comparisons from 2007–2009 to 2010–2012*. US Census, American Community Survey Briefs. November.

Florida, R. (2013). "America's Leading Metros for Venture Capital." *theAtlanticCities.com*. Posted online June 17.

Gallagher, J. (2012). "Tight market for downtown Detroit apartment rentals." *Detroit Free Press*. Posted online Sept. 26.

Galster, G. (2013). *Driving Detroit: The Quest for Respect in the Motor City*. Philadelphia: University of Pennsylvania Press.

Global Detroit. (2014). *Detroit Demographic Report*, re-release. (March 25).

Gray, K. and J. Guillen. (2014). "Detroit Bankruptcy Legislation Calls for 20 Years of Oversight." *Detroit Free Press*. (May 14).

Guillen, J. (2013). "Information technology: Upgrade needed for obsolete, inefficient systems." *Detroit Free Press*. (June 16).

Henderson, S. (2014). "Detroit's Rebirth Must Include More than Downtown, Midtown." *Detroit Free Press*. (March 2).

Henderson, T. (2013). "With new programs, boost in talent, TechTown returns focus to tech startups" *Crains Detroit*. Posted March 21.

LeDuff, C. (2013). *Detroit: An American Autopsy*. NY: Penguin Books.

Lavelle, M. and E. Ogbonna. (2013). "Comparing Detroit's Commuting Patterns with Other Cities.'" *Michigan Economy*. Federal Reserve Bank of Chicago, Detroit Branch. Posted online Dec. 4.

Maciag, M. (2014). "Cities Consider Taxing Commuters to Drive Up Revenue." *Governing*. (March 5).

Martelle, S. (2012). *Detroit: A Biography*. Chicago: Chicago Review Press.

Maynard, M. (2013). "4 Revelations from the Detroit Bankruptcy Trial." *Forbes*. (Oct. 26).

Muller, D. (2013). "Housing Activists Say Detroit Lost $1.3 Billion to Mortgage Crisis Last Year." *Mlive*. (May 16).

Perry, S. (2014). "Proposed Detroit Grants Test Limits of Philanthropic Aid to Cities," *Chronicle of Philanthropy*. (Jan. 14).

Ryan, B. (2012). *Design After Decline: How American Rebuilds Shrinking Cities*. Philadelphia: University of Pennsylvania Press.

Segal, D. (2013). "A Missionary's Quest to Remake Motor City." *New York Times*. (April 13).

Sugrue, T. (2005). *The Origins of the Urban Crisis: Race and Inequality in Postwar Detroit*. Princeton, NJ: Princeton University Press.

Williams, P. (2014). "Drop Dead, Detroit." *New Yorker*. (Jan. 27).

11

A Community Wealth-Building Vision for Detroit—*and Beyond*

Gar Alperowitz and Steve Dubb

At the behest of state-imposed Emergency Manager Kevyn Orr, the City of Detroit filed for Chapter 9 bankruptcy protection on July 18, 2013. Many observers place the blame for the crisis at the feet of the city itself with the main source of the problem defined as corrupt officials or inept bureaucrats. Other analysts have challenged this explanation, arguing that the bankruptcy was less the result of the City of Detroit being unable to pay its bills per se, but rather the product of a political agenda that used cash-flow challenges as an excuse to reduce pension obligations to union retirees and privatize the water system (Turbeville 2013: 9). Regardless of cause, however, the bankruptcy filing was the latest indicator of a remarkable decline for what was once one of America's wealthiest cities.

In the 2000 census, Detroit had a population of 951,270 residents, marking the first time since 1920 that the city's population had dipped below one million. By 2011, the city had 706,585 residents, an additional decline of more than 25 percent. All told, Detroit's population has fallen by more than 60 percent from the city's population of 1.85 million in 1950. As a direct result of this population decline over the past several decades, many neighborhoods in Detroit have suffered immense disinvestment and deterioration. This loss in population and jobs flows from the declining manufacturing base of the region, especially of the Big Three automakers and the even faster shrinkage of industry parts suppliers. And, of course, the process of disinvestment has been deeply abetted by white flight, as well as state policies that over the course of decades have helped create and systematically favored Michigan's white suburbs over its African American urban neighborhoods (Joyce 9/3/13).[1]

The city's poverty rate in 2011 was an astounding 40.9 percent, compared to 15.9 percent for the nation as a whole. For Detroit's children, 57.9 percent were in poverty. Unemployment in Detroit is also high (AlHajal 9/21/12). Even in May 2014, five years after the Great Recession peak, unemployment in the City remained an estimated 14.5 percent (Ross 5/29/14). Moreover, the unemployment figures vastly understate the extent of the challenge. A comparison of forty-one major US cities in 2010 found that Detroit had the lowest labor force participation rate of those polled. While Detroit unemployment in 2010 was 17.8 percent, labor force participation for Detroiters aged sixteen to sixty-four stood at 49.8 percent, more than 20 percentage points less than in many US cities (Gallagher and Seidel 4/8/12). These numbers are even more astonishing when viewed in the context of the past several decades. In 1950, more than 211,000 Detroiters worked in auto industry jobs; by 2012, fewer than 10,000 did. The numbers are only slightly better when one includes all manufacturing jobs. Again, the drop is dramatic: In 1950, nearly 349,000 Detroiters worked in manufacturing; in 2012, fewer than 28,000 did (Green 12/12/13).

Detroit is arguably the nation's leading example of our "throwaway city" habit: city infrastructure that once sustained two million people now serves a city of barely seven hundred thousand. Detroit's dramatic decline offers an opportunity to think seriously not only about the specific challenges facing the Motor City, but to consider serious long-term options for many cities, and for our nation, which faces a range of economic and environmental issues that cry out for creative solutions. What stands out is our historical lack of a national capacity to target major jobs to help stabilize rather than throwaway important communities. What is needed is, first, a bottom-up community wealth–building vision and strategy anchored by employee- and community-owned enterprises; and, second, a linking of that strategy to longer-range national sectoral planning, connected to public procurement of mass-transit vehicles and other publicly acquired goods and services.

Economic Development in Detroit: The Search for Easy Answers

The failure to build a new economic base for Detroit is not for a lack of effort. The Detroit Regional News Hub, an organization led by executive director Marjorie Sorge, recently pointed out that in the past decade, more than $15 billion in private dollars has been invested downtown in sports and entertainment venues, gaming casinos and hotels, major new Class A offices for General Motors, Compuware, and Quicken Loans, residential developments (single-family, condos, and lofts), retail, restaurants, and nightclubs (Detroit Regional News Hub 2014). Clearly, money is being invested in Detroit, although the types of investments being made are hardly the most likely candidates for addressing the deep issues of economic dislocation and structural poverty that Detroit faces.

City dollars—again, whether spent wisely or not—have helped subsidize a good portion of this investment. For example, the new baseball stadium (Comerica Park) received $145 million in City largesse. The new football stadium (Ford Field) received a more modest City contribution of $95 million, still enough to cover 31.7 percent of total project costs. Money dispensed by the City government came out of a mix of hotel and rental car taxes and general fund revenues (McCarthy 2014). Two new sports stadiums, three new casinos. What more can be done to support city economic development? Even in the midst of a municipal bankruptcy filing, perhaps adding a third new sports stadium to match the number of casinos? Although this may seem like an odd way to rebuild a city that has filed for bankruptcy, in 2014 an estimated $285 million in state and local public funds is dedicated for the purpose of providing the Red Wings hockey team a new stadium (Drape 10/14/13). Among the advocates of this public expenditure is none other than Emergency Manager Orr, who said days after the bankruptcy filing: "I know there's a lot of emotional concern about should we be spending the money [on the new arena]. But frankly that's part of the economic development" (Orr, quoted in Isidore 7/26/13). Orr advocates this subsidy even though Red Wings owners Marian and Mike Ilitch and family have a net worth estimated at $3.7 billion (Forbes 2014).

Philanthropic investment has also been significant. Foundation dollars have not been without positive impact, but to date the high levels of foundation spending has not been matched by proportionate results. For example, in January 2008, the philanthropic community pledged $100 million to create a "New Economy Initiative" fund that aimed to "help southeast Michigan attain a position of leadership in the new global economy." Ford, Kresge and Kellogg foundations each committed $25 million, with the remaining $25 million coming from the Knight, Hudson-Webber, Max and Marjorie Fisher, C.S. Mott, Skillman, the Community Foundation for Southeast Michigan, and the McGregor Fund (Knight Foundation 1/8/08; Howes 9/14/07). According to the *Chronicle of Philanthropy*, total grantmaking has been considerably greater, roughly $628 million in total between 2007 and 2011 (Perry 10/20/13). This total evidently does not include expenditures since 2011, including the approximately $360 million that foundations pledged in 2014 to mitigate public pension cuts and spare art from the city-owned Detroit Institute of Art from hitting the auction block, nor an additional $40 million pledged to continue the New Economy Initiative (Welch 2/6/14, The Planning Report 2014).

The billion-plus dollars of philanthropic investment over the past decade, combined with even greater private investment, has fostered considerable new development in downtown and in Midtown, a district that is home to many of the area's leading hospitals and universities—notably Henry Ford Health System, the Detroit Medical Center, and Wayne State University. A prominent sign of reinvestment in the area is the opening of a Whole Foods store at the corner of Mack and Woodward in June 2013 (Abbey-Lambertz 6/5/13). But of course the majority of Detroit residents are not shopping at Whole Foods! Tonya Allen, CEO of the Skillman Foundation, while lauding the progress to date in Midtown and Downtown, noted that the city's neighborhoods continue to "struggle with unparalleled despair. Residents bear the burdens of a broken city, as they work hard to stay put and hold it together. . . . Essentially, we have two Detroits. The new Detroit and the legacy Detroit" (Allen 1/28/14).

Slowly—and surely we need to add here the phrase *painfully slowly* —the need to think beyond conventional approaches is beginning to be acknowledged. Leslie Lynn Smith, president and CEO of TechTown Detroit, calls out this disparity explicitly. Citing Albert Einstein's definition of insanity as "doing the same thing over and over again and expecting different results," Smith points out that current "economic development strategies almost entirely neglect the city's neighborhoods. In Detroit, that's where 95 percent of city residents live. The jobs located in downtown information technology hubs are most often not jobs, certainly not good jobs, created for the vast majority of city residents" (Smith 2014).

Smith adds: "We've learned that businesses and jobs are just parts of what create healthy environments. We also have to figure out how to turn lights on, inspire high school kids, make streets safe, move slumlords out, remove blight and create community. We have to have the courage to challenge institutional perspectives, like the commonly shared view that suggests all people have an equal chance to receive a great education, job and pathway to family wealth. Because, candidly, that's not true" (Ibid.). But if more and more people have to come to acknowledge that conventional economic development approaches are not enough to rebuild Detroit, what is?

Beyond Throwaway Cities

A good starting point for understanding what response might make sense in Detroit is having a clear understanding of America's "throwaway city" habit and how we got here. Simply put, as jobs move in and out of cities in uncontrolled ways we literally throw away housing, roads, schools, hospitals, and public facilities—only to have to build the same facilities elsewhere at great financial, energy, and carbon costs. After all, the people needing these facilities did not disappear; they simply moved out of cities like Detroit into suburbs or other urban centers where everything must be rebuilt anew. All the while, the instability created by this political, economic, cultural, and social churning makes it impossible to carry out coherent transportation, economic and city planning.

Detroit provides a dramatic example, but it is not alone. In 1950, the United States had 112 cities with populations of 100,000 or more, Detroit ranking as the nation's fourth most populous city at the time. Of those cities, 56—fully half of them—had experienced population decline by 2008; this is true even though the nation's population more than doubled during the same period (Williamson, Dubb, and Alperovitz 2010: 37). Detroiters who could get out generally moved elsewhere, sometimes to the suburbs and sometimes to different parts of the country, where all the usual facilities had to be built anew to serve them—and, built under conditions that were likely to be subject to future instability and disruption. Many cities, of course, have begun to regain population since 1990 as urban centers have gained new popularity due to a mix of social, economic and cultural changes, but, even so, Detroit is hardly unique in suffering continued decline. Between 1990 and 2008, thirty-five of these cities suffered further losses, including, in addition to Detroit, cities such as Cleveland, Pittsburgh, Cincinnati, Syracuse, Birmingham, and Norfolk.

Given that the economic fate of most cities is dependent on decisions made by mobile investors of capital, putting an end to the practice of throwaway cities will require major efforts, first, to improve quality of life within cities; second, to reduce gaping social disparities within cities (a major cause of "urban decline"); and third, and critically, to stabilize the economic underpinnings of cities—that is, the job base.

The Community Wealth–Building Approach

One slowly expanding approach to addressing these challenges involves fostering community wealth building, an asset-based strategy that builds upon existing local talents, capacities, facilities, capital, and expenditure flows to develop locally owned—and often community owned—anchored businesses that can help sustain the local economy. Community wealth building is not flashy. It rejects mindless "smokestack chasing"—the use of tax incentives to "attract" business investment. *Annual* state and local tax abatements of this kind now total over $80 billion nationally (Story 12/2/12).

It also eschews megaprojects (such as casinos or new sports stadiums). Instead, community wealth–building centers on two key tactics: 1) leveraging existing flows of dollars—such as the spending and investment of place-based public and nonprofit "anchor" institutions; e.g., hospitals, universities, city government, museums and local foundations—and then capturing and 2) anchoring those flows by designing businesses that can meet the needs of those institutions, and where viable, embed those businesses in ownership structures that are unlikely to move and that broadly share the wealth generated among community members.

Community wealth building can occur through a wide range of legal forms, including employee, nonprofit, and public ownership. One key goal of community wealth building is to increase the proportion of capital held by actors with a long-term commitment to a given locality or region. In publicly traded firms, the central objective is to maximize profit for shareholders, whether it involves moving from one city to another or not. Community wealth, on the other hand, is tied to place. Public enterprises, employee-owned firms, neighborhood-owned enterprises, and nonprofits all are rooted in particular communities. The people who own and control the businesses live there. And the people who have lived in these communities for decades have the opportunity to build and keep wealth for themselves, their families, and their communities.

The overall economic impact of place-based, community wealth building has become increasingly important in recent years. More than ten million employees, for instance, own all or part of 10,900 companies through employee stock ownership plans (ESOPs)—firms that employees finance and increasingly own through pension contributions. These ESOPs have so far generated equity benefits of $870 billion for their employee-owners (National Center for Employee Ownership 2014). Cooperatives, according to a 2009 University of Wisconsin study, now operate 73,000 places of business throughout the United States, own $3 trillion in assets, employ 857,000 people, and generate over $500 billion in revenue for their member-owners (Deller et al., 2009). Importantly for Detroit, which is 82 percent African American, there is a deep and rich history of cooperative ventures and other forms of economic solidarity in black communities (Gordon Nembhard 2014). Past ventures in Detroit include a campaign to create a five-hundred-unit integrated Schoolcraft Gardens housing cooperative in 1950 (Wayne State 2001); the Cass Corridor Food Co-op, which operated in Detroit from 1972 to 2004 and had at its peak over 2,000, largely African American, member–owners (Clark 2014: 20–21, Gilmore 2009); and the formation of church-based credit unions that continue to exist today (HBCU Money 2014).

Community-based ownership also has the potential to yield far more long-term employment than traditional corporate strategies. Traditional employers have an incentive to keep labor costs low and hence will use workers only for as long as they are needed on a particular job (such as weatherizing homes). Community enterprises, in contrast, aim to maximize employment over the long term. Instead of treating employees as disposable, such employers commonly seek ways to find new work for their workforce when one line of work slows or ends.

Communities with a higher proportion of such capital are better positioned to achieve economic stability and create jobs. There are also additional benefits. For instance, a community wealth–building strategy can greatly assist in planning effectively for a low-carbon future. This is true because community-based businesses, anchored in place, provide the economic stability necessary to make transportation and housing patterns considerably more predictable and sustainability planning thereby more effective.

Further, community wealth–building strategies aim to achieve neighborhood revitalization benefitting existing residents rather than moving people around. Reducing poverty also improves the quality of life both in the central city and older suburban neighborhoods, making them more attractive options, thereby also helping to achieve stability.

Important policy support has also been developing in different regions of the nation. An example is the Ohio Employee Ownership Center (OEOC), based at Kent State University, which has used a relatively modest amount of state funding (less than $1 million annually in its best years) to facilitate employee takeovers of firms whose owners are retiring or that are threatened with closure. Such firms, owned by workers, are city (and tax base) stabilizers: they do not get up and move. The OEOC has created enormous economic returns—retaining employment over a twenty-five-year period at an estimated cost of $772 per job and helping stabilize over fifteen thousand jobs in Ohio cities (OEOC 2011).

A dramatic illustration of the community wealth–building approach has been developed in Cleveland, historically one of the leading cities of American capitalism. Home to John D. Rockefeller, Cleveland was once known as the "nuts and bolts" capital of the world. At one time, it was second only to New York City in headquartering Fortune 500 companies. In 1950, Cleveland's population exceeded 914,000. But times have changed. By the 2010 US census, Cleveland's population had fallen below 400,000. However, the legacy institutions remain—namely, the city's leading hospitals and universities, as well as its community foundation and a wide array of cultural institutions. Daily, more than 50,000 people commute to the Cleveland Clinic, University Hospitals, Case Western Reserve University, and the other so-called anchor institutions ("eds," "meds," and other place-based, mainly public or nonprofit institutions) within the University Circle, a relatively compact business district located roughly four miles northeast of downtown Cleveland. The purchasing power of these institutions—not including salaries and construction—exceeds $3 billion a year. Surrounding the University Circle, however, are low-income neighborhoods with 43,000 residents, whose median household income is only $18,500.

Can such disparities be altered? The economic consequences in low-income neighborhoods are devastating, and there are equally damaging consequences (sprawl, etc.) from an environmental standpoint. Over the past decade, the Cleveland Foundation, in cooperation with neighborhood groups, major hospitals and universities, as well as city government, has begin to develop an effort, known as the Greater University Circle initiative, that has the audacious goal of seeking to reverse both the economic and environmental devastation. (The Democracy Collaborative, home to the authors of this chapter, was involved in planning the cooperative business development component of this strategy.) There are many elements to the strategy, too numerous to detail here, including housing and retail development, public transit, education, community building, and workforce development components. Here we focus on the community wealth–building effort, which provides a marked contrast to the conventional approach of subsidies and megaprojects that marks so much of what passes for economic development in the United States today.

In what has come to be called the Cleveland model, one key program goal is to leverage the city's existing anchors—in this case, hospitals and universities—to provide a long-term market for new worker-owned cooperatives while at the same time providing living-wage jobs and access to business ownership to employee-owners situated in surrounding low-income, largely African American communities. The first point is to recycle purchasing power to achieve greater stability. The second—and critical—point is to target firms owned by (and anchored by) people who live in the community in order to create an ongoing stabilizing effect.

The first of Cleveland's network of cooperatives opened its doors for business in September 2009. The co-op industrial-scale laundry is a state-of-the-art, ecologically green commercial facility that cleans more than seven million pounds of health care linen a year, while providing its employee-owners a living wage and health benefits. In October 2009, a second employee-owned, community-based company began large-scale installations of solar panels for the city's significant scale nonprofit health, education, and municipal buildings. The company also provides home weatherization and LED (light-emitting diode) installation services. A third business, which opened in February 2013, is a year-round hydroponic greenhouse that is ramping up production and aims to produce more than three million heads of lettuce and approximately three hundred thousand pounds of basil and other herbs a year. Additional enterprises are in the planning stage.

Each business focuses on the specific procurement needs of hospitals and universities as well as the local market. Local foundations, anchor institutions, and city government have all committed resources to stimulate business growth. A cooperative development fund, initially capitalized by a $3 million grant from the Cleveland Foundation, has helped support a growing network of cooperatives. These are linked together in a structure that aims to help achieve community-wide benefits by generating a common fund that can reinvest in additional co-op development.

The cooperative development work has been buttressed by complementary strategies that seek to redirect anchor institution procurement at various levels of the supply chain—along with City policies that support and encourage others to do so as well. Steve Standley, chief administrative officer at University Hospital (UH), has estimated that the hospital had "essentially doubled [its] spending in Cleveland" between 2008 and 2011. An illustration of this approach is UH's five-year strategic growth plan, called Vision 2010, which centered on building five major facilities, as well as outpatient health centers and expansion of other facilities. The total cost of the plan was $1.2 billion, of which about $750 million was in construction. In implementing Vision 2010, University Hospital intentionally sought to target and leverage its expenditures to directly benefit the residents of Cleveland and the overall economy of northeast Ohio, setting goals for local, minority and female business contracting and the hiring of local residents. As a result of the effort, UH awarded contracts to 110 minority- and female-owned businesses and employed over nine hundred Cleveland city residents. More than 90 percent of all subcontractors participating in Vision 2010 were locally based, far exceeding the 80 percent target (Dubb and Howard 2012: 13; Serang, Thompson, and Howard 2013: 35).

Municipal policy has also helped to reinforce this shift in business orientation. Natoya Walker Minor of Mayor Frank Jackson's office noted that in 2010 the City of Cleveland passed into law Ordinance 187A, which created two certifications to promote city government procurement through local and sustainable businesses. Businesses in a five-county area (or food producers within a fifteen-county area) can qualify for a Local Producer Enterprise (LPE) designation, which gives these companies a 2 percent bid discount; the law also allows firms with sustainable practices to be certified as Sustainable Business Enterprises (SUBE). A firm with both designations can get a 4 percent bid discount. In 2013, 187 LPE- and/or SUBE-certified firms participated in City projects as either a prime or a subcontractor, with total contracts exceeding $93 million—i.e., more than 31 percent of City spending. In 2013, City Council passed new legislation that requires 20 percent of workers on construction projects to be city residents, with at least 4 percent being low-income city residents (Minor 2013).

The Cleveland model is important not only because of its local impact but because it points in the direction of using community-based economic planning to support the development of long-term, stable jobs. The relatively informal arrangements of the Cleveland model, in which nonprofits cooperate with public institutions and private employers, also indicates that "planning" need not mean remote government officials drawing up blueprints and then imposing them. Rather, community economic planning can be collaborative, with multiple institutional actors involved—indeed, if such planning is going to succeed, it will need to be.

Other cities have taken notice. In Atlanta, Georgia, and Washington, DC, philanthropy has financed feasibility studies, which are leading to efforts to develop employee-owned businesses patterned on the Cleveland effort, with the first businesses expected to begin operations in both cities by 2015. In Jacksonville, Florida, Mayor Alvin Brown sponsored a March 2014 Community Wealth Building Roundtable, attended by over one hundred Jacksonville residents; a City task force to implement recommendations was formed in October 2014. In Richmond, Virginia, Mayor Dwight Jones in April 2014 established an Office of Community Wealth Building to coordinate a $3.3-million-plus antipoverty initiative, focused on social enterprise development.

Building Community Wealth in Detroit

The potential for rebuilding significant parts of the Detroit economy in a like manner certainly exists. Back in 2008, Maggie De Santis, founding executive director of Warren/Conner Development Corporation, which developed a shopping center and other facilities, observed that the work of community development groups is the only strategy that has kept the city from dying completely in these last 15 years. But, De Santis added, "folks don't understand that. We don't market ourselves. Detroit has never had a progressive community development atmosphere" (DeSantis, Interview 2008). One could go further and suggest that the relative lack of support for community wealth building infrastructure has been a contributing factor in Detroit's decline. For decades, even as the Big Three and manufacturing largely abandoned the city, civic leaders have search for a "big project" that might turn things around. Meanwhile, community groups largely had to fend for themselves.

The long-term solution is clearly twofold: one key step is to buttress local community-based efforts, which are growing throughout the city. The second, profiled later in this chapter, is to link these community efforts to regional and national planning that helps the nation meet critical public goals, such as reducing carbon emissions to mitigate climate change. Either policy, in isolation, would have greatly mitigated Detroit's decline. In combination, such policies can help forge a more vibrant Detroit economy as well as a healthier national economy.

A myriad of projects suggest growing grassroots capacity to undertake community wealth–building efforts—a capacity that is building experience, too, for larger efforts: For example, Church of the Messiah, located on Grand Boulevard, has supported the development of four social enterprises. One of the most interesting, notes Reverend Barry Randolph, "is Nikki's Ginger Tea. It was started by a single mother in the church who was raising her daughter and decided that she didn't want to be on general assistance of any type. . . . All of her employees, 10 people, are young people from the community. The tea is made in the church's commercial kitchen" (Randolph, Interview 2013). "Another one," Reverend Barry adds, "is called Basic Black. That is a t-shirt and design company. . . . That is a community-based business inside the church: It is run by people who are in the community, who have an interest in manufacturing clothing and who are interested in art design. It employs about seven people." Additional church-located businesses are Lawn King, a landscaping company that employs seven people, and a thrift store called Repeat Boutique, employs six people. Nikki's business is privately owned, but for the other three, "the proceeds go back into the ministry of the church and are used primarily for job training" (Ibid.).

The Church of the Messiah is part of a much broader array of grassroots-based efforts that speak to the creative potential of citizens to craft innovative, small-scale solutions to the economic challenges they face. Reverend Barry captures this spirit well. Asked about the impact of the city's bankruptcy filing, the church pastor responded "We as a church concentrate on the good news. We don't deny the bad news. We do defy it. We use it to motivate us" (Ibid.).

Another prominent grassroots project involves the work of the Detroit Black Community Food Security Network. The Network, notes Executive Director Malik Yakini, was founded in 2006 with six goals: 1) promote urban agriculture, 2) promote sound policy; 3) promote cooperative buying; 4) promote healthy eating; 5) promote cooperation among members; and 6) promote youth involvement in this work. One of the group's achievements is the creation of D-Town farms, a "7-acre farm and agro-tourism destination. We are training a cohort of 10 new urban farmers. We are concerned about developing African American farmers." D-Town forms part of a vibrant urban agriculture movement, one that Yakini estimates involves 1,400 gardens and small farms citywide (Yakini 2013). The Network is also investigating the possibility of developing a food cooperative in the city's North End neighborhood (Yakini 2014).

Another leading force is longtime community leader and nonagenarian Grace Lee Boggs, who leads the Boggs Center, which has established the Detroit Summer program. One key goal of the Detroit Summer organizing effort, Boggs noted, is to recreate neighborhoods "where we grow our own food, where we help one another, where people see themselves as bringing the neighbor back into the 'hood'" (Boggs 11/9/11).

Still other prominent neighborhood-based developments include growing networks of local small businesses, particularly in Southwest Detroit (also known as Mexicantown) and in the North End, where a number of local businesses have been developed, including Slow's BBQ, owned by Phil Cooley, and the socially responsible Avalon Bakery, founded by Jackie Victor and Anne Perrault in 1997. Journalist Frank Joyce notes that, "Cooley has now added a Detroit business incubator to his restaurant and real estate interests [while] Avalon recently acquired a huge abandoned factory in the city to service their growing business" (Joyce 9/3/13).

At still another level, an effort to develop "Mondragón in Detroit"—an explicit attempt to emulate the well-known Spanish worker cooperative network that today employs eighty thousand (Howard, Dubb, and McKinley 2014)—is starting to take shape. A Detroit-based group called the Center for Community-Based Enterprises (*full disclosure: author Steve Dubb is a member of its board*), which has pursued that mission, has begun to gain some traction, working with the Church of the Messiah and other partners. The United Food and Commercial Workers union is also exploring community wealth–building, both using employee-ownership to support grocery-store development and through its support of Restaurant Opportunities Center (ROC) which is initiating a co-op academy to provide basic education to encourage worker cooperative development. In February 2014, a group of Detroit community activists also released a document titled *A People's Plan for Restructuring a Sustainable Detroit,* which called for a wide range of actions, including launching an urban homesteading program to enable people to claim ownership of abandoned properties contingent on investing to restore them. It also called for a participatory budget process to give Detroit residents a direct say in the allocation of municipal capital expenditures (A People's Plan 2014).

"Some people look at the physical destruction of Detroit and see only the blight," Frank Joyce wrote in 2013: "What I see is amazing resourcefulness on the part of the remaining residents to prevail against overwhelming odds." Joyce (9/3/13) adds:

> That economy includes increasingly sophisticated urban agriculture and a growing network of alternative schools. It is neighborhood based conflict resolution; do-it-yourself solar street lighting; community based manufacturing using the newest fab lab technology and alternative transportation systems. It is new art and new music and new media. It is time-banking, co-ops and other forms of creative finance.

Boggs sounds a similar note, summing up the larger challenge and opportunity: "Detroit is a city of Hope rather than a city of Despair. The thousands of vacant lots and abandoned houses provide not only the space to begin anew but also the incentive to create innovative ways of making our living—ways that nurture our productive, cooperative, and caring selves" (2011: 105).

Rebuilding Detroit in a Broader Context

Nonetheless, community wealth building, while necessary, is clearly not sufficient to create a flourishing Detroit economy that meets the needs of the majority of its population in the neighborhoods. A prosperous community wealth–building economy in Detroit also needs to be linked to new forms of regional and national planning that bring community resident strategies together with regional and national economies and goals.

Americans often like to pretend that government planning does not exist. Of course, in reality, economic planning takes place pervasively throughout our government. The Pentagon, as economists Robert Pollin and Dean Baker (2010) have argued, is a very impressive national planning agency. Additionally, regulatory and incentive programs, as well as public infrastructure investment (hydroelectric projects; environmental cleanup; water and sewage infrastructure; road construction and maintenance; and the construction of ports, airports, schools, and other government buildings) are also powerful planning instruments. A comprehensive agenda to rebuild a sustainable economy that can help support Detroit and other abandoned areas of the nation requires drawing on such existing policy instruments in a coordinated manner.

A central premise of contemporary urban policy encourages communities to become more attractive investment sites. Even when this approach succeeds, however, the communities concerned remain fundamentally dependent on the decisions of outside parties, whose concern is profit making, not community well-being—and often with little regard for sustainability. Or they lead to corporations playing off one city against another to gain subsidies.

Regional planning precedents can be found in European traditions of bolstering economically depressed cities, regions, and industrial areas. Although far from perfect, the European Union has employed a variety of "cohesion," "solidarity," and development funds aimed at redressing inequalities across countries so as to create an elevator to the top rather than a race to the bottom in terms of labor, environmental, and regulatory standards. Regions and nations with per capita gross domestic products below 75 percent of the EU-wide average, for instance, are eligible for "structural" assistance. The funds also assist communities harmed by natural disasters and provide support to middle-income and more affluent regions seeking to remain competitive. All together such funds amount to one-third of the EU's total budget (European Commission 2006).

A critical principle of regional planning is the preservation and stability of existing communities and their productive capacities—a principle that properly understood could include locating businesses with quality, accessible jobs in neighborhoods with high unemployment. Such strategies could be implemented with deep community partnerships.

A major element in next stage policy work is likely also to involve the continued use of productive capacities where conversion to a different product or industry is possible. A significant next stage option would be for Detroit to tap into the rapidly growing interest in and awareness of the connection that might be built between a healthier urban America and climate change. Detroit, which helped create the twentieth-century automobile economy, could pivot and help lead development of a green economy in the twenty-first century, a significant portion of which also involves transportation.

Using Public Transit—and Planning—to Build a New Economic Base

In 2009, the crisis of the American automobile industry became one of the most visible challenges facing the nation. Federal funds were committed to bail out Chrysler and General Motors—with the government taking significant ownership stakes in both companies. The Obama Administration, to its credit, took advantage of its extraordinary leverage over the industry to push through an increase in fuel efficiency standards, which will reach thirty-six miles per gallon by 2016. The move was an important step after two decades in which the auto industry had consistently blocked higher standards, although many other steps would be needed for the United States to approach its official goal of a 50 percent reduction in carbon emissions by 2030.

Fuel efficiency, however, should not have been the only environmental component of the "auto bailout." Government policy was more concerned with reconstituting GM as a profitable private enterprise than with preserving the communities in which GM plants were located—many of which were sacrificed even as GM was "saved." The environmental consequence of failing to preserve the plants was to force families to pick up roots and have new houses (and roads, sewers, community facilities, and other infrastructure) built, at considerable carbon expense, elsewhere. A better policy might have helped secure the economic viability of existing communities by keeping productive facilities in use. Stating matters this way does not mean that policy ought to have kept every automobile plant open. The crucial (unasked) question was whether, once factories stop making cars, could anything else be done with the idle facilities? Sadly, there was little interest in making productive use of this existing physical infrastructure, to say nothing of the considerable human capital that had been built up over workers' lifetimes in formerly thriving manufacturing hubs like Detroit—resources that might have served as the basis for building new productive capacity. Generally, the choice most former employees faced involved either joining the unemployment rolls or the ranks of low-wage service workers.

The crisis of the auto industry during the Great Recession represented an important missed opportunity to preserve and restore communities and to establish a powerful new precedent and principle. One obvious place where manufacturing capacity might have been utilized would have been in developing mass transit and rail infrastructure. Among transportation and planning experts there is widespread consensus that the scale of mass transit and both inter-city and intracity rail in the United States must expand very substantially to meet basic carbon-emission goals. This means that transit systems will need to make massive investments and acquire large quantities of new equipment.

High-speed rail is one area where public investment could pay handsome returns. Of course, at the moment high-speed rail is largely stalled in the United States, both politically and economically. While nations such as China build high-speed rail networks extending thousands of miles, it currently remains questionable whether high-speed rail lines in the United States will be built even in such higher priority areas as the San Francisco-Los Angeles corridor in California or the Boston-Washington DC corridor in the Northeast.

But we should not allow the political challenges of the present moment blind us to the possibilities for a brighter future. What might a serious commitment to a national high-speed rail system look like? In 2008, Simon Fraser urban studies professor Richard Gilbert and Toronto transportation consultant Anthony Perl proposed that the United States build some 25,000 kilometers in dual track devoted to high-speed rail service between now and 2025, as well as additional, incremental upgrades of existing rail lines. They estimated a total of $2 trillion in investment (roughly $140 billion a year for fifteen years) in infrastructure and equipment would be required. Gilbert and Perl recommended financing this with large increases in the price of gasoline, programs to allow citizens to trade in older, less fuel-efficient cars, and efforts to make trains as comfortable as possible to help cushion the transition to what would in effect be a different transportation system (Gilbert and Perl 2008).

Few have drawn the obvious connection between increased investments in mass transit and what is still, despite the postrecession auto industry recovery, a chronically troubled industry. Yet factories that once made cars could be retooled to begin making mass transit vehicles, as well as electric and super-high-efficiency cars. Currently there is no American-owned manufacturer of high-speed rail vehicles, although some subway cars are assembled in the United States by foreign firms, and there is one small Oregon-based manufacturer of streetcars.

Like the automobile industry in its prime, transit vehicle construction has the potential to provide good jobs for people with less than a college degree in an industry that is growing. How might public policy go about establishing a domestic capacity to supply America's public transit authorities with needed subway and rail cars in cities like Detroit? One possibility is to create an entirely new public-private partnership in which a new firm is guaranteed long-term contracts and the government (and local unions) take an ownership stake in exchange. Another possibility is to restructure an existing firm such as General Motors, and again offer long-term contracts and assistance in transitioning assembly lines to produce the new vehicles in exchange for public equity. Employee ownership could be part of the equation here too.

A key principle underlying a community-oriented industrial policy must be the preservation of existing communities, their in-place infrastructure and community capital, and their productive capacities on a long-term basis. What is required is a policy that assures productive capacities stay in use, with assistance provided as necessary in cases where conversion to a different product is required. Often this will mean adopting some form of community, public, or worker ownership. Since these kinds of structures vest business ownership in the local area, they anchor ownership in place, creating strong incentives for these businesses to reinvest in productive capacities, so they can maintain employment—and, by extension, production capacity—in their communities.

Key to the planning effort and long-run viability would be to write public procurement contracts for transit and high-speed rail to favor firms that invest in the capacity (or have their subcontracting firms so invest) to produce buses, subway cars, and the like. A domestic content requirement for federal and state purchases of mass-transit equipment would instantly create demand for such equipment. Domestic content requirements are already common in federal purchases of vehicles and some cities; for example, the City of Chicago recently announced such requirements on its planned $2 billion-purchase of railcars (Jobs to Move America 7/24/14). While it is important that domestic manufacturers eventually compete with one another for some contracts, awarding a significant portion of long-term contracts to newly converted facilities is a sensible way both to allow those facilities to get off the ground economically and to create a domestic mass transit manufacturing capacity. It is also a way to save in place community capital, to say nothing of jobs.

Beginning to Define a New Long-Term Approach

The long-term goal, in short, would be for Detroit to participate in an integrated plan to build and sustain green, low-carbon communities over the next two generations. Achieving this would require a range of mechanisms that would raise the price of carbon emissions and, by doing so, also finance new green development. In theory, a cap-and-trade emissions program with stiff, steadily strengthening standards might achieve this. Or, it might be achieved more directly by carbon taxes or higher gasoline taxes. (The effective price of a gallon of gas in the United States is less than half that of the United Kingdom, largely because of higher British taxes.) Direct taxes on carbon or gasoline, as is widely recognized, should be accompanied by rebates for lower-income consumers to avoid regressive income-distributive effects.

A further step would be sharply increased public investment in research and development for alternative energy sources and improved carbon efficiencies in vehicles, buildings, agriculture, and other major sectors. A third important measure is direct public investment in green jobs that directly mitigate carbon emissions and increase energy efficiency, such as planting trees, weatherizing older homes, and supporting transit systems.

A fourth policy instrument involves direct public investments in a greener urban infrastructure. Clearly, the present gas tax will not be adequate to finance these investments; however, an increased carbon tax could help finance such investments.

A fifth long-term strategy involves taking on direct public control of firms in critical sectors, such as energy and vehicle production. To the extent that oil and other energy producers push for continued fossil fuel production subsidies and resist the development of renewable forms of energy, there is a strong case for turning them into public utilities. In the vehicle-production sector, again there is a potential conflict (as took place in the 1990s and early 2000s) between the public interest in dramatically increasing fuel efficiency and attractive profit-making strategies for manufacturers—which with US car producers led them to emphasize the sale of larger, more expensive, and less efficient vehicles (such as the SUV).

The Obama administration, in its takeover of General Motors, emphasized the need for the reconstructed GM to build smaller cars. But that recommendation has not removed the structural conflict between the interests of car producers and the need to reduce carbon emissions. A privately owned GM will want to see more cars on the road and more highways, regardless of the public interest. Public ownership of large vehicle manufacturers would facilitate a transition from cars to transit and rail infrastructure.

Sixth, government could help create a market for this transition by modifying operations to minimize the carbon footprint and support community economies. Potential action in this regard include green building policies, integrating facility locations with sustainability plans, systematically using procurement to favor alternative energy sources and more sustainable communities, and changing behavior with respect to energy and transport use.

The policies listed above are not exhaustive, but are indicative of a reinvigorated political imagination—i.e., new directions for the long haul. An effective approach to foster economic stability in Detroit and other communities would likely also require the creation of new institutional regional planning bodies that can pay close attention to local economic conditions and trends—perhaps ten to twelve regional units, akin to the regional organization of the Federal Reserve Bank. Such agencies, of course, would have to have access to resources adequate to carrying out this mission. As an initial estimate, ten regional development entities could be capitalized at $5 billion a year each, rising over time to $10 billion a year to be able to carry out more extensive, longer-term efforts. Participating states and localities might be required to end "beggar-thy-neighbor" tax incentive programs aimed at raiding jobs from other localities as a precondition to be eligible to receive regional planning investment dollars. Specific tasks regional bodies might undertake include feasibility studies for refurbishing closing or closed facilities; providing financial support to help workers or other local groups acquire ownership of such facilities; equity investments in new or emerging firms in targeted localities; support for targeted job training for displaced or marginalized workers; and a range of other investments aimed at bolstering targeted cities' long-term viability.

Creating the Basis for a Truly Sustainable Detroit

The opportunities for Detroit to rebuild are great—and, indeed, despite the prominence of bankruptcy in the news, many grassroots rebuilding efforts are already under way. Reflection on ecological and transportation issues, the nation's experience with temporary ownership of General Motors, and the principles implicit in the nascent Cleveland effort all point to the possibility of an important new long-term strategic approach. It is one in which economic policy related to activities heavily financed by the public, such as the construction of mass transit, is used to create, and give stability to, enterprises that are more democratically owned, to target jobs to communities in distress or to deal with important environmental issues.

To date, official and community efforts in Detroit have often not been aligned. However, with the on-the-ground grassroots work now under way, Detroit has the potential to build toward a new economy that puts community wealth at the center of what Detroit does. "We know we can't do business as usual," Reverend Barry Randolph observes. "The days of working for the corporation are limited and gone. We know those days are gone. Co-op brings together the opportunity for community development, employment and entrepreneurship. It creates the type of community where every individual has a stake and a voice. . . . [I]t is also about changing the mindset. People are cynical—when you create the opportunity in a co-op, everyone has a stake and vested interest. That's so important in a city that is neglected. It actually brings about empowerment" (Randolph, Interview 2013).

Such first steps, taken seriously, could—indeed, should—help stimulate much broader strategies of importance not only for Detroit, both for our nation's economic and environmental future. A new approach, that builds community wealth at the local level, supported by regional and national policy to develop a less carbon-intensive economy, is clearly needed. Detroit, in large measure because of the disinvestment it has suffered, may arrive sooner at this conclusion than most cities. Of course, forging this path will not be easy. But there are signs that a new path is slowly, painfully emerging. Like the experimentation that went on in the state and local "laboratories of democracy" that later became the basis of many national-scale New Deal policies, we are witnessing extraordinary developments at the local level that could help clarify principles for much larger future change. The lessons learned in Detroit—and suggested by what might expand upon them—might well help inform the development of a new economy that extends far beyond the city limits.

Note

1. For a key foundational work on this topic, see Thomas Sugrue, *The Origins of the Urban Crisis: Race and Inequality in Postwar Detroit*, Princeton, NJ: Princeton University Press 2005. The authors gratefully acknowledge the very helpful comments of Chris Schildt of PolicyLink, who reviewed an earlier draft of this chapter.

References

A People's Plan for Restructuring a Sustainable Detroit. (2014). Detroit, MI. (February 25), http://www.d-rem.org/peoplesplan, accessed April 15, 2014.

Abbey-Lambertz, K. (2013) "Whole Foods Detroit Was 15 Years in the Making: Developer Peter Cummings of Ram Looks Back," *Huffington Post*, (June 5), http://www.huffingtonpost.com/2013/06/05/whole-foods-detroit-developer-peter-cummings_n_3388891.html, accessed June 9, 2014.

AlHajal, K. (2014). "Detroit has half the median income, three times the poverty rate of nation, new Census numbers show," *MLive*, September 21, 2012, http://www.mlive.com/news/detroit/index.ssf/2012/09/detroit_has_half_the_median_in.html, accessed June 8, 2014.

Allen, T. (2014). "Allen: 5 keys to make Detroit an 'Our Detroit'," *Knowledge Center,* Detroit, MI: The Skillman Foundation, January 28, 2014, http://www.skillman.org/Knowledge-Center/A-Rose-for-Detroit-Blog/Tonya-Allen-Our-Detroit-Framework, accessed June 8, 2014.

Boggs, G. L. (2011). *The Next American Revolution: Sustainable Activism for the Twenty-First Century*, Berkeley, CA: University of California Press.

———. (2011). Address to PolicyLink conference, Detroit, Michigan: November 9, 2011.

Clark, H. (2014). *Co-op Grocery Stores: More than Food—Building a Self-Determined Food Community in Detroit.* Detroit, MI: Detroit Black Community Food Security Network. (February).

Deller, S., A. Hoyt, B. Hueth and R. Sundaram-Stukel. (2009). *Research on the Economic Impact of Cooperatives*, Madison, WI: University of Wisconsin Center for Cooperatives. (March).

DeSanits, M. (2008) Interview by Steve Dubb, College Park, MD: The Democracy Collaborative. (January 2008).

Detroit Regional News Hub. (2014). *Transformation Detroit Fact Sheet*, Detroit, MI: Detroit Regional News Hub.

Drape, J. (2014). "Bankruptcy for Ailing Detroit, but Prosperity for Its Teams," *New York Times*. (October 14), http://www.nytimes.com/2013/10/14/sports/bankruptcy-for-ailing-detroit-but-prosperity-for-its-teams.html?_r=1&&pagewanted=all, accessed June 9, 2014.

Dubb, S. and T. Howard (2012). *Leveraging Anchor Institutions for Local Job Creation and Wealth Building*, Berkeley, CA: University of California, Institute for Labor Research and Employment, p. 13.

European Commission. (2006). *Investing in Europe's Member States and regions: After the European Council's Agreement on the Financial Perspectives: Putting EU Cohesion Policy into practice 2007–2013*, Brussels, Belgium, EC, (January).

Forbes Magazine (2014). #451 Michael & Marian Ilitch & family, New York, NY: Forbes.com, 2014, http://www.forbes.com/profile/michael-marian-ilitch/, accessed June 9, 2014.

Gallagher, J. and J. Seidel. (2014). "Detroit's workforce lacks job skills; it's called a 'huge problem'," *Detroit Free Press*, April 8, 2012, http://www.freep.com/article/20120408/BUSINESS06/204080539/Detroit-s-work-force-lacking-job-skills-it-s-called-a-huge-problem, accessed June 8, 2014.

Gilbert. R. and A. Perl. (2008). *Transport Revolutions: Moving People and Freight Without Oil*. London, UK: Earthscan, 2008.

Gilmore, I. (2009). "Goodwells: Little Grocer Brings Big Organic Goodness to Midtown," *Model D*, July 14, 2009, http://www.modeldmedia.com/features/goodwells19909.aspx, accessed October 6, 2014.

Gordon Nembhard, J. (2014) *Collective Courage: A History of African American Cooperative Economic Thought And Practice*. University Park, PA: Pennsylvania State Press.

Green, J. (2013). "No Longer Motor City: Detroit Sinks as Auto Industry Soars," *Quick Take: Bloomberg*, (December 12, 2013), updated May 2, 2014, http://www.bloomberg.com/quicktake/no-longer-motor-city/, accessed June 8, 2014.

HBCU Money. (2014). *HBCU Money's 2014 African American Owned Credit Union Directory*, hbcumoney.com, March 4, 2014, http://hbcumoney.com/2014/03/04/2014-african-american-owned-credit-union-directory, accessed October 6, 2014.

Howard, T., S. Dubb, and S. McKinley. (2014). "Economic Democracy," in D. Rowe, ed., *Achieving Sustainability: Visions, Principles, and Practices*, Macmillan Reference USA, January 2014, 231–239.

Howes, D. (2007). "100M to help region's economy: Ford Foundation, others aim to move Michigan jobs away from manufacturing," *Detroit News*, (September 14, 2007), http://community-wealth.org/content/100m-help-regions-economy-ford-foundation-others-aim-move-michigan-jobs-away-manufacturing, accessed June 9, 2014.

Isidore, C. (2013). "New $444 million hockey arena is still a go in Detroit," *CNNMoney,* July 26, 2013, http://money.cnn.com/2013/07/26/news/economy/detroit-bankruptcy-arena, accessed June 9, 2014.

Jobs to Move America. (2014). "Chicago Transit Authority Restarts $2 Billion Rail Car Procurement with Strong Manufacturing Job-Creating Approach," *Jobs to Move America News*, (July 24), http://jobstomoveamerica.org/chicago-job-creating-approach, accessed October 10, 2014.

Joyce, F. (2013). "The real story of Detroit's economy: A Motor City native explains why "Detroit is exactly where we want to be," *Alternet*, (September 3, 2013), http://www.salon.com/2013/09/03/the_real_story_of_detroits_economy_partner, accessed June 10, 2014.

Knight Foundation. (2008). *New Economy Initiative Launches $100 Million Effort to Strengthen Southeast Michigan Economy*, Miami, FL: John S. and James L. Knight Foundation, January 8, 2008, http://www1.knightfoundation.org/press-room/press-release/new-economy-initiative-launches-100-million-effort/, accessed June 9, 2014.

McCarthy, S. (2014). Summary of Total Cost and Public Subsidy for MLB Stadiums Constructed or Significantly Renovated Since 1990. *League of Fans*, Washington, DC. http://www.leagueoffans.org/mlbstadiums1990.html, accessed June 8, 2014.

Minor, N. W. (2013). *City of Cleveland's Self-Help Strategy: policies that ensure localist economic development*, presentation to the Business Alliance for Local Living Economies (BALLE) conference, Buffalo, New York (June 13).

National Center for Employee Ownership. (2014). *A Statistical Profile of Employee Ownership*, Oakland, CA: NCEO, January 2014, http://www.nceo.org/articles/statistical-profile-employee-ownership, accessed June 8, 2014.

Ohio Employee Ownership Center (2012). *Annual Report, FY2011 - July 1, 2010 - June 30, 2011*, Kent, OH: OEOC.

Perry, S. (2014). "Detroit Tests What Foundations Can Do To Rescue Troubled Cities," *Chronicle of Philanthropy*, (October 20), http://philanthropy.com/article/Can-Philanthropy-Rescue/142415, accessed June 9, 2014.

Planning Report. (2014). "Kresge Foundation's Trudeau Deftly Invests in Detroit's Reinvention" (interview of Laura Trudeau), *The Planning Report*, (June) , http://www.planningreport.com/issue/june-2014, accessed June 5, 2014.

Pollin, R. and D. Baker. (2010). "Reindustrializing America: A Proposal for Reviving U.S. Manufacturing and Creating Millions of Good Jobs," *New Labor Forum,* Volume 19, (Spring), pp. 17–34.

Randolph, B. (2013). Interview by Steve Dubb, Takoma Park, MD: The Democracy Collaborative, (October).

Ross, P. (2014). "Detroit Plan To Raze Blight Would Cost Over A Billion And Create Just 430 Jobs," *International Business Times*, (May 29), www.ibtimes.com/detroit-plan-raze-blight-would-cost-over-billion-create-just-430-jobs-1592164, accessed June 8, 2014.

Serang, F. J., P. Thompson, and T. Howard. (2013) *The Anchor Mission: Leveraging the Power of Anchor Institutions To Build Community Wealth*, Cambridge, MA and College Park, MD: Massachusetts Institute of Technology and the University of Maryland, (February).

Sugrue, T. (2005).*The Origins of the Urban Crisis: Race and Inequality in Postwar Detroit*, Princeton, NJ: Princeton University Press.

Smith, L. L. (2014). "No Victory Without Inclusion," *The Catalyst*, New York, NY and Washington, DC: Living Cities, http://www.livingcities.org/blog/?id=303, accessed June 8, 2014.

Story, L. (2012). "As Companies Seek Tax Deals, Governments Pay High Price," *New York Times*, (December 2), p. A-1, http://www.nytimes.com/2012/12/02/us/how-local- taxpayers-bankroll-corporations.html, accessed February 11, 2013.

Turbeville, W. C. (2013). *The Detroit Bankruptcy*, New York, NY: Demos, (November).

Wayne State University. (2001). Detroit African-American History Project, Detroit, MI: WSU, http://www.daahp.wayne.edu/1950_1999.html, accessed October 6, 2014.

Welch, S. (2014). "New Economy Initiative to target innovation, entrepreneurs with 2nd round of funding," *Crain's Detroit,* February 2, 2014, modified February 6, 2014, http://www.crainsdetroit.com/article/20140202/NEWS/302029991/new-economy-initiative-to-target-innovation-entrepreneurs-with-2nd, accessed June 9, 2014.

Williamson, T., S. Dubb, and G. Alperovitz (2010). *Climate Change, Community Stability and the Next 150 Million Americans*, College Park, MD: The Democracy Collaborative.

Yakini, M. (2013). Keynote address to the North American Students of Cooperation (NASCO) annual conference, Ann Arbor, Michigan: (November 2).

————. (2014). personal conversation, Oakland, California: (June 11).

12

The Cooperative City: New Visions for Urban Futures

David Fasenfest

We are ever faced with recurrent periods of expansion and contraction as cities go through cycles of growth and decline, and we imagine these are the normal workings of the forces of economic change. At times we consider whether the consequences can be avoided, and worry about the impact of these forces on the lives of the residents of cities. Often, decline is accompanied by out-migration and renewal brings with it new residents and different challenges. David Harvey's (1989) notion of the built environment within the urban experience resonates with Schumpeter's (1976) ideas of creative destruction: for the latter the old must be destroyed so the new can be created; for the former, the destruction is essential as a way of creating new investment opportunities for capital accumulation. Market forces invariably create winners and losers, no more so than among the cities, which increasingly face the prospect of becoming urban outcasts as populations become trapped in a state of advanced marginality (Wacquant 2008).

This essay is a discussion of the limitations of relying on traditional forms of investment and economic activity, an exploration into how a city might conceptualize responses to urban decline, and a counterfactual example of a solution that might have enabled Detroit to create the core of a viable local subeconomy, one without the dependence on an increasingly unstable and certainly uncontrollable globalized political economy. How, we ask, can residents of a community organize work around democratic principles, an organization within which decisions are made on behalf of and by its members (in this case workers and citizens of the city)? What is needed are not just single efforts, but rather a cohesive and interconnected system of enterprises and organizations, a cooperative city if you will, all sharing resources and working to secure the ongoing well-being of the city's residents, and functioning to insulate the city from, or at least minimize the effects of, economic forces beyond their control. To start this effort, the essay will end with a speculation about how the creation of a worker's cooperative, when confronted with another plant closing and plans for a new production facility, might have acted differently and blunted the industrial decline that characterizes Detroit's recent history.

In his closing of the Sermon on the Mount, Jesus warns against the man who builds his house on a foundation of sand, a foundation that will inevitably fail to support the house in times of trouble. We can ask if perhaps cities, rooted in a single vision of how they should be organized, would be well served to consider what sorts of foundations they are built upon. Is the market, and with it capitalist social relations, the sole and necessary basis on which to organize production and the lives of its residents? Are there other models that can break the cycle of prosperity and decline that is inflicted by markets upon cities during economic transitions? These are not trivial concerns, as evidenced by the financial sector's focus on declining consumer demand as a result of market forces (remember that selling in the marketplace is, after all, the way capitalists realize their gains). For example, a recent report by Morgan Stanley documents how the rising inequality negatively impacts consumption, pointing out that the "US Gini coefficient has increased by more than 20% from 1968 to 2013" (Morgan Stanley 2014: 4). It goes on to state, "(s)low wage growth over time has exacerbated inequality because lower and middle-income households rely more heavily on labor market income compared with their higher-income counterparts," and "(s)ince the labor market recovery began in early 2010, we estimate that roughly 65% of net new jobs created have been concentrated in low wage paying industries" (Morgan Stanley 2014: 5). Markets are in trouble if they cannot find consumers, and the solution may not be greater reliance on the market to make a change. Marx reminds us that people make their own histories, "but they do not make it as they please" (1994). If we limit ourselves to market solutions, we are likely to be revisited by these same problems at a later date.

It is an open question whether the many and varied nonmarket solidarity economy initiatives of the past decades in Europe, North and South America are as clear sighted and devoid of superstitions about the past as they will need to be to survive. The hope is that solidarity economy initiatives are a manifestation of Polanyi's "double movement" where extension of the market system provokes countervailing challenges when they threaten to overwhelm humans' need for a stable habitat. In these initiatives, based on the notion of self-management and more egalitarian working relationships, there are no employers or employees but rather an environment where decisions are taken jointly and all share in the profits equally. These associations come about as people form groups, cooperatives or associations around work. Singer (2002), the father of solidarity economics in Brazil and elsewhere, sees these efforts as operating in the tradition of utopian socialism, where individuals are encouraged to carve out space and opportunities for making a living within the existing social order, but according to more communal, socialized property and work relations.

There is another perspective on solidarity economic projects, one derived from those categories with which Polanyi was fully familiar but chose to abandon in his work, from the *Great Transformation* forward (Dale 2010). This perspective draws on the double movement identified by Marx in his diagnosis of capitalism (especially Volume 1 of *Capital*) where capital accumulation (today often referred to as economic growth) is simultaneously the accumulation of profit on the one hand and the accumulation of surplus labor (displacement of living labor via intensification of work, technical change, etc.) on the other. From the perspective of this double movement, solidarity economics appears to be as much about the disposition as the disposal of the laborers made redundant via neoliberal patterns of investment and employment.

Marx's double movement is more useful than that of Polanyi because it offers a more precise and empirically relevant diagnosis of how capitalism works. It provides exactly those conceptual tools abandoned by Polanyi, specifically the labor theory of value and the related forms (metamorphosis) in which capital manifests itself in the empirical world. Rather than treating land and labor as "fictitious" commodities, they are more properly regarded as necessary fictions, once we appreciate the insight about how capitalist commodity production itself obscures the role of laborers in profit creation. What is important here is that we must understand how the market operates, and perhaps question whether the market is the center of all social and economic life. After all, one of the main accomplishments of the neoliberal march of the past several decades is a return of the market as some sort of ideal state, that market societies represent a utopian vision of society. Whereas Marx offers us an understanding of how markets necessarily operate, the renewed interest in Polanyi reflects a desire to figure out how to save us from the worst aspects of markets without throwing out markets themselves.

Whether the dispositions of those engaged with solidarity economy projects become increasingly anticapitalist remains to be seen; whether the modes of self-provisioning that emerge come to have some degree of autonomy from market forces is an open question. Moreover, whether their current scale and scope of these efforts are sufficient to allow us to regard them as constituting a turning point in the long night of the twenty-first century may not be discernable, as yet. What is certain is that market economies produce huge inequalities, and neoliberal goals have eroded democracy as decisions are made in support of those goals (witness the ongoing devastation of austerity policies). And in the increasingly global nature of the contemporary economy, cities increasingly define winners and (more often) losers. As Harvey reminds us, "the levers of political, institutional, judicial, military and media power are under such tight but dogmatic political control" (2011: 228), leaving little room for change in a world that is increasingly urban.

Detroit: Past and Future

Detroit's story is an artifact of the centralization and concentration of the relations of capital in the first part of the twentieth century, and as capital began its departure half a century or more ago there was no market "recovery" based on a Polanyian countermovement. Even today, one could say whatever arc of recovery can be found in Detroit is based on efforts by individuals and groups of individuals to make something for themselves. Investments by capital are narrowly focused geographically, and the benefits projected do not appear to serve most of Detroit's residents. Relying on private capital markets to now return and regenerate the city's economy will achieve little beyond the pillaging of the public purse, promoting crackpot realism, and generating speculative bubbles rather than sustained growth or development.

The Detroit decline narrative is well rehearsed by others in this volume, in academic journals, and in the pages of the press. The range of causes for the current state of affairs in Detroit runs the gamut from public corruption and poor leadership, racism and city-suburb social/political conflict, white and/or economic flight over half a century, and social and physical infrastructure decline and neglect, to the most common trope of Detroit's reliance and dependence on an industrial mono-culture, and with its decline the subsequent job loss (for a recent recap of these causes, see Eisinger 2014). Regardless of its roots, it is undeniable that Detroit is in decline, and its population is now no more than a third of what it was at its peak in the middle of the twentieth century. Though Eisinger may still question whether or not Detroit is dead, others have not been so hesitant in pronouncing over its corpse (LeDuff 2014, Martelle 2014). The fact remains that Detroit, spread out on almost 139 square miles currently with a population density under 5,000 persons per square mile (see http://quickfacts.census.gov/), is shrinking. At its peak in the 1950s its density was over 13,300 people per square mile, comparing favorably with a city like Chicago (228 and 11,841 respectively). To put this into perspective, other Midwest industrial cities experiencing long periods of decline, like Cleveland (78 square miles with a density of 5100/sq mile), Buffalo (40 and 6470) and Pittsburgh (55 and 5521), do not feel as desolate, with so much empty space. The question of urban restructuring and shrinking cities is of general concern in this era of globalization (Martinez-Fernandez 2012), and solutions for restructuring and rebuilding these cities, and particularly Detroit, abound (Ryan 2012).

Bill Tabb (forthcoming) points out that most accounts of why Detroit is in its current state ignore the importance of race, noting that its population decline is not just about white flight (as Sugrue 1996, so persuasively demonstrates). Furthermore, race plays a role in both local and state politics. For example, according to the Michigan Department of the Treasury, there are now eleven cities under some form of receivership or emergency management in the State of Michigan—and in the biggest, Detroit, the emergency manager has taken the city into bankruptcy. What is significant is that in a state with about 1.4 million African-Americans, comprising just over 14 percent of the total population, over half of all African Americans live in cities under this nondemocratic rule. All decisions are made by appointed officials who move forward in the best interest of bond holders rather than its citizens, all in the name of bringing fiscal responsibility to the community. Political democracy fails the State of Michigan's poorest residents, and offers little hope of a change in policies. Central to everyone's assessment of Detroit's current woes are its unemployment levels and the absence of jobs within reach for residents in a city with no meaningful mass transit system and a low rate of automobile ownership. According to a Brookings report, "only 7.3% of jobs in the metropolitan area are located within three miles of the central business district, while 77% are beyond the 10-mile radius . . ." (as cited in Eisinger 2014: 3). Coupled with that, the change in the local labor market and outmigration of those able to find work elsewhere has left the city with a shortage of skilled workers (Carey 2013). Yet employment does not seem to be a focus of many of the proposals currently put forth.

Political solutions to Detroit's ills are questionable. Efforts by Detroit-based community groups to form wider regional coalitions in order to alter the political agenda and bring much-needed cooperation and support to Detroit are mixed (Rusch 2012). Perhaps the sentiments and level of support the region has for the city and its problems are best summed up by the title of an article in *The New Yorker* at the start of 2014 (Williams 2014): "Drop Dead, Detroit." This article was a profile of Oakland County's chief executive, L. Brooks Patterson, who directs a county that is the richest among the five counties surrounding Detroit, with a median household income that is four and a half times that of the city (according to the Census Bureau estimates,

$65,637 versus $14,861). Patterson's position vis-à-vis Detroit's problems is echoed regionally, and the impetus to both see the problems of the city and any solution as beyond a regional concern has been well established. Indeed, Logan (2011), reporting on the 2010 Census, finds that Detroit remains one of the most segregated US cities on several dimensions, most notably on the Isolation Index "despite the region's overall loss of black residents in the last decade" (2011: 7). On a practical level, for example, the refusal of the surrounding counties to support a regional mass transit system is fed by and feeds into the racism on the part of many who worry too many Detroit residents using that system will bring all the social problems of the city out to the suburbs if they had a way of getting there. Little concern is expressed over the fact that without one, Detroiters can't get to the jobs in those outlying counties. And without jobs or the prospect of an income, local retailers will struggle, more people will fail to make basic payments (witness the recent debacle as the city cuts off water to the homes of thousands of its poorest residents because of delinquent water bills), and the city will have little hope of generating revenue over the long term.

The politics and economics of place are further stymied by changes in political power as the economy declines. Looking at what Siemiatycki (2012) calls labor geography, the decline and restructuring of the US auto industry—vitally important to Detroit—has meant that the UAW has lost political power and influence. He goes on to say, "(t)here are few industries in which the implications of globalization and increasing competitions are seen more clearly than in the auto industry. . . . Permanent restructuring . . . is more inherent to the logic and imperatives of capitalism in an era of globalization" (Siemiatycki 2012: 469). With the decline of the power of the UAW, workers for the few jobs available now are hired according to a multitiered scale with reduced benefits, and retirees are forced to accept renegotiated benefit packages. The spinoffs are significant. Communities like Pontiac and Flint, kept afloat during the decline of auto by retired workers living with gold standard pensions, experience an accelerated decline. The regional health care industry, long a bright spot, now scrambles as insurance plan changes pay for fewer services at lower levels, and more people turn to self-medicating and care through over-the-counter pharmaceuticals (in poorer communities, it is not uncommon to see a chain drugstore on each corner of a major intersection).

There are several concrete proposals that seek to revive Detroit's stagnating economy. One solution put forth for Detroit is to combine all the empty space (akin to the eighteenth-century enclosures) and turn to urban commercial farming, an effort led by Hantz Farms Detroit (http://www.hantzfarmsdetroit.com), looking to create the world's largest urban farm. Reminiscent of earlier proposals to "right-size" Detroit (Glaeser 2010), this plan would require a degree of reorganizing existing space, perhaps relocating segments of the community to increase density in the more "viable" parts of the city, and creating an enterprise that essentially hires local unemployed residents at low wages. In one sense, current activities, such as clearing abandoned buildings is preparing for this kind of solution (Hackman 2014). By contrast, there are increasingly viable community gardening initiatives designed to improve access to quality food (until recently Detroit was a food desert) while empowering poor residents to work in their own interests (see White 2010, 2011a, 2011b). But can these gardens "sustain the community? Are they meant as a replacement of the old manufacturing base?" (Gottfried 2014: 99). These efforts do little to change the context of decline, or even organize consistently for change. Rather, these are important but uncritical activities of self-defense and personal development. Whether we look to corporate farming or community gardens, neither will address the question of employment that offers either living wages or the potential for payroll taxes that will provide the city with the resources it needs to rebuild its system of services, repair its infrastructure, and most importantly restore its educational system.

This brings us to some of the current proposals for how Detroit might move forward through real estate development. All of those solutions currently focus on market-based efforts, informed by the logic of neoliberal austerity. Eisinger (2014) points to the potential of public-private partnerships, as exemplified by plans to finally build a limited light-rail system along one of the city's main arteries, Woodward Avenue, to bring people into the city center—though that system won't reach into the close-in suburbs in Oakland County to the northwest, further along the avenue. Many see the speculative real-estate investments made by people like Dan Gilbert (owner of Quicken Loans) or Michael Ilitch (whose family owns both the Detroit Tigers and the Detroit Red Wings) as a sign of impending improvement. For example, the city (and state) is going forward with plans to underwrite a new hockey stadium in the downtown with a subsidy, even as Detroit seeks court approval to cut pension obligations on the basis of its fiscal crisis. Both Gilbert and Ilitch present themselves at visionaries that will bring life back to Detroit. Gilbert sees a vibrant city of businesses and cultural venues spring forth from his real-estate ventures (Segal 2013) while Ilitch plans on a grand revitalization as he pledges to pay for 44 percent of the projected cost of the new arena; the State of Michigan is issuing a $450 million Michigan Strategic Fund bond sale, backed by taxpayer dollars (Cristoff 2014) in support of this project. In addition, Ilitch promises to invest another $200 million to develop the surrounding neighborhoods with residential buildings, restaurants and retail outlets. The resulting speculation is indeed driving up the price of real-estate for properties in the path of these plans, and some long empty and derelict properties are now selling (or have sold) at respectable prices. Perhaps this can regenerate a depressed market, essential if the city hopes to increase important property tax revenue streams. And the city appears to be getting attention from investors far and wide looking to put their increasing store of cash to work. One has to wonder, therefore, whether investment from as far away as China (Kaiman 2014) signals a real change for Detroit, or further evidence of the speculative bubble that is emerging in parts of the city.

However, there are two realities that must be recognized with regard to these proposals. The first is that the scope of these changes is very narrow, focused as it is on a very small area within the center of Detroit. Even a casual examination of the urban space, as Bill Tabb and I did recently, reveals that all this sports-based construction (Clay Ford's NFL Lions, and Ilitch's MLB Tigers and NHL Red Wings play in downtown stadiums) constrains this city—should it suddenly spring back to life—because it no longer has the real-estate to create a vibrant urban downtown. On game day, one encounters a mainly white suburban audience streaming into the city, perhaps dining in local establishments, and then departing once the game is over. Most Detroit residents are hard pressed to spend the dollars on sports entertainment, when one counts ticket and concession prices. What is lacking, as a plan to revitalize Detroit, is a coordinated effort at development throughout the city. How will investment and development in a very small area around the central city and its business district resonate with the desolation and decline throughout the city? An interesting solution to this problem was posed when Chicago faced the same situation three decades earlier. Harold Washington, elected mayor of Chicago at a time when the city was hurting economically, proposed a redevelopment plan that required developers to link downtown real-estate investments with projects in the outlying neighborhoods. In Chicago downtown development resulted in corresponding positive change in outlying communities. As Betancur and Gills pointed out, ". . . significant overlapping existed between race and poverty and between neighborhood deterioration/disinvestment and racial minority status, community development in these areas was linked to a larger, national, and race-based movement for equal opportunity and access, for political representation, and for inclusive social change" (2004: 93). No such plan is in place for Detroit, and it would appear the only vision for the future is one that does not include its current residents.

The second reality is that once again the solution is rooted in market speculation. As so recently experienced, a real-estate bubble can burst (after all, the Great Recession destroyed a lot of built-up equity in real estate), teams go through periods of decline with loss of attendance, there may not be enough well-paying jobs to attract the people who will occupy this new upscale housing planned for these developments, and, like all markets, there is a reliance on the ability to sell the products on offer. It is not the nature or failure of public policies that interfere with markets, and there may not be Polanyian movements that bring markets back in line. Rather, as Marx points out, markets are the mechanism that permits capitalists to realize surplus extraction, the means through which commodity exchange operates. Investors will only realize their profits if either rents remain high or they sell at an advantageous price. Most people in Detroit cannot participate in this market, and so even if developers operate within the neoliberal utopian view that markets bring all things to all people, this is true only for those in the game. In the case of the Gilbert and Ilitch plans, what happens if they do not attract the young professionals so crucial to making their visions into a reality? What, then, might nonmarket solutions look like? How might the city reinvent itself with an eye toward economic democracy, and not look to some sort of political democracy to protect everyone's interests?

Toward a Cooperative Solution

Can we escape the market? Certainly not immediately, and not until there is a major upheaval in a global system that inexorably drives greater and greater inequality and poverty through its neoliberal austerity (Stiglitz 2014). The current market-based system may deliver the goods writ large, but the allocation of the benefits in the form of surplus is very limited, flowing as it does to only a small portion of the population. We cannot expect it to do otherwise. But we can mitigate some of these effects by focusing on economic democracy (Dahl 1985, Held 1993, Malleson 2014) and crafting solutions that put decisions about investments and the distribution of work into the hands of direct producers (Ringen 2004, Warren 1992). This will, however, require rethinking the political frames through which we consider forms of economic activities (Hirst 1994, Johanisova and Wolf 2012).

Worker cooperatives can reorient how we value work performed, and consider arrangements that maximize the lives of people both in and out of work (see Iuviene et al. 2010 for an overview of worker cooperatives). If we imagine a different way of organizing economic activity (Parkinson 2003), we can also imagine how work can have a positive impact on community. For example, by spreading the work among more people, workers might trade time at work with time at home, in their neighborhoods, building community. It is not trivial to ask for new work arrangements, and it is only utopian if we think it is unimaginable. After all, we must never forget that the ideal market is also a utopian vision; even though markets are modeled to function effectively and efficiently, markets routinely result in less than optimal solutions. If workers direct the allocation of surplus and provide living wages and less work, we might find that "the small measures of freedom from work that the demands for basic income and shorter hours might enable could also make possible the material and imaginative resources to live differently" (Weeks 2011: 222).

Before we speculate about what might have been as a model of what could be, a quick review of cooperative efforts in North America is in order. Canada has a long, if not always untroubled, relationship with cooperatives (Laycock 1989). Co-operatives and Mutuals Canada is an organization that represents over eighteen million co-op members participating in over nine thousand cooperative organizations (http://canada.coop/). They go on to list on their website a range of the types of cooperative efforts found in Canada: consumer (food, credit unions, housing, etc.); worker (operating in forestry, leisure, manufacturing, etc.), producer (pooling equipment, agricultural co-ops, advising, etc.), multi-stakeholder (home care, health services, community services, etc.), and worker-shareholder (manufacturing, technology, etc.). Overall, it is estimated that over seventeen million Canadians are co-op members, cooperatives employ over 150,000 workers and have CN\$275 billion in assets (http://coopzone.coop/en/coopsincda). Formalized under the Canada Cooperatives Act of 1998 (http://laws-lois.justice.gc.ca/PDF/C-1.7.pdf), which states that "cooperatives work for the social and economic development of their communities through policies approved by their members," a Canadian House of Commons report claims without cooperatives there would be more unstable income to farmers, uncertain access to high-quality inputs, less opportunity for Aboriginal people, less consumer choice, retail competition and restricted access to goods and services, and more uncertainty about access to affordable housing (Richards 2012: 6).

The United States has had a long history of cooperatives promoting economic democracy (Blasi and Kruse 2006), and many continue to exist. According to a survey conducted by the University of Wisconsin Center for Cooperatives (http://uwcc.wisc.edu/), there are almost thirty thousand cooperatives operating in the United States, with over \$3 trillion in assets, generating over \$500 billion in revenues employing over two million workers. The Center's website offers details on revenue, employment, and other key data on the firms in their survey. As impressive as these overall figures may be, still, only about 1 percent of all cooperatives are worker cooperatives (Abell 2014: 5). US cooperatives vary in size from very large regional associations to small-scale operations. For example, the Valley Alliance of Worker Co-ops is an assembly of cooperatives across parts of western Massachusetts and southern Vermont, linking together firms providing a variety of services. The Co-operative Home Care Associates in the South Bronx has been in existence for the past three decades, bringing together home care workers providing services to the community. What makes these examples relevant to any discussion about Detroit is that they bring together several cooperatives across a specific geography, or they engage in a large number of workers. A common assumption is that cooperatives are economically risky enterprises, but a study comparing survival rates of worker cooperatives and traditional firms (Olsen 2014) shows that they perform as well, if not better. Another study finds that worker cooperatives "display a well-defined and positive relationship between wages and employment" (Burden and Dean 2009: 526) when compared to traditional capitalist firms. Rather, Olsen speculates, it is not economic performance that restricts the number of worker cooperatives in the United States, but structural factors like credit constraints and what he calls entrepreneurial rents that partially explain their low formation rates.

Any firm, regardless of its ownership structure, must deal with some key questions: what will be produced, how it will be produced, who is the target for the product, and how the firm will enter that marketplace. Owners of traditional firms can decide to change the product mix, resulting in a change of staffing, can decide to adopt labor augmenting technology based on increased productivity and a desire to reduce their labor costs by laying off employees, and can choose to close a profitable firm if they feel there are better profits to be made elsewhere, with no regard for the workers they employ or the community in which they are located. Detroit is the case study for what can happen to any community as a result of these kinds of decisions. Worker cooperatives differ on two main dimensions: production decisions and the distribution of revenues. The key benefits of cooperatives organized along the principles of worker control and self-management is the ability to decide what to produce, how to produce it, how to allocate work in the production process, and what to do with the social surplus (or even worry about profits at all so long as costs are met, though there is no reason to assume a worker cooperative is uninterested in generating a profit). It is the decisions about how profits are used that matter—for example, providing non-enterprise supports like communal childcare, agreeing to have shorter work weeks to allow for more community involvement, or more traditionally expanding production or investing in new plants or equipment.

In short, cooperatives could operate just like any other firm in the economy, deal with the larger political economy, yet not be at risk if investors decided the return to capital is not sufficiently high, or that they no longer want to operate in a particular locale. And unlike state-run enterprises (and in this we may as well include social services—since many cooperatives around the world perform social service functions) that respond to policy shifts and external electoral whims, worker run cooperatives focus first and foremost on the collective will and interest of the workers who make all decisions (see Wolff 2012). By focusing on worker interests, a cooperative necessarily concerns itself, implicitly or explicitly, with the conditions of the communities in which workers live. What is important here is that once we change the decision making criteria from maximizing profits and the return on capital investment to maximizing employment and worker satisfaction, we change the vulnerability of a community to market forces.

Everyone is aware of the size, scope, and expanse of the Mondragón Corporation, an immense cooperative founded in 1956 in the Basque town of Mondragón, which today employs almost 75,000 people in over 250 companies operating in almost every sector of the economy. They are internally organized as worker cooperatives, though they must interact with and operate within the global market economy. A key to Mondragón's early success was its focus on local sources for labor and inputs and local outlets for its products. This cooperative grew as a result of its focus on the interests of its workers and the communities in which they operated, and not because of any targeted return on investment (Whyte and Whyte 1991). Other, less well-known examples, are the various worker cooperatives that arise out of the solidary economy movement in Latin America (most frequently in Brazil and Argentina), where workers reclaim bankrupt or abandoned enterprises to operate as self-managed entities, usually producing the same goods or services of the abandoned company. In the first example, a community organized itself to make something where there was nothing, rejecting the capitalist model (in part, we might speculate, due to an absence of investment capital). In the second, workers decided to continue operating existing firms that shut their doors for reasons that had more to do with inadequate rates of return or the simple abandonment of capital by their owners. Both situations can be said to exist in Detroit.

Perhaps more instructive is a review of the cooperative movement in Italy. There is a long history of cooperative activity, most recently with a focus on what they call social cooperatives (see Carini et al. 2012 for a detailed discussion). What is most important for our discussion is that these social cooperatives achieve objectives of social importance, undertake activities that do not necessarily provide an acceptable rate of return on investment, and they fulfill important functions in society. It is also the case that often these enterprises' products and services are of higher quality, the enterprises exhibit higher productivity levels, and mostly they are geographically located in underserved parts of the country. Several keys factors contribute to the success of the Italian cooperatives. First, through successive legislation a variety of grant schemes and financial arrangements exist giving cooperatives access to low cost finance and capital. Italian law also permits municipalities to participate as capital partners to sustain local cooperatives. These laws that form and support cooperatives have broad support across all political parties because of the importance of cooperatives in Italy in their success in creating jobs operating in all sectors of the economy. Italian cooperatives in the north central Emilia Romagna region of Italy are especially relevant as a model for Detroit (Fitch 1996); they employ over four million people with about 7,500 cooperatives generating about 35 percent of the region's GDP, providing high standards of living and striving for full employment in the region. In essence, "(c)ooperation has been the most essential characteristic of political life in Emilia-Romagna, enabling it to pursue its goal of increased autonomy and providing for its economic and political success" (Ferri and White 1999: 94).

The City of Detroit has made small strides toward fostering and building cooperative endeavors in the city. Organizations, like the Center for Community Based Enterprise (http://c2be.org/), that seeks to provide education and technical assistance, and the

Detroit Community Cooperative, one that is a grass roots organization bringing together worker cooperatives to coordinate activities (see their "Declaration of Interdependence" at http://c2be.org/wp-content/uploads/2011/09/DCC_Declaration_of_Interdependence. pdf), reflect efforts to change the city through the promotion of community based activities. But the record for Detroit is mixed. Notable worker cooperatives are Avalon Bakery supplying restaurants and food markets and operating a coffee shop and bakery, and the The Hub dedicated to providing both training and low cost bicycles in the city. Service-oriented cooperative networks include the Greater Detroit Cooperative Nursery Council (http://www.gdcnc.org/), providing help to parents wanting to get involved in early education, and the Blackstone Manor Cooperative (http://www. blackstoneco-op.org/) and the Hyde Park Cooperative (http://hydeparkcoop.org/), both examples of several cooperatives addressing the need for affordable housing. For the most part, these efforts do not reflect significant change in the underlying political and economic structures of the city. Reviewing two films featuring Detroit's decline, Gottfried states that messages of hope are "repeated by residents who are engaged in transforming the city from the bottom up" (2014: 97). These efforts, and others like them, try to address very local needs on a limited scale. As one commentator remarked about Detroit's opportunity crisis, "(t)here are queer-owned, women-owned, cooperatively run businesses getting together" (Llanes 2011). However, these are, in reality, only coping activities and they operate at a small scale doing little to change the larger socioeconomic landscape in Detroit.

A Historical Thought Experiment

Cooperatives have been shown to have as much success as tradition firms, and one of the most important barriers for worker cooperatives is access to capital. The benefits of worker-run cooperatives can improve job quality, may improve job creation and retention, cluster in more labor intensive sectors, and are able to use simpler production technologies. Worker cooperatives "have produced real economic and social benefits for their members and communities" (Dickstein 1991: 29). Pointing out that worker cooperatives don't have the singular purpose of maximizing profits, an International Labour Office (ILO) report finds that they balance competing and at times contradictory goals of "job security, reinvestment, higher wages and benefits, health and safety" (Logue and Yates 2005: 53) along with profit sharing and patronage dividends. The Italian experiences noted above demonstrate that worker cooperatives provide needed products and services to underserved communities, and demonstrate more civic engagement for firms that are part of the communities in which they operated. Another ILO reports finds that cooperatives are effective in reducing poverty. Reviewing a number of examples of worker cooperatives from both developed and developing countries, Birchall finds that they "succeed in helping the poorest and most vulnerable people to become organized. . . . Where there are alternative, for-profit alternatives the cases demonstrate that the cooperative is—for the aim of poverty reduction—superior" (2003: 62).

So why can't we envision worker cooperatives as the broad solution for Detroit's ills? After all, Detroit certainly contains some of the poorest and most vulnerable population in this country. What keeps this model of organizing work from becoming a reality?

Two key elements can be identified: enabling legislation and financial support. The first would require a set of laws, as was passed in Italy, that permitted if not encouraged municipalities to partner with cooperatives. This would enable local governments to help direct and encourage the formation of a range of activities that could serve the interests of the wider community, and promote coordination among cooperatives that formed. The greatest obstacle to this kind of legislative initiative is the strong adherence to a market logic that dictates public sector competition with private sector firms is unfair—or put another way, private sector provisioning is always assumed to be the best way and most efficient form of operating. Even so-called public/private ventures are, at the core, ways that private sector actors can draw upon the public's funds to finance their operation. It shifts the risks from private investors onto taxpayers, and one might even suggest that it encourages less prudent financial decision-making as a result of those guarantees.

Financing can be seen as a bigger obstacle, especially for a bankrupt city like Detroit. Where might potential cooperatives find the capital to begin operation? The solution is not that far away—it only requires a bit of revamping of the current practices and policies rooted in market-driven frames. For example, consider the reality of public-sector support for private-sector activities. Current news reports are full of the struggle over minimum wage and living wage efforts to ensure that workers can support themselves. There is a public cost to low-wage work in the form of social supports such as food stamps and other needs-tested programs for workers in many industries, and these concerns are not limited to the United States (see Huttunen et al. 2010). Studies of both the fast-food industry (Allegretto et al. 2013) and retail (Democratic staff 2013) demonstrate that the only real benefits that accrue as a result of implicit public sector subsidies to low wage workers are to the bottom line of these corporations. In effect, the public sector, through its tax revenues, provides capital to market-based private sector firms. This not only runs counter to the notion of a free market for factors of production (the rationale for rates of return, but oddly not the cost of labor), but also has the adverse effect of increasing inequality in society (Traub and Hiltonsmith 2013).

During a year spent at the University of Hamburg's Center for Comparative Urban Research, I had the opportunity to meet with the Lord Mayor of Bremen. In the mid-1990s the shipbuilding industry located in Bremenhaven was under pressure (most would eventually close), and I was curious why the city decided to provide cash subsidies to underwrite (and effectively lower) wages for those employees. It seemed, to my US-centric idea of the role of government, illogical and counter to rational (i.e., market) decision-making. Mayor Henning Scherf explained to me (on reflection, patiently and somewhat gently) that from a social perspective, the potential costs per worker of the full range of social consequences should the shipyards fail far exceeded the costs of the subsidy. That is, unemployment insurance payments, the costs associated with the rise in crime and delinquency, the impact on greater demand for social housing due to loss of earnings, the dissolution of families, and so on—all problems familiar to cities in distress—are much greater than the cost of the subsidies to the corporations. In other words, it was a matter of whether the public pays now to augment and secure employment in the community, or pays later to deal with the social dislocations and problems that arise as a result of loss of employment. There was not a sense that somehow because the public sector was operating in the private sector that such supports are unwarranted or even not allowed. As we note above, the public sector in our unambiguous neoliberal market society functions in much the same way, though not so explicitly, as the mayor of Bremen (Bremen is one of several city-states in Germany, and as such acts with the full power and limitations of any other state).

As a thought exercise, let us consider what a cooperative outcome might have looked like had Detroit opted (or been able to opt) out of a market solution. The Dodge Main plant was located in both Detroit and Hamtramck, Michigan (an independent city on the east side that, due to the nature of annexation laws in the state, is fully within the larger boundaries of Detroit). Chrysler Corporation shut the plant and offered it and the land around it to Detroit. In turn, the city identified that site and embarked on a program to provide GM with land cleared and developed to accommodate plans to build a new GM plant. The company was departing from the multistory automobile plants common in the city at that time for one modeled on newer plants built in the rural areas of the Midwest and the South. The Dodge Main plant was so named because it was the heart of the Dodge Motor Company's operations (an interesting aside: in 1926 it was sold by the heirs of the Dodge brothers to a Wall Street firm for $145 million, and they in turn sold it in 1929 to the Chrysler Corporation for $170 million—a forerunner of a more common practice today). It was a well-built and relatively good place to work, though by 1980 the plant required major renovations. The decision by Chrysler to effectively abandon the plant is a prime example of how capital can just leave a community in response to local and global changes in the market.

The ensuing struggle over the proposed site, and the planned destruction of a viable community commonly known as Poletown that called for the relocation of "3438 residents, 1362 households, 143 institutions or businesses (including 16 churches, a hospital and 2 schools) and demolish 1176 buildings" (Fasenfest 1986: 110) is well documented (Wylie 1989). What is relevant for this exercise is that Detroit committed about $300 million (in today's dollars approximately $866 million) to demolish the plant and the surrounding structures, prepare the site for the new GM plant, and turn the plant over to GM. The rationale for the project was that GM would go someplace else to build their plant and take with it the much-needed jobs for the city. Already hemorrhaging jobs, the city decided the cost of clearing and preparing the site through the investment of public dollars was appropriate. In addition, before the new plant was built GM asked for, and got, additional tax incentives and other concessions. In return, GM made several promises regarding how many workers in how many shifts would be located in that new location. In reality, once the site was turned over to GM, market forces and new technology (this was at the dawn of full-scale automation and robot production) changed both the timing of the opening of and employment levels at the new plant. A cost-benefit analysis of this project (Fasenfest 1986) demonstrated that only under a very specific set of circumstances would the city be justified in making its investment, but no performance guarantees or conditions were imposed to ensure that the anticipated return would materialize.

This could well have been a prime example of going with a (quasi) non-market alternative solution to a serious situation. Mayor Young was certainly correct when he argued the city had to act, albeit somewhat cavalier to the needs of the residents of Poletown. But what if instead of investing those funds to the benefit of GM, the city instead decided to use the facility to create a worker-run cooperative. The skilled workforce was still in place—it was a time when there were still sufficiently trained but laid-off UAW workers, and the UAW was still in a position to support, through training and placement, a supply of workers. The physical plant and surrounding land was owned by the city—albeit renovations and investment in equipment would be required (though there would be no imperative to get state-of-the-art machines, a strategy that works well for budding enterprises outside of Europe and the United States). And there were versions of automobiles—specifically a knock-off of the Dodge Dart, a popular and relatively indestructible vehicle—that could be manufactured.

The problem of capital could have been addressed by allocating the $200–300 million committed to the site preparation plan, plus redirecting the social welfare and unemployment insurance payments made to the estimated six thousand workers who would have found work in the plant. Plus, the car could have been offered at a reasonable price if it were sold at the factory gate rather than having to rely on a large dealer network, national advertising, and guaranteeing a rate of return on investment capital. The jobs in the community would have been saved, and payroll taxes that ended up being lost could have been earmarked for operating expenses. The city already agreed to provide a tax abatement for the new plant. At the same time, a worker-directed cooperative would have meant that decisions could be made on how to distribute profits (or whether to generate profits rather than raise wages), would have ensured the viability of a community in place and the neighborhoods from which those workers came, and it could have served as a model for more ventures radically altering the economic and social landscape of Detroit. Granted, that would have been difficult under the existing legislative structure, but as was shown in Italy, not impossible to bring about. Finally, a worker cooperative would mean that the city would not be vulnerable to capital flight due to the demands of the market or the requirements of rates of return on investment, workers would not be in fear of losing their jobs as long as they continued to produce a quality product, communities would not see the desolation of out-migrations as families moved to find work elsewhere, resulting in the abandonment of housing, and the city would have some reasonable expectations that payroll and property taxes would continue to flow in support of city services.

Concluding Comments

It is not possible to avoid markets when the dominant mode of production operates under the rules of capitalism, which relies on market allocations of factors of production and the surplus produced. Neoliberal austerity policies are, if nothing else, a utopian dream that markets are effective and efficient, and they serve to reverse social policy legislation aimed at mediating the worst aspects of markets. In an earlier time one might imagine owners knowing their workers and experiencing some small concern for the impact of their decisions. However, the history of capitalist development is littered with discarded workers, families, communities, and even cities as market forces drove decision-making. In an age of global capitalism, the forces at work reach far beyond the geographical horizons of city limits, state borders, and national boundaries, creating winning and losing regions and even countries.

Detroit has become the poster child for capitalist and market processes. At its height, it represented the power of capital to generate profits, provide good standards of living, build the urban infrastructure, and use some of the surplus to support and construct a world-class set of cultural institutions. The city became a magnet for migrants looking to achieve the American Dream, and early migrant waves found well-paid employment in the automobile industry. These workers had children who often found work in these same plants, and from one generation to the next families and communities prospered. But when market forces turned, when the global economic landscape shifted and technological changes resulted in a restructuring of the industry, Detroit became the symbol of what happens when capital leaves. We could take issue with how that transition was managed, find fault with leadership that made bad decisions, criticize financial institutions that preyed on cities like Detroit ensnaring them in bad debt, and worry about the impact and meaning of race to understand how events unfolded as they have.

What is possible is to reduce the immediate threats of market forces with respect to local investments and production. While any enterprise—as large as Mondragon with its global reach and as small as a bakery collective in a neighborhood—must contend with market forces to sell its products and stay in business, worker cooperatives provide some security from the seemingly arbitrary investment (and divestment) decisions by owners of capital. By considering what might have been, had Detroit supported a worker's cooperative to maintain auto production and the jobs it provided, we can get a glimpse as to how, on a small scale, the city might have begun to shield itself from market forces. The search for a solution and the designs for Detroit's resurrection that rely on the same mechanisms that brought the city to its knees may well be a fool's errand. Much as the city prospered under capitalism's operating principles in the past, it will remain vulnerable to reversals of fortune over which it has little or no control. And in the interim, investors and developers will continue to seek new ways of extracting the resources that remain in the city, whether in the form of reducing pensions to repay private sector bond obligations, minimizing private capital risks through public sector guarantees, or enhancing capital's rate of return through tax waivers. The residents of Detroit, on the other hand, will remain vulnerable to the vagaries of markets.

References

Abell, H. (2014) "Worker Cooperatives: Pathways to Scale" *The Democracy Collaborative*. June. Available at http://community-wealth.org/sites/clone.community-wealth.org/files/downloads/WorkerCoops-PathwaysToScale.pdf.

Allegretto, S., M. Doussard, D. Graham-Squire, and K. Jacobs. (2013). *Fast Food, Poverty Wages: The Public Cost of Low-Wage Jobs in the Fast-Food Industry*. (October 15). University of California Berkeley Labor Center and the University of Illinois Department of Urban and Regional Planning. Available at: http://laborcenter.berkeley.edu/publiccosts/fast_food_poverty_wages.pdf.

Bella, R. N. (1968). "Civil Religion in America," in W. G. McLoughlin and R. N. Bellah (eds.), *Religion in America*. Boston: Houghton Mifflin.

Bendick, Jr., M. and M. L. Egan (1995) "Worker Ownership and Participation Enhances Economic Development in Low-Opportunity Communities" *Journal of Community Practice*. 2 (1): 61–85

Betancur, J. J. and D. C. Gills. (2004). "Community Development in Chicago: From Harold Washington to Richard M. Daley," *Annals of the American Academy of Political and Social Science*, Vol. 594, Race, Politics, and Community Development in U.S. Cities (July), 92–108.

Birchall, J. (2003) "Rediscovering the Cooperative Advantage: Poverty Reduction Through Self-Help" Cooperative Branch. Geneva: International Labour Office. Available at http://www.acdivocacoopex.org/acdivoca/CoopLib.nsf/dfafe3e324466c3785256d96004f15a8/e23f0c803fc6060485256ef400575ed8/$FILE/Rediscovering%20the%20Cooperative%20Advantage.pdf.

Blasi, J. R., and D. L. Kruse. (2006). "The Political Economy of Employee Ownership in the United States: From Economic Democracy to Industrial Democracy?" *International Review of Sociology* 16 (1): 127–47.

Burdin, G. and A. Dean (2009) "New Evidence on Wages and Employment in Worker Cooperatives Compared with Capitalist Firms." *Journal of Comparative Economics*. 37 (4): 51.

Carey, N. (2013) "Detroit Jobs Might Return, but Workers Still Lack Skills," *Huffpost Detroit*. August 2. Available at http://www.huffingtonpost.com/2013/08/02/detroit-jobs-_n_3693303.html?.

Carini, C. C. E., M. Carpita, and M. Adreaus. (2012). The Italian Social Cooperatives in 2008: A Portrait Using Descriptive and Principal Component Analysis. *European Research Institute on Cooperative and Social Enterprises*. Eurice Working Paper N.035/12.

Christoff, C. (2014). Red Wings Owner, Needing Hockey-Arena Neighborhood, Builds One, *Bloomberg* (August 6). (available at http://www.bloomberg.com/news/2014-08-06/red-wings-owner-needing-hockey-arena-neighborhood-builds-one.html).

Dahl, R. A. (1985). *A Preface to Economic Democracy*. Berkeley : University of California Press.

Dale, G. (2010). *Karl Polanyi: The Limits on the Market*. London: Polity Press.

Democratic Staff of the United States House Committee on Education and the Workforce, (2013). Low Wage Drag on Our Economy: Wal-Mart's low wages and their effect on taxpayers and economic growth. (May). Available at: http://democrats.edworkforce.house.gov/sites/democrats.edworkforce.house.gov/files/documents/WalMartReport-May2013.pdf.

Dickstein, C. (1991) "The Promise and Problems of Worker Cooperatives." *Journal of Planning Literature*. 6 (1): 16–33.

Eisinger, P. (2014). "Is Detroit Dead?" *Journal of Urban Affairs* 36 (1): 1–12.

Fasenfest, D. (1986). "Community Politics and Urban Redevelopment: Poletown, Detroit and General Motors," *Urban Affairs Quarterly*, 22 (1): 101–123.

Ferri, M. and T. J. White. (1999). "Regionalism, Cooperation, and Economic Prosperity: Effective Autonomy in Emilia-Romagna," *Mediterranean Quarterly* 10 (3): 89–106 (also available at http://muse.jhu.edu/journals/mediterranean_quarterly/v010/10.3ferri.html).

Fitch, R. (1996). "The Cooperatives Economics of Italy's Emilia-Romagna Holds a Lesson for the US," *The Nation* May 13, pp 18–21.

Fung, A. (2004). *Empowered Participation : Reinventing Urban Democracy*. Princeton, NJ : Princeton University Press.

Glaeser, E. L. (2010) "Shrinking Detroit Back to Greatness." *The New York Times*. March 16. Available at http://economix.blogs.nytimes.com/2010/03/16/shrinking-detroit-back-to-greatness/?_php=true&_type=blogs&_r=0.

Gottfried, H. (2014) "Dystopia or Utopia? Alternative Visions of the City of Detroit: *Detropia* and *We Are Not Ghosts*." *New Labor Forum*. 23 (3): 96–99.

Hackman, R. (2014) "Detroit Demolishes its Ruins: 'The capitalists will take care of the rest'." *The Guardian*. (September 28). Available at http://www.theguardian.com/money/2014/sep/28/detroit-demolish-ruins-capitalists-abandoned-buildings-plan.

Harvey, D. (1989). *The Urban Experience*. Baltimore: John's Hopkins University Press.

———. (2011). *The Enigma of Capital and the Crisis of Capitalism*. New York and Oxford: Oxford University Press.

Held, D. (1993). "Liberalism, Marxism, and Democracy." *Theory and Society* 22 (2): 249–281.

Hirst, P. Q. (1994). *Associative Democracy : New Forms of Economic and Social Governance*. Amherst : University of Massachusetts Press.

Huttunen, K., J. Pirttilä, and R. Uusitalo. (2010). The Employment Effects of Low-Wage Subsidies. Discussion Paper No 4931 (May) Bonn: The Institute for the Study of Labor (IZA) Available at http://ftp.iza.org/dp4931.pdf.

Iuviene, N., A. Sitely and L. Hoyt (2010) "Sustainable Economic Democracy: Worker Cooperatives for the 21st Century" Community Innovators Lab, MIT available at http://cyberjournal.org/Documents/Coops-CoLabOct2010.pdf.

Johanisova, N., and S. Wolf. (2012). "Economic Democracy: A Path for the Future?" *Futures* 44 (6): 562–70.

Kaiman, J. (2014). "Does Multimillion Dollar Chinese Investment Signal Detroit's Rebirth?" *The Guardian*, (July 22) (available at http://www.theguardian.com/cities/2014/jul/22/does-multimillion-dollar-chinese-investment-signal-detroits-rebirth).

Laycock, D. (1989). "Representative Economic Democracy and the Problem of Policy Influence: The Case of Canadian Co-Operatives." *Canadian Journal of Political Science / Revue canadienne de science politique* (4): 765.

LeDuff, C. (2014). *Detroit: An American Autopsy*. New York: Penguin Books.

Leftwich, A. (1993). "Governance, Democracy and Development in the Third World." *Third World Quarterly* (3): 605.

Llanes, C. (2011) "A Cooperative Economy: The Time is Now" *CommonDreams* August 26 available at http://www.commondreams.org/views/2011/08/26/cooperative-economy-time-now.

Logan J. R. and B. J Stults (2011) "The Persistence of Segregation in the Metropolis: New Findings from the 2010 Census" *Census Brief prepared for Project US2010* March 24. Available at http://www.s4.brown.edu/us2010/Data/Report/report2.pdf.

Logue, J. and J. Yates (2005) "Productivity in Cooperatives and Worker-Owned Enterprises: Ownership and Participation Make a Difference!" Employment Sector. Geneva: International Labour Office, available at http://dept.kent.edu/oeoc/OEOCLibrary/Preprints/LogueYatesProductivityInCooperativesAndWorkerOwnedEnterprises2005.pdf.

Malleson, T. (2014). *After Occupy: Economic Democracy for the 21st Century*. Oxford: Oxford University Press.

Martelle, S. (2014). *Detroit [A Biography]*. Chicago: Chicago Review Press.

Martinez-Fernandez, C., I. Audirac, S. Fol, and E. Cunnigham-Sabot. (2012). "Shrinking Cities: Urban Challenges of Globalization." *International Journal of Urban and Regional Research*. 36 (2): 213–25.

Marx, K. (1994) [1852]. *The Eighteenth Brumaire of Louis Bonaparte*. New York: International Publishers

Morgan Stanley (2014). "Inequality and Consumption" *US Economics*. September 22. Available at http://www.morganstanleyfa.com/public/projectfiles/02386f9f-409c-4cc9-bc6b-13574637ec1d.pdf.

Olson, E. K. (2014). "The Relative Survival of Worker Cooperatives and Barriers to Their Creation." *Advances in the Economic Analysis of Participatory & Labor-Managed Firms* Volume 14: Sharing Ownership, Profits, and Decision-Making in the 21st Century, 83–107.

Parkinson, J. (2003). "Models of the company and the employment relationship," *British Journal of Industrial Relations* 41 (3): 481–509.

Richards, B, MP (2012) "Status of Co-operatives in Canada." Report of the Special Committee on Co-operatives, House of Commons, Canada. September. Available at http://www.parl.gc.ca/content/hoc/Committee/411/COOP/Reports/RP5706528/cooprp01/cooprp01-e.pdf.

Ringen, S. (2004). "A Distributional Theory of Economic Democracy." *Democratization* 11 (2): 18–40.

Rusch, L. (2012). "Going Regional: The Evolution of an Organizing Strategy in Detroit." *City & Community*. 11: 1: 51–73.

Ryan, B. D. (2012). *Design After Decline: How America Rebuilds Shrinking Cities*. Philadelphia: University of Pennsylvania Press.

Segal, D. (2013). A Missionary's Quest to Remake Motor City, *New York Times*. (April 13) (available at http://www.nytimes.com/2013/04/14/business/dan-gilberts-quest-to-remake-downtown-detroit.html?pagewanted=all&_r=0).

Schumpeter, J. A. (2008) [1942]. *Capitalism, Socialism and Democracy*. New York: HarperCollins Publishers.

Siemiatycki, E. (2012). "Forced to Concede: Permanent Restructuring and Labour's Place in the North American Auto Industry," *Antipode* 44: 2: 453–473.

Singer, P. (2002). "The Recent Rebirth of the Solidary Economy in Brazil," In de Sousa Santos, Boaventura (ed.), *Produzir para viver: os caminhos da produção não capitalista*. Rio de Janeiro: Civilização Brasileira, (translation available, accessed June 12, 2014, at http://www.ces.uc.pt/emancipa/research/en/ft/difusao.html)

Stiglitz, J. (2014). "The Age of Vulnerability." *Social Europe Journal*, (October 13) (available at http://www.social-europe.eu/2014/10/vulnerability/).

Sugrue, T. J. (1996). *The Origins of the Urban Crisis: Race and Inequality in Post-War Detroit*. Princeton: Princeton University Press.

Tabb, W. K. (forthcoming) "If Detroit is Dead Some Things Need to Be Said at the Funeral." *Journal of Urban Affairs*.

Traub, A. and R. Hiltonsmith (2013). "Underwriting Bad Jobs: How Our Tax Dollars Are Funding Low-Wage Work and Fueling Inequality." New York: Demos (available at http://www.demos.org/publication/underwriting-bad-jobs-how-our-tax-dollars-are-funding-low-wage-work-and-fueling-inequali).

Wacquant, L. (2008). *Urban Outcasts: A Comparative Sociology of Advanced Marginality*. Malden, MA and Cambridge: Polity Press.

Warren, M. (1992). "Democratic Theory and Self-Transformation," *American Political Science Review* 86 (01): 8–23.

Weeks, K. (2011). *The Problem with Work*. Durham and London: Duke University Press.

White, M. M. (2011a). "D-Town Farm: African American Resistance to Food Insecurity and the Transformation of Detroit." *Environmental Practice*. 13 (4): 406–417.

———. (2011b). "Sisters of the Soil: Urban Gardening as Resistance in Detroit." *Race/Ethnicity: Multicultural Global Contexts* 5 (1): 13–28.

———. (2010). "Shouldering Responsibility for the Delivery of Human Rights: A Case Study of the D-Town Farmers of Detroit," *Race/Ethnicity: Multicultural Global Contexts*, 3 (2): 189–212.

Williams, P. (2014). "Drop Dead, Detroit," *The New Yorker*. (January 27): 32–39.

Wylie, J. (1989) *Poletown: Community Betrayed*. Chicago: University of Illinois Press.

Whyte W. F. and K. K. Whyte (1991) *Making Mondragon: The Growth and Dynamics of The Worker Cooperative Complex*. Ithaca: Cornell University Press.

Wolff, R. (2012). *Democracy at Work: A Cure for Capitalism*. Chicago: Haymarket Books.

13

Which Way, "Detroit"?

Peter Marcuse

Looking to the future, Detroit can go in five possible directions. It can: (I) go the conventional urban austerity route, by way of (II) the Growth game, (III) the Global Cities game, and (IV) the Identity game. Or, alternately, it could (V) try to become a model of something new, different, and better—a New Social Detroit.

The approach used here parallels in many ways the approach suggested by the editors in their introduction, although here owing perhaps more to Karl Marx than to Karl Polanyi. As summarized by the editors, Polanyi holds that "urban shrinkage is not the inevitable result of inexorable economic forces, but rather is the outcome of sociopolitical choices, struggles and negotiations at various scales. Ultimately, [such] struggles . . . hinge on the proper relationship between markets, communities, and the state" (Kirkpatrick and Smith, this volume). In Detroit, this struggle is largely waged by and for three social segments that constitute "Detroit": a Corporate Detroit, a Working Detroit, and an Excluded Detroit.

While my approach in this article is not inconsistent with the Polanyian view, it frames the issue more in terms of actors with competing interests. It suggests a "Multiple Detroits" analysis, (see Appendix) and begins by examining the Urban Austerity route, and the three games—Growth, Global City, and Identity—most frequently put forward as the determinant of Detroit's future, and finally examines what a New Social Detroit approach might look like. It examines each in its impact on the different Detroits and concludes that each, in its own way, is both limited and biased toward one Detroit over another. It then suggests that a new approach might begin with a clear discussion of the values and goals desired for the city, summarizing them as Justice, Abundance, and Democracy. It then examines what is blocking the path to the realization of such values. It argues that clear agreement on concrete proposals for adoption by the City of Detroit and by the state and federal governments could form a practical agenda for a possible transformation and creation of a New Social Detroit. It concludes by discussing possible political strategies that might make the realization of those concrete proposals, as steps to broad comprehensive changes, feasible.

The Multiple Detroits

"Detroit" is in quotes in the above paragraph because any discussion must start with the realization that "Detroit" is not one homogeneous thing, or actor. Rather, the word can have a variety of meanings: the city government, the power structure or regime, the territory of the formal jurisdiction, its metropolitan area, the business community located within that territory, the population residing within it with its multiple divisions by class, race, ethnicity, occupation, etc. As used here, unless another meaning is clear, "Detroit" means its regime, those ultimately with the power to influence the direction in which its government, economy, and social character will go, and the assortment of residents and businesses and groups directly affected by the problems created by its "shrinkage" and desiring to influence government's response to it. Detroit, in other words, is not, as such, an actor, but rather an aggregation of variously conflicting forces, constituting different "Detroits" whose interaction determines what the city government of Detroit will do. The point is not academic nitpicking. As the discussion will show, each of the alternatives facing the City, each of the routes and games that are possible, has very different results when analyzed by the various Detroits in what constitutes "Detroit." Moreover, any analysis of the alternatives needs to highlight the differences of impact on "Detroit's" parts.

In the Appendix to this chapter I suggest a systematic way of analyzing those patterns, although one only partially implemented here for lack of space. The basic idea is that there is a Detroit of business and work, and a Detroit of residences and community—roughly analogous to Jürgen Habermas's system world and life world, and that in turn each of these Detroits is divided by income, by ethnicity, by genders, by age, by education, by occupation—divisions largely represented by concepts of class.[1] Thus the identity of "Detroit" encompasses many Detroits, and their identities and futures vary dramatically. The identity of which—rather, whose—Detroit is always a question that can be quite fraught with controversy. One needs to examine, then, the five ways "Detroit" can go.

The Urban Austerity Route

By far the most widespread official response, from the United States to Germany, from Greece to Argentina, from Japan to Australia, is Urban Austerity. It attributes the economic issues of cities like Detroit to government spending "beyond its means," and ends by cutting such spending, reducing taxes to prevent discouraging private investment, transfers as much economic activity from the public to the private sector as possible. Previous chapters have dealt trenchantly with the economic aspects of the policy (see, for instance, Peck, this volume). Often considered an essential characteristic of neoliberal policies, it turns out the spending that is cut is spending in Working Detroit, and the taxes that are cut are for Corporate Detroit. The very term "*urban* austerity" betrays the bias: when Dick Morris, a key policy advisor to President Clinton, was asked at a forum why the administration did not have a national urban policy, he replied, "Why, we do. We have an urban policy. It is welfare reform." The reading of "urban" is clear.

The Growth Game: Shrink-Proofing Detroit

The most frequent single formulation of what's wrong with Detroit is that it is shrinking: losing population. While the loss may be attributed to a variety of factors, the resultant goal is implicit: return to growth. Success would mean programs that make Detroit, in effect, shrink proof.

But growth should be a means, not an end in itself. The conventional view of growth sees it as the priority goal of public policy, and sees the path to it in a market inevitably embedded in Polanyi's sense. If one looks at the indicators that are most frequently used to measure whether growth or shrinkage is taking place, population is probably the most prominent. More expanded discussions include indictors that might be summed up as the local equivalent of GNP, or Gross City Product. They include rising average or gross income, regardless of whether the rise is among top earners or low earners, rising real estate prices regardless of their impact on affordability, sometimes but not always declining unemployment regardless of the quality of the jobs involved, rising school graduation rates regardless of the content of the education received, declining rates of reported crimes regardless of the treatment of those charged, population gain regardless of the quality of life of the residents, a balanced public budget regardless of the cutbacks in the quality or quantity of services produced by the cuts.

The only response to shrinkage that the conventional view of growth can imagine is to reverse each of these indicators, never asking whether shrinking in any of these indicators might in fact be healthy for some or most of Detroit's residents, never minding the critical environmental and ecological limits to growth, never minding the distributional justice or injustice of particular anti-shrinking/pro-growth policies might produce, and never exploring what alternatives might be possible to the interrelated processes that create the real problems that should be addressed.

Playing the Growth Game is without a point if what is targeted for growth is not specified concretely: specifically, which Detroit is to be targeted, which activities, which land uses, the power and welfare of which groups. And by the same token, what growth is not desired must be examined. Decisions must be made in the interests of the overall goals of the policies being advocated.

How much and what kind of growth is then desirable? There's the story of the two old friends who meet unexpectedly on the street. "How's business?" one asks. "Well," says the other, "it's growing. I lose money on every item I sell, but I figure if I grow even more and sell even more, I'll make it up on volume." That clearly doesn't work. When people talk about growth as an objective for a city, that's not the kind of growth they have in mind. In fact, if the kind of growth that is desired is not specified, if growth is pursued for its own sake, growth as an end rather than as a means to an end, it is likely to disproportionately benefit the established order of things, the established interests, the upper rather than the middle or lower classes, the Corporate rather than the Working or Excluded "Detroit."

The most frequent response to those arguing for at least environmental limits on growth is that a balance must be found between recognition of and dealing with environmental consequences, on the one hand, and the economic necessity of growth to increase social welfare and eliminate poverty, on the other. The argument is that increasing the size of the pie benefits all participants, and is the best way to benefit the poor, i.e., to end poverty. But factually that argument is simply wrong. The historical evidence is that as economies have grown, the share of increased income going to the top 1 percent is steadily increasing, as is their enhanced position compared to those at the bottom, even as the size of the whole, measured at least by conventional standards, is growing.[2]

The Global Cities Game: Out-Competing Other Cities

Focusing on global relations and functions is a ubiquitous, if bifurcated game, which both shrinking cities and global cities play, with inverted logics. For "shrinking cities,"[3] the argument is that they have to climb out of shrinking status by competing with other cities for their rescue and economic growth in a globally competitive market. For "global cities" the argument is that they have to defend and expand their competitive position in a globally competitive market or they will lose the economic growth that they currently enjoy. In both cases, the means adopted tend to be the reduction of government regulations of business activities, the distribution of grants and loans to businesses seen as competitive in return for their commitment to stay in the city, the promotion of labor relations effectively based on an unacknowledged competitive race to the bottom as to wages and labor standards, the assurance of a business-friendly climate with free and easy access by business to government and restrictions on unionization and worker militancy, with land-use policies that support gentrification of the most desirable locations and gerrymandering that reduces the political influence of minorities and lower-income neighborhoods—am I missing anything? In other words, this includes the full panoply of neo-liberal policies at the local level, in effect focusing on benefiting the 1 percent for the possible ultimate trickle-down benefit of the 99 percent.

Perhaps oddly, a similar ideology is used to support such policies in both shrinking and globalizing cities. The language is familiar: "growth" is good, and is defined as economic growth, which in turn is defined in levels of financial flows, incomes, real estate values, and jobs, regardless of the quality or social value of the activities measured as positive. "Global" is a mantra hotly pursued in both, the wave of the future, spearheaded by the financial industry, which is seen as the ultimate motor of progress. Consensus is desired, although the definition of the "stakeholders" among whom consensus is sought may vary. Stakeholders, in any event, do not include predictable troublemakers, and public participation, which while espoused in theory, will be held under actual tight control on its impact. "We" is used liberally: "we must do this if we want that," with no attention to which "we" is referred to among the thicket of conflicting interests in a city.

The net result of such policies, in both shrinking and globalizing cities, is predicable. Business interests are favored, with financial connections and profitability supported with money subsidies, low-interest loans, tax concessions, zoning manipulation, public infrastructure provision, and insulation from populist-type measures and demands. Welfare costs need to be held down, public programs and social welfare benefits limited by austerity, the homeless made to disappear, schools privatized and run for private profit at the expense of the majority relegated to an underfunded public school system, workers' pensions cut back and worker organization discouraged, militant protest by the poor, the excluded, the under-paid, the displaced, strictly limited. Public safety and security are provided by the police and the penal system. The full and "free" reign of the market is the Holy Grail, although its proper functioning is heavily dependent on government action.

The Globalizing Cities game is one systematically tilted to push Polanyi's double movement in one direction only. The effect of public policies designed to keep and lure businesses to their particular city is to favor all businesses at the expense of both their own and competing cities' ability to fund social welfare expenditures; the rich are benefited at the expense of the poor. As in Detroit, the fact of shrinkage is used as justification for public measures desired to achieve economic results disproportionately beneficial to specific business interests—just as essentially parallel measures in globalizing cities are justified on similar grounds. The urban austerity route is consistently followed.

The "Detroit" that benefits from playing the global cities game, focusing its path on competing to be a global city, is a small sociopolitical part of the city proper, heavily occupied by a financial and commercial elite, most of whose members live not in the city itself but in its suburbs, some perhaps in gated and/or fortress-type developments.

The Identity Game: Imagining a Single Identity

The past of a city can be used in two ways in looking at its future. It can be seen as defining "the" city, establishing a single identity, setting the path along which its future will, and should, move. Or it can be used to look for seeds and sprouts that can contribute, as in an experimental greenhouse, to future growth along new lines that show promise for a new and better identity, a contribution to something new rather than a revival of something past.

The tendency of shrinking cities like Detroit to look nostalgically at their past before shrinkage began, and to set their sights on recovering their past glory, is very understandable. The better past is known, and its loss is regretted. Any measure that lets their residents recapture what they feel they have lost seems a logical starting point for dealing with their present. But it is a movement that can end up going in two quite different directions. It can focus on the past, trying to revive the city as it was, or, in the search for something new and more viable in a new period, it can look for elements fostering changes in new direction, preserving what is desired, building, in greenhouses if necessary, on what was vibrant and enduing in its past.

And indeed a city's history in all its complexity can be a good source for ideas and actions. Most residents of any given city have roots there. Even given the high mobility of urban residents, the instinct to identify with the actual place of current residence is very powerful psychologically. Marshaling that feeling, the pride of place, even with a "well, it wasn't perfect, but what the hell, it's ours, we have to do what we can to keep it" feeling, supports an energy for action that is essential to any city's prosperity. New York City recognized this in funding an aggressive public relations campaign for the slogan "I love New York" on ads and bumper stickers. And specifically it is a feeling political leaders can draw on for support for their own election and continued power, putting local government behind a recapture of the past program.

There is much to be said for taking those feelings into account and making the most of them. The preservation of historic sites, for instance, can be both a reinforcement of such feelings of belonging and identity and constitute possible tourist attractions. Local museums can do the same. Continuing or begetting cultural festivals, ethnic jamborees, local sports, repaving downtown streets with bricks or cobblestones, going for urban awards and good city rankings, exploring and teaching local history, can all help. But there are limits to how far such an approach can revive a shrinking city. The image of the past is always that of a community,[4] something remembered in the present with the eyes of the present. In reality, different people remember the past differently; indeed different people have different paths, and remember different Detroits.

And therein lies the rub.

The Single-Identity Solution

Two rubs, in fact. One is the illusion of the city as a single organic entity, ignoring the conflicts among the multiple entities, the multiple Detroits. The other is that the focus on a single unique characteristic or part of its history may be treacherous, if that characteristic held to define its identity is in fact not a very viable one for future use. Glorifying the past, seeking to value it for its own sake, using the ideological claim to a single identity to establish priorities for the future, is a form of recapturing the past. We might call it the Single Identity approach to the Identity Game. At its ideological heart is the conception that there is only one Detroit, that of its dominant forces and people and industries, the Detroit stereotyped as a Fordist trailblazer with the automotive mass-production as its heart and a mass consumption as its lifeblood, led by pioneers of a new industrial age of mass production, automotive transportation, suburbanization, technological innovation as its heart, a prosperous working class fully dependent on its economic success as its base, globally preeminent in what it did.

Rather than conceding that Detroit was always a city—as most every city was and is—of multiple cities, multiple classes, multiple ideals, disparate incomes and wealth and education, the Single Identity approach portrays Detroit as one city, where whatever benefits one benefits all, where "'We' are all in it together" and all must cooperate for any progress to be made. The Single Identity approach, however, in practice, serves the interests of the upper class, the corporate hierarchy, the large real estate interests, the existing power elite, in C. Wright Mills's terms. There are losers as well as winners in this identity game, which playing it conceals. Playing it tends to perpetuate and strengthen the status quo.

For indeed Detroit has had multiple pasts, multiple identities. It has a past of labor organization, of industrial strife, of racial division, of radical political leanings, whose interests are not naturally identical with those of the dominant economic and political and cultural leadership in the city.

And then, and this is the second rub, the usefulness of pushing a single identity for a city depends very much on what that city's past in fact was. For many cities, in fact probably most cities, are doing the same thing, and some pasts are easier to glorify than others. Every city has some particular history, location, population, climate, language, customs, that are the fabric of its self-imaged identity. They support one particular identity for that city: Detroit as auto capital of the world, strongest magnet for African

Americans leaving the rural south during industrialization, crossroads of the Midwest, home of the factories that nurtured burgeoning radical unionism.

But relying on that one historical identity as the basis for its future development and prosperity could well be a major mistake. Auto production can be a deceptive lure in an industry whose environment has radically changed to become global; luring workers seeking industrial employment can create a quagmire for unhappy unemployed residents; shifting transportation technology can change locational advantages and disadvantages; globalization, financialization, climate change, all matter. That Detroit was a magnet for African Americans fleeing a racist South of limited opportunities in the past does not mean it will be a Mecca for them in the future. Past identity can become a prison of ideas for the future. Importantly, shifting economics and national political patterns will change class relations, affecting the relative power of capital and labor.

That recalling of past identity can of course also be made into a tourist attraction, and thus an economic boost to various tourist-related businesses in the city; Lowell, Massachusetts, is a good example, as is New York City's making a museum of old working-class tenement housing. But memorializing a past can only go so far. It can become "ruin porn,"[5] a tourist attraction to show how bad things can get, the lives of the losers, a tourist attraction for those who have it better.

Even more, the economic aspects of a "recapture the past" approach can be treacherous. The larger truth is that what has shaped the majority of the shrinking cities in countries like the United States is manufacturing and its associated patterns of economic activity, transportation dependence, skill sets, sources of profitability, and educational offerings. But all this has changed, as a result of forces far beyond any local city's leadership to change. The economic logic of preserving old factories and seeking to attract old industries back into using them and basing their production there is weak; the pressures to realize a greater profit from the use of such spaces, buildings but particularly land, by converting them to housing, or even shopping or, rarely, office use, are too great.

The conservative identity winners in the Identity Game attempt to restore, to reclaim, the past, perhaps modernizing it a bit here and there where obviously necessary. But seeing the future as necessarily as not only recognizing and building on the past, but further having that same past identity be the guide for future development, is equally limited. All the seeds for the future are not necessarily contained in that past that gave the city its historic identity. New ideas, new technologies, new desires, new residents, new geographical relationships, new answers to old and new problems—in short, change, even dramatic change, are desirable.

So there are dangers in a focus on the past if it is seen as necessarily the best seedbed for its future. Politically and socially, it can feed extreme parochial thinking; to put it bluntly, regret for an imagined former all-American, all white, all native city. The undesirable new aspects of change—pressure on public budgets and hence taxes and consequent austerity, everything from potholes to street crime to shuttered stores and overcrowded underfunded schools, eroding moral values and divided communities—can be blamed on new immigrants, racial change, sexual looseness, and other un-American trends and activities. Neoliberalism is close by to rear its ugly head. If only these recent weeds can be eradicated, the old plants, or their seeds, will flourish anew.

Even on the purely economic front, planning that harkens back to what once was a city's economic base has its limits. Detroit will not be a world center of automobile production again, and extreme efforts to revive such surviving aspects of its past auto-related activities are building on a shaky foundation, out of the city's control. Certainly there is a reservoir of knowledge, skills, experience, even perhaps some tools and machinery that can still be kept in productive use, but the effort will be defensive, and unlikely to reverse the causes of shrinkage.

So there is indeed a Detroit that was once the center of thriving and progressive automobile development and manufacturing sector, and its history may still play a useful role in a new Detroit. But there is another Detroit for whom that history is, if anything, a distant memory, one that contains few hints for a realistic new progressive future. It is a Detroit whose identity harks back to the social achievements of the New Deal era, to the labor organization of the automobile workers, to the militant strikes and mass organization of unskilled as well as semiskilled and skilled workers in one union, and the inspired leadership of the civil rights movement.

Illustrative of the different approaches to "Detroit's" past might be the current controversy over selling off the Detroit Institute of Arts collection, including famous radical Diego Rivera murals, as compared to the handling of the city's social welfare programs, symbolized by the cutting off of municipal water connections for those unable to pay fees charged. Either of these might be seen as key parts of the identity of one or another Detroit, but they relate to different pasts, different identities. Each of these ways Detroit could go is likely to produce losers and winners, to benefit one Detroit over other Detroits. So key choices must be made. What is the best way to proceed, to decide among the competing Detroits or in favor of yet other alternatives? Some principles must be established clearly as to what the goals are. This is the first, necessary step toward a New Social City.

Setting the Goal: A Social City of Justice, Abundance, and Support

"Inventing a New Detroit" might distinguish itself from "Reinventing Detroit" by suggesting the task is not a matter of simply doing the old all over again in a new way, but that fundamental historical change may be required. Repeating Detroit's history all over again but better is not the goal. As the saying that accompanies any marketing of stock has it, "past performance is no guarantee of future results." The goal is not to design a new museum of the past, but rather to create a new future: one that honors the past, builds on it, but seeks what may be an entirely new and different contour for its future. A new Detroit, one without the pains of unwanted shrinkage, will be a different one from the old—perhaps Detroit as a Social City.[6] But what would a new model Social Detroit look like?

To begin with, the goal must be clear. What it is and what it isn't, what are means and what are ends. The goal is not "growth" for its own sake. Growth is a means to an end, not an end in itself.

Yet it is clear that in many ways growth does remain a necessity if shrinkage, which is of course a matter of size, is seen as the problem. Yet I would suggest a redefinition of both the quantitative and the qualitative change that is desirable would relegate the issue of shrinkage to secondary importance. With an eye to an extensive discussion of this project, one might consider three overarching objectives: Social Abundance, Justice, and Democracy. Formulating any such goals for a city, specifically for the public policies desired that best represent the wishes and needs of is residents, is a tricky business, especially given the conflicts among the positions of various groups within the city. At a high level of abstraction there would probably be widespread agreement on some formulations such as, in shorthand form: (1.) *Justice*: A fair distribution of the benefits of living in the city and security in their enjoyment taking into account the diversity of their needs and abilities and wishes; (2.) *Abundance*: An adequate supply of what is felt to be necessary to lead a good life, taking into account both the possibilities and the limitations of existing technologies and resources and the environmental impact of the various processes of supply, turning what are now commodities into non-rivalrous (public) goods; (3.) *Democracy*: Provision of arrangements, economic, social, political and spatial, including provision for full and democratic participation in the making of decisions that affect the general good and that support relations among residents of respect, friendship, mutual understanding, and helpfulness, reinforcing commitments to the provision of just distribution of the abundance society is capable of producing.

These are admittedly goals that have been historically considered utopian, but it has been well argued that advances in technology and understanding have now made a goal of abundance for all a matter of political and economic, rather than of technical, limitations. And goals are, after all, guides for the direction actions should take, the roads to be taken, not blueprints to be followed line by line to build a fully elaborated structure. In more detail:

Social Justice

The literature on justice is vast, and reasonable people have disagreed about its definition for centuries.[7] For present purposes, no single definition needs to be accepted by all; the important point is that giving priority to the importance of such a concept as a key criterion for public policy is necessary. And the distinction between individual justice and social justice should be kept in mind. There will always be individuals unhappy at the results of some individual competition (e.g., for the love of another), but the resolution of such competitions is not a matter of social, but individual, justice, often through a judicial system. Social justice does not guarantee universal happiness.[8] When the disputes are essentially among social groups (e.g., as to police racial attitudes in the treatment of African Americans or the just division of business profits between owners and workers in the setting of minimum living wages), then it is important that concepts of social justice be a major consideration.

Social Abundance

The concept of social abundance might be a more useful term for what's desired than the unspecified term Growth. A social definition of abundance means abundance as a sufficient quantity and quality of the goods and services and relationships necessary not only to sustain life but to support a standard of living and the possibility of full development of all people's faculties in a peaceful and harmonious world—an abundance flowing with milk and honey and goodwill among men and women, not McMansions and yachts and conspicuous consumables. Such values have deep roots in religion as well as in secular philosophy. It is in one view utopian, but not really utopian in the sense of the unattainable, given the level of technological development attained in the developed world. Materially, in fact, providing redress for severe social inequality in its many forms—including shrinking cities—is now easily within reach.[9] (It should be noted that for the majority of the world's people, the problem of urban development is not shrinkage, but explosive growth, yet abundance is still not in sight, but that's a different question.) The concept of social abundance is important for three reasons.

First, as a general goal of desirable public action in cities, social abundance should surely be one of the cardinal objectives of any civilized society that has the capability to provide it. It includes the achievement of a minimum but truly adequate standard of living for all: the elimination of hunger, of poverty, of homelessness, of illiteracy, of cramped and insecure choices, and their replacement to the standards a technologically developed, free, and democratic society would determine to be appropriate. Social abundance is a matter of simple justice for the residents and users of the city, and contributes to the peaceful coexistence of all within its borders.

Second, the achievement of abundance for all at such a level helps answer the difficult question of the treatment of those wanting even more—more than has been democratically agreed upon to be provided. The simple rule could be, once abundance for all has been achieved, those wanting more are free to pursue getting it, as long as it does not interfere with the provision of abundance for others. In welfare economic terms, once a commodity becomes a public good, is abundant enough to be non-rivalrous, so that its consumption by one does not reduce the amount available to others, there is no reason to restrict its consumption other than constraints of resources and environmental impact. That may well create some problems of interpretation, since the impacts may not all be immediately apparent; for example, allowing more upscale housing that some may desire while there is a market allocation of residential space is likely to make neighboring space more expensive and less affordable, but that kind of problem can be dealt with by suitable remedial measures or restrictions, in a planning system concerned with the equity of its outcomes. One might imagine that debates on adopting such policies might be conducted, once each participant's personal needs are satisfied, in a communicative and rational democratic and participatory manner, along agonistic, rather than antagonistic, lines.

Third, and perhaps most important of all, in a city in which abundance prevails, the problem of those wanting even more is likely to be radically diminished or disappear entirely. It is one of the classic and well-known dilemmas of political science and of the philosophical underpinnings of democracy that to have a free and democratic society, you need free and democratic citizens, but to create free and democratic citizens, you need a setting in which freedom and democracy are already extant. To provide public support for some at the expense of others is likely, today, to arouse opposition from those others. But if the others are themselves guaranteed all that they need, and are secure in that knowledge, they have no reason to resist providing for those still in need, and are more likely to be willing to share their own benefits with those having less. The dangers of a Tea Party, or racist conservatism, are likely to be far reduced—there will not be tensions between the haves and the have-nots when there are no have-nots.

Democracy

If there is one principle that would have virtually universal support it is the principle of democracy, even though its precise meaning may vary considerably. Its implementation at the local level is generally recognized as an essential component of a free society. Democracy is both a means and end in itself—a simple expression of the dignity and equal worth of all citizens, and a rejection of power as a determinant of their relations with each other. And it is valuable also as a means to other ends, obtaining the collective wisdom of assemblies of citizens, thus making better decisions. But it is important not to equate democracy with a formal system of electoral procedures, but to see it as a substantive aspect of the relationship among individuals and groups (see Kirkpatrick, this volume).

And democracy is valued also as contributing to building communities and solidarity among different people and groups, united in an effort to achieve a common good. All communities have a component that is partly or entirely imagined.[10] Community again is a concept with a vast literature, but there is general agreement that relationships of solidarity, of mutual help and support and respect, are an essential part of it. The emphasis on identity, depending on how it is defined and advanced (as discussed above), can be negative, but also positive, and democracy can contribute to the creation of a positive image of communities of solidarity through their common allegiance to the ideal and practice of participatory democracy.

Implementing such ideas clearly requires a quite different role for the market than now prevails. If we agree with Polanyi, and indeed with most economists, that the unregulated market (whether because of imperfections or inherently) is responsible for the current inequities in the distribution of goods and services, then restricting sharply the role of the market, at least till the desired level of abundance is reached, is an appropriate part of the answer. Other standards than distribution on the basis of ability to pay must be found, at least until abundance is achieved. *Need*, fully and humanely considered, is the obvious alternative. After abundance is achieved, merit, or effort, or contribution, might also be considered. Debates over such standards, once each participant's personal needs are satisfied, should be feasible in a communicative and rational manner in a democratic and participatory city.

Analyzing the Conflicts Blocking Social Values

Assuming widespread agreement on these values, why then are they not implemented in Detroit and cities like it today? The answer lies in the conflict of interests that separate the multiple Detroits, and the unequal power exercised by each. To overcome the blockages that stand in their way, their nature must be better understood.

Abundance for all might seem unobjectionable to any, though there might be some restrained annoyance that some are benefiting from that abundance though they have not "earned" it—as in Reagan's "welfare queens" blast and the frequent theme of right-wing populists on Fox News. While such blasts sometimes appeal to a part of working-class Detroit, the objection to abundance for all from significant parts of Corporate Detroit is more directly effective in shaping public policies, for they profoundly influence government actions. The corporate sector benefits from low wages, from high unemployment, from unmet needs that create markets. They produce incentives to work that increase the profits of employers and help constraint demands for higher pay. If there were abundance for all, the excluded would no longer be excluded, no longer serve as a reserve army of the unemployed. So abundance for all, even if technologically feasible today, is a controversial call.

Justice is obviously also a controversial objective. Social justice is explicitly a call for a distribution of goods and benefits among social groups, following principles to be agreed on or put into effect democratically (see discussion below) that will result in some redistribution from one group or groups to others, from one Detroit to other Detroits, from the Corporate to the Working and Excluded. It would be surprising if those whose interests were threatened would not object, and do everything in their power to block said redistribution.

A key principle in a just redistribution is to recognize principles for the distribution agreed on publicly, including factors such as need, effort, equality, and social impact. A redistribution using such criteria calls into question the primary reliance on the private market to set its terms. It necessarily would see the market as servant, not as master deciding who gets what. Use of the market as the natural form for the production and distribution of goods and services would thus not be taken for granted. Instead, the default form might well be public provision, rather than private profit motivated, most clearly in those sectors where the goods and services are necessities of life, moving gradually to the point where abundance for all can be guaranteed. Thus in the provision and distribution of food, shelter, education, health care, sanitation, clean air and water, public safety, facilities for sports, and participation in government, the responsibility should be in the first place on the public shoulders, not dependent on income or wealth, the market determinants. Since again not all Detroits are affected similarly by a replacement of market criteria by those of social justice, a conflict among Detroits may be expected.

Democracy is pivotal because it is absolutely necessary for the implementation of the other two goals. Democratic processes include mechanisms for establishing majority preferences, implementing them, and procedures for their free and informed expression and debate about them. Since government plays a key role in determining what happens in the city and the distribution of resources within it, including how widely spread the abundance will be among the Detroits, it is only to be expected that that those in Detroit actually today having the most power will do everything they can to shape democratic processes so that it may maintain their power—including the limitation of democracy itself. The appointment of a powerful technocratic emergency manager to replace the normal decision-making processes in the city is an example of the way one Detroit clearly sees its interests as conflicting with full-fledged democracy. And other Detroits clearly see that appointment quite differently, and fight it.[11]

Looking at the measures currently being imposed in Detroit, the centrality of austerity as opposed to abundance, of market-based policies as opposed to welfare policies, and outside imposed unelected management of the city as opposed to participatory democracy, it seems that Working Detroit has been unable to overcome these blockages to the effectuation of the key values suggested above, which are likely to be more the values of Working Detroit than of its Corporate counterpart. Might that situation be reversed? After the first step, setting the goals of a city, giving priority to Justice, Abundance, and Democracy, has been widely advanced and agreed upon, what might the next steps be overcoming the obstacles that stand in the way?

Given the present situation, goals such as those outlined above are not likely to be achieved in the foreseeable future and may even seem utopian today. But if it they are indeed desirable and acknowledged as long-term goals, as the embodiment of a New Social Detroit, then how to get there? Suggestions can be made for what is immediately feasible (or at least conceivable!). A concrete agenda for immediate action, the second crucial step, entails developing initial measures leading to transformative long-term change. What follows is then a concrete set of suggestions for an alternate way of dealing with the pains of shrinkage that such a long-term perspective would put on the table for consideration.

Developing a Policy Agenda at the National Level: Supporting Local Social Goals

The major factors that have led to Detroit's problems today are in fact out of its direct control at the local level. They include processes related to globalization, which boost the ability of firms to locate where the costs of production are lowest, including wages.[12] Also contributing to urban decline is the reluctance of governments—under pressure, locally, nationally, or internationally—to deliberately influence and control the social effects of global business activities (Tabb, this volume). Further, cities such as Detroit have been negatively impacted by the declining power of labor and social movements vis-à-vis capital, of the 99 percent vis-à-vis the 1 percent, fueled by the financialization of business activities and the use of credit to deepen the cultural effects of consumerism.

The division of functions among different levels of government needs to be seriously addressed in order to deal with such problems. All of the fundamental issues, are supra-city, supra-metropolitan, super-regional, many national, and often have global aspects. Contrary to the subsidiarity principle, which holds that decisions and actions should be taken at the lowest feasible jurisdictional level, supra-local needs to be dealt with at supra-national levels from the outset, and tackled directly. Cities need to band together and create an effective interurban political force in order to deal with the numerous issues they cannot effectively deal with alone.

Consequently, a large part of an agenda for change must involve organizing along with other municipalities and nationwide movements and pressure groups for common action. Programmatic goals, at various higher levels of government than Detroit, but for which Detroit might lead the way, might include legislation that would prohibit competitive use of tax incentives or subsidies to attract business enterprises to their jurisdiction, beggaring local governments for the net benefit of profitable business, necessarily operative on at least the metropolitan level, ideally state or nationally. Forging a new national policy agenda would also involve redefining the criteria for the granting of federal contracts to local communities, taking into account not only normal factors of cost effectiveness, but also social concerns, such as level of employment, use of underutilized existing facilities, wage levels (inversely), and racial disparities. Following a paradigmatic shift of this sort, federal urban interventions might also include:

1. Enforcement of fair housing laws, both via restrictions and via affirmative actions.
2. Consideration of the domestic spatial and social consequences of international treaties on trade.
3. Review of patent and intellectual property laws to examine their impact on the opportunities for individual inventiveness and creativity of the type so sought for within their borders by most local governments.
4. Federal absorption of the additional costs of welcoming and supporting immigrant education, employment, social services, health care, antidiscrimination provisions.
5. Direct federal funding of infrastructure provision, not only of supra-local but also of local importance, realizing that the tax basis of federal dollars is significantly more progressive and equitable that local taxation.
6. Major federal funding of public transportation, with an eye to both equity and environment impacts.
7. Where federal funding flows are involved, flexible provisions permitting control of the manner of provision, and the provider, to be left in local hands, providing standards for procedures for the allocation of contracts to avoid corruption, and encouraging the development of local public and nonprofit government-owned entities to permanently engage in such activities.
8. Establishment of a generous and uniform minimum wage for all employment, wherever located and by whatever employer.
9. Measuring achievement not by change in gross city product or population size but by quality and extent of school completions, infant mortality, life expectancy, adequacy of mental health, elimination of substandard housing conditions.

Few would argue about the desirability of such actions at the appropriate levels of government (with the possible exception of some right-wing ideologists). For Detroit, the task would be to help organize and lead political support nationally for the development of the substantive content of such proposals.

At the Local Level: Pursuing a New Social Model

There have been, recently, other efforts to organize democratic decision-making along urban lines—in New Orleans, after Katrina; in New York City after 9/11, for example—but with limited success. In such cases, it has been a specific disaster that has provided the impetus. Detroit's disaster is of longer duration, but it finds a city in not such catastrophic condition, and its potential to be at the leading edge of such efforts, with national attraction, should be excellent. Its long history of active political engagement, both ruly and unruly, should be an added impetus for movement in this direction. However difficult the endeavor and however awkward the compromises needed along its way, it will, even in the effort itself, help put Detroit on the map as a national model of a city trying something new, adventurous, forward looking, and just. Programmatic goals might include:

1. Maximizing transparency and participation in all governmental decisions, including particularly land uses and budgeting. Techniques of participatory budgeting are being slowly explored elsewhere; Detroit could, with

imagination, principle, and energy, show the way—the Porto Alegre of the northern hemisphere.

2. Dramatically revising the local electoral system might become a model for what truly democratic representation can mean. Limits on the role of money in elections, the provision of public support for candidates to get their messages out and stage substantive debates, facilitation of voting, including provisions for proportional representation, can be experimented in with new forms of public participation developed and implemented as their feasibility is established.

3. Providing public space not only for conventional park and ecological purposes, but also to facilitate communication and organization among residents, optimizing the opportunities for active participation by the residents in city government. Public space might thus include not only outdoor open space but also indoor or sheltered community use space, available for anything from political meetings to private parties to exhibitions to farmer's markets to public lectures or public entertainment to planning charrettes.

4. Fostering public agreement on the purposes of government is an important necessity, both logically and politically. The relationship between government and private activities is a fundamental and unsettled political issue, at least in the United States. A campaign of public participation in government, permitting intelligent, interactive collective discussion of what government does, can go far in ensuring widespread support for any of the above proposals. Examples, drawn from experience in New York City, might include participatory budgeting, or community board review roles in zoning and land use decisions, or in operating budget priorities. The ideological legitimacy of socially oriented governmental activity needs to be aggressively argued.

5. Public educational and research institutions can play a major role in planning and implementing many of the above suggestions, and are in and of themselves major contributors to the goals of a desirable and Social City. They should receive maximum public support, and be appropriately high in the priorities of political and private campaigns for funding and encouragement.

6. At the private level, to foster cooperation in the economy, forms and institutions of private but socially oriented collective action and cooperation should be strongly encouraged.[13] But this should be within a necessary framework. Public-private partnerships, at least in the prevailing models, in which the assumption is that the public sector should only do what the private sector cannot, are destructive of the very premises on which social values can be given priority and implemented. Historically, and understandably, public-private partnerships have increased the role and power of Corporate Detroit at the expense of Working and Excluded Detroit, which must and should be able to rely significantly on public governmental support for their health and well-being. That at least is the social purpose of government, and it differs from the appropriate profit-making purpose of the private sector.

What then should the role of nongovernmental private enterprise be in a New Social Detroit? It would primarily focus on a principled expansion of alternative models of cooperative organization. These models should be developed and formed with an eye on the conversion of private profit-driven operations into worker-owned and -run activities, with manner of provision, including working conditions under the control of workers themselves, but the social utility of the products and services should be subject to influence by more general democratic public procedures.

But realism is required in the hopes for that expansion. Cooperative and worker-owned enterprises are vulnerable to the risk of self-exploitation as they compete with less socially oriented private firms.[14] Two possible measures may promote such protected activities. One is their development in areas traditionally noncompetitive financially, i.e., already largely in the public non-market sector, such as education or health care or public safety or regulatory inspection activities. The other answer is to put them directly under the shield of public ownership, with large worker input, as for instance tenant involvement in both the provision and management of maintenance services in public housing, or workers' councils in municipal services.

The Transformative Aspect

The above programmatic proposals are each individually high priority. Each meets immediate needs, each is a significant step forward to reach a major goal. To become part of a New Social Detroit, however, more is needed than individual moves to individual changes—what is needed is further seeing these individual changes both as connected with each other and as part of a single movement, a movement toward a single goal that is more than the sum of each separately. Call the goal social transformation, from the old Detroit to a new Detroit, including a qualitative as well as quantitative change, with the relation between the multiple Detroits significantly reformed. Is such transformation even remotely conceivable, moving from the almost hopelessness of today's Detroit to a virtual nirvana of ideals and hopes? It does seem unlikely, but on the other hand every attempt to move toward it is useful by itself. By regularly, constantly, almost obsessively, linking present smaller steps, of the kind listed above, to the larger goal of a transformed New Social Detroit, even more will have been accomplished.

Who will be the actors that could move Detroit in this direction, and with what chance of success? Critical, of course, are the people of Working and Excluded Detroit themselves. They face major obstacles: first and foremost, lack of power under present institutional relationships, and then the day-to-day pressures of the fight for survival, often a tough and energy-consuming task in itself. And there are ideological obstacles. Not only the massive pressure of the media, (and not only the media) telling them to lift themselves by their own bootstraps, go get an education, work harder, don't ask government to do for you what you ought to do for yourself. But widespread ideological acceptance of concepts such as the American Dream of homeownership, employers as job creators, government as "them" taking money out of "our" pockets, also get in the way. Yet, ultimately, the material facts of life, the observable and omnipresent markers of inequality and injustice, will also have their effect. That, after all, is what the belief in the value of democracy is all about.

And there is a long history of such democratic action by the people of Working and Excluded Detroit, a history in which Working Detroit played a leading role nationally, influencing key aspects of the New Deal and its social programs, prominent among cities nationally in marshaling support for change, part of a national movement which changed Detroit as part of a national movement for reform. As this is written, the day before the elections of November 2014, the nation seems almost equally divided between limited progress and regression. What happens on the national level (and with it the international) will ultimately be decisive for Working Detroit's fate. But Detroit itself can and should play an important role with many similarly situated communities in determining that fate.

And academics, intellectuals, students, artists, many of whom may be economically part of Corporate Detroit but whose hearts lie with Working and Excluded Detroit, will be among them. They can have a real role to play in this process. Erik Olin Wright, in a wide-ranging discussion, summarizes it as three tasks:[15] diagnosis and critique; formulating alternatives; and elaborating strategies of transformation.

Conclusion—The Political Priorities

Because Detroit is in so many ways today at the nadir (one hopes!) of its contemporary decline, it is an unwelcome but highly visible model of what other cities, to one extent or another, are experiencing or need to watch out for. But, by that very token, if it made itself a model of forward change, it could attract nationwide attention and support. It could show that recapturing the past is not the way to go, that formulating clear and ambitious goals can be inspiring to actions that really make a difference, that immediate steps are feasible that would be, not simply a turnaround, but a movement forward. It will certainly take state action, and Detroit should be willing to share credit for its successes with the state level, and it should help mobilize the many other cities confronting similar problems to persuade the national government, and both political parties, that national action to undergird an urban renaissance will be to the benefit of all.

The priorities in any such effort are twofold: the restoration of democratic government for the municipality of Detroit and the end of the imposed restrictions imposed on it, and the unification of Working and Excluded Detroit behind an agenda that has both explicit central values of justice, abundance, and democracy, and as well a practical concrete political agenda pursued on the road to their full implementation. If such priorities are implemented, democracy will play its role. For, after all, justice, abundance, and democracy are ultimately values that benefit all members of society, in the long run.

Appendix

The Multiple Detroits

Which Detroit?	At Work	At Home	Attitudes and Politics
The Corporate 1% (10%?)	Financial, global,	High-rise downtown	Exploiting immigrants
	Upper class	Gated communities	Anti-public sector
The Working 99% (90%, 51%?)	Labor, union, small business	Economically, ethnically segregated	Fearful of immigrants; Ambivalent on public sector; pro-metropolitanization Antitax
	Middle class, working class	Suburban home ownership, rental,	
The Excluded (15%)	Unemployed, in poverty, African-American	Social housing,	
	Excluded, immigrant	Slums	

Notes

1. The literature here is voluminous. Foundational are the developed theories of Karl Marx and of Max Weber, and their detailed examination in contemporary industrial societies in the work of Erik Olin Wright would provide a rich basis for examine the differences among the many Detroits referred to here (*Classes*. London: Verso, 1985.)
2. This, of course, is the major thrust of Thomas Piketty's *Capital in the Twenty-First Century*, 2014 Arthur Goldhammer (Translator), Cambridge: Belknap Press/Harvard University Press.
3. The quotation marks are to call attention to the point, made in the Introduction, that not everyone or everything in shrinking cities is shrinking or is globally related. For convenience, they will be implied, rather than printed, hereafter. [My computer has obviously caught my attitude to the subject of this paper, and, before I corrected it, typed "shitking" for "shrinking."]
4. In Benedict Anderson's vivid phrase, which he applied to the concept of nationalism, but is equally applicable at the urban level. *Imagined Communities: Reflections on the Origin and Spread of Nationalism*, 1983, London, Verso.
5. "Detroit's Abandoned Ruins Are Captivating, But Are They Bad For Neighborhoods?" *The Huffington Post* | Kate Abbey-Lambertz | Posted 01.23.2014 | HuffPost-Home, available at http://www.huffingtonpost.com/news/detroit-ruin-porn/.
6. Other cities see their being a model as a strong attraction also, and have for long. For a recent example, referring to a quite different model, see, for Ecuador, *Yachay, the City of Knowledge*, 1970, pp. 62–82. http://www.miamiherald.com/2014/07/12/4233299/ecuador-is-betting-1-billion-that.html.
7. Susan Fainstein's *The Just City* (2010) Ithaca: Cornell University Press is an excellent broad discussion of both the philosophical background and the practical interpretations of the concept in an urban policy context.
8. See Marcuse, Peter. "Justice in Planning," *Oxford Handbook of Urban Planning*, ed. Rachel Weber and Randall Crane, Oxford: Oxford University Press, pp. 141–165.
9. Herbert Marcuse, 1999, The End of Utopia, in Marcuse, Herbert. "The End of Utopia." [*Ramparts*, April 1970, pp. 28–34] in Five Lectures: Psychoanalysis, Politics, and Utopia. Boston: Beacon Press, and in Herbert Marcuse, 2014, *Marxism, Revolution and Utopia*, London: Routledge, pp. 249–263 and Peter Marcuse, "From Immediate Demands to Utopias via Transformative Demands," at pmarcuse.wordpress.com, Blog 58a:.
10. Benedict Anderson, *Imagined Communities*.
11. See for instance *Detroiters Resisting Emergency Management*, http://www.d-rem.org/.
12. Sassen, Saskia. 2012. *Cities in a World Economy*. Pine Forge Press, updated 4th ed. (1st ed. 1994).
13. The New Economy Movement, the work of Gar Alperovitz and his colleagues, elements of the traditional cooperative movement and its newer adaptations in campaigns as for community land trusts, provide groundbreaking ideas and examples. (See Alperovitz, Gar, *What Then Must We Do?: Straight Talk about the Next American Revolution*, (Chelsea Green, 2013).
14. See for instance, as a typical comment, John McNamara 2010, *The Co-operative and Its Workers*, at http://www.cooperativeconsult.com/blog/?p=323.
15. Erik Olin Wright, 2010, *Envisioning Real Utopias*, London: Verso Books, p. 6. I have used a similar formulation in writing of the tasks of progressive planning: "Expose, Propose, Politicize," in "Other Cities are Possible," *Progressive Planning*, Spring, 2010, no. 171, pp. 33–34.

References

Abbey-Lambertz. (2014). "Detroit's Abandoned Ruins Are Captivating, But Are They Bad For Neighborhoods?" *The Huffington Post* Posted 01.23.14 | HuffPost-Home, available at http://www.huffingtonpost.com/news/detroit-ruin-porn/.

Alperovitz, G. (2013). *What Then Must We Do?: Straight Talk about the Next American Revolution*. White River Junction, VT: Chelsea Green Publishing.

Anderson. B. (1983). *Imagined Communities: Reflections on the Origin and Spread of Nationalism*, 1983, London, Verso.

Fainstein. S. (2010). *The Just City*. Ithaca: Cornell University Press.

McNamara, J. (2010). *The Co-operative and Its Workers,* at http://www.cooperativeconsult.com/blog/?p=323.Marcuse, H. (1970). "The End of Utopia," in H. Marcuse. *Ramparts*, (April): 28–34.

———. (2014) *Marxism, Revolution and Utopia*. London: Routledge.

Marcuse, P. (2010). "Expose, Propose, Politicize," *Progressive Planning*, (Spring) No. 171: 33–34.

————. (2012)."Justice in Planning." in R, Weber and R. Crane, eds., *Oxford Handbook of Urban Planning*, Oxford: Oxford University Press: 141–165.

————. (2014). "From Immediate Demands to Utopias via Transformative Demands." at pmarcuse. wordpress.com, Blog 58a, Posted on September 26.

Piketty, T. (2014). *Capital in the Twenty-First Century*. A. Goldhammer (Translator), Cambridge: Belknap Press/Harvard University Press.

Sassen, S. (2012). *Cities in a World Economy*. Thousand Oaks, CA: Pine Forge Press, updated 4th edition (1st ed. 1994).

Wright, E. O. (1985). *Classes*. (London: Verso).

————. (2010). *Envisioning Real Utopias*, London: Verso Books.

About the Contributors

Gar Alperovitz, Lionel R. Bauman professor of political economy at the University of Maryland, is cofounder of The Democracy Collaborative and a former fellow of the Institute of Politics at Harvard and of King's College, Cambridge University. He has served as a legislative director in the US House of Representatives and the US Senate, and as a special assistant working on United Nations matters in the Department of State. Earlier he was president of the Center for Community Economic Development, and of the Center for the Study of Public Policy. Dr. Alperovitz's numerous articles have appeared in publications ranging from *The New York Times*, *The Washington Post*, and the *Atlantic* to *The Journal of Economic Issues*, *Foreign Policy*, *Diplomatic History*, and other academic and popular journals. Recent books include *What Then Must We Do?* (2013); *America Beyond Capitalism* (2011); *Unjust Deserts*, with Lew Daly (2008); *Making a Place for Community* (2002, with Thad Williamson and David Imbroscio), and *The Decision to Use the Atomic Bomb* (1995).

Patrick Cooper-McCann is a PhD candidate in urban and regional planning at the University of Michigan. His research concerns the transformation of local governance in cities in fiscal distress.

Mathieu Hikaru Desan is a PhD candidate in sociology at the University of Michigan, Ann Arbor. His dissertation is on the political transformation of a group of French socialists into fascists during the interwar period, with a particular focus on the mutation of socialist discourse and its interaction with the factional dynamics of the field of French socialism. He has also published on Marxism and Bourdieusian critical sociology.

Margaret Dewar is professor of urban and regional planning in the Taubman College of Architecture and Urban Planning at the University of Michigan. Her research focuses on American cities that have lost large shares of their peak population and employment and now have extensive blighted buildings and vacant land. She is the coauthor of *The City after Abandonment* (Philadelphia: University of Pennsylvania Press, 2012) and numerous articles on planning and policy in the context of extreme urban decline. She has degrees in urban planning from Harvard University and the Massachusetts Institute of Technology.

Steve Dubb is research director of The Democracy Collaborative and has worked for the Collaborative since 2004. At the Collaborative, Dubb has led the development of the Community-Wealth.org web-based information portal and has been lead author or coauthor of a number of publications, including *Building Wealth: The New Asset-Based*

Approach to Solving Social and Economic Problems (Aspen, 2005), *Linking Colleges to Communities: Engaging the University for Community Development* (2007), *Growing a Green Economy for All: From Green Jobs to Green Ownership* (2010), and *The Road Half Traveled: University Engagement at a Crossroads* (2012). With Ted Howard, Dubb has also worked on the development of community wealth–building strategies in a number of cities, including Cleveland, Atlanta, Pittsburgh, and Washington, DC. Previously, Dubb was executive director of the North American Students of Cooperation (NASCO), a US and Canadian nonprofit association that provides education and technical assistance to university and community-based housing and retail cooperatives. Dubb received his Masters and PhD in political science from the University of California, San Diego and his Bachelor's in Economics (with honors) and Spanish from the University of California, Berkeley.

Peter Eisinger (PhD, Yale, 1969, political science) is retired from the Milano School of the New School, where he held the Henry Cohen Chair. He previously taught for nearly three decades at the University of Wisconsin-Madison. He directed its La Follette Institute of Public Affairs from 1991–1996. From 1997–2005 he lived in Detroit while he taught at Wayne State University and established and directed its State Policy Center. He has been a fellow at the Center for Advanced Study in the Behavioral Sciences in Palo Alto and a distinguished Fulbright chair in the Netherlands. He has written a number of books on topics including economic development policy in American states and localities, hunger and food assistance policy in the United States, and the response of white elites in Detroit and Atlanta to the rise of black political dominance. His more than sixty articles include studies of political protest, racial politics at the local level, cities in the federal system, municipal public-policy issues, and the nature of nonprofit grassroots organizations, among others. He lives in New York City and Wellfleet, Massachusetts.

Meagan Elliott has her Master of Urban Planning and is a PhD candidate in sociology at the University of Michigan. Her interest in gentrification and understanding growth in the midst of broader decline has led to research in Krakow, Poland; Germany's Ruhr Valley; and Detroit, Michigan.

Reynolds Farley is a research scientist at the University of Michigan's Population Studies Center and the Otis Dudley Duncan professor emeritus. He spent much of his career analyzing United States population trends with an emphasis upon racial issues. He teaches courses about the history and future of Detroit and maintains the website www.Detroit1701.org.

David Fasenfest (PhD, Michigan), associate professor of sociology and urban affairs, College of Liberal Arts and Sciences, Wayne State University, is an economist and sociologist who has written numerous articles on regional and urban economic development, labor market analysis, work force development, and income inequality. His work has appeared in *Economic Development Quarterly*, *Urban Affairs Review*, *International Journal of Urban and Regional Research*, and the *International Journal of Sociology*.

His edited publications include *Community Economic Development: Policy Formation in the U.S. and U.K.* (Macmillan Press, 1993), *Critical Perspectives on Local Development Policy Evaluation* (Wayne State University Press, 2004), *Engaging Social Justice: Critical Studies of 21st Century Social Transformation* (Haymarket, 2010), and *Social Change, Resistance and Social Practice* (Haymarket, 2011). In addition, he is currently the editor of the international journal *Critical Sociology* (http://crs.sagepub.com), and is the book-series editor of *Studies in Critical Social Science* published by Brill Academic Press (http://www.brill.nl/scss).

John Gallagher is a veteran journalist and author whose book *Reimagining Detroit: Opportunities for Redefining an American City* was named by the *Huffington Post* as among the best social and political books of 2010. His most recent book is *Revolution Detroit: Strategies for Urban Reinvention.* John was born in New York City and joined the *Detroit Free Press* in 1987 to cover urban and economic redevelopment efforts in Detroit and Michigan, a post he still holds. His other books include *Great Architecture of Michigan* and, as coauthor, *AIA Detroit: The American Institute of Architects Guide to Detroit Architecture.* John and his wife, Sheu-Jane, live along Detroit's east riverfront.

Lucas Owen Kirkpatrick is assistant professor of sociology at Southern Methodist University. He began investigating Detroit during his time as assistant professor of urban and regional planning (Taubman College of Architecture and Urban Planning) and postdoctoral scholar in the Michigan Society of Fellows at the University of Michigan. His research interrogates the political economy of urban decline, with a special focus on the relationship between urban austerity, the reconfiguration of urban citizenship, and the retrenchment of public space. His work has been published in *Politics & Society,* the *International Journal of Urban and Regional Research,* and the *Journal of Urban History.* His book, *Sovereignty and the Fragmented City: The Many Citizenships of Detroit, Michigan* (Wayne State University Press), is expected in 2016.

Peter Marcuse, a planner and lawyer, is professor emeritus of urban planning at Columbia University. He has a JD from Yale Law School, and a PhD in planning from the University of California at Berkeley. He was professor of urban planning at UCLA and president of the Los Angeles Planning Commission. He has been a member of Community Board 9M in New York City and former chair of its Housing Committee. He is currently focused on responses to mortgage foreclosures, the New York City Coalition for Community Land Trust Initiative, and the Occupy Wall Street and Right to the City Movements. His recent books include *Globalizing Cities: A New Spatial Order?* (Blackwell, 1999, coedited with Ronald van Kempen), *Of States and Cities: The Partitioning of Urban Space* (Oxford, 2002), and the coedited volume *Searching for the Just City* (Routledge, 2009). His most recent book, coedited with Neil Brenner and Margit Mayer, is *Cities for People, Not for Profit* (Routledge, 2011). He has a blog on issues of urban policy and social justice at pmarcuse.wordpress.com.

Jamie Peck is Canada research chair in urban & regional political economy and professor of geography at the University of British Columbia, Canada. His research interests include the political economy of neoliberalism, the politics of policy formation and mobility, economic governance, labor studies, and urban restructuring. Recent publications include *Fast Policy* (with Nik Theodore, Minnesota, 2015), *Constructions of Neoliberal Reason* (Oxford, 2010), and the coedited collections *Contesting Neoliberalism* (Guilford, 2007), *Politics and Practice in Economic Geography* (Sage, 2007), and *The Wiley-Blackwell Companion to Economic Geography* (Wiley, 2012). An elected Fellow of the Royal Society of Canada, an Academician in the Social Sciences, and a former Guggenheim Fellow, Jamie Peck is the recipient of the Royal Geographical Society's Back Award, for contributions to economic geography.

Eric Seymour is a PhD candidate in the Urban and Regional Planning Program at the University of Michigan. His research focuses on foreclosure, housing policy, and redevelopment initiatives in US shrinking cities.

Michael Peter Smith is distinguished research professor of community studies in the Department of Human Ecology at the University of California, Davis. His research focuses on the relationship between cities, the state, globalization, and transnationalism. He is coauthor of the award-winning book *Citizenship across Borders* (Cornell, 2008). His other books include *Transnational Urbanism: Locating Globalization* (Blackwell, 2001); *City State, & Market* (Blackwell, 1988); and *The City and Social Theory* (St. Martin's, 1979; Blackwell, 1980). He has also edited or coedited several influential anthologies, including *Cities in Transformation* (1984), *The Capitalist City* (1987), *The Bubbling Cauldron* (1995), *Transnationalism from Below* (1998), and The *Human Face of Global Mobility* (2006). Smith's research has been published in a wide array of interdisciplinary social science journals, including *Theory and Society, Politics & Society, Social Text, Political Geography, Global Networks*, the *Journal of Ethnic and Migration Studies, Ethnic and Racial Studies*, the *International Journal of Urban and Regional Research, City & Society, Urban Affairs Review,* and *Territory, Politics, Governance*. He is the series editor of Transaction's *Comparative Urban and Community Research* book series.

George Steinmetz is the Charles Tilly collegiate professor of sociology and German studies at the University of Michigan. He has also taught at the University of Chicago as a tenured professor of sociology and history and at the New School for Social Research and the École des hautes études en sciences sociales in sociology. He is a social theorist and a historical sociologist of states, empires, and social science. He is currently working on two main projects—a reconstruction of sociology as historical socio-analysis and a project on the historical sociology of sociology in Europe, North America, and postcolonial Africa. Here he looks at sociologists who have analyzed, criticized, and advised colonial and informal empires during the past 150 years. He has also worked on Germany and several of its former colonies (Namibia, Samoa, and Qingdao, China), on social policy at the local and central levels in imperial Germany, on visual sociology, and on the rise and fall of the city of Detroit. His most recent publications are *The Devil's Handwriting: Precoloniality and the German Colonial*

State in Qingdao, Samoa, and Southwest Africa (2007) and *Sociology and Empire: The Imperial Entanglements of a Discipline* (2013).

William K. Tabb is professor emeritus of economics at Queens College and of economics, political science, and sociology at the Graduate Center, City University of New York. His books include *The Restructuring of Capitalism in Our Time, Economic Governance in the Age of Globalization, Unequal Partners: A Primer on Globalization, Reconstructing Political Economy: The Great Divide in Economic Thought, The Postwar Japanese System: Cultural Economy and Economic Transformation, The Long Default: New York and the Urban Fiscal Crisis,* and *The Political Economy of the Black Ghetto.* Tabb is the author of over a hundred articles and book chapters. He may be reached at William.tabb@gmail.com.

Matthew D. Weber, MA, JD, is a doctoral candidate in urban and regional planning at the University of Michigan. As an attorney and law professor in Michigan and Wisconsin, he taught and practiced a mix of municipal and community-development law for nearly ten years before returning to graduate school. His research into the ways that population loss affects property relations in "shrinking" cities earned him the 2014 Alma H. Young Emerging Scholar Award from the Urban Affairs Association.

Index